MW01644071

Financial Accounting

Revised Edition

Financial Accounting

Revised Edition

Financial Accounting

Revised Edition

VINCENT C. BRENNER
Louisiana State University

RONALD M. COPELAND
Northeastern University

PAUL E. DASCHER
Drexel University

1991

Dame Publications, Inc.
P.O. Box 35556
Houston, TX 77235-5556

Artist: Anita Hester
Typographer: Jan Tiefel

P.O. Box 35556
Houston, TX 77235-5556

ISBN 0-87393-117-3
Library of Congress Catalog Card No. 90-84299

Printed in the United States of America.

PREFACE

Financial Accounting is an introductory level textbook, appropriate for a one-semester or a two-quarter elementary accounting course. No previous exposure to the material is assumed and the book is intended to be used alone or enriched with appropriate supplemental materials at the option of the instructor.

This text does not make a radical departure from the traditional approach to financial accounting. Instead, it focuses on the underlying theory of the discipline and enhances the presentation with an organization and approach that match the developing thrust of current practice. Consistent with this organization is the goal of presenting concepts and exploring underlying theory through discussion and generalized examples. The text is divided into five major sections.

Section one presents an introduction to accounting and is intended to orient the student. It begins by emphasizing the importance and usefulness of financial statements and develops a basic set—including balance sheet, income statement, and statement of cash flows—from a realistic example. In essence, this establishes parameters for the book and provides a context for the remaining chapters.

Section two leads into the fundamentals of the accounting process. The debit/credit, mechanism, journal, and ledger are introduced and explained. This section uses procedural illustrations to view accounting as processing system, developed and functioning in a manner parallel to other information systems.

Section three views the accounting process in the context of the income statement. At this point, the text begins to emphasize income determination.

Section four deals with particular issues involved in recording and reporting asset, liability, and equity items. These chapters, while developed with a recognition of the importance of reporting earnings, provide specific treatments on subjects that affect particular transaction-based accounts.

Section five presents topics that can enhance the student's grasp of accounting. The capstone of this section is a chapter dealing with the total financial report, including footnotes, and the auditor's opinion. Written at an understandable level, this section serves as a bridge to allow the student to enter the total context of the development, environment, and future of the accounting profession.

Although the chapters are organized on the basis of subject content, attention has been given to the amount of material included. Several chapters are subdivided into two or more *parts* to provide flexibility of coverage. This division into parts also enables the instructor to continue the pace of assignments at a constant rate.

The order of chapter sequence has been developed to reflect the structure of the instructional goal. Other arrangements and sequences may be developed by instructors without altering the flow of the material. Individuals can structure chapter assignments to meet goals of particular courses or to accommodate professorial individuality. This text has been prepared to complement the instructor, not to restrict or inhibit teaching style in any way.

Assignment materials are important elements of introductory textbooks. The assignment materials here are divided into *questions, exercises,* and *problems* and are provided in sufficient numbers to ensure adequate selection. Questions are designed to focus on concepts, definitions, and descriptions. Exercises generally require data-manipulating steps that relate to chapter illustrations in a straightforward manner. Problems are based on the textual material but present reasonably complex analytical or discussion stituations. All of the assignment materials have been class tested to ensure their reliability and relevance. While appropriate for the level of the text, the assignment items draw on realistic situations and develop problems from pertinent data.

Several learning materials are available to aid instructors and students using *Financial Accounting*. A *Student Study Guide to Accompany Financial Accounting* and *Working Papers* are available. The *Instructor's Manual* contains extensive teaching notes for each chapter and a set of simple demonstration problems for class use. Blank *transparencies* are also available for users.

PREFACE

Financial Accounting is an introductory level textbook, appropriate for a one-semester or a two-quarter elementary accounting course. No previous exposure to the material is assumed and the book is intended to be used alone or enriched with appropriate supplemental materials at the option of the instructor.

This text does not make a radical departure from the traditional approach to financial accounting. Instead, it focuses on the underlying theory of the discipline and enhances the presentation with an organization and approach that match the developing thrust of current practice. Consistent with this organization is the goal of presenting concepts and exploring underlying theory through discussion and generalized examples. The text is divided into five major sections.

Section one presents an introduction to accounting and is intended to orient the student. It begins by emphasizing the importance and usefulness of financial statements and develops a basic set—including balance sheet, income statement, and statement of cash flows—from a realistic example. In essence, this establishes parameters for the book and provides a context for the remaining chapters.

Section two leads into the fundamentals of the accounting process. The debit/credit, mechanism, journal, and ledger are introduced and explained. This section uses procedural illustrations to view accounting as processing system, developed and functioning in a manner parallel to other information systems.

Section three views the accounting process in the context of the income statement. At this point, the text begins to emphasize income determination.

Section four deals with particular issues involved in recording and reporting asset, liability, and equity items. These chapters, while developed with a recognition of the importance of reporting earnings, provide specific treatments on subjects that affect particular transaction-based accounts.

Section five presents topics that can enhance the student's grasp of accounting. The capstone of this section is a chapter dealing with the total financial report, including footnotes, and the auditor's opinion. Written at an understandable level, this section serves as a bridge to allow the student to enter the total context of the development, environment, and future of the accounting profession.

Although the chapters are organized on the basis of subject content, attention has been given to the amount of material included. Several chapters are subdivided into two or more *parts* to provide flexibility of coverage. This division into parts also enables the instructor to continue the pace of assignments at a constant rate.

The order of chapter sequence has been developed to reflect the structure of the instructional goal. Other arrangements and sequences may be developed by instructors without altering the flow of the material. Individuals can structure chapter assignments to meet goals of particular courses or to accommodate professorial individuality. This text has been prepared to complement the instructor, not to restrict or inhibit teaching style in any way.

Assignment materials are important elements of introductory textbooks. The assignment materials here are divided into *questions, exercises,* and *problems* and are provided in sufficient numbers to ensure adequate selection. Questions are designed to focus on concepts, definitions, and descriptions. Exercises generally require data-manipulating steps that relate to chapter illustrations in a straightforward manner. Problems are based on the textual material but present reasonably complex analytical or discussion stituations. All of the assignment materials have been class tested to ensure their reliability and relevance. While appropriate for the level of the text, the assignment items draw on realistic situations and develop problems from pertinent data.

Several learning materials are available to aid instructors and students using *Financial Accounting*. A *Student Study Guide to Accompany Financial Accounting* and *Working Papers* are available. The *Instructor's Manual* contains extensive teaching notes for each chapter and a set of simple demonstration problems for class use. Blank *transparencies* are also available for users.

We are indebted to many people for their ideas and assistance in preparing this text. Graduate students, Barbara Lane and Gisele Jackson of Louisiana State University, were invaluable in preparing the manuscript.

A special measure of thanks is due to the staff of Dame Publications, Inc. for their interest in and commitment to this project.

Finally, we welcome comments from the users of this text.

1991

Vincent C. Brenner
Ronald M. Copeland
Paul E. Dascher

We are indebted to many people for their ideas and assistance in preparing this text. Graduate students, Barbara Lane and Gisele Jackson of Louisiana State University, were invaluable in preparing the manuscript.

A special measure of thanks is due to the staff of Dame Publications, Inc. for their interest in and commitment to this project.

Finally, we welcome comments from the users of this text.

1991

Vincent C. Brenner
Ronald M. Copeland
Paul E. Dascher

TABLE OF CONTENTS

1 The Accounting Information System 2

INTRODUCTION. INFORMATION AND ACCOUNTING. Accounting Defined. ELEMENTS OF THE ACCOUNTING MODEL. A Business Venture. Accounting Entity. Transactions. Accounts. USERS OF ACCOUNTING INFORMATION. ECONOMIC DESCRIPTIONS. Assets. Equities. Changes in Assets and Equities. ACCOUNTING REPORTS. The Balance Sheet. The Income Statement. The Cash Flow Statement. SUMMARY. KEY DEFINITIONS. APPENDIX—THE ACCOUNTING PROFESSION. INTRODUCTION. FINANCIAL ACCOUNTING. AUDITING. TAXATION. COST AND MANAGERIAL ACCOUNTING. INTERNAL AUDITING. NOT-FOR-PROFIT ACCOUNTING. OTHER ACCOUNTING EFFORTS. QUESTIONS. EXERCISES. PROBLEMS.

2 Accounting Principles and Information Processing 24

INTRODUCTION. THE ENVIRONMENT OF ACCOUNTING. Complexity. Ownership and Control. Public Information. Efficiency. PROCESSING ACCOUNTING DATA. An Example. INFORMATION REPORTING. TRANSACTIONS AND FINANCIAL STATEMENTS. The Accounting Equation. Expanding the Equation. CLASSIFYING INFORMATION. An Example. Recording the Events. Revenues and Expenses. STATEMENT PREPARATION. SUMMARY. KEY DEFINITIONS. APPENDIX—THE DEVELOPMENT OF GENERALLY ACCEPTED ACCOUNTING PRINCIPLES. INTRODUCTION. The Securities and Exchange Commission. The American Institute of Certified Public Accountants. The Financial Accounting Standards Board. QUESTIONS. EXERCISES. PROBLEMS.

3 The Accounting Cycle 50

INTRODUCTION. THE GENERAL LEDGER. Maintaining Accounts. Format of the Ledger. DEBITS AND CREDITS. Normal Account Balances. Double-Entry Recording. ANALYZING TRANSACTIONS. REVENUE AND EXPENSE TRANSACTIONS. Revenue. Expenses. Recording Revenues and Expenses. THE GENERAL JOURNAL. Format of the Journal. THE COMPLETE RECORDING PROCESS. The Trial Balance. The Closing Process. SUMMARY. KEY DEFINITIONS. APPENDIX—FORMS OF BUSINESS ORGANIZATIONS. INTRODUCTION. PROPRIETORSHIPS. PARTNERSHIPS. CORPORATIONS. FINANCIAL STATEMENTS AND FORMS OF ORGANIZATION. QUESTIONS. EXERCISES. PROBLEMS.

4 Financial Statement Relationships and Adjustments 78

INTRODUCTION. ACCRUAL ACCOUNTING. FINANCIAL STATEMENT INTERRELATIONSHIPS. Assets, Expenses, and Equities. The Effects of Errors. THE ADJUSTMENT PROCESS. EXPENSE AND ASSET ADJUSTMENTS. Prepayments. Utilization. EXPENSE AND LIABILITY ADJUSTMENTS. Utilities Expense. Salary Expense. REVENUE AND ASSET ADJUSTMENTS. Interest Revenue. REVENUE AND LIABILITY ADJUSTMENTS. ADJUSTMENTS IN PERSPECTIVE. PROCESSING ADJUSTMENT DATA. THE WORKSHEET. An Example. Completing the Worksheet. Trial Balance. Adjustments. Adjusted Trial Balance. Income Statement. Balance Sheet. USING THE WORKSHEET. Closing Entries. SUMMARY. KEY DEFINITIONS. APPENDIX—REVERSING ENTRIES. INTRODUCTION. ADJUSTING ENTRIES AND STANDARD OPERATING PROCEDURES. ADJUSTMENTS AND ENTRIES IN THE FOLLOWING PERIOD. REVERSING ENTRIES FOR EXPENSE ACCRUALS. REVERSING ENTRIES FOR REVENUE ACCRUAL. QUESTIONS. EXERCISES. PROBLEMS.

5 The Income Statement: Revenues and Realization **118**

INTRODUCTION. BUSINESS INCOME. The Matching Concept. Accounting Income. THE INCOME STATEMENT. An Example. REVENUE REALIZATION. SALES. Cash Sales. Credit Sales. SALES RETURNS AND ALLOWANCES. SALES DISCOUNTS. Trade Discounts. Cash Discounts. OTHER INCOME ELEMENTS. Other Revenue. Other Expense. Extraordinary Items. An Example. Recording the Information. Reporting the Results. FORMS OF THE INCOME STATEMENT. SUMMARY. KEY DEFINITIONS. APPENDIX—SPECIAL JOURNALS AND SUBSIDIARY LEDGERS. INTRODUCTION. SUBSIDIARY LEDGERS. SPECIAL JOURNALS. Sales Journals. Cash Receipts Journal. Cash Disbursements Journal. Other Special Journals. QUESTIONS. EXERCISES. PROBLEMS.

6 The Income Statement: Expenses **152**

INTRODUCTION. COST OF GOODS SOLD. Statement Presentation. INVENTORY SYSTEMS. Periodic Inventory Method. Perpetual Measurement. RECORDING PERIODIC INVENTORY DATA. Adjusting Entries. RECORDING PERPETUAL INVENTORY DATA. OPERATING EXPENSES. BAD DEBT EXPENSE. ESTIMATING BAD DEBTS. Sales Volume. Age of Accounts. RECORDING BAD DEBT ESTIMATIONS. Recording Aged Information. Bad Debts. ADMINISTRATIVE EXPENSES. COMPLETING THE INCOME STATEMENT. RETAINED EARNINGS STATEMENT. An Example. Recording the Information. Statement Presentation. SUMMARY. KEY DEFINITIONS. QUESTIONS. EXERCISES. PROBLEMS.

7 Cash, Temporary Investments, and Receivables **176**

INTRODUCTION. CASH. CONTROL OF CASH. Control Procedures. BANK CHECKING ACCOUNT. BANK RECONCILIATION. An Example. PETTY CASH. TEMPORARY INVESTMENTS. ACCOUNTING FOR TEMPORARY INVESTMENTS. Investment Income. Valuation of Investments. Disposition of Temporary Investments. RECEIVABLES. ACCOUNTING FOR NOTES RECEIVABLE. DISCOUNTING NOTES RECEIVABLE. An Example. SUMMARY. KEY DEFINITIONS. QUESTIONS. EXERCISES. PROBLEMS.

8 Inventory Measurement and Reporting 202

INTRODUCTION. PHYSICAL FLOWS. PREPETUAL INVENTORY SYSTEMS. PERIODIC INVENTORY SYSTEMS. THE VALUATION PROCESS. Specific Identification. Average Cost Method. First-in, First-out Method. Last-in, First-out Method. COMPARISON OF COST FLOW ASSUMPTIONS. COST FLOW IN PERPETUAL SYSTEMS. Average Cost Method. LIFO Method. INVENTORY ON THE BALANCE SHEET. LOWER OF COST OR MARKET. INVENTORY ESTIMATION. SUMMARY. KEY DEFINITIONS. QUESTIONS. EXERCISES. PROBLEMS.

9 Noncurrent Assets 228

INTRODUCTION. LAND. PLANT AND EQUIPMENT. Measurement of Cost of Plant and Equipment. MEASURING COST EXPIRATIONS. DEPRECIATION ACCOUNTING AND REPORTING. DEPRECIATION METHODS. Straight-Line Depreciation Method. Double-Declining-Balance Depreciation Method. Sum-of-the-Years'-Digits Methods. Comparison of Methods Measuring Life in Years. Units of Production. Partial Year's Depreciation. Consistency. Maintenance. DISPOSITION AND PLANT AND EQUIPMENT. NATURAL RESOURCES. INTANGIBLE ASSETS. RESEARCH AND DEVELOPMENT. LONG-TERM INVESTMENTS. DEFERRED CHARGES. SUMMARY. KEY DEFINITIONS. QUESTIONS. EXERCISES. PROBLEMS.

10 Current Liabilities 258

INTRODUCTION. CHARACTERISTICS OF LIABILITIES. Specific Obligations. Definite Obligation. Specific Due Date. CLASSIFICATION OF LIABILITIES. OBJECTIVES IN ACCOUNTING FOR CURRENT LIABILITIES. EFFICIENT INTERNAL MANAGEMENT. Costs of Credit. Timely Payment. INFORMATION FOR FINANCIAL STATEMENT USERS. The Measurement Issue. The Reporting Issue. TYPES OF CURRENT LIABILITIES. Accounts Payable. Notes Payable. Interest-Bearing Notes. Noninterest-Bearing Notes. PAYROLL LIABILITIES. Payroll Deductions. Employer Payroll Taxes. ACCRUED LIABILITIES. DEFERRED REVENUES. THE TIME VALUE OF MONEY: COMPOUND INTEREST AND PRESENT VALUE. FUTURE AMOUNT AND COMPOUND INTEREST. DISCOUNTED PRESENT VALUE. SUMMARY. KEY DEFINITIONS. QUESTIONS. EXERCISES. PROBLEMS.

11 Long-Term Liabilities **290**

INTRODUCTION. WHY INCUR LONG-TERM DEBT? BONDS PAYABLE. ACCOUNTING FOR BONDS PAYABLE. BONDS ISSUED AT FACE VALUE. DETERMINING BOND ISSUE PRICE. BONDS ISSUED AT A DISCOUNT. Straight-Line Amortization. Effective-Interest Amortization. BONDS ISSUED AT A PREMIUM. BONDS ISSUED AFTER DATE ON BOND CERTIFICATE. The Amortization Problem. Interest for the Short First Period. ACCRUED BOND INTEREST EXPENSE. INVESTMENT IN BONDS. NOTES PAYABLE. LEASE LIABILITIES. RECLASSIFYING THE CURRENT PORTION OF LONG-TERM DEBT. OTHER SIGNIFICANT LIABILITIES. ADEQUATE DISCLOSURE. SUMMARY. KEY DEFINITIONS. QUESTIONS. EXERCISES. PROBLEMS.

12 Accounting for Owner's Equity **316**

INTRODUCTION. CORPORATIONS. CHARACTERISTICS OF A CORPORATION. Limited Liability. Continuity of Life. Centralization of Management. Ease of Transferability of Ownership Interests. ADVANTAGES AND DISADVANTAGES OF THE CORPORATE FORM. ACCOUNTING FOR STOCKHOLDERS' EQUITY. TYPES OF STOCK. Common Stock. Preferred Stock. ISSUANCE OF STOCK. TREASURY STOCK TRANSACTIONS. OTHER SOURCES OF CONTRIBUTED CAPITAL. ACCOUNTING FOR RETAINED EARNINGS. Statement of Retained Earnings. Prior-Period Adjustments. ACCOUNTING FOR DIVIDENDS. Stock Dividends. Stock Splits. ADEQUATE DISCLOSURE. SUMMARY. KEY DEFINITIONS. APPENDIX—PROPRIETORSHIPS AND PARTNERSHIPS. PART I: SOLE PROPRIETORSHIPS. PART II: PARTNERSHIPS. LEGAL CHARACTERISTICS. Voluntary Contractual Association. Limited Life. Mutual Agency. Unlimited Liability. DECISION: SHOULD WE ORGANIZE AS A PARTNERSHIP? ALLOCATING PARTNERSHIP PROFIT AND LOSS. PARTNERSHIP DRAWINGS. PARTNERSHIP FINANCIAL STATEMENTS. PARTNERSHIP CHANGES AND LIQUIDATIONS. SUMMARY. QUESTIONS. EXERCISES. PROBLEMS.

13 Statement of Cash Flows **354**

INTRODUCTION. Definition and Classification of Cash Flows. Operating Activities. Investing Activities. Financing Activities. Noncash Transactions. Format of the Statement of Cash Flows. Preparing Statement of Cash Flows. An Example. Operating Activities. Investing Activities. Financing Activities. SUMMARY. KEY DEFINITIONS. APPENDIX—WORKSHEET FOR STATEMENT OF CASH FLOWS. INTRODUCTION. Analyzing Changes. QUESTIONS. EXERCISES. PROBLEMS.

14 **Financial Statement Analysis** 382

INTRODUCTION. THE ANALYTIC PROCESS. PLAN OF ANALYSIS. Measurement Base. Data Collection. Comparison. ANALYTIC TECHNIQUES AND INTERPRETATION. Comparative Analysis. Limitations. Common-Size Analysis. Limitations. Ratio Analysis. An Example. PROFITABILITY RATIOS. Profit Margin on Sales. Rate of Return on Assets. Rate of Return on Common Stock Equity. Earnings Per Share. LIQUIDITY RATIOS. Current Ratio. Acid-Test Ratio. Receivables Turnover. Inventory Turnover. SOLVENCY RATIOS. Debt to Total Assets. Times Interest Earned. MARKETABILITY RATIOS. Price Earnings Ratio. Payout Ratio. SUMMARY OF RATIOS. LIMITATIONS OF RATIO ANALYSIS. IMPACT OF ACCOUNTING METHODS. SUMMARY. KEY DEFINITIONS. QUESTIONS. EXERCISES. PROBLEMS.

15 **Long-Term Equity Investments and Consolidations** 412

INTRODUCTION. LONG-TERM STOCK INVESTMENTS. Cost and Equity Compared. OWNERSHIP AND CONSOLIDATION. CREATING A PARENT-SUBSIDIARY RELATIONSHIP. Transfer of Assets. Stock-for-Stock Exchange. Purchase Transactions. Excess Cost Over Net Book Value. Consolidation of a Purchased Subsidiary. CONSOLIDATION WORKSHEETS. CONSOLIDATED INCOME STATEMENT. REPORTING PARENT-SUBSIDIARY RELATIONSHIPS. MINORTIY INTERESTS. SUMMARY. KEY DEFINITIONS. QUESTIONS. EXERCISES. PROBLEMS.

16 **Analysis of Other Disclosures and International Operations** 442

INTRODUCTION. PART I: ANALYSIS OF OTHER DISCLOSURES. FOOTNOTE DISCLOSURE. Significant Accounting Policies. Changes in Accounting Principle. Contingencies. Description of Liabilities Outstanding—Credit Agreements. Information Regarding Stockholder's Equity. Long-Term Commitments. Subsequent Events. Other Useful Disclosures. THE AUDITOR'S REPORT AS AN INFORMATION DISCLOSURE. Scope of the Audit. The Opinion. INTERIM REPORTING. REPORTING FOR SEGMENTS OF A BUSINESS. Problems in Providing Segment Data. Disadvantages of the Reporting Company. Usefulness of Segment Data. PART II: ACCOUNTING FOR INTERNATIONAL OPERATIONS. Foreign Accounting Principles. Accounting for Multinational Transactions. Translation of Foreign Balances. SUMMARY. KEY DEFINITIONS. QUESTION. EXERCISES. PROBLEMS.

Index 467

Financial Accounting

Revised Edition

Learning Objectives

Chapter 1 presents a basic overview of accounting and introduces the basic financial statements. Studying this chapter should enable you to:

1. Define accounting and describe its general function or purposes.
2. Identify the various elements of the accounting model and discuss their interrelationships.
3. Define the terms: assets, liabilities, owner's equity, revenue, and expense.
4. Construct simplified versions of the balance sheet, the income statement, and a statement of cash flows.
5. List some questions that could be answered with data contained in the typical accounting reports.

1

The Accounting Information System

INTRODUCTION

Everyone regularly uses the services of different information specialists. News and weather reporters study data and provide news and weather forecasts to the general public. Medical doctors review diagnostic information and report to patients about their health problems. Lawyers advise clients about the legal ramifications of certain actions after reviewing the relevant laws and court decisions. Accountants also are information specialists. They collect, process, and report economic information about specific financial events for business or noncommercial activities. Some reports issued by accountants become part of the public domain and are available for use by anyone who is interested in financial statements.

Actually, accounting originated several thousand years ago when human beings first developed a need to accumulate information about economic resources such as land, livestock, and other personal property.[1] Throughout history, the accounting profession has continued to grow in response to the financial information needs of individuals and societies. Today, in the United States, several hundred thousand individuals are engaged in profes-

[1] Accounting records dating from 5000 B.C. have been discovered in the ruins of the ancient Babylonian and Egyptian civilizations.

sional accounting activities; millions of others throughout the country depend on accountants for information that affects their personal and professional lives.

The need for accounting information grew rapidly when businesses expanded and had to rely on capital raised from individuals who were not active in managing the business. These absentee owners and creditors had to rely on accounting reports to provide information regarding the financial aspects of the company. The evolution of the corporate form of business organization had the greatest impact on financial accounting. In a corporation, there may be millions of stockholders who rely on corporate financial reports as their primary source of information concerning a company's operation. These reports are so important to investors, creditors, and others, that accountants that are outside and independent of the company are required to review the reports and give an opinion as to the reasonableness of the financial statements. Such financial statements are called certified financial statements.

INFORMATION AND ACCOUNTING

We can collect many types of data about an object or activity. For example, when considering a building, we can note its age, height, volume, location, cost, or structual composition. For any given purpose, some data are extremely useful, while other data are irrelevant. When buying a new car, the price of the vehicle and the purchaser's available cash are important pieces of data, but the expiration date of the purchaser's driver's license is not. However, if the purchaser plans to operate the new car, the license expiration date is extremely important. Thus, data can be useful or not, depending on the situation or on the decision to be made. Useful data are termed *information*, and information represents the goal, or desired end product, of an information system.

All human activity depends on information. Ordinarily, more information is used to make important decisions than is used to make trivial ones. Business decisions often require economic information that is provided by the accounting system.

Accounting Defined

The accounting information system includes all of the procedures, techniques, methods, and resources needed to collect and disseminate relevant economic information to interested users.

Accounting is a system of identifying, measuring, and communicating economic information to be used in making informed judgments and decisions.

The accounting system provides financial reports, the objectives of which are:

> . . . begin with a broad focus on information that is useful in investment and credit decisions; then narrow that focus to investors' and creditors' primary interest in the prospects of receiving cash from their investments in or loans to business enterprises and the relation of those prospects to the enterprise's prospects; and finally focus on information about an enterprise's economic resources, the claims to those resources, and changes in them, including measures of the enterprise's performance, that is useful in assessing the enterprise's cash flow prospects.[1]

ELEMENTS OF THE ACCOUNTING MODEL

The traditional accounting model, or the basis for the accounting process, relies on three major assumptions about business and commerce. The first is that business activity is conducted by distinct entities or identifiable business units. Second, it is assumed that business activity is conducted through economic transactions that may be observed and measured. Finally, the assumption is made that a transaction can be described meaningfully in terms of standard units of information, or accounts. A better understanding of these assumptions may be gained by considering a specific business venture.

A Business Venture

Two longtime friends, Harry Hawke and William Wizzard, decide to start a business upon graduation from college. Each has a limited amount of cash to invest, but they have received assurances of a sizable loan from a local bank. After a brief period of negotiation, they receive authorization to act as a local distributor for a manufacturer of electronic games. The terms of the distributorship agreement call for Hawke and Wizzard to form a company that will buy the games at a wholesale price from the manufacturer and, then, resell them at a higher price. The agreement specifies that they can add 75 percent to the wholesale price to arrive at a retail selling price.

During the month of June, the business was organized. The owners of the business, Hawke and Wizzard, each invested $5,000 in the venture and named their company Fun N Games. Recognizing that the business needed a supply of games for inventory, the owners, acting through Fun N Games, borrowed $10,000 from the local bank. The terms of the loan called for the business to pay 12 percent annual interest, or $100 each month that the loan was outstanding ($\$10{,}000 \times 0.12 \times \frac{1}{12}$).

During the month of August, Fun N Games opened for business, and several things happened quickly. First, the company rented a store for $500 a month and promptly paid the first month's rent. Store furnishings of $5,000

---

[2] *Statement of Financial Accounting Concepts No. 1*, "Objectives of Financial Reporting By Business Enterprises" (Stamford, Conn.: Financial Accounting Standards Board, 1978), par. 32.

and games worth $7,000 (the wholesale price) were purchased for cash. A salesman was hired at a salary of $700 per month. At the end of the month, the first $100 interest payment was made to the bank and the salesman was paid. During the month, the salesman sold $3,000 worth of the games for a retail price of $5,250 ($3,000 cost + 75% of $3,000), which was promptly collected from the customers.

Accounting Entity

An accountant seeking to compile information about this particular business would first clearly identify the business organization for which to account. The specific organization under consideration is referred to as the *accounting entity*. Therefore, Harry Hawke, as an individual, may be an accounting entity; financial data pertaining to Harry may be collected, measured, and reported. Similarly, Fun N Games, the company owned by Hawke and Wizzard, may be an entity. Fun N Games is the entity of interest in this example.

All accounting entities are treated independently of one another. Thus, data relating to the entity Harry Hawke (the individual) are not confused with, or included in, data concerning Fun N Games (the company). This assumption—which restricts the accountant's attention to a specific individual or organization—is known as the *separate entity assumption*. Under the separate entity assumption, a business is treated as being separate and distinct from its owners. The accounting records of Fun N Games should reflect economic events relating solely to that entity.

Transactions

After an entity has been identified, the accounting model measures the economic effect of transactions on the business. A *transaction* is a simultaneous exchange between the accounting entity and other parties such as customers, suppliers, employees, or owners. The exchange is characterized by each party giving and receiving something of value. Thus, an exchange of economic value must take place for a transaction to occur.

Examples of transactions would include the following:

1. Sale of goods for cash—an exchange of property for cash took place.
2. Purchase of store furnishings for cash—the firm received store furnishings and exchanged (gave) cash for it.
3. Paying a salesperson's salary—the business received the salesperson's services and gave cash in return.

The transactions concept relies on the assumption of a rational, economic individual; people and organizations are always assumed to exchange things of equal value. For example, if a college student buys a best-selling novel for $15, it is assumed that the book was worth $15 to the student, or he or she wouldn't have exchanged his or her money for it. The same logic prevails with respect to the seller of the book and with all business transactions included in the accounting system.

Such an assumption of economic rationality aids in valuing accounting transactions; once one element of a transaction is valued, the value of the other element is also known. Thus, if $3,000 is paid for store furnishings, the furnishings will be valued at $3,000 by their new owners. The transaction concept also adds to the definition of an entity. An accounting entity must be an economic unit capable of entering into transactions.

A list of transactions for Fun N Games during its first month of operations is given below. Observe that the dollar impact of the objects given and received is the same. Each transaction between a business and another party can be characterized in a similar fashion.

Objects or Services Received	*Objects or Services Given*	*Dollar Impact*
Money	Promise to repay bank (note)	$10,000
Use of store (rent)	Money	500
Furnishings	Money	5,000
Salesman's labor	Money	700
Use of bank's money (interest)	Money	100
Money	Games	5,250

Furthermore, most business transactions are evidenced by source documents that describe the event. For example, a promissory note is a legal instrument that provides evidence of borrowing money. A purchase order, sales slip, shipping invoice, and cancelled check all evidence the acquisition of furnishings. Business forms, documents, and memos reflect each transaction. Creating source documents coincident to a business transaction lies at the heart of most accounting systems, since these documents usually activate the accounting process.

Accounts

Accounting systems classify transactions into broad groups such as sales transactions, purchase transactions, and borrowing transactions. Data relating to each type of transaction is accounted for, or recorded and processed, in the same manner as all other transactions of the same class. They are recorded consistently. For example, identical accounting procedures are applied to all sales for cash no matter what product is being sold. Preprinted source documents or business forms ensure that corresponding data are collected for similar transactions.

Information in the accounting system is recorded in accounts that reflect the characteristics of various types of transactions. Accounts are used to accumulate information about both elements of each transaction—that is, what an entity receives and what it gives in a transaction. An *account* identifies the name under which information about a specific element of data is recorded. Accounts represent the names of objects or activities that are accepted as part of the recording vocabulary. Similar transaction components are recorded in the same account. Thus, all information relating to cash will be reflected in the cash account. The ability to record, classify, and summarize information in accounts is fundamental to the operation of all accounting systems.

USERS OF ACCOUNTING INFORMATION

Although accounting information can be collected for any organization, we will concentrate on accounting for business organizations. A wide cross section of our society uses accounting information. Most of these users, however, fall within the following general classes:

1. Managers or decision-makers within the business organization.
2. Stockholders or owners who do not play an active managerial role and consequently are considered to be outside of the organization.
3. Governmental regulating agencies.
4. Labor unions and individual employees of the organization.
5. Creditors.
6. Private regulatory bodies, such as a stock exchange.
7. Potential investors in a business.

This list could be expanded greatly, since many individuals have some interest in the present and potential future performance of business enterprises.

ECONOMIC DESCRIPTIONS

Reporting information to interested users requires that the accounting system describe various aspects of a firm's economic condition as well as the activities that a firm initiates. Part of this description includes identifying and measuring the value of resources owned by the business. These resources are termed *assets* by the accountant.

Assets

Assets are resources, or things of value, owned and controlled by the business. Assets have probable future service potential or economic value to the firm and they result from past transactions. Thus, a building, future occupancy rights, or a debt owed by a customer (future economic value to be collected) are assets. Normally, the accountant will establish specific accounts to summarize data on each type of asset, such as cash, land, or buildings.

An accountant initially measures assets at their dollar cost to the firm. This is consistent with the description of a transaction. For example, if $10,000 cash is given for a plot of land, the land is measured at $10,000. In the previous example, when Fun N Games started operations, it had one asset: cash that was valued at $20,000.

Equities

Our free enterprise system recognizes the private ownership of property; and our courts determine property rights whenever questions of ownership arise. Businesses are "owned" in varying degrees by those who supply the assets and those who therefore have legal claims against them. If Fun N Games were to cease operations at the beginning of the month, the following legal claims would be honored against its $20,000 of assets: the local bank, $10,000; Harry Hawke, $5,000; and William Wizzard, $5,000.

As this example shows, there are two parts, or distinct sides, to an accounting description of this or any business. On one side, there are the assets, or resources, with which the firm may operate. These resources are owned or controlled by the firm. On the other side, there are the claims against the assets of the firm. Claims correspond to sources of the assets of a business, in that suppliers of assets have corresponding claims. Accountants refer to these claims as equities.

Legally, these claims are divided into two distinct types or classifications—*liabilities* and *owners' equity*. Liabilities are probable future sacrifices of economic benefits that result from past transactions. They are claims by creditors of a business and commit the firm to convey assets or perform services at some future time. Liabilities are usually definite in amount and rank high in priority. Equity is the residual interest in the assets of the enterprise that remains after deducting its liabilities. Owners' equity represents all of the claims of owners that are recognized under our system of private enterprise. Among other rights, there is the right of owners to designate who will manage the business, as well as the rights to profits earned by their firm. In the case of Fun N Games, Hawke and Wizzard are owners, and their claims are classified as owners' equity; whereas the local bank is a creditor, and its claim is classified as a liability. Normally, the claims of creditors take priority over the claims of owners.

Economic information associated with two transactions of Fun N Games is shown below:

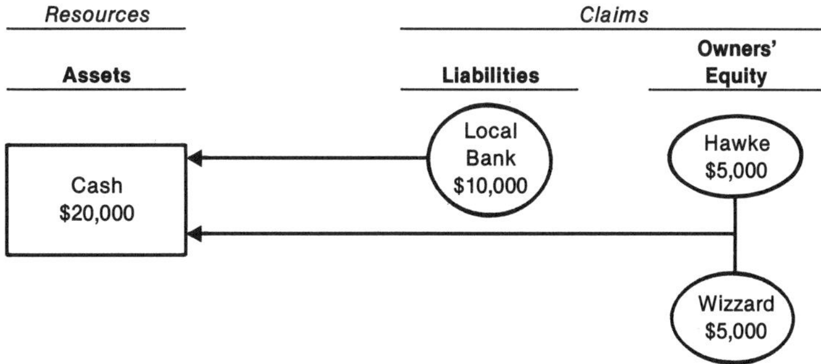

The $20,000 of assets are matched in amount by corresponding claims of creditors and owners.

Changes in Assets and Equities

During the first month of its operations, Fun N Games engaged in several transactions that changed the asset and equity descriptions of the business. At the end of the month, the asset cash has been reduced to $11,950. This resulted from payments made by the company for rent ($500), store furnishings ($5,000), games ($7,000), salary ($700), and interest ($100), and from collections by the company from its customers ($5,250).

While cash decreased, two additional assets were recognized. The company acquired $5,000 worth of store furnishings and has $4,000 of games remaining at the end of the month ($7,000 were purchased and $3,000 were sold). The effect of these changes in the assets of the firm could be portrayed as shown in this figure.

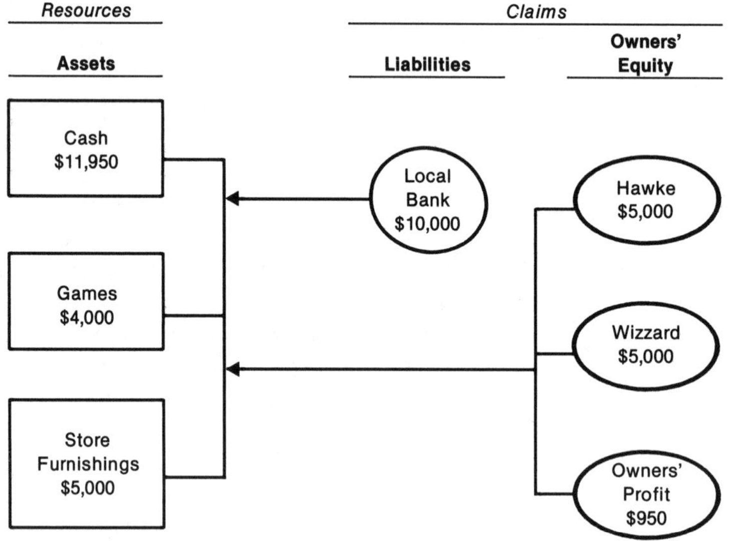

The total dollar value of assets has increased from $20,000 to $20,950. The increase in assets resulting from successful business operations is called *profit*, or *net income*, and belongs to the owners. Therefore, it is reflected as a corresponding increase in the owners' accounts.

Generally, all increases and decreases in assets resulting from business operations are reflected by corresponding changes in the claims of owners. This characteristic of owners' equity differentiates it from liabilities; owners' claims change in reaction to business success or failure, while creditors' claims remain constant until they are paid.

Individual ownership rights and liabilities are related to all of the assets in general. The cash balance is not sufficient to satisfy all of the claims. Thus, all of the assets must be used to satisfy all of the claims against these assets. Since the size of owners' claims change with business success, the total amount of claims will always equal the total amount of the assets.

ACCOUNTING REPORTS

Although schematic presentations can reveal information about a business venture, they are limited. A thorough understanding of most business organizations and their activities demands other means of reporting. Accounting reports attempt to present relevant information about a specific entity. These reports culminate several activities, including:

1. *Measurement*—economic information about business transactions is measured and quantified.
2. *Collection*—Pertinent economic information is collected and entered into the accounting system.
3. *Summarization*—data in the accounting system are summarized to facilitate reporting.
4. *Classification*—summarized data are classified and combined to prepare accounting reports.

Three kinds of accounting reports are prepared regularly to address different aspects of a business.

The Balance Sheet

On August 31, the owners of Fun N Games, Harry Hawke and William Wizzard, wanted to know the status of their investment in the venture. Accordingly, their accountant prepared a *balance sheet* or *statement of financial position* (shown in Illustration 1).

The balance sheet shows the specific assets, or resources, of the venture and the specific claims against these assets at one particular point in time. The report is called a balance sheet because it discloses the "balances," or summaries, of the various assets and claims.

The balance sheet identifies the balances of specific asset, liability, and equity accounts as of a specific date. Since account balances change in response to additional transactions, balance sheets at different dates present different balances. Therefore, the balance sheet usually is prepared on a regular schedule, such as annually, quarterly, or monthly, and it reflects the final position as of one period in time.

Consider the example of Hawke and Wizzard. The August 31 balance sheet reflects the items of economic value controlled by Fun N Games: three assets—cash, games, and store furnishings. Also, the balance sheet discloses the nature and extent of claims against these assets: a bank claim of $10,000 and the owners' claims of $10,950. Although this information is important,

Illustration 1
Fun N Games
Balance Sheet
August 31, 19x6

Assets		*Claims (Equities)*	
Cash	$11,950	Liabilities—	
Games	4,000	Bank loan	$10,000
Store furnishings	5,000	Owners' equity—	
		Hawke investment	5,000
		Wizzard investment	5,000
		Owners' profit	950
Total assets	$20,950	Total claims	$20,950

it does not relate directly to questions about the efficiency of the business venture. For example, the cash balance decreased from an initial balance of $20,000 to its current level of $11,950. Although the balance sheet reports a $950 profit, the owners could question how this profit was determined. An *income statement* relates information about a venture's profitability.

The Income Statement

As its name implies, the income statement presents information about the profitability, or income, earned by a business venture. An income statement for Fun N Games is presented in Illustration 2. This statement shows the results for the first month of operations—August. Basically, it is a summary of sales activity (distributing goods and services to customers) and expense activity (utilizing goods and services to generate sales).

The income statement first identifies the sales made during the period, which is measured by the total amount of cash that was or that will be received from customers. This portion of the statement shows the amount customers paid or promised to pay the business for the product or service that they received. In accounting terminology, this is called *revenue*, or *sales revenue*, or *sales*.

The next section of the income statement focuses on the cost of providing the product or service to customers of the business. These costs are referred to as *expenses*. The expenses of Fun N Games included the cost to the company of the games sold during the month, the rental fee for the store, the salesman's salary, and the interest on the bank loan. These expenses represent the cost of doing business for the month of August.

The last section of the income statement shows the difference between revenues and expenses, or the *profit*. Common synonyms for profit are *earnings* and *income*. In this case, the specific point figure indicates that Fun N

Illustration 2
Fun N Games
Income Statement
For the Month of August 19x6

Sales to customers (as measured by cash received or promised)—revenue		$5,250
Cost of operation (as measured by cash paid or promised to be paid to make sales to customers)—expenses:		
Cost of games sold	$3,000	
Rental of store	500	
Salesman's salary	700	
Interest paid on loan	100	
Total cost of operation		$4,300
Profit on month's operations		$ 950

Games earned $950 more than the expenses incurred to distribute the product to its customers. Profit can be considered as the return to owners for initiating the business. The $950 profit compensates the owners for investing $10,000 in the business, lending their managerial skills and time to the venture, and performing an entrepreneurial function—that is, starting a business and assuming any risks that may be involved.

The income statement provides management with an insight into strategies for price policy. It gives answers to questions such as: "Are prices high enough to recover costs?" The income statement also provides the user with the information needed to review expenses and evaluate their magnitude and relationships. The summarization and classification included in the statement makes this task feasible.

Owners of a business may also want to know how resources were used during a particular period of time. For example, Hawke and Wizzard might be concerned about the decrease in the cash balance from $20,000 to $11,950 during the month of August. The *cash flow statement* describes the changes that affect cash during a time period.

The Cash Flow Statement

A cash flow statement for Fun N Games shown in Illustration 3. This statement isolates activities that affected the asset cash during the month of August. Sources and uses of cash are identified, and the change from the beginning balance to the ending balance is explained.

After establishing the beginning balance, all sources and uses of cash are presented in the statement. The difference between the sources and uses represents the change in the cash balance (cash decreased by $8,050 from

Illustration 3
Fun N Games
Cash Flow Statement
For the Month of August 19x6

Cash balance—August 1, 19x6		$20,000
Sources of cash during the month:		
Received from customers		5,250
Total cash available to be used during the month		$25,250
Uses of cash during the month:		
Purchased calculators	$7,000	
Store furnishings	5,000	
Store rental	500	
Salesman's salary	700	
Interest payment	100	
Total uses of cash during the month		$13,300
Cash balance—August 31, 19x6		$11,950

$20,000 to $11,950). The cash flow statement for Fun N Games for the month of August was very similar to its income statement, but this merely reflects: (a) the low number of transactions initiated during August, (b) that most of these transactions dealt with revenue or expense activities, and (c) that none of the transactions involved the use of credit. In a more typical example, the cash flow statement reflects activities different from those shown on the income statement.

The three accounting reports for Fun N Games illustrate a complete set of the financial accounting information that is normally prepared by all business enterprises. The complexity and the size of the reports will increase as the size of the business increases.

SUMMARY

This chapter considered the importance of information to individual decision-makers. Information, defined as useful data, must possess certain general characteristics to be of value to a user. These characteristics include relevance, verifiability, timeliness, clarity, conciseness, freedom from bias, and comparability.

Accounting information specifically relates to economic data about organizations. This information is used by individuals in a wide cross section of society. The accounting information system encompasses all of the procedures, techniques, methods, and resources necessary to produce and distribute relevant financial information to interested users.

The means of transmitting this information is through accounting reports. Three basic accounting reports—the balance sheet, the income statement, and the cash flow statement—were discussed in this chapter. The balance sheet reports, as of a particular moment in time, the resources (assets) of a business organization, and the claims (liabilities and owner's equity) against these resources. The income statement, often considered to be the most important financial statement, summarizes output and input activity as the revenues and expenses that relate to business operations during a particular time period and discloses the profit or loss. Finally, the cash flow statement details the changes in a firm's cash resources that occurred during the period under consideration.

These three statements are important to virtually all decision-makers associated with a business. Although these reports can become more complex as the size of a business increases, their basic forms and purposes remain the same. A major part of the total accounting effort is devoted to processing the underlying transaction data to produce these reports.

KEY DEFINITIONS

Account—where information about a specific element of data is recorded.

Accounting—a system of identifying, measuring, and communicating economic information to be used in making informed judgments and decisions.

Accounting entity—the concept that views a business as separate and distinct from its creditors and owners.

Assets—resources that have probable future service potential to the firm.

Balance sheet—a financial statement that shows the assets, liabilities, and owner's equity as of a specific date.

Cash flow statement—a financial statement that reflects sources and uses of cash during a specific time period.

Expenses—costs of providing goods and services to customers or carrying out other activities that constitute the entity's ongoing major or central operation.

Income statement—a financial statement that show the revenues and expenses for a period of time.

Information—data that is useful for decision-making.

Liabilities—probable future sacrifices of economic benefits that result from past transactions.

Owner's equity—the residual interest in assets of an enterprise that remains after deducting liabilities.

Profit (income)—revenues less expenses.

Revenues—increases in assets resulting from selling goods or rendering services to customers.

Transaction—an exchange between two or more parties where consideration is received and given.

Appendix

The Accounting Profession

INTRODUCTION

The potential users of accounting information include all individuals involved in any form of economic decision-making. This ranges from personal decisions to situations involving large, multinational corporations such as General Motors, General Electric, or Exxon. The broadness of this user base and the diversity of the resulting information needs has fostered specialization within the accounting profession.

FINANCIAL ACCOUNTING

Financial accounting is concerned with collecting, recording, classifying, and reporting business information about economic events that have involved a specific accounting entity. Financial accounting is based on a set of *generally accepted accounting principles*, which provide a framework for the accountant's activities. The output of the process is a financial history of an organization, primarily reported to users through three main financial statements—the balance sheet, the income statement, and the statement of cash flows. Each year, copies of these reports are distributed to corporate stockholders. Our government, acting through the Securities and Exchange Commission, has imposed public reporting requirements on large, publicly owned businesses. The Federal Trade Commission demands and receives financial accounting reports from selected entities that are in a position to initiate monopolistic or anticompetitive practices. All stock exchanges and most banks require client businesses to submit timely financial statements. Most metropolitan newspapers devote daily space to data obtained from annual reports of selected companies. In other words, widespread attention is focused on financial accounting data.

The public accounting profession, acting especially from associations with three formal institutions, has had a tremendous impact on establishing accounting standards. The American Institute of Certified Public Accountants (AICPA), a professional association of CPAs, has a long history of involvement in financial accounting, and its related principles, in the United States. More recently, a seven-member Financial Accounting Standards Board (FASB) has assumed quasi-regulatory authority for the development and promulgation of generally accepted accounting principles. However, the ultimate control over American accounting practice rests with the Securities and Exchange Commission (SEC), an agency of the U.S. Government that has legal authority to specify accounting principles and to demand that any business falling under its jurisdiction must follow them. For the most part, the FASB and SEC work in concert in the development of contemporary accounting standards for financial reporting.

AUDITING

The auditor provides an independent, third-party evaluation of financial accounting reports and certifies to their fairness, consistency, and conformity to predetermined standards through the issuance of an opinion. Thus, auditing extends the financial accounting function and lends credibility to the results.

Independent audits are conducted by *Certified Public Accountants* (CPAs) retained by a company to express an opinion on its financial statements. These opinions accompany the firm's financial statements that are presented to stockholders and, in many instances, to the public. CPAs are licensed by the individual states; they are professionals who have passed a comprehensive examination (the *Uniform CPA Examination*) and have met certain education and experience requirements.

CPAs rely on generally accepted accounting principles, acceptable auditing standards, and the official pronouncements of the Financial Accounting Standards Board, the Securities and Exchange Commission, and other authoritative sources as an indication of proper reporting by a company. The CPA bears personal legal liability for his or her work and may be sued by stockholders and other interested parties if he or she performs in an unprofessional or negligent manner.

TAXATION

Personal and corporate income tax payments are based on calculations using certain accounting information. The purpose of tax accounting is to determine the proper amount of a tax payment and to aid in future tax planning so that tax benefits (in the form of a reduced liability) may be obtained. Tax accounting then, combines the techniques of accounting with the requirements of various federal, state, and local laws. Normally, corporate tax accountants report to the management of an organization and will interact with the taxing body on the behalf of the organization. Tax accounting also comprises a large part of a public accounting practice. Here the CPA assists clients in tax return preparation and tax planning.

COST AND MANAGERIAL ACCOUNTING

Another distinct phase of accounting relates to reporting information useful to management decision-makers within the firm. Managers charged with planning and control of an enterprise have different information needs than do investors or the general public. Forecasts, budgets, cost reports, performance reports, and special analyses characterize these needs.

This type of information is normally supplied by a cost, or managerial, accountant working within the firm. The managerial accountant relies on economic decision models, quantitative techniques, and an appreciation of the specific needs of users to arrive at an acceptable report for each request.

INTERNAL AUDITING

Larger companies have a staff of internal auditors. These accountants perform a variety of functions. They audit company records and activities to determine if the business is being operated in accordance with policies and procedures established by top management. They normally report directly to a committee of the board of directors and thus, may report on activities of management as well as other employees of the corporation. The internal auditors also review controls to determine if proper safeguards have been implemented to protect the company's employees and assets. Part of the focus of the internal auditor also is to evaluate operations and make recommendations to management concerning areas where efficiency can be improved.

NOT-FOR-PROFIT ACCOUNTING

Governmental units and other not-for-profit organizations pursue different goals than the typical business organization. Basically, they are not profit-oriented; instead, they seek to deliver a particular product or service to satisfy social needs. Most of the accountants engaged in not-for-profit accounting refer to specific laws for guidance in their work.

OTHER ACCOUNTING EFFORTS

Like other professions, accounting is performed in many environments under a variety of situations. There are accounting historians and accountants engaged in law enforcement (special agents of the Federal Bureau of Investigation, for example). Accountants contribute services to the National Aeronautics and Space Administration and they are also involved in environmental monitoring. Accounting firms engage in feasibility studies, systems design or installation, and personnel recruitment activities. While the accounting discipline has far-reaching interests and innumerable opportunities for service, financial accounting—the subject of this book—focuses on the narrower range of activities described in this chapter.

QUESTIONS*

1-1 Define the word *accounting*.

1-2 Define the word *information*. Do accounting reports provide information?

1-3 List three elements of the accounting model.

1-4 What is the purpose of a source document?

1-5 Describe the components of an accounting information system.

1-6 Specify three assumptions about business that are implied in the accounting model.

1-7 What does the separate entity assumption entail?

1-8 Define *transaction* and explain the exchange concept embodied in the definition.

1-9 Give some examples of users of different types of accounting information.

1-10 Define assets, liabilities, and owner's equity.

1-11 What is net income?

1-12 Compare the content of the balance sheet and the income statement. How does the bottom line of the income statement relate to the balance sheet?

1-13 What does the cash flow statement disclose?

1-14 Which organization has ultimate control over American accounting practice?

1-15 What does an auditor contribute to financial accounting reporting?

1-16 Define *revenue*. On which financial statement is revenue reflected?

1-17* List some areas of specialization in accounting.

***Note:** Questions marked with an asterisk relate to the Appendix.

EXERCISES

E1-1 Indicate whether each of the following situations constitutes an accounting transaction.

a. Company A bought a machine from a supplier for $100.
b. Company A agreed to supply Company B with widgets for the next ten years.
c. Land reflected on the books of Company A at $1,000 has been recently appraised at a fair market value of $5,000.
d. Company A paid rent of $500 for office space to Company B.
e. Company A bought $200 of supplies from Company B and agreed to pay within thirty days.

E1-2 Determine which of the following accounts are listed on the balance sheet and which are on the income statement. The company manufactures and sells boats.

a. Cash on hand.
b. Sales for the year.
c. Equipment used for manufacturing boats.
d. Boats in stock.
e. Salary paid to salesman.
f. Rent paid for office space.
g. The owner's investment in the business.

E1-3 List the following transactions under the three headings: *Objects/Services Received, Objects/Services Given*, and *Dollar Impact*.

a. Owner invested $5,000 in business.
b. Company paid $200 for office supplies.
c. Company promised to pay $300 in thirty days for merchandise that was obtained for resale.
d. Company borrowed $1,000 from the bank.
e. Company pays rent of $200 for use of office space.

E1-4 Some financial statements report the financial activities of a firm over some period of time, while others report the condition of a firm at one point in time. Classify the income statement, balance sheet, and cash flow statement as to whether they report activities over a period of time, such as a year, or whether they report the condition of a firm at one point in time.

E1-5 During 19x4, Ace Company had an increase in assets from $100,000 to $125,000. What sources could have attributed to this growth?

E1-6 Assuming that no loans were made and no investment equity was issued in E1-5, what caused the increase?

E1-7 During the month of June, The Art Shop Company had the following transactions: borrowed $10,000 from the bank, rented a shop and made an obligation to pay rent of $1,000 for the first year, purchased paintings costing $15,000, sold some of the paintings for $22,000. List each transaction, and determine what was received and given and the dollar impact.

E1-8 Assuming that Jay Company had the following account balances, arrange the information into a balance sheet: cash—$8,200, inventory—$3,200, other assets—$500, Jay's investment—$10,000, liabilities—$200, and profit?

E1-9 Determine whether each of the following accounts would be classified as asset, liability, or owner's equity accounts on the balance sheet of a firm:

a. Cash.
b. Wages payable.
c. Land.
d. Property, plant, and equipment.
e. Jane Webber, equity (Jane owns the business).
f. Interest payable.
g. Note payable.
h. Office furniture and fixtures.

E1-10 A statement of cash flows for AAA Company reflects a beginning balance of $20,000, sources of cash of $8,000, and uses of cash of $6,000. What amount is the ending cash balance?

E1-11 Gordon's Barber Shop has the following transactions during the month of June: revenues from hair cuts—$1,205, wages paid—$350, rental expenses for shop—$250, supplies used—$30, utilities—$105, interest expense on bank loan paid—$20, union dues paid by business—$20. Prepare an income statement for Gordon's Barber Shop for the month of June using the format shown in Illustration 2.

E1-12 Complete the blanks in the following table:

Case	*Assets*	*Liabilities*	*Owner's Equity*
1	$ 3,000	$ 1,900	
2	15,600		6,800
3		47,000	3,800
4	12,000		9,600
5	62,000	47,000	

E1-13 Haried Company received $6,000 in cash from customers during the month of July and paid $500 in rent, $1,000 in salaries, and $3,500 for an automobile during the month of July. Prepare a cash flow statement for the company assuming its beginning cash balance on July 1, 19x5, was $2,700. Use the format shown in Illustration 3.

PROBLEMS

P1-1 John Smart operates his own business. He sells tires. Last year John had revenue from sales of $14,000. Repairs last year for the delivery truck cost him $150. He uses the truck to transport his tires from the manufacturer to his place of business, which is 250 miles round trip. He makes this trip four times a year and buys 200 tires each trip at $20 for each tire, selling them at $28 each. John pays $.50 per gallon of gas and his truck gets twenty-five miles to the gallon. He sold 500 tires during the year.

Required:

Prepare an income statement as shown in Illustration 2.

P1-2 Rita Wright owns and operates her own business. She writes and sells a CPA exam guide. Her cash account on January 1, 19x8, had a balance of $5,000. The following business events occurred during January 19x8.

a. Sold fifty guides for $2,000 in cash.
b. Borrowed $10,000 cash from the bank.
c. Sold forty guides for $1,500 on credit.
d. Bought a new printing press for $30,000, half of which was paid for in cash.
e. Rita invested $4,000 additional cash in the business.
f. Promised to sell guides to students next month for $4,000 in cash.
g. Paid rent of $500 in cash.

Required:

Prepare a simple statement of cash flows for the month of January as shown in Illustration 3.

P1-3 Ben and Mary Higgins operate a shoe shop. Their balance sheet accounts at year end, December 31, 19x6, had the following balances:

Cash	$ 2,600
Supplies	600
Land	10,000
Buildings	21,000
Store furnishings	3,900
Bank loan	25,000
Higgins' equity	6,000
Owners' profit	7,100

Required:

Prepare a balance sheet for the Higgins Shoe Shop as of December 31, 19x6, as shown in Illustration 1.

P1-4 Redman Brothers Pharmacy is interested in acquiring additional funds to expand the business. Susan Olsen is considering investing in the business and is interested in getting answers to these questions:

a. What is the current financial condition of the business?
b. How profitable is the business?
c. How much are employees paid in salary?
d. How much does the firm pay in rent?
e. Is the cash flow of the business positive (inflows exceed outflows)?
f. How much is owed to creditors?
g. How much cash is currently available for expansion of the business?

Required:

Indicate which financial statements will provide answers to these questions.

P1-5 Wayne Plumbing Company's account balances as of December 31, 19x4, are as follows:

Cash	$ 1,210
Supplies	1,800
Tools	2,240
Office furnishings	1,300
Bank loan	500
Waynes' equity	1,000
Revenues	13,680
Salary expense	5,800
Supplies expense	2,780
Interest expense	50

Required:

Prepare an income statement and a balance sheet for the year ended December 31, 19x4, for Wayne Plumbing Company.

P1-6 The Hemphill Company's cash account details the following transactions for the first month the business is in operation:

Owner's investment in business	$3,000
Purchased equipment	1,200
Rented office space	700
Received from customers	1,500
Paid wages	1,100
Purchased store furnishings	1,400
Paid interest	40

Required:

Prepare a statement of cash flows for Hemphill Company for this month.

P1-7 Henderson Dry Cleaners is owned by George Henderson. George rents all his equipment and store space and uses a calendar year for the business. The account balances for Henderson Dry Cleaners are shown below as of December 31, 19x4:

Accounts payable	$ 1,200
Accounts receivable	6,900
Advertising expense	2,000
Cash	18,200
Insurance expense	600
Miscellaneous expense	210
Rent expense	18,000
Sales	41,400
Salaries payable	300
Salary expense	14,300
Supplies	8,100
Supplies expense	3,900
Taxes expense	3,050
Utilities expense	4,250
Henderson—equity	36,610

Required:

a. Prepare an income statement for Henderson Dry Cleaners for 19x4 using the format shown in the chapter.
b. Having calculated owner's profit, prepare a balance sheet for Henderson Dry Cleaners as of December 31, 19x4.

P1-8 Below are the account balances for Midland Service Company as of June 30, 19x7, its fiscal year-end:

Accounts payable	$ 12,000
Accounts receivable	20,000
Advertising expense	21,000
Cash	15,000
General operating expense	13,000
Interest expense	2,000
Land, buildings, and equipment	10,000
Salary wage expense	75,000
Sales	250,000
Rental expense	60,000
Selling expenses	57,000
Owners' equity	11,000

Required:

a. Prepare an income statement for Midland Service Company for the year ended June 30, 19x7.
b. Prepare a balance sheet for Midland Service Company as of June 30, 19x7.

P1-9 A summary of important events and transactions for the Victor Company for the month of June 19x8, is shown below.

a. Purchased a car for company use, paying $1,000 and signing a note for $6,000.
b. Paid wages, $3,700 in cash.
c. Purchased supplies, $650 in cash.
d. A small fire destroyed supplies costing $100 that had been acquired in a prior month.
e. Sales to customers totalled $16,000; half was received in cash, the remainder was recorded as accounts receivable.
f. Collected accounts receivable, totalling $3,800 during the month.
g. Signed a new rental agreement, requiring $600 per month in rents. Paid the June rental.
h. Owners invested $1,000 in the business.

Required:

Prepare a statement of cash flows for the Victor Company for June 19x8, assuming its opening cash balance was $3,500.

Learning Objectives

Chapter 2 presents a discussion of how data is collected and how basic financial statements are prepared. Studying this chapter should enable you to:

1. Describe the business environment that affects accounting.
2. Explain selected, generally accepted accounting principles.
3. Relate specific accounting principles to the data collection, data processing, and information reporting processes.
4. State the accounting equation and explain its underlying relationship.
5. Extend the accounting equation (by adding revenue, expense, owners' investment, and withdrawal variables to the previous elements), and use the equation to record transactions.
6. Construct financial statements from accounts balances.

2

Accounting Principles and Information Processing

INTRODUCTION

When writing a book, a term paper, a business letter, or a note to a friend, certain rules and procedures must be followed. Communication is possible only with a common understanding of the meaning of words and a system to interrelate such words. English grammar and syntax combine with definitions to provide meaning to communicated expressions. Form is also an important part of the communication process. In English, we write from left to right and from top to bottom. These accepted procedures enable the reader to follow the flow of thought intended by the author.

The accounting process also is based on predetermined rules, procedures, and form. These concepts and standards which underlie financial accounting are referred to as *Generally Accepted Accounting Principles*, or *GAAP*. The development of GAAP has been an evolutionary process. Specific principles were developed in response to changes in available data, information processing technology, and the information needs of users. Financial accounting practices in the United States are fairly well specified in the pronouncements of the Securities and Exchange Commission (SEC), the American Institute of Certified Public Accountants (AICPA), and the Financial Accounting Standards Board (FASB).

GAAP is very important to investors and other users of financial statements in that they provide some consistency and comparability between financial statements of different companies. Imagine you have savings to invest in a stock and that you are trying to select a company by comparing their financial statements. If GAAP did not exist, your comparison would be very difficult. One company may record assets at cost, another at estimated market value, and another at unexpired cost. Without GAAP, you would not know what measurement basis the companies employed and you would not be able to make meaningful comparisons. With GAAP, each company's statements are prepared under the same set of general principles and comparability is enhanced. Thus, GAAP aids in making the financial statements more useful.

THE ENVIRONMENT OF ACCOUNTING

Accounting principles result from needs and reflect the environment of the profession. Several factors characterize the environment of accounting: the complexity of modern business organizations, the separation of business ownership and control, the public's *"right to know,"* and a concern for *efficiency* fostered by the profit motive of free enterprise.

Complexity

Most business enterprises operate as individual proprietorship or partnership ventures. These forms of organization generally limit the size and scope of activities that can be undertaken. However, the greatest bulk of business volume is conducted by entities that adopt the corporate form of organization. The corporation provides a means for many individuals to pool their financial resources for large scale commerical ventures. For example, the growth of the areospace, computer, steel, and automobile industries in this country is directly related to the ability of individual investors to collectively invest.

By combining vast amounts of resources in a single organization, corporations can become huge. Size and complexity create a need for significant quantities of accounting information. Many modern corporations operate in multinational markets, adding additional dimensions to accounting information needs.

Ownership and Control

As business operations expand, those who supply economic resources to the organization become farther removed from directly controlling the resources. For example, when a neighborhood laundry adds a truck for pickups and deliveries, the owner of the laundry (the supplier of the resources) relinquishes direct control of that delivery truck (a resource) to a driver. In large, corporations directed by professional managers, the owners (stockholders) effectively relinquish all direct control to the managers. Managers of large organizations require information about the business operations, while the owners require information about the resource stewardship of management.

Public Information

In organized societies, governments exercise control over many aspects of life for the betterment of those who are governed. Such control requires information. The significant impact of business on modern society has heightened the need for government to be informed of business activities and to monitor compliance with laws and regulations. The administrative complexities of societal controls have magnified requirements for accounting information.

Efficiency

Businessmen have always been concerned about the efficient use of economic resources of immediate concern to their own business, such as materials, labor, plant, and equipment. Efficient use of these resources is directly reflected in accounting-derived profit measurements—a widely recognized performance index in both socialistic and capitalistic economies. Historically, less concern was directed at measuring the consequences of employee safety, pollution, and other ecological factors. Today, however, a growing social awareness has broadened the focus and concerns of the accounting field.

PROCESSING ACCOUNTING DATA

Financial accounting is primarily concerned with historical events. Data relating to completed transactions represent the focus of accounting attention. Measurements are primarily based on *historical costs*, or values recorded at the time a transaction was completed, instead of current or future values. Under the historical cost concept, land that was acquired by an entity in 1950 for $120,000 would be reflected in the accounts at $120,000 today, despite known changes in real estate values. The use of historical cost provides an objective measurement for processing accounting data—the recorded value of the land is $120,000 because it was purchased for this amount in 1950. While striving for objectivity, accountants will sometimes record estimates and other judgments if the presentation enhances the usefulness of resulting reports.

There are various ways to record descriptions of transactions. Qualitative descriptions rely heavily on judgment and interpretation. For example, if a friend says, "I paid a lot of money for my new car," he has described a transaction in qualitative terms. However, the phrase "a lot of money" can be interpreted quite differently by different individuals; contrast the reactions of an eight-year-old and someone earning a salary in excess of $100,000 per year.

Quantitative descriptions leave no room for judgmental errors or misinterpretations. "The car cost $15,000" conveys the same meaning to everyone. Therefore, accountants focus on the available quantitative information about transactions. The *monetary unit* or *measurement scale* identifies money as a common denominator and the basis for quantifying transactions.

The usefulness of historical costs is related to the *going concern assumption*. This assumption directs the accountants to treat each entity as though it were to continue in existence indefinitely. But since information users require periodic reports to make informed decisions, the concept of *periodicity* supports the preparation of periodic accounting reports about a business. While periodic reports could be prepared for periods spanning any interval, almost all entities prepare an annual report. The business year is called a *fiscal year* and it may or may not coincide with a calendar year. A fiscal year could run from July 1 through June 30 or any other contiguous twelve-month period.

Periodic reporting requires that income for the business entity under consideration be calculated. Two classes of accounts are important in making such an income determination:

1. *Revenue*—results from the sale of a product or service. Revenue is measured by the corresponding increase in assets (or resources) received as payment for the item sold.
2. *Expense*—is associated with the goods or services consumed by the revenue generation process. They are measured as a decrease in the assets (or resources) that result from making a sale of a product or service, that is, the historical cost of the assets given up in the sale or consumed to make the sale.

In preparing a periodic income statement, expenses are related to revenues for the particular period in question. The *matching concept* relates expenses with corresponding revenues during a period and reports the difference between them as net income (or loss). Expenses are recognized and reported when revenue is generated. The income statement is intended to reflect the interrelationship of expenses being incurred to generate revenues. When revenues are reported, all expenses necessary to generate the revenue should also be reported, even if the expense is a future cost such as a product warranty cost.

An Example

The foregoing concepts are used in accounting practice to determine how data are collected and processed in the accounting system. The following example illustrates how these concepts are employed by the accountant.

On June 1, 19x6, Nancy Byrne and Jane Rice opened the Campus Book Store and hired an accountant. In this case, the accounting entity is the Campus Book Store and its *fiscal year* will run from June 1, 19x6, through May 31, 19x7. The accountant is interested in recording transactions data relative to this business.

Throughout the year, the following business events occurred.

1. A store was purchased for $20,000.
2. Books costing $15,000 were purchased from publishers.
3. One-half of the books were sold for $12,000.
4. The remaining 980 books were unsold at the end of the year—one wholesale book company offered to buy them for $3,000 and another offered $5,000, but Jane felt that they were worth about $9,000.

5. A part-time salesman was paid $4,000 in salary for the year.

In reviewing this information throughout the year, the accountant did several things. Using historical costs and monetary *units of measure*, he recorded the store at $20,000, the books at $15,000, and the salesman's services at $4,000. He assumed that the business would keep going in the future (going concern concept); thus, he ignored the offers of the wholesale book companies. The only information that he recorded concerned completed transactions.

To provide the owners with information, he employed the concept of *periodicity* and produced reports at the end of the fiscal year. One report, the income statement, *matched* revenues and expenses. *Revenue*, valued at $12,000, related to sales made during the year. The *expenses* matched to this revenue were books of $7,500 (one-half of the total cost of all the books) and salaries of $4,000. When these were *matched*, they resulted in net income of $500.

INFORMATION REPORTING

Once transaction data have been collected, other accounting characteristics are introduced to the reporting process to help assure that the reported information is useful. The first is the *cost benefit* characteristic under which the benefits expected to be derived from the reported information is greater than the cost of collecting and reporting that information.

The information should be *relevant* (i.e., the information should have some bearing on the decision to be made by the statement reader). To be relevant, the information must have *feedback value* and *predictive value.* Feedback value means the information confirms prior information or expectations. Predictive value means that the information is useful to the statement user in predicting future economic information about a company. To be relevant, accounting information must also be *timely*. The information must be available to decision-makers before it loses its capacity to influence decisions.

Accounting information must also be *reliable*. To be reliable it must have *representational faithfulness*, *verifiability*, and *neutrality*. Representational faithfulness means that there should be correspondence or agreement between the reported information and the phenomenon it intends to represent. In other words, if a financial statement reflects equipment, the company should actually own the equipment. Verifiability means that the reported information can be confirmed. For example, if a company reports inventory of $50,000, another accountant could go into that company and arrive at the same value. Neutrality means that the information is free from bias. The preparer does not try to overstate or understate his or her measurements or bring about a specific intended decision.

Financial statements provide a basis for *comparability* where data for two companies are compared or where the changes over time (between reports) of one company are isolated. *Consistency* is a necessary characteristic that promotes comparative analyses. Consistency requires the entity to use similar accounting procedures over time. Therefore, if a company acquires two similar assets in two consecutive years, it must classify the asset in similar fashion. To do otherwise is inconsistent and would hinder comparability.

While the accountant supplies useful information, expedients are taken so that time and money are not wasted on trivial problems. The concept of *materiality* calls for precise classification of all significant information and implies that insignificant data may be classified in an expedient fashion. For example, a large business organization might classify a newly acquired screwdriver as an expense rather than as an asset. Materiality is measured relative to the entity under consideration. Thus, the misclassification of $100 of assets may be significant, or material, to a small business. However, General Motors, with billions of assets, would consider a $100 misclassification as immaterial.

TRANSACTIONS AND FINANCIAL STATEMENTS

In Chapter 1, the three basic financial statements were introduced—the balance sheet, the income statement, and the cash flow statement. The balance sheet, or statement of financial position, discloses the nature and recorded value of the investment in assets, or resources, of the entity and the claims against these assets, referred to as liabilities and owners' equity. In a condensed fashion, this statement appears as follows:

Balance Sheet

Assets	*Liabilities + Owners' Equity*
Total Assets	Total Liabilities and Owners' Equity

The form of the statement approximates the letter "T", with assets on the left-hand side and liabilities and owners' equity on the right-hand side. The dollar value of the assets is exactly equal to the dollar value of the claims against those assets—liabilities and owners' equity. This fundamental interrelationship of assets, liabilities, and owner's equity is referred to as the *accounting equation.*

The Accounting Equation

In algebraic form, the accounting equation is expressed as:

Assets = Liabilities + Owners' Equity

Relying on this relationship, we can see that if any two parts of the balance sheet are known, the third may be found by substitution. For example, if assets are $100 and liabilities are $80, then owners' equity must equal $20 for the basic equation to hold. Knowing that liabilities are $200 and that owners' equity is $400, we can imply that assets must equal $600.

The accounting equation is related to the transaction concept. Transactions are characterized by giving and receiving consideration of equal economic value. Therefore, if the economic effects of transaction items given and received are recorded in the balance sheet, the equality of the accounting equation will hold.

For example, if a business buys a used truck for $1,000, the asset truck will increase in value by $1,000 and the asset cash will decrease by $1,000. Total assets are unchanged by this transaction and the equality of the accounting equation stays the same. If the business initially had $10,000 of cash, an $8,000 bank loan, and $2,000 of owners' investment, its balance sheet, expressed in equation form, looked like this before acquiring the truck:

Assets = Liabilities + Owners' Equity

	Cash	$10,000	Loan	$8,000	Owners' Investment	$2,000
Total		$10,000	=	$8,000	+	$2,000

After acquiring the truck, the equation underlying the balance sheet still holds as shown below:

Assets = Liabilities + Owners' Equity

	Cash	$ 9,000	Loan	$8,000	Owners' Investment	$2,000
	Truck	1,000				
Total		$10,000	=	$8,000	+	$2,000

The same equality will hold as long as the accountant consistently records all parts of a transaction. Assume that the company also buys a building for $20,000, paying $5,000 in cash and securing a $15,000 mortgage. Properly recorded, this information still maintains the equation:

Assets = Liabilities + Owners' Equity

	Cash	$ 4,000	Loan	$8,000	Owners' Investment	$2,000
	Truck	1,000				
	Building	20,000	Mortgage	15,000		
Total		$25,000	=	$23,000	+	$2,000

In this case, assets were increased by $20,000 due to the acquisition of the building. They were simultaneously decreased by $5,000 because of the outflow of cash. Liabilities were increased by the $15,000 mortgage. The overall effect of this transaction was to increase assets by $15,000 (from $10,000 to $25,000) and to increase liabilities by $15,000 (from $8,000 to $23,000).

Expanding the Equation

The accounting equation provides a basis for all accounting activity. The general form parallels the format of the balance sheet. The income statement explains, or elaborates on, part of the change that may occur between two balance sheets—specifically the effect of normal operations on a firm's financial position.

Owners' equity, or the owners' claim against the business, results from the net effect of the owners' investments in, and withdrawals from, the business plus any income (less any losses) from operations. In tabular form, these effects are summarized below:

Action or Event	*Effect on Owners' Equity*
Investment by owner	*Increase* in owners' equity
Withdrawal by owner	*Decrease* in owners' equity
Income from operations	*Increase* in owners' equity
Loss from operations	*Decrease* in owners' equity

Income is measured by matching *revenue* and *expenses*. To the extent that revenue exceeds expenses, income has been earned. If expenses exceed revenue, a loss has been incurred. The basic accounting equation can be expanded to reflect this detail as follows:

Assets = Liabilities + Owners' Equity

Assets = Liabilities + (Investment − Withdrawal) + (Revenue − Expenses)

The expanded equation includes the impact of the *net owners' investment* (investment − withdrawals) and the *net income* (revenue − expenses). In accounting terminology, the word "net" indicates that a subtraction has occurred.

CLASSIFYING INFORMATION

Fundamentally, the recording process is based on the accounting equation; each transaction involving the entity may be analyzed in terms of its impact on the equation. Parts of the equation may be subclassified into various types of assets, liabilities, and owners' equity items, while preserving the equality. Classifying the data in this manner facilitates the preparation of the financial statements. For example, changes in the asset "cash" may be separated from changes affecting the asset "building."

Illustration 1 provides a comprehensive example of this classification approach based on the following:

An Example

On September 1, 19x6, Mr. Phil Weiss decided to open a boat dealership named the Weiss Boat Company. During the month of September, the following economic events (transactions) occurred relative to this business:

Event	*Description*
1	Mr. Weiss invested $20,000 in the business.
2	A bank loan of $50,000 was obtained.
3	A store was rented for $2,000 per month, paid in cash.
4	$10,000 of equipment for use in the store was purchased for cash.

Illustration 1

Analyzing and Classifying Transactions

Event Number	Cash	Accounts Receivable	Boats (Inventory)	Equipment	Bank Loan	Accounts Payable	Sales Revenue	Rent Expense	Advertising Expense	Salary Expense	Cost of Goods Sold	Investment
	Assets				= Liabilities		+ Owner's Equity					
							+ Revenue −	Expenses				+ Owner's Investment
		+	+	+	=	+	+	−	−	−	−	+
1	$20,000											$20,000
2	50,000				$50,000							
3	(2,000)							$2,000				
4	(10,000)			$10,000								
5	(20,000)		$40,000			$20,000						
6	(500)								$500			
7a	75,000						$75,000					
7b			(30,000)								$30,000	
8	(2,000)									$2,000		
9a	1,000	$6,000					7,000					
9b			(3,000)								3,000	
10	(15,000)					(15,000)						
Totals	$96,500	$6,000	$ 7,000	$10,000	$50,000	$ 5,000	$82,000	$2,000	$500	$2,000	$33,000	$20,000

Note: Parentheses denote negative numbers and decreases.

Event	Description
5.	Boats costing $40,000 were purchased. Mr. Weiss paid the supplier $20,000 in cash and agreed to pay the balance in sixty days.
6.	$500 was spent on advertising in local papers.
7.	Six boats which cost $30,000 were sold for $75,000.
8.	Salaries of $2,000 were paid.
9.	A boat which cost $3,000 was sold for $1,000 in cash, with the purchaser's promise to pay $6,000 in thirty days.
10.	$15,000 of the amount owed to the boat supplier was paid.

These transactions are analyzed in Illustration 1. The accounting equation has been expanded to provide subclassifications of the various asset, liability, and equity items affecting the firm. In this case, specific column names were selected and inserted as events were recorded. The columns are used to represent *accounts*, or classes of information, that will be captured by the accounting system. Thus, the column cash is an account that contains information about the movement of cash into or out of the business. Separate rows were used for each transaction to provide a chronological listing. Since transactions are characterized by inflows and outflows, each transaction row should have at least two entries in account columns. Because the accounting equation underlies the entire process, the equation should remain in balance after each row is complete.

Recording the Events

The accounting analysis for each of the ten transactions involving the Weiss Boat Company is explained in the following list. You may relate the description to the record in Illustration 1.

1. *Event 1*—The business (which is the accounting entity) received $20,000 in cash and gave Mr. Weiss a corresponding $20,000 ownership claim. Thus, the asset cash is increased by $20,000 and the owner's investment account is also increased by $20,000.

2. *Event 2*—The business received $50,000 in cash, reflected by an increase in this amount in the cash account. The corresponding claim is not held by an owner, but by a creditor. Therefore, the liability Bank Loan is increased by $50,000.

3. *Event 3*—The $2,000 store rent represented an outflow of cash; the cash account was decreased by this amount. A corresponding increase was made to the rent expense account, since the "right to use the store" was acquired. Recognize that the increase in the expense account represents a decrease in owner's equity; thus, the accounting equation maintains its equality.

4. *Event 4*—Equipment, valued at $10,000, was received by the entity and recorded as an increase in the equipment account. Another asset, cash, is reduced by $10,000, reflecting its outflow from the business.

5. *Event 5*—The acquisition of boats increases the inventory account by the amount of their cost, $40,000. Two distinct outflows relate to this event: a $20,000 reduction of cash and a $20,000 promise to pay the supplier. This type of promise to pay is commonly called an accounts payable. Because the supplier is a creditor, the $20,000 increase in accounts payable is placed as a liability.
6. *Event 6*—Advertising is a business expense. Thus, the $500 payment is reflected by an increase in the advertising expense account and a decrease in the asset cash.
7. *Event 7*—The entry to record this sale is shown in two parts: 7a and 7b, respectively, although it could have been combined on a single line. The business received $75,000 in cash, which is shown as an increase in the cash account. The $75,000 represents a receipt from a customer for a product or service; so it is shown as an increase in the sales revenue account. The cost of goods sold is shown in row 7b. The account boats is reduced by $30,000; this reflects the historical cost of the boats that were sold. Since these resources (boats) are of no future benefit to the firm (i.e., no longer belong to the firm), they are included as an increase of $30,000 in the cost of goods sold (expense) account.
8. *Event 8*—The receipt of labor services from employees is an expense to the firm. Thus, the account salary expense is increased by $2,000. Since the salaries were paid in cash, the cash account is reduced by a corresponding amount.
9. *Event 9*—Like Event 7, the entry for Event 9 is separated into two parts: 9a and 9b. The total revenue to be recognized is $7,000, including a $1,000 increase in the cash account and a receipt of the purchaser's promise to pay $6,000. Such promises are termed accounts receivable, and this account is increased by $6,000. The $7,000 revenue is recorded by an increase to the sales revenue account. The value of the boat that was sold, $3,000 is shown as a decrease in the inventory account and an increase in the cost of goods sold (expense) account.
10. *Event 10*—Making a payment to the supplier reduced the cash. Thus, the cash account is decreased by $15,000. Also, the outstanding promise to pay, accounts payable, has been reduced by $15,000.

Revenues and Expenses

One further point should be mentioned concerning the disclosure of revenues and expenses. Examine Event 7. The entry could have increased the cash by $75,000, decreased boats by $30,000, and increased owner's equity by $45,000—the gain or profit on the sale. However, this approach obscures the revenue and expense information needed to prepare an income statement. By separating the entry into two parts, and separately identifying revenues and expenses, income reporting is facilitated. Recognize that both methods have the same effect on the balance sheet. Once revenue of $75,000 is matched with expenses of $30,000, the resulting net income of $45,000 belongs to the owner and eventually becomes part of the owner's equity.

STATEMENT PREPARATION

After all of the transactions for the fiscal period have been recorded, financial statements can be prepared. As a first step, all accounts are totalled to determine their balances. Check that the sum of the asset account balances equals the sum of the liability account balances plus the owner's equity account balances. The transactions information has been *recorded* (in a form paralleling the account equation), *classified* (chronologically by transaction and by class and type of account), *summarized* (totalled by account) and is also available for reporting.

The income statement discloses revenues, expenses, and net income. Revenue and expense account balances for the Weiss Boat Company were used to prepare an income statement as shown in Illustration 2. Recognize that the form of this statement differs from previous examples. Cost of goods sold has been separated from the cost of operating the business (operating expenses), as is commonly done. *Gross margin* represents the difference between the amounts a company pays for its goods and the price it charges its customers.

Illustration 2
Weiss Boat Company
Income Statement
For the Month Ended September 30, 19x6

Sales revenue		$82,000
Cost of goods sold		33,000
Gross margin on sales		$49,000
Operating expenses:		
Rent expense	$2,000	
Advertising expense	500	
Salary expense	2,000	4,500
Net income		$44,500

The balance sheet presents the balances of those accounts not included in the income statement. Instead of reporting details of revenues and expenses, the balance sheet carries forward net income or net loss as part of owner's equity. A balance sheet for the Weiss Boat Company is presented in Illustration 3. Note that the term, investment, is used to represent the owner's financial contribution to the business. Other terms are commonly used as

Illustration 3
Weiss Boat Company
Balance Sheet
As of September 30, 19x6

Assets		*Liabilities*		
Cash	$ 96,500	Accounts payable	$ 5,000	
Accounts receivable	6,000	Bank loan	50,000	
Boats (inventory)	7,000	Total liabilities		$ 55,000
Equipment	10,000			
		Owner's Equity		
		Owner's investment	$20,000	
		Net income*	44,500	
		Total owner's equity		64,500
Total assets	$119,500	Total liabilities and owner's equity		$119,500

***Source:** Income statement, Illustration 2.

synonyms, the most frequent of which is *capital.* Capital, owner's equity, and other terms introduced later in the text will be used interchangeably, as is widespread in business practice.

SUMMARY

Financial accounting practices and techniques are based on generally accepted accounting principles. Transactions for specific accounting entities are the focus of attention. The principles of historical cost, going concern, monetary unit of measure, and periodicity all relate to processing accounting data. Periodic income determination requires that revenues and expenses are clearly identified and matched to yield net income. Conservatism, consistency, and materiality are guides for the reporting process.

All accounting activities are based on the accounting equation:

Assets = Liabilities + Owners' Equity

This equation can be modified to reflect additional classifications of owners' equity:

Assets = Liabilities + (Investment − Withdrawals) + (Revenue − Expenses)

Properly recorded transaction information maintains the equality of the accounting equation. Account balances provide a basis for preparing the income statement and the balance sheet of the entity.

KEY DEFINITIONS

Accounting equation—Assets = Liabilities + Owner's Equity.

Comparability—the information is comparable between years and between companies.

Consistency—requires that the entity use similar accounting methods over time.

Cost benefit—the concept that indicates that information should have more benefit than the cost of providing it.

Feedback value—the information confirms prior information or expectations.

Generally accepted accounting principles—the conventions, rules, procedures, and methods used to define accepted accounting practice.

Going concern—the concept that assumes the business will continue in existence indefinitely.

Gross margin—sales less cost of sales.

Historical costs—values recorded at the time a transaction is completed.

Matching—the concept that indicates that the income statement should match expenses with their related revenues.

Materiality—accounting information is concerned with only significant dollar amounts.

Monetary unit—the concept that identifies money as the common denominator for recording business transactions.

Neutral—the information is free from bias.

Periodicity—the concept that indicates that accounting reports should be prepared at specific time intervals.

Predictive value—the information is useful in future predictions.

Relevant—accounting information should have predictive or feedback value and be timely.

Reliable—the information is representationally faithful, verifiable, and neutral.

Representationally faithful—there should be agreement between the reported information and the actual item it intends to report.

Verifiable—the information can be confirmed.

Appendix

The Development of Generally Accepted Accounting Principles

INTRODUCTION

Accounting emerged in response to the need for information about economic resources of distinct entities.

Accounting information is used by many people to make a variety of economic decisions. The growth of large and diverse corporations during the early 1900s emphasized some inadequacies in existing accounting practices. Following the stock market crash of 1929, general dissatisfaction with then current accounting practice stimulated the accounting profession, the government, and the major stock exchanges to take a more active interest in regulating and controlling accounting practice.

The accounting profession practices self-regulation through various professional organizations, the most notable being the *American Institute of Certified Public Accountants (AICPA)*. As an extension of private, professional control, the *Financial Accounting Standards Board (FASB)* was authorized to establish generally accepted accounting principles. Governmental control of financial accounting is exercised primarily through the *Securities and Exchange Commission (SEC)*.

The Securities and Exchange Commission

The Securities and Exchange Commission, a federal regulatory body, was created in the 1930s to oversee all activities related to public securities markets, including the financial reporting practices of companies that are traded on the various stock exchanges. SEC initiates its regulatory power by requiring that subject companies submit periodic reports. This reported information then becomes publicly available. In addition, SEC also requires that each business under its jurisdiction issue periodic reports to its stockholders. These reports must be examined by a certified public accountant who certifies that the reports were prepared in conformity with generally accepted accounting principles. By this action, SEC delegated power to the CPAs to control the financial reporting practices of publicly owned companies.

The Securities and Exchange Commission has the legal power and practical ability to formulate accounting principles. However, over the years, the commission has used this power sparingly, relying on the accounting profession itself to play a leadership role in developing and promulgating accounting principles.

The American Institute of Certified Public Accountants

The AICPA is the national professional association of Certified Public Accountants in the United States. Since the early 1900s, the institute has sought to codify and promote generally accepted accounting principles. Through a variety of special and continuing committees, the AICPA has addressed itself to the areas of accounting principles and auditing standards.

In 1938, the AICPA (then called the American Institute of Accountants) established the Committee on Accounting Procedure. This committee was formed to develop generally accepted accounting principles. The committee issued Accounting Research Bulletins (ARBs) and Terminology Bulletins. The committee issued fifty-one ARBs until, in 1959, the AICPA formed the Accounting Principles Board.

In 1959, the AICPA created the *Accounting Principles Board (APB)* to advance the development of accounting principles and to reduce the existing inconsistencies which characterized common practice. Over its fourteen-year existence, the APB issued a series of thirty-one opinions. These opinions constituted official pronouncements by the board about specific areas of controversy. All members of the American Institute of Certified Public Accountants in the United States were bound to adhere to these principles and procedures in preparing financial statements. Responsibility for establishing accounting standards shifted in 1973 from the APB to the Financial Accounting Standards Board, an independent body. However, the AICPA has retained its control over the establishment of auditing standards and continues to support a variety of research and professional educational endeavors that are aimed at continually enhancing the profession and its members.

The Financial Accounting Standards Board

The Accounting Principles Board was composed of members of the AICPA. Over the years, it received substantial criticism concerning its lack of independence and its inability to respond quickly to emerging problems. Following the recommendations of a study group, the AICPA supported the establishment of an independent organization to promulgate accounting principles. FASB was established to meet this need.

The Financial Accounting Standards Board consists of seven full-time members drawn from public accounting, industry, education, and government. The board is supported by an extensive staff and has the ability to research, evaluate, and react to new situations in a reasonable time. The board's activities are structured to provide the broadest base of input into their deliberations concerning accounting principles.

Like its predecessor, the Accounting Principles Board, the Financial Accounting Standards Board promulgates reporting and disclosure principles for use by the profession. The board has received the cooperation and support of the Securities and Exchange Commission, which has legislative authority to force compliance.

Other organizations, boards, and commissions also have an influence on accounting practice. Because of the breadth of the profession, the focus of some of these activities is not restricted to financial accounting. The impact on the financial records of an entity may be indirect in nature. Advanced study in accounting will expose students to information about many of these organizations, their activities, authority, and accomplishments.

QUESTIONS

2-1 Name three organizations that specify rules for financial accounting practices.

2-2 Which factors characterize the environment of accounting?

2-3 Distinguish between qualitative and quantitative descriptions. Which is most applicable to accounting?

2-4 What assumptions underlie the use of historical costs for financial statements?

2-5 Define the terms, *revenue* and *expense*.

2-6 What characteristics are applied in accounting to help assure that reported information is useful to statement users?

2-7 What is *relevance*? *Reliability*?

2-8 Why is the principle of consistency necessary for the evaluation of comparative financial statements related to consecutive periods?

2-9 How is insignificant data treated under the concept of materiality? Give an example.

2-10 Describe the format of a conventional balance sheet.

2-11 Distinguish between the "accounting equation" and the "expanded accounting equation."

2-12 List four events that can affect owner's equity.

2-13 What steps are taken in the preparation of financial statements to assure that correct information is reported?

2-14 Define the term *gross margin*, and explain what information can be derived from it.

2-15 Discuss the powers and duties of the three organizations that regulate the accounting profession.

2-16 Explain the matching concept.

2-17 Identify the concept that is associated with the preparation of *annual* financial statements.

2-18 Name the accounting concept that instructs that all measures listed in financial reports prepared for distribution in the United States be stated in terms of dollars.

2-19 From which sources do CPAs obtain information required in their work? Are CPAs legally liable to clients for the quality of their work?

2-20 Describe the objectives of three accounting reports listed in this chapter.

2-21 Accounting reports are used in making various business decisions. List three examples of decisions that are commonly based on accounting information.

EXERCISES

E2-1 Just prior to going out-of-business, the Smith Corporation prepared a balance sheet as follows:

Assets (no cash)	$50,000
Liabilities..........................	30,000
Owners' equity	20,000

Assets were subsequently sold for $40,000 in cash.

Required:

a. Prepare a balance sheet immediately after the sale of assets.
b. Explain how the cash should be distributed.

E2-2 On January 1, 19x6, the inventory account of the Harper Company showed a balance of $100,000. During the year, the company purchased $50,000 worth of inventory, and delivered $55,000 of goods to customers. What is the balance of the inventory account on December 31, 19x6?

E2-3 The Jones partnership was established on July 1, 19x6. It adopted a June 30 year-end. Each of three partners contributed $1,000 on July 1, 19x6. On June 30, 19x7, the following amounts were determined: (a) $2,050 was in the checking account, (b) amounts due from customers for services rendered—$1,000, (c) office supplies on hand—$2,000, (d) $1,500 in notes payable owed to a local bank, and (e) amounts due to suppliers of $500.

Required:

a. Using the accounting equation, what is the balance of the partners' capital accounts (in aggregate) at June 30, 19x7?
b. Prepare a balance sheet for the Jones partnership at June 30, 19x7.

E2-4 Barbara James and Heather Holmes opened Dallas Used Cars, Inc. They hired an accountant at the end of their first year of operations who determined that the following transactions took place during the year:

a. A bank account was opened with a deposit of $70,000.
b. Used cars were purchased for $60,000.
c. Cars that cost $20,000 were sold for $30,000.
d. The remaining cars had fair market value of $80,000.
e. Barbara's brother-in-law was paid $6,000 salary as a part-time salesman.

Required:

Perform an analysis similar to the one shown in Illustration 1.

E2-5 Below are independent events. Indicate the effect (increase, decrease, no effect) and the amount on assets, liabilities, and owner's equity:

a. In starting a new business, owners contribute $100,000 cash, a building worth $50,000, and land worth $40,000.
b. Office furniture and calculators were purchased for $5,000.
c. A mortgage of $30,000 was taken out on the building.
d. Salesmen's commissions are paid by cash—$200.
e. Inventory was purchased on account—$500.

E2-6 Westward Photographers, Inc. has a fiscal year closing of June 30. For fiscal year 19x7, you have determined the following account balances:

Sales	$100,000
Cost of goods sold	60,000
Advertising expense	5,000
Rent expense	7,200
Salary expense	10,000

Required:

Prepare an income statement for Westward Photographers, Inc.

E2-7 The Vivian Company balance sheet on December 31, 19x1, contains the following totals:

Assets	*Liabilities*	*Owner's Equity*
$10,000	$1,000	$9,000

Keep a cumulative running total showing the effect each of the following transactions has on the totals of the balance sheet as in Illustration 1.

a. Bought truck for $5,000 cash.
b. Owner invested $10,000 of additional cash in business.
c. Business borrowed $10,000 on a note to the bank.
d. Sold merchandise for cash—$3,000.
e. Paid off a note to the bank—$1,000.

E2-8 Show the effects (increase + decrease − or no change 0) in the proper columns of the balance sheet—assets (A), liabilities (L), owner's equity (OE)—for the following transactions.

a. Owner withdaws cash.
b. Equipment sold for cash.
c. Bought truck on credit.
d. Truck purchased for cash.
e. One owner sells his or her interest to another owner.
f. A bank loan is obtained to pay an overdue bill.

E2-9 a. The assets of a company total $2 million and the owner's equity totals $1.4 million. What is the amount of total liabilities?
b. The total liabilities of a company are worth $100,000. This figure is 50 percent of the total assets. What is the amount of owner's equity.

E2-10 Determine whether each of the following events constitutes a recordable transaction.

a. Owners invested $10,000 cash into the business.
b. Purchased truck for $8,000, payment to be made next year.
c. Employed salesman at $1,000 per week. He or she will start work tomorrow.
d. Paid $400 for telephone bill for previous month.
e. Paid for truck in (b).

E2-11 Indicate whether the effect on each of the following transactions is to increase, decrease, or have no effect on the total assets of the business as shown on its balance sheet.

Transaction	*Asset Increase*	*Asset Decrease*	*No Effect*
a. Owners invest cash in business	______	______	______
b. Customers pay cash for services	______	______	______
c. Business purchases supplies for cash	______	______	______
d. Business purchases equipment for cash	______	______	______
e. Supplies are purchased for credit	______	______	______
f. A liability is paid in cash	______	______	______
g. Owners withdraw cash	______	______	______
h. An asset is destroyed by fire	______	______	______

E2-12 Show the effect of each of the following transactions on owner's equity by completing the following table.

	Effect on Owner's Equity		
Transaction	*Asset Increase*	*Asset Decrease*	*No Effect*
a. Owner invested cash	______	______	______
b. Business purchases land	______	______	______
c. Business pays rental expenses	______	______	______
d. Customers pay cash for services	______	______	______
e. Owners withdraw cash	______	______	______
f. A liability is paid	______	______	______
g. A creditor satisfies his or her claim by becoming an owner	______	______	______

E2-13 Compute the unknown amounts on each of the four unrelated business balance sheets.

	A	*B*	*C*	*D*
Accounts receivable		$ 400	$1,000	$ 3,000
Accounts payable	$ 9,000	800	1,000	8,000
Cash	12,000		1,300	7,000
Equipment	32,000	9,000	6,000	13,000
Land	6,000	8,000	2,000	5,000
Salaries payable	8,000	600		2,500
Supplies	500	1,000	1,000	1,500
Owner's equity	46,000	20,000	8,000	

PROBLEMS

P2-1 Below are transactions for the Rogers Company for the month of April 19x9:

1. Clay Rogers invested $50,000 in the business.
2. $5,000 of equipment was purchased for the business for cash.
3. $50,000 of merchandise was purchased for resale on account.
4. Clay Rogers invested $50,000 of additional cash in the business.
5. Advertising of $500 was paid with cash.
6. Merchandise costing $10,000 was sold for $40,000 cash.
7. Rent of $10,000 for the company's office building was paid for in cash.
8. Merchandise costing $20,000 was sold for $50,000, $10,000 of which was paid in cash, and the rest was owed on account.
9. Salaries of $25,000 were paid in cash.
10. Clay Rogers withdrew $10,000 cash from the business.
11. $10,000 of the amounts owed the company were paid in cash.
12. Merchandise costing $3,000 was sold for $6,000 cash.

Required:

a. Set up an expanded accounting equation in the same form shown in Illustration 1. Record the transactions for the Rogers Company.
b. After all transactions have been recorded, prepare a simple income statement and balance sheet.

P2-2 The balance sheet for the Blackburn Company on January 1, 19x9, is as follows:

Blackburn Company
Balance Sheet
January 1, 19x9

Assets		*Liabilities*	
Cash	$10,000	Accounts payable	$ 2,000
Accounts receivable	15,000	Notes payable	4,000
Inventory	4,000		$ 6,000
Equipment	17,000	*Owner's Equity*	
		Net investment	$40,000
	$46,000		$46,000

The following transactions took place during 19x9:

a. Sold merchandise costing $1,000 for $5,000 cash.
b. Bert Blackburn, owner, invested additional cash of $20,000 in the business.
c. Received $10,000 in cash as payment of accounts from customers.
d. Bought merchandise for $10,000 on account.
e. Advertising of $500 for the year was paid in cash.
f. Equipment was purchased for $1,000 cash.
g. Sold merchandise costing $5,000 for $15,000, $10,000 of which was paid in cash.
h. Paid off $3,000 of note payable with cash.
i. Paid salaries of $10,000 with cash.

Required:

Prepare income statement and balance sheet for Blackburn Company.

P2-3 Prepare a balance sheet for the McCummen Company for December 31, 19x9, using the following infomation:

Accounts payable	$14,000
Accounts receivable	8,275
Buildings	64,000
Land	30,000
Cash	?
Equipment	2,100
Notes payable	30,000
Truck	3,420
Jim McCummen—capital	80,000

P2-4 The financial data for the Howard Company (an electronics servicing firm) for the month of April are summarized in equation form below. Each line shows the effect of each transaction on the equation.

	Cash	+ *Accounts Receivables*	+ *Supplies*	+ *Equipment*	= *Accounts Payable*	+ *Capital*	+ *Revenue*	− *Expense*
Balance	$11,000	$4,000	$450	$ 6,000	$4,450	$17,000		
1	2,000						+ $2,000	
2	− 100				− 100			
3			− 200					+ $200
4	− 400		+ 400					
5	+ 1,000					+ 1,000		
6	− 200							+ 200
7	− 1,500					− 1,500		
8				+ 4,000	+ 4,000			
9		+ 300					+ 300	
10	+ 2,000	− 2,000						
	$13,800	+ $2,300	+ $650	+ $10,000	= $8,350	+ $16,500	+ $2,300	− $400

Required:

a. Describe the probable nature of each transaction.
b. What is the net change in cash and owner's equity for the month?
c. What is the net income for the month?

E2-5 Below are transactions for the Howard Company for the month of May:

May	1	Ann Howard, owner, invested $40,000 cash.
	3	The company borrowed $8,000 cash from bank on a note payable.
	4	The company buys $20,000 worth of equipment, pays $10,000, and promises to pay the other $10,000 within thirty days.
	12	Cash received for services is $12,000.
	14	Services performed for customers who agree to pay within thirty days is $4,000.
	16	Salaries are paid in cash, totalling $4,500.
	19	The company pays $2,000 of the note payable owed to the bank.
	22	The company pays $50 of interest on note with cash.
	24	Customers pay $1,000 of amount owed to company.
	27	An order is received from a customer for services to be rendered next week, which will be billed at $1,000.
	31	Utilities bill of $560 is paid in cash.

Required:

a. Using the following form of the expanded accounting equation, enter each transaction.

Date	*Cash*	+	*Accounts Receivable*	+	*Equipment*	=	*Accounts Payable*	+	*Notes Payable*	+	*Owners' Equity*	+	*Revenue*	−	*Expenses*

b. Calculate net income for the month of May.

E2-6 Given below are the statements of financial position and the income statement of the Logan Company.

Logan Company
Statement of Financial Position

	April 30, 19x8	*May 31, 19x8*
Assets:		
Cash	$ 8,000	$12,000
Accounts receivable	12,000	10,000
Prepaid rent	3,000	2,000
Total assets	$23,000	$24,000
Liabilities and Owner's Equity:		
Liabilities	$ 6,000	$ 3,000
Total owner's equity	17,000	21,000
	$23,000	$24,000

Logan Company
Income Statement
For the Month Ended May 31, 19x8

Revenue		$15,000
Expenses:		
Utilities	$10,000	
Rent	1,000	11,000
Net earnings		$ 4,000

Required:

Assume that all revenues earned were received in cash. State the probable cause of the changes in each of the statements of financial position accounts during May.

E2-7 Below are the transactions of Lightfoot Service Company for the month of March 19x4:

1. Received $800 for services performed for customers, not previously billed.
2. Paid $300 accounts payable.
3. Paid rent of $300 for March.
4. Received $1,000 on account from customers.
5. Purchased $200 of supplies, paying cash.
6. Purchased $2,000 of equipment on account.
7. Withdrew $200 for owner's personal use.
8. Paid wages in cash—$1,300.
9. Paid utilities in cash—$100.
10. Used $100 in supplies.

Required:

a. Complete the following expanded accounting equation for each of these transactions:

	Cash	+	*Accounts Receivable*	+	*Supplies*	+	*Equipment*	=	*Accounts Payable*	+	*Capital*	+	*Revenue*	–	*Expenses*
Balance:	$12,000	+	$3,000	+	$500	+	$6,000	=	$2,000	+	$19,500	+	________	–	________

b. Prepare a balance sheet as of March 31, 19x4.

E2-8 Savannah TV Repair Company's records show the information listed below for 19x3 and 19x4:

	December 31, 19x3	*December 31, 19x4*
Accounts receivable	$9,000	$6,000
Accounts payable	4,000	1,500
Cash	6,000	7,200
Equipment	8,800	7,700
Supplies	1,500	900
Notes payable	3,000	2,000
Owner's investment......	?	?

Required:

a. Prepare a balance sheet for Savannah TV Repair Company for each year.
b. Assuming that the owner withdrew $1,000 during 19x4 for personal needs, calculate net income for 19x4.

E2-9 The transactions for the Mint Company for the month of October 19x2 are shown below:

a. Purchased auto for business use on credit.
b. Billed customer for services provided.
c. Paid rent for the month.
d. Collected cash from customer for rendering services.
e. Received amount due from customer.
f. Paid wages.
g. Purchased supplies for cash.
h. Withdrew cash for owner's personal use.
i. Paid utility bills when received.

Required:

Show the effect of each of these transactions on the balance sheet totals of assets, liabilities, and owner's equity.

Learning Objectives

Chapter 3 describes how journals and ledgers are maintained and illustrates the accounting cycle. Studying this chapter should enable you to:

1. Describe the format and purpose of the general ledger.
2. Record transactions in the ledger, giving proper consideration to debits and credits.
3. Prepare general journal entries.
4. Prepare a trial balance.
5. Complete the accounting cycle by journalizing and posting closing entries.

3

The Accounting Cycle

INTRODUCTION

All complex activities require organization if they are to achieve their intended goal. A baseball or football game would deteriorate into chaos if they were not organized. Organization implies a predetermined system or set of related procedures that govern the activity. In a baseball game, the rules specify who is at bat, who is in the field, and what specific actions may be taken at a given time. Rules organize the game.

The organization of many related parts is referred to as a system. A system regulates activities and functions in such a way that an overall goal may be attained. The accounting system directs all accounting activities toward a goal of reporting useful information. The sequence of activities followed in an accounting system is referred to as the *accounting cycle*, and it includes procedures to collect, record, and process financial data into a report of meaningful economic information. The process is continuous and ongoing, leading to the use of the term "cycle."

THE GENERAL LEDGER

An *account* is a unit of information about a particular economic object or event: in a physical sense, it is a form on which data are summarized. Thus, a cash account would maintain information about increases and decreases in cash. A personal checkbook could serve as an account; increases and decreases in available cash are recorded on the checkstub. The checkstub also summarizes (produces a balance) all transactions involving items classified as cash, that is, all checks and deposits. Like a checkstub, an account facilitates recording, summarizing, and classifying information about any one element of a transaction.

Maintaining Accounts

To properly record all of the transactions of an entity, many accounts are needed. Specifically, a separate account is kept for each item on a firm's balance sheet and income statement. Thus, there can be many asset, liability, and owner's equity accounts, plus revenue and expense accounts.

Accounts are kept and maintained in a *ledger*. In manual accounting systems, the ledger is a large book with a separate page for each account. In computerized systems, the ledger is a set of reserved storage locations with sublocations reserved for each acount. In either case, the ledger provides a summarization of how transactions affect a particular account.

Format of the Ledger

Each ledger account should provide the following information:

1. *Account Name*—Each account is identified by a name consistent with that used in the financial statements. Without becoming too restrictive, the number of accounts is normally limited to provide a reasonable amount of summarization.

2. *Account Number*—In most accounting systems, ledger accounts are numbered. Numbering aids in indexing and locating accounts, as the numbering system may be structured to identify groups of related items. For example, all assets could be identified with three digit numbers where the first digit is always a "1." By sorting on this digit, assets could quickly be identified. Liability account numbers might start with the numeral "2," owner's equity with a "3," and so on.

3. *Date Column*—The date of record is noted for every entry in the account. Dating each entry allows balances to be determined as of a specific date, knowledge that is absolutely necessary for preparing financial statements.

4. *Explanation Column*—The explanation column in the ledger provides room to describe the underlying transaction that affected the account. In many cases, explanations will be unnecessary as the reference column entry will provide an adequate description of the event.

5. *Reference Column*—The reference column indicates the source and location of the data that was recorded in the ledger. This is a control procedure to facilitate cross checking the original recording of the transaction with the summarization.

6. *Amount Columns*—Each ledger has two amount columns: one for increases in the account, the other for decreases from the account. The double-column format reduces possibilities for error associated with using plus and minus signs in a single column.

7. *Balance Columns (optional)*—Ledger accounts may include specific columns for maintaining a running total of the account balance. The balance is the difference between the debits and credits. When a balance column is not used, the account is periodically totalled, or *footed*, to facilitate reporting.

8. *Number of Accounts in the Ledger*—The number of accounts contained in the ledger is determined by the amount and type of information demanded by the organization. Additional accounts are added when more information is required. Organizational form also influences the number of accounts contained in the ledger, as described in the Appendix at the end of this chapter. For example, information about the equity of a sole proprietorship is contained in one account called owner's equity, while equity accounts for a corporation are titled common stock and retained earnings.

A standard, three column ledger account will appear as shown in Illustration 1.

Illustration 1
Ledger

Account Title			Account Number		
Date	Explanation	Post Ref.	Debit Amount	Credit Amount	Balance

Specific forms of ledger accounts can vary, depending on the particular business environment in which they are used. However, each will have the general characteristics identified above. A ledger account can be represented by the letter "T:"

Account Title	
Debit Amount	Credit Amount

While form is important and should not be ignored, the T-account representation is an excellent way to illustrate the effect of transactions on the accounts. We shall employ the T-account format to illustrate how transactions affect accounts.

DEBITS AND CREDITS

Amount columns of general ledger accounts have been identified as *debit* and *credit*, respectively. Literally, these terms refer to the side of an account where an entry is to be placed. *Debits* relate to entries on the left-hand side of an account, and *credits* relate to entries on the right-hand side. Such entries will either increase or decrease an account, depending on whether its normal balance is a debit or credit.

Normal Account Balances

The normal balance of an account depends on its traditional classification and placement on the balance sheet. By treating the balance sheet as a large T-account, with left- and right-side balances, and by superimposing specific accounts on it, the normal account balances become obvious as shown in Illustration 2.

Assets that appear on the left side, or debit side, of the balance sheet are increased by debits and have a normal debit balance. Conversely, the normal balances of liability and owner's equity accounts are credits and credit entries will increase them. In a summary fashion, the relationships between the accounts and debits and credits can be expressed as follows:

1. Asset accounts:
   a. Normal balance is on the left side—debit.
   b. Increases are recorded by debit entries.
   c. Decreases are recorded by credit entries.
2. Liability accounts:
   a. Normal balance is on the right side—credit.
   b. Increases are recorded by credit entries.
   c. Decreases are recorded by debit entries.
3. Owner's equity account:
   a. Normal balance is on the right side—credit.
   b. Increases are recorded by credit entries.
   c. Decreases are recorded by debit entries.

Double-Entry Recording

A transaction was defined as an exchange in which the entity gives and receives consideration of equal economic value. Therefore, any transaction must be recorded by entries to, at least, two accounts—one showing what was given in the transaction and the other what was received. Furthermore, the debits recorded for a transaction must equal the recorded credits, since accountants equate values for both parts of the transaction.

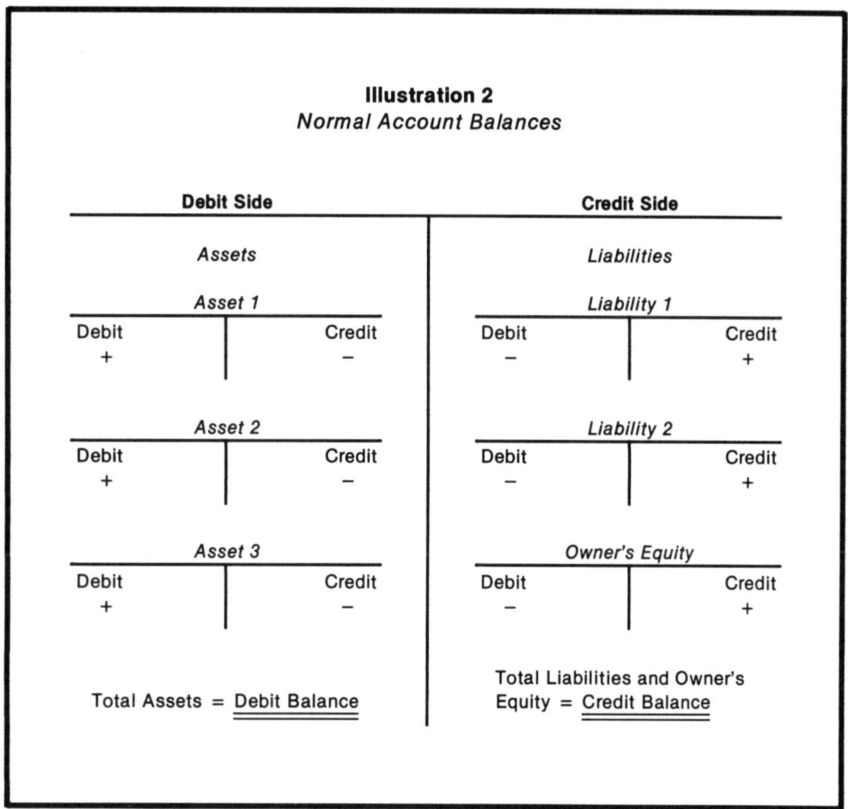

The duality of this process—debits equals credits—is the basis of double-entry accounting, where each transaction results in, at least, two entries—a debit and a credit of equal value. Verification of the equality of debits and credits in each transaction provides the accountant with some assurance that the complete effect of transaction was recorded.

ANALYZING TRANSACTIONS

The accountant must analyze transactions to: (1) determine which accounts are affected, and (2) determine the proper debit and credit amounts needed to record the transaction. An advantage of the general ledger is its flexibility; accounts may be added as needed. The following transactions illustrate how information is recorded in the general ledger. Each transaction assumes that the accounts do have sufficient amounts of their normal balance to facilitate the exchange. Account names include the parenthetical notation of A, L, or OE, representing asset, liability, or owner's equity, respectively. Also, the debit and credit captions include a notation of either + or − to indicate the effect on the normal balance of this type of account.

1. *Type*—Receipt of an asset for owner's equity.

   Example—An owner invests $20,000 cash in the business. (Cash increases, owner's equity increases).

Cash (A)	
Debit (+)	Credit (−)
$20,000	

Owners' Equity (OE)	
Debit (−)	Credit (+)
	$20,000

2. *Type*—Exchange of an asset for an asset.

   Example—A new truck is purchased for $6,000 cash. (Truck asset increases and cash decreases).

Truck (A)	
Debit (+)	Credit (−)
$6,000	

Cash (A)	
Debit (+)	Credit (−)
	$6,000

3. *Type*—Receipt of an asset for a liability.

   Example—Land, costing $28,000, is purchased through a mortgage. (Land increases and mortgage payable increases).

Land (A)	
Debit (+)	Credit (−)
$28,000	

Mortgage Payable (L)	
Debit (−)	Credit (+)
	$28,000

4. *Type*—Reduction of a liability in exchange for an asset.

   Example—Cash for $10,000 is paid to reduce an outstanding mortgage. (Cash decreases and mortgage payable decreases).

Cash (A)	
Debit (+)	Credit (−)
	$10,000

Owners' Equity (OE)	
Debit (−)	Credit (+)
$10,000	

5. *Type*—Reduction of owner's equity in exchange for an asset.

   Example—An owner withdraws $4,000 of his or her investment from a business. (Cash decreases and owner's equity decreases).

Cash (A)	
Debit (+)	Credit (−)
	$4,000

Owners' Equity (OE)	
Debit (−)	Credit (+)
$4,000	

6. *Type*—Reduction of a liability in exchange for owner's equity interest.

   Example—A creditor, to whom the company owes $8,000, is permitted to invest that amount in the business in exchange for cancelling the liability. (Accounts payable decreases and owner's equity increases).

Accounts Payable (L)	
Debit (−)	Credit (+)
$8,000	

Owners' Equity (OE)	
Debit (−)	Credit (+)
	$8,000

In each of the forgoing transactions, the complete entry required the debits to equal the credits, thus maintaining the equality of the accounting equation.

REVENUE AND EXPENSE TRANSACTIONS

Revenue and expense transactions have not been analyzed to this point. Data obtained from recording these activities become the central elements of an income statement.

Revenue

When resources are acquired, they are recorded at their cost to the firm. When resources are sold by the firm, they are recorded at their sale price. The selling price is termed *revenue*, and it is measured as the amount received by the firm in exchange for the resource given up. Revenue results from business activities where a product or a service is sold. Examples of revenue-producing transactions include sales of merchandise or products manufactured, providing services, renting property, interest earned on investments, etc.

Expenses

When a business incurs a cost, it is valued at what the firm paid for it. The cost may provide the company with future benefits, present benefits, or, in some cases, no benefit. As Illustration 3 presents, when a cost has future benefit (such as the cost of a new truck), it is recorded as an asset. If the cost benefits only the current year (such as the cost of electricity), it is recorded as an expense. A cost that has no benefit (such as the cost of a fire) is recorded as a loss.

Assets are reported in the balance sheet while expenses and losses are recorded in the income statement. Sometimes a cost is initially recorded as an asset and later becomes an expense. For example, if a company purchased some merchandise in one year to be sold in the next year, the cost of the merchandise would be recorded as an asset in the first year because it will benefit the future (i.e., the next year when it is sold). In the second year, when the merchandise is actually sold, the cost becomes an expense because it is now benefiting only the current year. Thus, in the second year, the cost has to be reclassified from asset to expense. This reclassification is part of the adjustment process which will be explained in detail in Chapter 4.

Recording Revenues and Expenses

Revenue and expense accounts are used to calculate net income as reported on the income statement. Revenues increase and expenses decrease net income. Recall from Chapter 2 that income adds to owner's equity in the balance sheet. Since owner's equity has a credit balance, revenue (which increases income) must also have a credit balance and expenses (which decreases income) must have a debit balance. The effects of debits and credits on these accounts are summarized as follows:

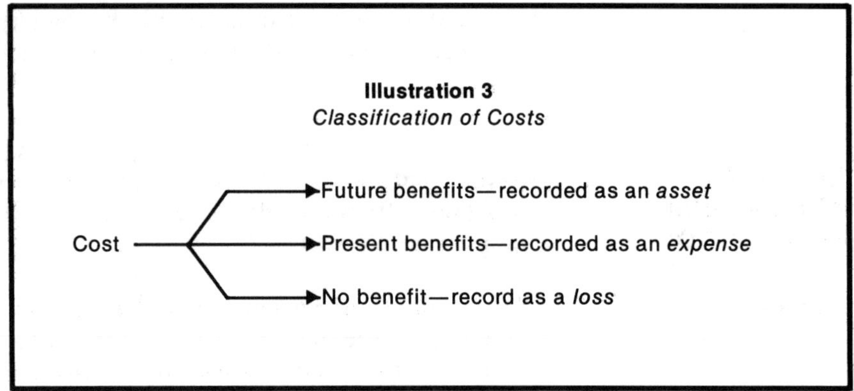

1. Revenue accounts:
   a. Normal balance is on the right side—credit.
   b. Increases are recorded by credit entries.
   c. Decreases are recorded by debit entries.
2. Expense accounts:
   a. Normal balance is on the left side—debit.
   b. Increases are recorded by debit entries.
   c. Decreases are recorded by credit entries.

To illustrate, assume an automobile dealer sells a car to a customer for $10,000. Also assume the car cost the dealer $6,000. The parenthetically noted R and E refer to revenue and expense accounts, respectively, and the debit and credit captions include a notation showing the effect on the normal balance of the accounts.

1. Reclassifying costs from assets to expenses—assets must be reduced by $6,000 and expenses must be increased by $6,000.

Car (A)	
Debit (+)	Credit (−)
	$6,000

Cost of Goods Sold (E)	
Debit (+)	Credit (−)
$6,000	

2. Recognizing the revenue from the sale—assets must be increased by $10,000 and revenue of $10,000 must be recognized.

Cash (A)	
Debit (+)	Credit (−)
$10,000	

Sales Revenue (A)	
Debit (+)	Credit (−)
	$10,000

THE GENERAL JOURNAL

In the previous examples, transactions were recorded directly into the general ledger accounts. While this method facilitates the preparation of financial statements, it is not conducive to recording *transaction activity* in an orderly fashion. Assume that 100 transactions are recorded in the ledger, the details of any particular transaction would be obscured, since the general ledger classifies activity by type of account rather than by transaction. One of the entries for the cash account may be an increase (debit) of $5,000. If we wanted to know the source of this $5,000, we could not determine it from the ledger account because it shows only one side of the transaction. To get this information we would need to view the whole transaction. Transaction data is recorded in the *journal*. The journal contains a chronological listing of each transaction. Transactions are initially recorded in the journal. Hence, the journal is a place of original entry.

The information recorded in the journal is then transcribed or recorded in the ledger format. The process of taking transaction data from the journal and putting it in the ledger is called *posting*. Thus, in accounting there are two types of records. The journal provides a listing of transactions and allows us to view both what was received and what was given in each transaction. However, if we had only a journal, it would be difficult to determine the current balance in an account, such as cash, without going back over every transaction to determine its effect on cash. It is for this reason that a second record, the ledger, is kept. The ledger summarizes, in one location, the effect of all transactions on a specific account. If management wants information regarding a particular transaction, it is found in the journal while information concerning a specific account is found in the ledger.

Format of the Journal

The general journal normally is structured to provide the following information:

1. *Date Column*—The date when each transaction occurred is recorded in the date column.
2. *Accounts*—The names of the ledger accounts to be debited and credited are recorded in this section.
3. *Reference*—The reference column identifies the ledger account number of each account to be posted. Normally, these numbers are inserted when posting occurs, thereby providing a control over the posting process.
4. *Amount Columns*—Separate columns are maintained for recording the debit and credit accounts corresponding with each account.

A standard journal will appear in the following form:

Date	Accounts	Ref.	Debit	Credit
19x1 July 15	Land Cash To record the purchase of building lost number A-176	10 1	$4,200	 $4,200

Recognize two additional characteristics of the journal entry. First, the debit account in the accounts column is slightly left adjusted and the credit account is slightly right adjusted. This placement represents a generally used form for recording journal entries. Second, the entry itself is followed by a brief description of the transaction. These descriptions are used sparingly, when necessary, to provide details about a transaction or to disclose important information about the transaction not evident from the journal entry.

THE COMPLETE RECORDING PROCESS

To place the entire recording process in context, consider the following transactions of the Tell-A-Phone Answering Service:

19x1	
June 1	Mr. William Tell invested $5,000 in the Tell-A-Phone Answering Service.
2	The business bought a store for $20,000, paying $4,000 in cash and getting a mortgage for the balance.
2	The business leased telephone equipment for $1,000 a month and paid the first month's charge.
7	The business negotiated a $7,000 bank loan and received the cash.
8	An employee was paid a salary that totalled $300.
10	Collections from customers for answering services amounted to $1,000.
11	Customers were billed $3,000 for answering services.
15	An employee was paid a salary of $300.
16	Customers billed on June 11 paid $1,000, one-third of the balance due.

These transactions are recorded in the general journal of the business, or *journalized*, as shown in Illustration 3. The first transaction is recorded by debiting cash (increasing it) since the company received cash in the transaction. The source of the cash was the owner and owner's equity is increased by crediting it. The transaction can then be posted to the ledger (see Illustration 5). In the ledger, account no. 1 (cash) is debited for $5,000. Once the cash portion of the transaction has been posted, the account number is placed

Illustration 4
General Journal

Page 1

Date	*Accounts*	*Ref.*	*Debit*	*Credit*
19x6				
6/1	Cash	1	$ 5,000	
	Owner's equity	6		$ 5,000
	Investment in business by Mr. Tell			
6/2	Store	3	20,000	
	Cash	1		4,000
	Mortgage payable	5		16,000
	Purchase of a new store			
6/2	Equipment expense	9	1,000	
	Cash	1		1,000
	Rental charge for new telephone equipment			
6/7	Cash	1	7,000	
	Bank loan payable	4		7,000
	Loan of $7,000 from the Smith Bank			
6/8	Salary expense	8	300	
	Cash	1		300
	Weekly salary was paid			
6/10	Cash	1	1,000	
	Service revenue	7		1,000
	Cash collections from customers			
6/11	Accounts receivable	2	3,000	
	Service revenue	7		3,000
	Owed by customers for service performed			
6/15	Salary expense	8	300	
	Cash	1		300
	Weekly salary was paid			
6/16	Cash	1	1,000	
	Accounts receivable	2		1,000
	Collections of account from customers			

in the reference column of the journal. This reference serves two purposes. First, it informs the individual doing the posting that this item has been posted. Second, it provides a trail to show where the item has been posted in case there is a question concerning the posting or the transaction effect on the account. Next, the owner's equity account in the ledger is credited (increased) for $5,000. The account number, 6, is then put in the reference column. In the second entry, a store was purchased for cash and a mortgage. In the journal, the asset account store is debited (increased) for $20,000 and cash is credited (decreased) for the $4,000 down payment and a second credit (increase) is made to the liability account, mortgage payable. When an entry involves more than one debit and credit, as in this case, it is called a *compound* entry. After journalizing this transaction, it is posted to the ledger accounts. The process continues until all transaction have been recorded and posted.

For purposes of this illustration, the ledger format used was a simplified T-account form rather than the formal ledger format shown previously in Illustration 1. Had the more detailed form been used, there would also be a reference column in each ledger account. The source of the posting, such as J-1 (meaning journal, page 1), would be entered. The use of reference columns in both the journal and the ledger provides a quick cross-reference between the two records.

The Trial Balance

After transactions have been posted in the ledger, ledger accounts are periodically footed, or totalled. A single line through the account indicates that a balance appears on the following line. Balances are set out by a double underline. Recognize that some accounts have a debit, or left side, balance, while others have a credit, or right side, balance.

Partial verification of journalizing and posting accuracy is obtained from a *trial balance*. The trial balance is a listing of all of the account balances as of a particular date. The total dollar amount of accounts with debit balances should equal the total of accounts with credit balances. If they are not equal, a journalizing or posting error has been made. The accountant should locate and correct the error.

Equality of trial balance debits and credits does not insure that the recording process has been correctly performed. Instead, it indicates that certain errors have not been made. Among the errors which a trial balance will not detect are:

1. A transaction posted to the wrong account.
2. An incorrect dollar value used consistently in both the debit and the credit of a transaction.
3. Recording a transaction more than once.
4. Correctly posting a transaction that was incorrectly journalized.
5. Failure to record a transaction.

Illustration 5
Ledger Accounts

Cash (A) — No. 1

Debit (+)		Credit (−)	
6/1	$5,000	$4,000	6/2
6/7	7,000	1,000	6/2
6/10	1,000	300	
6/16	1,000	300	6/15
	$8,400		

Accounts Receivable (A) — No. 2

Debit (+)		Credit (−)	
6/11	$3,000	$1,000	6/16
	$2,000		

Store (A) — No. 3

Debit (+)		Credit (−)	
6/2	$20,000		

Bank Loan Payable (L) — No. 4

Debit (−)		Credit (+)	
		$7,000	6/7

Mortgage Payable (L) — No. 5

Debit (−)		Credit (+)	
		$16,000	6/2

Owner's Equity (OE) — No. 6

Debit (−)		Credit (+)	
		$5,000	6/1

Service Revenue (R) — No. 7

Debit (−)		Credit (+)	
		$1,000	6/10
		3,000	6/11
		$4,000	

Salary Expense (E) — No. 8

Debit (+)		Credit (−)	
6/8	$300		
6/15	300		
	$600		

Equipment Expense (E) — No. 9

Debit (+)		Credit (−)	
6/2	$1,000		

A trial balance as of June 30, 19x1, for the Tell-A-Phone Answering Service is shown in Illustration 6.

The Closing Process

Revenue and expense account balances are not cumulative. These accounts are maintained on an annual basis (i.e., start with a zero balance and accumulate data for a whole year) to facilitate the preparation of an income statement. At the end of the period, revenue and expense accounts are "closed out," or turned back to zero, so that they can start off with a fresh start for the next period. The closing process also helps confirm the net income calculation. The closing process can be used to transfer the net income

Illustration 6
Tell-A-Phone Answering Service
Trial Balance
June 30, 19x1

Account	*Debit*	*Credit*
Cash	$ 8,400	
Accounts receivable	2,000	
Store	20,000	
Bank loan		$ 7,000
Mortgage payable		16,000
Owner's equity		5,000
Service revenue		4,000
Salary expense	600	
Equipment expense	1,000	
	$32,000	$32,000

to the owner's equity accounts. The process of determining net income and clearing the revenue and expense accounts is referred to as the *closing process*; the revenues and expense accounts are closed for the year.

The closing process introduces a special, temporary account called "income summary" as a vehicle for computing net income and transferring it to the owner's equity account. In a sequential fashion, the steps of the closing process are as follows:

1. Closing revenue accounts by *debiting* them for their balance and *crediting* income summary.
2. Close expense accounts by *crediting* them for their balance and *debiting* income summary.
3. Determine the balance of the income summary account. A debit balance indicates a loss. A credit balance indicates income.

   Close the income summary account with a *debit* balance by *crediting* income summary and *debiting* owner's equity. Close the income summary account with a credit balance by *debiting* income summary and *crediting* owner's equity.

When the closing process is complete, all revenue and expense accounts should have a zero balance and the net income or loss should be included in the owner's equity account. Three closing entries would be necessary for the Tell-A-Phone Answering Service:

Date	Accounts	Debit	Credit
June 20	Service revenue....................	$4,000	
	Income summary		$4,000
	To close the revenue account		
30	Income summary	1,600	
	Salary expense		600
	Equipment expense		1,000
	To close the expense accounts		
30	Income summary	2,400	
	Owner's equity		2,400
	To close the income summary account		

Illustration 7 shows the general ledger after the closing entries have been posted and final balances taken. The closing entries are identified by a parenthetical "c."

After the closing process is complete, any account with a nonzero balance is reported on the balance sheet. The revenue and expense accounts, as well as the income summary account, all have zero balances. These accounts supply data used in preparing the income statement.

SUMMARY

The accounting cycle consists of a periodic process that encompasses all account events from the recording of original transactions to the ultimate preparation of financial statements. Each transaction is analyzed in terms of its effect on two or more accounts. These effects are chronologically listed in the general journal, a formal book of original entry that identifies account names, as well as debit and credit dollar amounts. Every entry in the journal specifies whether an account is to be increased or decreased, an effect related to the traditional (but arbitrary) "normal" balance of an account. Normally asset and expense accounts maintain debit balances, while liability, owner's equity, and revenue accounts have credit balances.

Subsequent to the original entry, data from the journal is transcribed or posted in the ledger. The ledger is a collection of accounts, each of which has a title (name) and account number, and columns for debit, credit, and balance entries. Posting from the journal to the ledger sorts all transaction effects by account name, so that each account balance represents the accumulated summary up to a particular point in time. A trial balance summarizes debit and credit account balances and provides a limited validity check on the recording process.

Revenue and expense accounts are periodically closed, or transferred, to a special account called income summary. Income summary is used to compute the net income or loss resulting from a series of transactions and to clear the balances of the revenue and expense accounts for future accumulations of transactions activity. The income summary account is closed by transferring its balance to the owner's investment account. After the closing process is complete, accounts with remaining balances are reported on a balance sheet. The revenue, expense, and income summary accounts are used to prepare the income statement.

Illustration 7

Final General Ledger Balance

Cash (A) — No. 1

$5,000	$4,000
7,000	1,000
1,000	300
1,000	300
$8,400	

Accounts Receivable (A) — No. 2

Debit (+)	Credit (−)
$3,000	$1,000
$2,000	

Store (A) — No. 3

Debit (+)	Credit (−)
$20,000	

Bank Loan Payable (L) — No. 4

Debit (−)	Credit (+)
	$7,000

Mortgage Payable (L) — No. 5

Debit (−)	Credit (+)
	$16,000

Owner's Equity (OE) — No. 6

Debit (−)	Credit (+)
	$5,000
	2,400 (c)
	$7,400

Service Revenue (R) — No. 7

Debit (−)	Credit (+)
(c) $4,000	$1,000
	3,000
	0

Salary Expense (E) — No. 8

Debit (+)	Credit (−)
$300	$600 (c)
300	
0	

Equipment Expense (E) — No. 9

Debit (+)	Credit (−)
$1,000	$1,000 (c)
0	

Income Summary — No. 10

Debit	Credit
(c) $1,600	$4,000 (c)
(c) 2,400	
	0

KEY DEFINITIONS

Account—a unit of information about a particular object or event.

Closing process—entries made to zero out revenues, expenses, and dividend accounts.

Credits—increases in liabilities, equity, and revenues and decreases in assets and expenses.

Debits—increases in assets and expenses and decreases in liabilities, equity, and revenues.

Journal—a chronological record of transactions.

Ledger—a record of accounts.

Posting—transcribing transaction data from the journal to the ledger.

Trial balance—a listing of account balances used to check the accuracy of postings.

Appendix

Forms of Business Organization

INTRODUCTION

Virtually all of the millions of businesses in the United States are organized and operated as proprietorships, partnerships, or corporations. While proprietorships represent the largest number of businesses, domestic corporations generated the majority of the total business receipts in the United States. Features of the organizational forms can explain these results. Although the basic accounting framework applies to all organizational forms, each form does require some few unique accounting procedures.

PROPRIETORSHIPS

Proprietorships are organized around a single owner of the business venture. In the legal sense, a proprietorship is not considered to be separate and distinct from its owner; thus, it is treated as an extension of the individual. Nevertheless, a proprietorship is treated as a distinct accounting entity.

Proprietory ventures may be started without prior legal authorization and may, therefore, be initiated or terminated quickly. Taxes are levied against the owner at individual tax rates, and business and personal income are combined. Most proprietorship ventures are fairly small, because they operate on the capital, or investment, of a single owner.

There are two major disadvantages to the proprietorship form of business organization, including the following:

1. *Legal Liability*—The business venture is not considered independent of its owner. Therefore, creditors may satisfy debts and other claims against the business by seizing or attaching the owner's personal property, such as home or car.
2. *Limited Life*—Proprietorships lack continuity, because they are associated with a particular individual. When the individual leaves the business, either through sale or death, the proprietorship ceases to exist.

In spite of these limitations, over ten million business ventures are organized as proprietorships—probably because of the ease of formation.

PARTNERSHIPS

The partnership is a form of business organization where ownership is shared among two or more co-owners (called partners). Although some minimal legal controls over a partnership are imposed, it, like a proprietorship, is considered to be an extension of its owners.

Taxes are levied against partners as individuals, and partnership income is combined with personal income in determining the annual tax liability. In contrast to proprietorships, partnerships can be quite large, because many individuals may combine their individual resources under this form of organization. Many certified public accounting firms and law firms are organized as partnerships, some of which have over a thousand partners.

Although partnership form permits the investment of several individuals, it still has the same disadvantages as does the proprietorship:

1. *Legal Liability*—Each partner is individually and personally liable for all of the debts of the partnership.
2. *Limited Life*—Each partnership represents a combination of specific individuals. When a partner dies, retires, or sells an interest in the business, the old partnership is terminated; continuity requires the formation of a new partnership.

It is estimated that over one million businesses are organized as partnerships in the United States.

CORPORATIONS

A corporation is legally defined as being separate and distinct from its owners; it is considered to be an artificial legal entity. Any number of individuals may simultaneously invest in a corporation by buying shares of its capital stock. These shares represent a proportionate ownership interest in the business. An individual investor's liability for debts of a corporation is legally limited to the amount he or she originally invested in the share of stock.

Shares of stock, or ownership interests, are freely traded on stock exchanges throughout the country; transferability of ownership is easily facilitated by the corporate form of organization. Also, the death of any stockholder does not terminate the business, since the stock can be sold or given to someone else; thus, continuity of ownership is promoted.

For these reasons, corporations have been able to attact significant amounts of investments over the years. Many large corporations have assets (resources) measured in the billions of dollars.

There are disadvantages to the corporation including the following:

1. *Organizational Costs*—Corporations must be chartered or approved by either a state government or by the federal government. Significant amounts of legal work, involving time and money, are generally required to secure this approval.

2. *Taxation*—Corporations are taxed on their earnings before they are distributed to the owners (investors). When earnings are distributed, they are taxed again to the individual recipients as personal income. Thus, corporate earnings are, in effect, taxed twice.

Corporations clearly dominate other forms of organization in terms of volume of business activity. Many investors feel that the advantages outweigh the disadvantages.

FINANCIAL STATEMENTS AND FORMS OF ORGANIZATION

The income statement and statement of cash flows of a business would not, in themselves, provide an indication of the form of organization used by the business. The reported information in these statements is not dependent on organizational form.

However, one section of the balance sheet will vary with the form of organization. While resources (assets) and creditor claims (liabilities) are independent of the organizational form, the owners' equity is not. The owners' equity section of the balance sheet reflects the particular type of owners' claims that are outstanding; these claims are related to the form of business organization.

Illustration 1 presents three different forms of a hypothetical owners' equity section for proprietorships, partnerships, and corporations. In practice, only one form would be used to reflect the prevailing organization structure.

Illustration 1

The Hypo-Thetical Company
Balance Sheet
January 31, 19x6

Assets		*Liabilities*	
Cash	$ 50,000	Bank loan	$75,000
Inventory	40,000		
Delivery trucks	60,000		
Furniture	30,000		
Total assets	$180,000		

Proprietorship

Owner's equity:	
Investment and income	$105,000
Total liabilities and owner's equity	$180,000

Partnership

Owners' equity:	
Partner A—investment and income	$ 52,500
Partner B—investment and income	52,500
Total liabilities and owners' equity	$180,000

Corporation

Stockholder's equity:	
Capital stock	$ 90,000
Retained earnings	15,000
Total liabilities and stockholders' equity	$180,000

QUESTIONS

3-1 Describe the format and purpose of the general ledger.

3-2 Are debit or credit balances normally found in asset accounts? In liability accounts? In owners' equity accounts?

3-3 In posting to the ledger, will a debit or a credit perform the following functions?

a. Increase a liability.
b. Increase an owners' equity
c. Decrease an asset.
d. Decrease a liability.
e. Increase an asset.
f. Decrease an owners' equity.

3-4 Define the word transaction.

3-5 What must an accountant determine when analyzing a transaction before journalizing it?

3-6 In the following transactions, indicate whether assets (A), liabilities (L), or owners' equity (OE) increase (+), decrease (−), or remain constant (0). The business:

a. Receives an asset for a liability (e.g., borrows money from a bank).
b. Exchanges an asset for an asset (e.g., buys inventory for cash).
c. Satisfies a liability for an asset (e.g., pays off a debt).
d. Distributes money to an owner.
e. Receives money from an owner.

3-7 Explain the difference between an asset, expense, and loss. Give an example of each.

3-8 On which side (debit, credit) of the T-account are the following situations entered?

Normal balance—expense accounts
Increase—expense account
Increase—revenue account
Decrease—expense account
Normal balance—revenue account

3-9 Does the general ledger summarize account activity before or after entries are made in the general journal?

3-10 Describe the format and purpose of the general journal.

3-11 Specify the purpose of the reference column in the general journal.

3-12 List some of the errors a trial balance *will not* detect.

3-13 What is the purpose of the closing process in the accounting cycle?

3-14 List the steps in the closing process.

3-15 Why are revenue and expense accounts "closed out" at the end of the accounting cycle?

3-16 Why are asset and liability accounts not "closed out" at the end of the accounting cycle?

3-17 Which of the following accounting principles are most closely related to the accounting cycle: materiality, consistency, or matching?

EXERCISES

E3-1 Set up separate T-accounts as needed and record the following transactions. Assume accounts have sufficient beginning balances to facilitate the exchanges.

a. Equipment purchased for $4,000 cash.
b. Purchased merchandise worth $2,000 on account.
c. The owner withdraws $10,000 cash from the business.
d. Paid $8,000 cash to a creditor on account.
e. Owner invests $4,000 cash in the business.

E3-2 The cash account for ABC Company had a $5,000 balance on July 1. During July, cash sales amounted to $4,000, but the bookkeeper mistakenly recorded this amount in the cash account with a credit rather than a debit. By how much will the cash account be misstated as a result of this error?

E3-3 Set up the T-accounts as needed and record the following transactions in them.

a. Received $900 cash for services rendered.
b. Sold truck costing $8,000 for $8,000 cash.
c. Sold merchandise costing $200 *on account* for $400.

E3-4 The preliminary trial balance of Mouton Equipment Co. presented below does *not* balance. A review of the records shows that the:

a. Debits and credits in the cash account total $14,000 and $11,000, respectively.
b. The balance of the equipment account is $2,200.
c. Four hundred dollars of accounts receivable was not posted to the ledger accounts receivable account.
d. Each account should reflect a *normal balance*.

Mouton Company
Trial Balance
June 30, 19x0

Cash	$ 4,200	
Account receivable	3,000	
Prepaid insurance		$ 400
Equipment	2,000	
Land		4,000
Account payable		6,000
Notes payable	1,000	
K. Mouton—capital		6,000
Sales		400
Ad expense		200
Selling expense	200	
	$10,400	$17,000

Required:

Prepare a corrected trial balance.

E3-5 Give journal entries for the following transactions:

a. Paid $6,000 cash for a new truck.
b. Paid vendor $2,000 for outstanding accounts payable.
c. Bought inventory on account for $3,000.
d. Sold inventory that originally cost $5,000 for $20,000 cash.
e. Paid $2,000 for current rent.
f. Cash payment on mortgage was $10,000 consisting of principal $9,000 and interest $1,000.

E3-6 Give journal entries for the following transactions, for a new business, the National Bookbinders Company:

a. Deposited $50,000 in checking account in the formation of the business.
b. Borrowed $50,000 from the bank.
c. Purchased equipment on account for $40,000.
d. Paid $600 rent for the current month.
e. Paid $1,200 for wages.
f. Cash sales for the month amounted to $8,000.
g. Issued check for $20,000 in part payment of equipment purchased (see item c).

E3-7 Prepare ledger T-accounts and post the transactions journalized in E3-6.

E3-8 Specify the normal balance for the following accounts.

a. Cash.
b. Owner's equity.
c. Accounts payable.
d. Truck.
e. Insurance expense.
f. Prepaid insurance.
g. Sales.
h. Salary expense.
i. Income tax expense.
j. Income tax payable.
k. Land.
l. Notes payable.

E3-9 Prepare closing entries for the following accounts.

	Debit	*Credit*
Cash	$ 2,300	
Supplies	300	
Tools	3,500	
Bank loan payable		$ 500
Owner's equity		1,600
Sales		16,000
Wages expense	8,000	
Materials expense	1,600	
Rent expense	2,400	
	$18,100	$18,100

E3-10 Below are transactions for Susan's Beauty Shop for one month.

a. Sales totalled $1,440 in cash.
b. Purchased supplies for $200 cash.
c. Paid wages to employee—$400 in cash.
d. Purchased new equipment for $600 in cash.
e. Borrowed $1,000 from bank.
f. Paid $200 rent.

Required:

Prepare general journal entries for these transactions and post these to T-accounts.

E3-11 Prepare a trial balance for the following accounts, assuming all accounts have a normal balance. Then prepare a balance sheet and an income statement.

Cash	$ 6,100
Accounts receivable	850
Supplies	450
Land	18,000
Buildings and equipment	32,000
Bank note payable	5,000
Wages payable	3,200
Owners' equity	40,200
Sales	36,000
Wages expense	20,000
Materials expense	6,000
License fee expense	500
Interest expense	500

E3-12 From the following financial data, prepare a trial balance, and closing general journal entries.

Cash	$ 630
Accounts receivable	200
Materials	1,000
Equipment	1,800
Bank loan payable	300
Owners' equity	2,730
Sales	5,000
Wages expense	2,000
Materials expense	2,000
Rent expense	400

E3-13 Construct a balance sheet with T-accounts as shown in Illustration 1, with these accounts and normal balances: cash—$3,000, accounts receivable—$2,000, equipment—$8,000, accounts payable—$1,000, bank note payable—$1,000, and owner's equity—$11,000. Post each of the following transactions in the appropriate accounts and check to see that the balance sheet still balances:

a. Owner invests $3,000 cash.
b. Firm purchases supplies on account—$200.
c. Firm purchases equipment for $500 cash.
d. Customers pay $600 on account.
e. Firm pays $500 on bank loan.
f. Firm pays $700 on accounts payable.

E3-14 Which of the following accounts are *not* closed in making closing entries?

a. Cash.
b. Owner's equity.
c. Accounts payable.
d. Truck.
e. Insurance expense.
f. Prepaid insurance.
g. Sales.
h. Salary expense.
i. Income tax expense.
j. Income tax payable.
k. Land.
l. Notes payable.

E3-15 Prepare the necessary closing entries in general journal format for the following financial data for Goddard Company. How much is its net income?

	Debit	*Credit*
Cash	$13,000	
Accounts receivable	13,000	
Accounts payable		$ 5,000
Supplies	1,500	
Sales		80,000
Salary expense	21,000	
Supplies expense	15,000	
Insurance expense	1,000	
Rent expense	12,000	
Notes payable		12,000
Utilities expense	2,000	
Owner's equity		6,500
Equipment	25,000	

PROBLEMS

P3-1 The Johns Company repairs automobiles and began operations on December 1, 19x9. Transactions for the month of December 19x9 were:

Dec.	1	John invested $5,000 of cash to start the business. (The business is a proprietorship.)
	1	Received cash for services—$2,400.
	3	Customers billed for services—$2,800.
	5	Collected on customer account—$2,000.
	7	Bought supplies for cash—$400.
	9	Paid miscellaneous expenses—$200.
	12	Bought supplies on account—$400.
	15	Received cash for services—$8,000.
	18	Bought equipment for cash—$2,000.
	27	Paid wages to employees for December—$500.
	29	Paid miscellaneous expense for December with cash—$400.
	30	Supplies used during the month—$400.
	31	Rent for December is paid in cash—$400.

Required:

a. Prepare general journal entries to record these transactions.
b. Prepare a general ledger and post the journal entries to the accounts. (Assume that beginning balances are large enough to accommodate the new transactions.)
c. Prepare a trial balance *in good form*.
d. Prepare journal entries to close the revenue and expense accounts.

P3-2 The following transactions for the Darling Company, a computer dating service, were incurred in the month on April 19x2.

Apr.	1	Received cash for services—$8,000.
	4	Purchased supplies for $1,000 and equipment for $3,000 on account.
	5	Billed customers $10,000 for services rendered.
	8	Paid for advertising—$1,000.
	12	Paid cash to creditors on account—$2,000.
	14	Returned equipment that was faulty to seller for full credit—$500.
	16	Paid miscellaneous expenses—$100.
	18	Bought truck on account—$3,000.
	22	Received cash for services—$12,000.
	26	Paid cash to creditors on account—$4,000.
	30	Paid rent for April—$300.
	30	Paid wages to employees—$500.

Required:

a. Determine the account affected and the amounts debited and credited. Enter these amounts into properly labeled T-accounts. (Assume beginning balances exist in the accounts in amounts sufficient to accommodate the new transactions.)
b. Prepare trial balance from T-accounts as of April 30, 19x2, reflecting the results of the above transactions.

P3-3 Wheeler Company has the following trial balance on December 31, 19x4:

	Debit	*Credit*
Cash	$28,000	
Accounts receivable	18,000	
Supplies	4,000	
Equipment	30,000	
Prepaid rent	2,000	
Truck	8,000	
Accounts payable		$ 8,500
Notes payable		500
Owner's equity		55,000
Revenue		33,000
Rent expense	1,000	
Operating expense	500	
Insurance expense	2,500	
Administrative expense	3,000	

Required:

a. Indicate which accounts are balance sheet accounts and which accounts are income statements accounts.
b. Prepare journal entries to close out all appropriate accounts to the income summary.
c. Prepare journal entry to close income summary into owner's equity.

P3-4 Collins, Inc. was organized January 1 and carried out several transactions prior to opening for business on February 1.

Jan.	1	Ed Collins, owner, invested $90,000 in business.
	4	Purchased land worth $9,400 for $4,000 cash and issued note payable for balance.
	14	Purchased office building for $36,000.
	17	Purchased cash register for $1,600 from Bar and Co. on account.
	30	Paid $700 of account payable to Bar and Co.

Required:

a. Prepare a general journal and ledger. Record and post the transactions.
b. Prepare a trial balance.
c. Prepare a balance sheet as of February 1.

P3-5 Jim Rich is in the business of selling football equipment. The following list shows the account balances at June 30, 19x0.

Accounts payable	$ 7,410
Accounts receivable	2,850
Trucks	6,800
Owner's equity	50,000
Cash	?
Equipment	58,950
Furniture and fixtures	5,400
Warehouse	4,970
Land	16,740
Notes payable	79,800
Notes receivable	1,200
Office building	33,000
Office supplies	400
Net profit for month	6,270
Bonds payable	10,000

Required:

a. Prepare a trial balance. (Compute balance for cash.)
b. Prepare a balance sheet as of June 30, 19x0.

P3-6 Arens Company has the following transactions for the month of July that affect cash:

1. Paid rent—$600 (July 3).
2. Purchased supplies for cash—$350 (July 5).
3. Received $1,250 from customers on account (July 8).
4. Received $5,700 from customers for cash sales (July 16).
5. Paid wages—$3,000 (July 23).
6. Paid utilities—$170 (July 29).

Required:

a. Prepare general journal entries to record these transactions.
b. Prepare a four-column general ledger account for cash, and post these transactions to the cash account. Assume a beginning cash balance of $3,200.

P3-7 Wayne Plumbing Company has the following account balances as of December 31, 19x5:

Cash	$ 1,210
Accounts receivable	2,200
Supplies	1,800
Tools	2,240
Furniture and fixtures	1,300
Notes payable	500
Owner's equity	3,000
Sales	14,500
Rental expense	3,400
Salary expense	3,600
Supplies used	2,000
Interest expense	250

Required:

a. Prepare a trial balance for these accounts.
b. Prepare closing entries in general journal format.
c. Prepare a balance sheet and income statement.

P3-8 Harper Shoe Service had the following transactions for January 19x7:

1. Purchased supplies on account—$1,000.
2. Paid May rent—$400.
3. Paid utilities—$60.
4. Received $4,000 cash for services performed.
5. Billed customers $200 for services performed.
6. Paid wages—$1,200.
7. Purchased equipment on account—$3,000.
8. Paid $1,000 note.
9. Paid $50 interest on note in (h) above.
10. Used $1,000 in supplies.

Harper had the following account balances on January 1, 19x7:

Cash	$3,000	
Accounts receivable	100	
Equipment	3,000	
Supplies	1,500	
Accounts payable		$ 100
Notes payable		1,000
Owner's equity		6,500

Required:

a. Record the transactions for January in general journal format.
b. Post the journal entries to four-column general ledger accounts.
c. Prepare a trial balance for January 31, 19x7.
d. Prepare closing entries as of January 31, 19x7.
e. Prepare a balance sheet and income statement for the period ended January 31, 19x7.

Learning Objectives

Chapter 4 discusses how accounts are adjusted and financial statements prepared. Studying this chapter should enable you to:

1. Explain the relationship between costs and assets, expenses and losses.
2. Describe the interrelationships between accounts on the balance sheet and those on the income statement.
3. Relate accrual/deferral information to specific accounts.
4. Prepare adjusting entries. Identify effects of adjustments on financial statements.
5. Construct and complete an adjustment worksheet.
6. Prepare adjusting and closing journal entries.
7. Prepare financial statements.

4

Financial Statement Relationships and Adjustments

INTRODUCTION

Publicly owned companies publish and distribute annual financial reports. Most of these firms also distribute interim and special reports throughout the year. These reports are supplemented by other financial information filed by these companies with the Securities and Exchange Commission and the major stock exchanges. Millions of partnerships and proprietorships also prepare financial reports for use by owners, creditors, and other interested parties. Financial statements and accounting reports are the most widely distributed, regularly published source of financial information in the United States, aside from newspapers and news magazines.

Anyone attempting to use published financial information effectively must have a thorough knowledge of the accounting process. This chapter will describe the adjusting process and its effects on the financial statements.

ACCRUAL ACCOUNTING

Accounting records may be maintained under a cash or accrual basis. Under the *cash basis*, transactions are recorded only when cash is received or paid. Such a system does not provide meaningful financial statements because such statements would reflect only a part of the business's activities. For example, assume a company produced a product and sold it in 1991, but did not collect the cash until 1992. Under the cash basis, revenue would be reported in 1992 when the cash was collected rather than in 1991 when the revenue generating activities actually took place. Similar problems arise with expenses. Assume that in December, 1991, a company prepaid rent for the following six months. Under the cash basis, the rent would be recorded as an expense in 1991, rather than in 1992 when the benefits were actually received. The cash basis of accounting is also subject to manipulation because management can time revenues and expenses by determining when bills are sent to customers or checks are sent to suppliers.

Current accounting is on the *accrual basis* where revenues are recorded when earned and expenses recorded when incurred, regardless of when the cash is received or paid. The income statement is intended to reflect *a cause and effect* relationship. When a revenue is earned, it is reported in the income statement. The company incurred costs to generate the revenue and these costs should be deducted from their related revenue so that the net result of the operating activities can be viewed and the reported net income or loss. Thus, the income statement reflects the cause (costs incurred) and the related benefits (the revenue earned). To provide the most meaningful financial statements, it is essential that all revenues and expenses be recorded up to the date of the financial statement. *Adjusting* is the process of recording entries to bring the records up-to-date.

FINANCIAL STATEMENT INTERRELATIONSHIPS

Revenue transactions ordinarily affect both revenue and asset accounts. Expense transactions ordinarily affect expense and asset (or liability) accounts. Thus, "income activity" is inherently related to financial position. Transactions that affect an income statement also affect the balance sheet. Illustration 1 presents the relationships between accounts on both the income statement and the balance sheet.

Assets, Expenses, and Equities

Revenues affect both financial statements. Revenues increase reported net income, which, in turn, increase owner's equity on the balance sheet. Also, the corresponding inflows associated with recognizing revenue, cash, or receivables, lead to an increase in assets reported on the balance sheet. As assets are used, they are reclassified as expenses. This process reduces the assets reported on the balance sheet (i.e., inventory) and increases the expenses included in the income statement (i.e., cost of goods sold). The increase in expenses will reduce net income, and consequently, will lead to a reduction in owner's equity. These interrelationships are consistent with the equality of the accounting equation.

Assets		Liabilities	+ Owners' Equity
+ Cash or Receivables	=		+ Revenue
− Inventory or Other Assets			− Expense

Illustration 1
Relationships Between Accounts on Income Statement and Balance Sheet

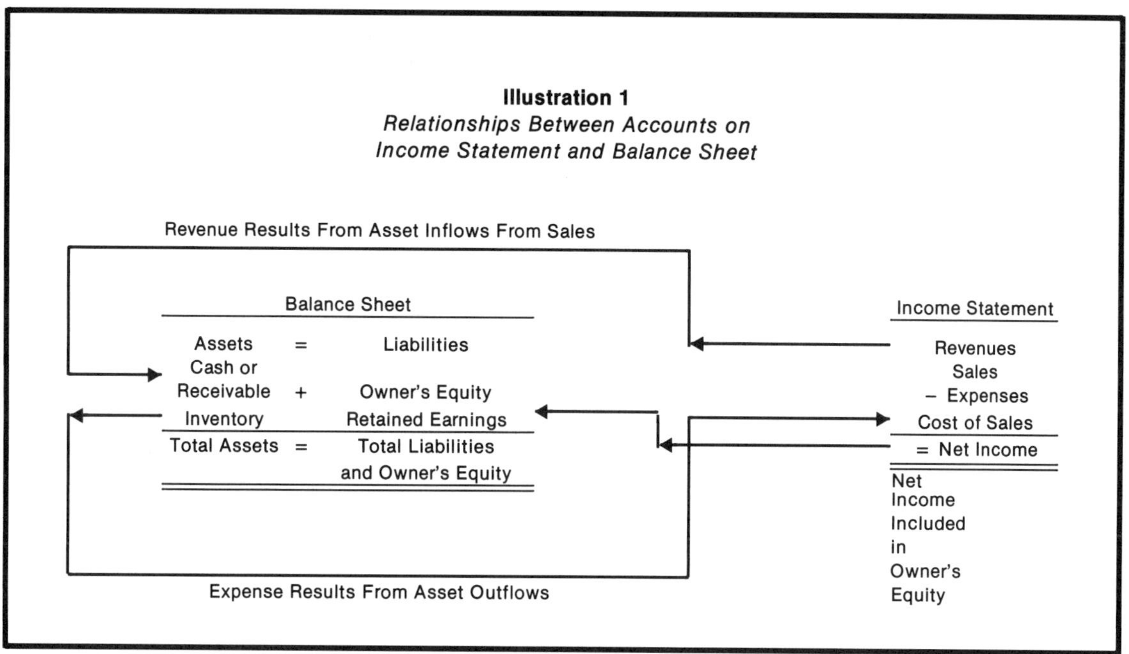

The Effects of Errors

A single error in recording a transaction can produce multiple effects, given the relationships that exist between the financial statements. For example, if an asset valued at $1,200 were consumed during the course of a business year but was not listed as an expense, the following errors in the financial statements would result:

1. *Assets*, reported on the balance sheet, are overstated by $1,200, because the consumed resource is still (improperly) shown as an asset.
2. *Expenses*, reported on the income statement, are understated by $1,200, because the consumed resource was (improperly) not expensed.
3. *Net income*, reported on the income statement, is overstated by $1,200, because a legitimate expense was not deducted from revenue.
4. *Owner's equity*, reported on the balance sheet, is overstated by $1,200, because net income, overstated by $1,200, was added to the beginning owner's equity balance.

In spite of these errors, the balance sheet will still balance, because both assets and owner's equity are overstated by $1,200.

Other errors can also have serious multiple effects on the financial statements.

If revenue, relating to a particular $2,000 sale, was not recognized in the accounts of an entity, a series of errors would again be introduced into the financial statements:

1. *Assets*, reported on the balance sheet, would be understated by $2,000, because the corresponding asset inflow associated with the revenue was not recorded.
2. *Revenue*, reported on the income statement, would be understated by $2,000.
3. *Net income*, reported on the income statement, would be understated by $2,000, because less revenue has been reported.
4. *Owner's equity*, reported on the balance sheet, would be understated by $2,000, because net income, understated by $2,000, was added to the beginning owner's equity balance.

The accounting system must be designed, implemented, and controlled to ensure that errors are not committed. Some errors can be minimized if the source documents that initiate accounting activity are automatically generated by transactions. However, errors will still occur if the accounts are not updated periodically to reflect all changes which have taken place, even if source documents are automatically generated.

THE ADJUSTMENT PROCESS

Companies normally record transactions when some event keys an entry. The event may be sending an invoice, receiving cash from customers, paying bills, etc. Frequently, revenues that have been earned and expenses that have been incurred are not recorded because the event keying the recording has not yet occurred. For example, a company may record wage expense when the employees are paid. If a company pays employees once a month on the fifteenth, any wages incurred from the fifteenth to the end of the month, will not be recorded until the next month. As a result, the wage expense reflected on the books for the month are understated because it does not include the wages for the second half of the month. The adjustment process would bring the books up-to-date and record the incurred wages as an expense and set up a payable to the employees. Through adjustment process, a company attempts to record all revenues earned and expenses incurred to the date of the financial statements.

Four common combinations of accounts are generally affected by adjusting entries. These include:

1. Expenses and assets.
2. Expenses and liabilities.

3. Revenues and assets.
4. Revenues and liabilities.

Three general steps are necessary to complete the adjusting process at the end of an accounting period:

1. Decide what *should* be the proper balance of an account.
2. Identify what is the *actual* balance of the account.
3. Make a journal entry to bring the *actual balance* to the *proper balance*.

EXPENSE AND ASSET ADJUSTMENTS

The most common expense and asset adjustments relate to prepayments for future services and utilization of resources that are owned. Failure to adjust the accounts for expiration of prepayments lead to misstatements of expenses and assets and multiple statement errors.

Prepayments

When advance payments are made, the common entry is to increase an asset account (debit) and to decrease the cash account (credit). At the end of the accounting period, that portion of the asset which has been consumed should be removed from the asset account and reclassified in the appropriate expense account.

Rent is often paid in advance, and no source document is received to indicate the expiration associated with use over time. Assume that the Ample Company rented a warehouse on June 1, 19x8, for $18,000 a year and paid the first year's rent in advance. The following journal entry would be made on June 1 to record this transaction:

Prepaid rent	$18,000	
Cash		$18,000
To recognize prepayment of one year's rent		

The asset, prepaid rent, was debited to record the inflow to the company. Ample Company received the right to use the warehouse for the next twelve months—a resource having future service potential.

By the end of December 19x8, seven-twelfths of the resource. prepaid rent, has been consumed by virtue of occupying the warehouse for seven months. Although no transaction has occurred, an adjusting reclassification is necessary. Since the $18,000 annual rental is equivalent to $1,500 per month ($18,000 ÷ 12), the five remaining months (after December 31) have an asset value of $7,500 ($1,500 × 5). Accordingly, the $10,500 difference between $7,500 and the $18,000 original balance of the account represents the amount of the rent expense (that portion of the asset that was consumed). The adjusting entry that reflects this information is:

Rent expense	$10,500	
Prepaid rent		$10,500
To reclassify expired prepaid rent		

Recognize that the balance of the prepaid rent account is $7,500 after the adjusting entry has been posted. The rent expense account has a balance of $10,500.

Insurance premiums are ordinarily paid in advance and represent another example of an asset (prepaid expense). *Prepaid expenses* are future expense items that have been acquired, paid for, and recorded prior to their use. Assume that Ample Company had purchased a three-year insurance policy for $3,600 on August 15, 19x6. The appropriate journal entry to record this transaction on August 15 would be as follows:

Prepaid insurance	$3,600	
Cash		$3,600
To recognize the acquisition of a three-year insurance policy		

The debit to the asset account, prepaid insurance, reflects the receipt of a resource—insurance protection for a three-year period.

If financial statements were prepared on December 31, the prepaid insurance account is overstated, because part of the coverage period has expired; therefore, an adjusting entry is necessary. The adjustment should reduce the asset account balance to the 31½ months remaining on the policy (36 − 4½) and also recognize insurance expense for 4½ months. The following adjusting entry would be appropriate:

Insurance expense	$450	
Prepaid insurance		$450
To reclassify expired prepaid insurance		

The amount of the adjustment was calculated by multiplying the monthly cost of insurance coverage—$100 ($3,600 ÷ 36)—by the 4½ months that elapsed between August 15 and December 31. The insurance account is adjusted to $450 and the balance in prepaid insurance is reduced to $3,150 as a result of the adjusting entry.

In the above insurance illustration, the prepayment was properly recorded in a prepaid insurance account. However, many times in practice such prepayments are recorded in an expense account in an entry such as the following:

Insurance expense	$3,600	
Cash		$3,600
To record acquisition of three year insurance policy		

In this situation, a different adjusting entry will be required to properly reflect the expense and asset accounts. Just as before, the records should still reflect $450 of insurance expense and $3,150 of prepaid insurance. Since the books currently reflect an expense of $3,600, the expense account must be reduced by $3,150 and an asset account established in that amount. The adjusting entry would be as follows:

Prepaid insurance	$3,150	
Insurance expense		$3,150
To adjust insurance accounts		

Notice that, after adjustment, both cases reflect the proper expense of $450 and an asset of $3,150. Before the accountant can make the adjusting entry, he or she must determine how the transaction was originally recorded. This can be done by looking at the original entry in the journal or, more simply, by looking in the trial balance to see if a prepaid or an expense account exists for the particular cost.

These adjustment alternatives are summarized in Illustration 2.

Utilization

Many assets used by a business in its operations, such as plant and equipment, lose value with the passage of time or with an amount of usage. A factory building may have a service life of forty or fifty years, after which it must be replaced. As time passes, the building loses its future service potential, and the financial statements should reflect this change in asset and expense accounts. Similarly, equipment may have a service life related to the number of units produced. A delivery truck, for example, may be able to accumulate 180,000 miles before it must be replaced. As more miles are actually driven, future service potential is lost, and an adjustment should be made to the asset and expense accounts. The process of allocating a long-lived asset's cost to the periods benefitted is termed *depreciation*.

Depreciation expense is the amount of an asset's cost that is deemed to have expired during the course of an accounting period. Instead of directly reducing a related asset account when recording depreciation expense, accounting practice supports the preservation of historical cost information through the use of a contra account commonly titled, *accumulated depreciation*. This *contra account* is directly related to the particular portion of the asset that is being reclassified as an expense, and it is used to reflect the cumulative amount of reductions in the asset. Contra accounts may be used to reduce the balance of asset, liability, or equity accounts. They permit the preservation of the initial balance in their related account. The asset and the contra asset accounts are always disclosed together in the financial statements, and the net difference between the two is reported as the net book value of the asset. Two accounts are used to reflect two different types of information: the historical cost reflected in the asset account is supported by facts (original acquisition price), but the balance reflected in the accumulated depreciation account is only an estimate.

Illustration 2
Expense and Asset Adjustments and Recording Alternatives

August 15, 19x6: A premium of $3,600 is paid on a three year insurance policy.

Record as an Asset			*Record as an Expense*		
Prepaid insurance	$3,600		Insurance expense.............	$3,600	
Cash		$3,600	Cash		$3,600

Prepaid Insurance		Insurance Expense		Prepaid Insurance		Insurance Expense	
$ $3,600						$3,600	

December 31, 19x6: Adjustment at the end of the year is necessary.

Insurance expense.............	$450		Prepaid insurance	$3,150	
Prepaid insurance		$450	Insurance expense...........		$3,150

Prepaid Insurance		Insurance Expense		Prepaid Insurance		Insurance Expense	
$ $3,600	$450	$450		$3,150		$3,600	$3,150
$3,150						$ 450	

After Adjustment

Results are the same

The balance sheet disclosure of a particular depreciated asset, using equipment as an example is shown below:

Balance Sheet Segment	*December 31 19x6*	*December 31 19x7*
Assets:		
Equipment (original acquisition cost)	$100,000	$100,000
Less: Accumulated depreciation (sum of annual depreciation charges)	1,800	3,600
Net book value of equipment...........	$ 98,200	$ 96,400

The historical cost of the asset, equipment, will not change over the life of the equipment. The annual charge to depreciation expense is accompanied by a credit to the contra account, accumulated depreciation, rather than directly reducing the asset account. While depreciation expense will be cleared annually in the closing process, accumulated depreciation (being an asset classification) will not be closed: its balance increases over the life of the asset. This cumulative balance is deducted from the historical cost to produce the *net book value* or carrying value of the asset.

To illustrate this process, assume that a company purchased a new building on January 1, 19x6, for $100,000. The building is expected to have a useful life of fifty years, at which time it is expected to have a *residual value* of $10,000; that is, after fifty years, the building may be salvaged or sold for $10,000.

On January 1, 19x6, the acquisition of the building would be recorded with the following entry:

Buildings	$100,000	
Cash		$100,000
To record acquisition of building		

Recognize that acquisitions are recorded at the historical cost regardless of expectations about residual values.

On December 31, 19x6, the amount of depreciation expense for this building must be determined, and an adjustment must be made. One method of calculating depreciation is called the *straight-line method*, which generates an even flow of expense over the life of the asset. Straight-line depreciation is computed as follows:

$$\text{Annual Depreciation} = \frac{\text{Cost} - \text{Residual Value}}{\text{Useful Life in Years}}$$

In terms of the example, the amount of depreciation expense would be:

$$\text{Annual Depreciation} = \frac{\$100{,}000 - \$10{,}000}{50}$$

$$= \underline{\underline{\$1{,}800}}\ \textit{Per Year}$$

Thus, the proper adjusting entry for 19x6 would be as follows:

Depreciation expense	$1,800	
Accumulated depreciation—buildings		$1,800
To record depreciation for one year		

The balance sheet would contain the following information in the asset section:

Assets:		
Buildings	$100,000	
Less: Accumulated depreciation—buildings	1,800	$98,200

If this method is followed consistently, net book value will equal the residual value of the asset at the end of fifty years. The balance sheet will appear as follows at that time:

Assets:		
Buildings	$100,000	
Less: Accumulated depreciation—buildings	90,000	$10,000

Adjustments for depreciation are essential if the income statement is expected to match against revenues the costs of all inputs that helped generate the revenue. The depreciation calculations rely on estimations of residual value and useful life; thus, depreciation expense is an estimate. However, an informed estimate of expired cost is better than completely ignoring the expiration of future service potential. Other acceptable methods of calculating depreciation will be discussed in a later chapter.

EXPENSE AND LIABILITY ADJUSTMENTS

Most expense and liability adjustments relate to transactions where goods or services are acquired by the entity *before* receipt of the documents that normally initiate the recording process. Two examples are utilities and salaries. If adjusting entries are not made at the end of an accounting period, the related expense accounts will be understated.

Utilities Expense

If utility payments for power or water are made when bills are received, the normal accounting treatment is to record the transaction at that time. Therefore, if a $12,000 electricity bill is received and paid on the tenth of the month, the entry to recognize an expense is:

Utility expense	$12,000	
Cash		$12,000
To record payment of utility bill		

However, if the accounting period extended to the end of the month, the account balances at the month end would not be correct, since utility expense for the period from the tenth through the thirtieth would not have been recorded.

An adjusting entry can correct the accounts for the proper amount of expense. Accordingly, the adjusting entry at the end of the month would estimate expense for two-thirds of the month:

Utility expense	$8,000	
Accrued utility payable		$8,000
To accrue unbilled utility liability		

The term "accrued" indicates that a transaction occurred and has been recognized, but that it has not been billed or paid. The next utility payment made on the tenth of the following month will recognize expense for the first ten days of that period, and will also satisfy the accrued liability for the last twenty days of last month.

Utility expense	$4,000	
Accrued utility payable	8,000	
Cash		$12,000
To record payment for first utility bill of the new period		

Thus, the adjusting process insures that utility expenses charged to both accounting periods are correct.

Salary Expense

In most businesses, employee salaries are paid on a regular basis—weekly, bimonthly, or monthly. The normal entry to record the payment of salaries is to debit salary expense and to credit the asset, cash; thus, the costs of securing employee services are recognized. However, when an accounting period ends before a regular payday, an adjusting entry is needed to recognize the full salary expense attributable to the period.

Assume that a company has a regular weekly payroll of $12,000, which is normally paid on Fridays, and that the last day in an accounting period is Wednesday. Two days will elapse after the period before salaries will be paid; however, salary expense for the first part of the week should be recognized as attributable to the period just ended. The following adjusting entry records salary expense incurred for the first three days in the week, which are attributable to the period just ended:

Salary expense	$7,200	
Accrued salaries payable		$7,200
To record unpaid salary liability		

Accrued salaries payable indicates a liability arising from the acquisition of labor services which have not been paid. When salaries are actually paid on Friday, the entry will recognize that this liability has been satisfied:

Salary expense	$4,800	
Accrued salaries payable	7,200	
Cash		$12,000
To record payment for the first payroll of the new period		

REVENUE AND ASSET ADJUSTMENTS

Adjustments to revenue and asset accounts are required when some revenue items are earned, even though no source document is received by the end of the accounting period. These revenues are generally collected on a regular basis, and the collection date falls in the next accounting period. Income determination requires that the full amount of revenue earned in the current period must be recognized.

Interest Revenue

Interest revenue increases gradually with the passage of time and therefore must be adjusted if the collection date does not coincide with the last day of the accounting period. Throughout the period, revenue would be recognized whenever an interest payment is collected. For example, consider the collection of a semiannual interest payment on a $100,000, 8 percent loan: receipt of the $4,000 interest would be recorded as follows:

Cash	$4,000	
Interest revenue		$4,000
Collection of semiannual interest ($100,000 × .08 × ½)		

If the fiscal year ended on December 31, but the semiannual interest was due on September 30 and March 31, the interest revenue account will not reflect the actual amount of interest revenue earned by the end of the fiscal year. An adjusting entry can correct revenue to the amount earned for the period. The entry must record three months of interest revenue and a corresponding accrued receivable reflecting that the revenue has been realized (earned) but not collected.

Accrued interest receivable	$2,000	
Interest revenue		$2,000
To accrue three months of interest		

Part of the interest collected on March 31 pertains to the receivable and the remainder is treated as revenue.

Cash	$4,000	
Accrued interest receivable		$2,000
Interest revenue		2,000
Collection of semiannual interest		

Thus, the adjusting entry divided an interest payment into two parts, half as revenue in the new accounting period and half as revenue in the old period.

REVENUE AND LIABILITY ADJUSTMENTS

Whenever payment is received in advance for a product or a service to be supplied over time, revenue and liability accounts should be adjusted at the end of the accounting period. Generally, revenue is recognized in the accounting records when bills are distributed or cash is received. If an accounting period ends before all of the revenue has been earned, an adjustment must be made.

For example, on September 1, the New Say Magazine Company received 1,000 annual subscriptions at $12 each for their monthly news journal. The entry to record this collection is as follows:

Cash	$12,000	
Subscription revenue		$12,000
To record receipts for new subscriptions		

The company has fulfilled one-third of its publication commitment by December 31. Consequently, revenue is overstated by $8,000 (⅔ × $12,000). An adjusting entry will reduce revenue and establish a liability for future commitments; the company must deliver magazines to its subscribers for the following eight months. The proper adjusting entry would be:

Subscription revenue	$8,000	
Unearned subscription revenue		$8,000
To adjust the revenue account		

The account, unearned subscription revenue, is a liability account. Unlike other liabilities, unearned subscription revenue will be satisfied by providing goods or services, rather than by cash payments. Unearned implies the postponement of income recognition. In the example, $8,000 of revenue is deferred until the next accounting period. Deferred revenue or deferred expense accounts are reflected on the current balance sheet but eventually will be recognized in future income statements.

In the previous subscription example, the company credited subscription revenue when it received the $12,000 cash. As an alternative, the company could have credited the liability account as follows:

Cash	$12,000	
Unearned subscription revenue		$12,000
To record receipts for new subscriptions		

When this approach is used, an adjusting entry is still needed because the liability is overstated and the revenue account understated by the amount of subscription revenue that was earned through December 31 ($4,000). Therefore, the following adjusting entry is needed:

Unearned subscription revenue	$4,000	
Subscription revenue		$4,000
To adjust the liability and revenue accounts		

In order to determine which type of adjusting entry will be needed, one should look for either the unearned revenue or the revenue account in the trial balance.

The above adjustment alternatives are similar to the expense and asset adjustments discussed earlier. The alternatives for revenue and liability adjustments are summarized in Illustration 3. As with the expense and asset adjustment alternatives, these alternatives also result in after-adjustment ending balances that are the same. The adjusting entry in the next year would be the same no matter how the entry was originally recorded because, after the first year adjustments, there is no difference in the account balances.

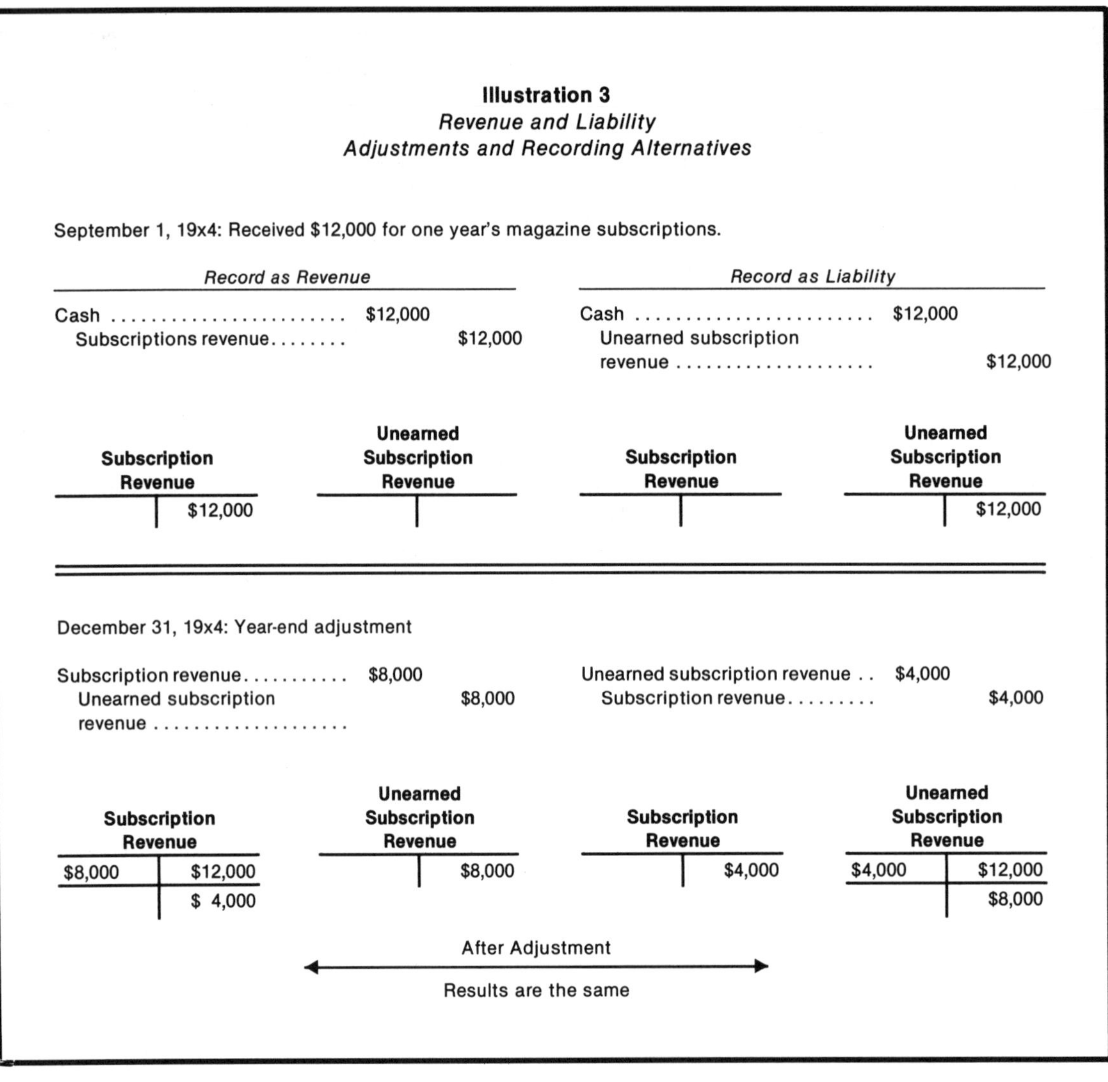

Illustration 3
Revenue and Liability
Adjustments and Recording Alternatives

September 1, 19x4: Received $12,000 for one year's magazine subscriptions.

Record as Revenue			*Record as Liability*		
Cash	$12,000		Cash	$12,000	
Subscriptions revenue		$12,000	Unearned subscription revenue		$12,000

Subscription Revenue: credit $12,000
Unearned Subscription Revenue: (no entries)
Subscription Revenue: (no entries)
Unearned Subscription Revenue: credit $12,000

December 31, 19x4: Year-end adjustment

Subscription revenue	$8,000		Unearned subscription revenue	$4,000	
Unearned subscription revenue		$8,000	Subscription revenue		$4,000

Subscription Revenue: debit $8,000; credit $12,000; balance credit $ 4,000
Unearned Subscription Revenue: credit $8,000
Subscription Revenue: credit $4,000
Unearned Subscription Revenue: debit $4,000; credit $12,000; balance credit $8,000

After Adjustment
Results are the same

ADJUSTMENTS IN PERSPECTIVE

Adjustments can be classified as *accruals* or *deferrals*. Accruals build up gradually from continuous activity associated with the passage of time. They are unrecorded prior to adjustment, because no source document has been received to initiate the accounting process. Both revenues and expenses can be accrued. Recognition of accrued revenues results in the creation of a receivable (asset). Recognition of an accrued expense results in the creation of a liability.

Many business transactions relate to continuous activities. Rent is associated with an ongoing right to use property owned by another entity; interest relates to the right to use a sum of money for a period of time. Other activities requiring accruals are associated with the accounts utilities, income taxes, and labor. In these cases, expenses and revenues build up as a function of time or usage, even though bills are received or payments occur later. Transactions ordinarily are recorded when a source document initiates the accounting process; however, continuous activity frequently occurs well before the receipt of a source document. If an accounting period ends before the source document for a continuous activity is received, an adjusting entry must be made to correctly state the account balances. Adjusting entries insure that income statements reflect earned revenue and expired costs and that unearned revenue or unexpired costs are reflected on the balance sheet.

Deferred costs or revenues are associated with prepayments. Deferred costs are assets that are unexpired at the end of the period; deferred revenues are precollected but unearned. Deferred cost adjustments reclassify expenses to assets. Deferred revenue adjustments reclassify revenues to liabilities.

PROCESSING ADJUSTMENT DATA

The accounting system includes various procedures to assist the accountant in manipulating data. These procedures also provide for efficient processing information. The worksheet helps accountants organize data for the adjusting process. The worksheet is an intermediate processing device employed to develop meaningful information for other accounting uses. Worksheets are prepared solely for use within the accounting function and are rarely shown to report users.

THE WORKSHEET

The *worksheet* is a document prepared by and for accountants as a part of the process of preparing adjusting entries and formulating financial statements. Deferral and accrual entries are first prepared on a worksheet before they are officially recognized by the journalizing and posting process. In effect, the worksheet becomes the source document for recognition of adjusting entries.

A tabular format is used to construct the worksheet. Account titles and preadjustment balances are obtained from the ledger. Adjusting entries are formulated from this and other supporting data and entered in the appropriate debit/credit columns. Combining the original account balances with the adjusting amounts will produce an adjusted trial balance. This trial balance provides the data used to develop the balance sheet and income statement, which are also presented in a columnar fashion. Note that the choice of information to be recorded in the worksheet requires accounting expertise and judgments.

An Example

The fiscal year for High Way Air Freight Company ends on December 31. At the end of 19x8, the accountant prepared the worksheet presented in Illustration 4. The unadjusted account balances on the worksheet came from the general ledger. The following pertinent information was also available:

1. On September 1, one year's rent of $12,000 was paid in advance for the use of a terminal building.
2. Equipment, which cost $100,000, is to be depreciated on a straight-line basis at the rate of $10,000 per year.
3. Wages and salaries of $2,000 per week are normally paid on Fridays. December 31 is a Tuesday.
4. The company had loaned some of its surplus cash to an officer of the firm in exchange for an interest-bearing note. The note provides for interest payments of $500 to be made to the firm twice a year, on March 31 and September 30.
5. One customer paid $1,000 in advance for ten shipments. At the end of the year, four of these shipments had been made.
6. All other expenses were paid as incurred, and all other revenues were collected as realized.

Completing the Worksheet

Completing a worksheet is somewhat mechanical, although accounting judgment is needed to interpret the data. The worksheet is arranged with titles of specific accounts listed vertically in the first column. Columns are provided to record specific monetary amounts for the trial balance, adjusting entries, an adjusted trial balance, the income statement, and the balance sheet.

Trial Balance

Throughout the year, information concerning specific transactions was recorded in the journal and posted to the ledger. At the end of the year, the ledger accounts were *footed*, or summed, and the balances were developed into a trial balance. This trial balance is reproduced in the first two columns of the worksheet. The equality of the debits and the credits ($304,200 and $304,200) tends to support the integrity of the accounting system. The trial balance provides the basis for initiating adjustments.

Illustration 4

High Way Air Freight Company
Worksheet
For the Year Ended December 31, 19x8

	Trial Balance		Adjustments		Adjusted Trial Balance		Income Statement		Balance Sheet	
Account Titles	*Debit*	*Credit*	*Debit*	*Credit*	*Debit*	*Credit*	*Debit*	*Credit*	*Debit*	*Credit*
Cash	$ 35,300				$ 35,300				$ 35,300	
Accounts receivable	22,400				22,400				22,400	
Prepaid rent	12,000			(a) $ 4,000	8,000				8,000	
Notes receivable	12,500				12,500				12,500	
Equipment	100,000				100,000				100,000	
Accumulated depreciation		$ 30,000		(b) 10,000		$ 40,000				$ 40,000
Accounts payable		6,600				6,600				6,600
Unearned service revenue		1,000	(e) 400			600				600
Capital stock*		80,000				80,000				80,000
Retained earnings*		45,400				45,400				45,400
Service revenue		140,700		(e) 400		141,100		$141,100		
Interest revenue		500		(d) 250		750		750		
Salary expense	102,000		(c) 800		102,800		$102,800			
Insurance expense	5,700				5,700		5,700			
Maintenance expense	11,500				11,500		11,500			
Miscellaneous expense	2,800				2,800		2,800			
	$304,200	$304,200								
Rent expense			(a) 4,000		4,000		4,000			
Depreciation expense			(b) 10,000		10,000		10,000			
Accrued salaries payable				(c) 800		800				800
Accrued interest receivable			(d) 250		250				250	
			$15,450	$15,450	$315,250	$315,250	$136,800	$141,850	$178,450	$173,400
Net income							5,050			5,050
							$141,850	$141,850	$178,450	$178,450

*These accounts represent owners' equity in a corporation. They are explained in more detail in the Appendix of Chapter 3.

Adjustments

Using the trial balance information and supplemental data, the accountant formulates specific adjustments that should be made to the accounts. "Journal entries" reflecting these adjustments are recorded in the two adjustment columns. The debit and credit parts of each adjusting entry are coded together [(a) through (e)] for future reference. If additional accounts are needed in the adjusting process, they are added to the list of account titles. The High Way Air Freight Company required five adjusting entries:

1. *Entry a—Prepaid Rent*—The unadjusted trial balance reported prepaid rent as an asset. However, four months have elapsed since the rental payment was made. Therefore, one-third of the prepaid rent should be reclassified as rent expense to indicate that it has been consumed. This may be accomplished by debiting rent expense and crediting prepaid rent.

2. *Entry b—Depreciation*—The annual charge for depreciation is reflected in the adjusting entry which increases depreciation expense (debit) and increases the account accumulated depreciation (credit). Since the account depreciation expense was not included in the trial balance, it was added to the account title column.

3. *Entry c—Accrued Salaries*—The end of the accounting period fell between company paydays. Consequently, it is necessary to recognize an expense and a corresponding liability for that amount of salary which has been earned, but not yet paid. The adjustment to salary expense is $800, representing two-fifths (2 days out of 5 days) of the $2,000 weekly payroll. The adjusting entry includes a debit to salary expense and a credit to accrued salaries payable.

4. *Entry d—Accrued Revenue*—The company received an interest-bearing note on March 31 of this year. To date, $500 of interest revenue has been recognized, because an interest payment was received on September 30. However, at the year-end. $250 of interest has been earned but not received. To properly include this information in the financial statements, it is necessary to establish an accrued asset, accrued interest receivable (debit) and to increase the interest revenue account (credit).

5. *Entry e—Unearned Revenue*—Sometime during the year, the company received an advanced payment from a customer for services to be provided in the future. At that time, the advanced payment was recorded as an unearned, or deferred revenue, and treated as a liability. At the year-end, 40 percent of the service has been provided (4 shipments were made out of the 10 that were contracted). Therefore, a corresponding percentage of the revenue (40%) should be recognized as earned. This may be accomplished by an adjusting entry which decreases the unearned service revenue account (debit) and increases the service revenue account (credit).

After all the adjusting entries have been completed, the two adjustment columns (debit and credit) are summed and checked for equality. While not conclusive, this provides some assurance that all parts of the adjustments were recorded.

Adjusted Trial Balance

The adjusted trial balance debit and credit columns are next. The account balances in these columns represent the extension across or horizontal summation of the trial balance and adjustments columns. Note that the summation of debits and credits to the same account requires a subtraction [e.g., prepaid rent (a)]. The summation of two debits or two credits is accomplished by addition [e.g., salary expense (c) and accumulated depreciation (b)].

For example, the account cash had a debit balance of $35,300 and was not affected by the adjusting entries. Therefore, a debit balance of $35,300 was extended over to the adjusted trial balance. Prepaid rent had a trial balance total of $12,000. However, a credit adjustment of $4,000 was made to this account. The combined effect ($12,000 debit and $4,000 credit) results in a debit balance of $8,000, which was extended over to the adjusted trial balance.

The adjusted trial balance provides a summary of account balances prior to the preparation of financial statements. Therefore, all of the accounts listed on the adjusted trial balance will either be reported on the balance sheet or on the income statement.

Income Statement

The income statement provides disclosure for all of the revenue and expense accounts. The revenue and expense account balances reported in the adjusted trial balance are carried over to the income statement columns. Since the adjusted trial balance represents a summation of all previous activity concerning these accounts, the account balances in the income statement columns reflect all available information.

After the revenue and expense balances have been placed in the income statement columns, the columns are footed. If the credit column (revenue) exceeds the debit column (expense), net income has resulted. Conversely, if the debit column exceeds the credit column, a loss has resulted. The amount of the income (or loss) is inserted to offset the difference between the two columns (i.e., to bring both columns into balance). The debit of $5,050 equates both columns at $141,850.

Balance Sheet

The asset, liability, and equity accounts are all reported on the balance sheet. As with the income statement, account balances from the adjusted trial balance are extended to the balance sheet columns. No revenues or expenses that appeared in the income statement should also appear in the balance sheet.

After the account balances have been carried over, the debit and credit columns are footed. A difference between the columns equals the amount of the net income or loss for the period. For the example, net income of

$5,050 exactly balances the remaining two columns. This income will eventually be added to the equity account retained earnings. In the context of the worksheet, obtaining a final balance provides some assurance of consistency between the income statement and the balance sheet.

USING THE WORKSHEET

The worksheet provides the accountant with a focal point for analyzing adjusting entries and tracing their effects through to the financial statements. After the worksheet had been prepared, it is used as a guide for the clerical or bookkeeping tasks that remain.

The adjusting entries formulated on the worksheet must be reflected in the actual accounts. Consequently, these entries would be recorded in the journal and then posted to the ledger. The journal entries made for the High Way Air Freight Company are shown in Illustration 5.

Illustration 5
High Way Air Freight Company
Adjusting Entries

Date	*Accounts*	*Debit*	*Credit*
Dec. 31	Rent expense	$ 4,000	
	Prepaid rent		$ 4,000
31	Depreciation expense	10,000	
	Accumulated depreciation		10,000
31	Salary expense..................	800	
	Accrued salaries payable		800
31	Accrued interest receivable	250	
	Interest revenue		250
31	Unearned service revenue..........	400	
	Service revenue		400

The worksheet also contains information needed to construct the balance sheet and the income statement. The worksheet information should parallel the information found in the accounts after the adjusting entries have been posted. The balance sheet and income statement for the High Way Air Freight Company are shown in Illustrations 6 and 7, respectively.

Closing Entries

After the adjusting entries have been made and the financial statements have been prepared, the worksheet provides direction for journalizing closing entries. The income statement columns provide annual balances for the

Illustration 6
High Way Air Freight Company
Balance Sheet
December 31, 10x8

Assets		
Cash		$ 35,300
Accounts receivable		22,400
Prepaid rent		8,000
Accrued interest receivable		250
Notes receivable		12,500
Equipment	$100,000	
Accumulated depreciation	40,000	60,000
Total assets		$138,450
Liabilities and Stockholders Equity		
Liabilities:		
Accounts payable	$ 6,600	
Accrued salaries payable	800	
Unearned service revenue	600	
Total liabilities		$ 8,000
Stockholders' equity:		
Capital stock	$80,000	
Retained earnings*	50,450	
Total stockholders' equity		130,450
Total liabilities and stockholders' equity		$138,450

*Beginning retained earnings balance ($45,400) plus net income ($5,050) will equal the closing retained earnings balance.

revenue and expense accounts. These accounts must be closed to the appropriate owner's equity account to complete the accounting cycle.

When the closing process is complete, all of the revenue and expense accounts will have a zero balance. In the case of the High Way Air Freight Company, the resulting net income will eventually be closed to the retained earnings account, since the company is a corporation. The closing entries necessary for this example are shown in Illustration 8.

Illustration 7
High Way Air Freight Company
Income Statement
For the Year Ended December 31, 19x8

Service revenue	$141,100	
Interest revenue	750	
Total revenue		$141,850
Operating expenses:		
Salary expense	$102,800	
Insurance expense	5,700	
Maintenance expense	11,500	
Miscellaneous expense	2,800	
Rent expense	4,000	
Depreciation expense	10,000	136,800
Net income		$ 5,050

Illustration 8
High Way Air Freight Company
Closing Entries

Date	*Accounts*	*Debit*	*Credit*
Dec. 31	Service revenue	$141,100	
	Interest revenue	750	
	Income summary		$141,850
31	Income summary	136,800	
	Salary expense		102,800
	Insurance expense		5,700
	Maintenance expense		11,500
	Miscellaneous expense		2,800
	Rent expense		4,000
	Depreciation expense		10,000
31	Income summary	5,050	
	Retained earnings		5,050

SUMMARY

Resources and services acquired by an entity are valued at their cost and considered to be an asset as long as they have a future service potential. Assets are reported on the balance sheet. When the future service potential of an asset expires, either through the use or sale, the asset is reclassified as an expense and transferred from the balance sheet to the income statement.

Expenses are matched with revenues on the income statement. Revenues are valued at the dollar amounts exchanged for goods and services distributed to customers. Net income, a positive difference between revenues and expenses, leads to an increase in owner's equity. The financial statements are articulated, in the sense that revenue and expense transactions affect both the balance sheet and income statement. Errors in recording these transactions are likely to distort both financial statements.

Account balances may not be properly stated at the end of the period, because formal source documents that initiate the accounting process have not been received for all transactions. These situations require adjusting entries. Adjusting entries recognize new information and, accordingly, adjust account balances for accruals, deferrals, or reclassifications. For the most part, a need for adjustments results from a difference in timing that severs the two parts of a transaction, for example, the prepayment for goods or services, the early delivery of goods or services, or the gradual use of goods or services. Several common combinations of accounts are affected by the adjustment process. Accrual entries accelerate the recognition of new transaction information by journalizing events before the accompanying source documents arrive. Deferral adjustments postpone (accelerate) income by linking revenue-liability accounts or asset-expense accounts.

The primary objective of the adjusting process is to bring the accounts of an entity to their proper balances at a point in time. To achieve these balances, the accountant must review the available facts and exercise professional judgment.

The accountant may use a worksheet in the adjusting process. The worksheet provides a concise form on which to summarize and manipulate account data and to prepare draft copies of adjusting entries and financial statements. The worksheet then serves as the source document that authorizes the journalization of adjusting entries.

KEY DEFINITIONS

Accrual basis—a basis of accounting where revenues are recorded when earned and expenses when incurred, regardless of when the cash flow takes place.

Accruals—revenues or expenses that build up over time and are recognized periodically.

Accumulated depreciation—the total of depreciation taken on an asset to date.

Adjusting entries—entries made to bring the books up-to-date.

Cash basis—a basis of accounting that records revenues and expenses only when cash is received or paid.

Cause and effect—the income statement is intended to show that expenses generate revenues and should be matched with their related revenues.

Contra account—an account that directly related to another account and reduces that account.

Deferrals—revenues or expenses where the cash flow has taken place but the revenue has not been earned or the expense incurred as of the financial statement date.

Depreciation—the amount of cost of a long-lived assets that is expensed in the current period.

Net book value—the cost of an asset less its accumulated depreciation.

Prepaid expenses—expenses that are paid in advance.

Unearned income—income that has been collected in cash but has not yet been earned.

Worksheet—a document prepared to assist in the adjustment and financial statement preparation process.

Appendix

Reversing Entries

INTRODUCTION

The accounting departments of all but the smallest of organizations consist of several people performing a variety of complementary functions. Some of the tasks that are done require relatively low levels of accounting knowledge while other accounting operations require sophisticated insight into accounting theory and practice. For example, the process of journalizing recurring transactions in ongoing systems can be performed by persons with little technical knowledge, and thus function is usually done by clerks. The clerk who posts entries from the journal to the ledger accounts can be trained to do this function in less than one day. On the other hand, the person who prepares the end-of-period adjusting entries must make precise accounting judgments.

Clerks can journalize and post recurring entries in ongoing systems whenever standard operating procedures are developed and implemented. For example, the journal clerk can be trained to debit an expense account and credit a payable (liability) account whenever a bill is received, as would happen with the electric bill, the water bill, or employee time cards (i.e., the labor bill). These bills do represent expenses: in the normal course of business, custom specifies that the bill is to be determined only after the service has been delivered. On the other hand, the clerk can be directed to debit an asset account and credit a liability on receipt of an insurance premium notice, a rent bill, or an invoice for materials purchased: in the normal course of business, these bills usually are paid before the service is consumed. Journal clerks are trained to recognize specific accounts, and only those accounts, in response to the receipt of specific source documents: if no document arrives, no entry is made.

ADJUSTING ENTRIES AND STANDARD OPERATING PROCEDURES

Journal clerks who follow prescribed accounting standard operating procedures record the December electric, water, and labor expenses in January, when the bills are received, even though December and January may fall in different fiscal years. At the same time, the clerk typically would not record the expiration of prepaid insurance or rent, since no document will be prepared to initiate such a journal entry. In other words, the implementation of standard operating procedures in the typical accounting system creates end-of-period account balances that must be adjusted, and such adjustment requires the intervention of an accountant with relatively high levels of technical knowledge.

The exact nature of the adjustment made by an accountant depends on the directions given to the clerk who journalizes the original transactions, as described in the main body of this chapter under the heading, *Alternative Adjustments*. One set of adjustments is required if business costs are first recorded as assets, and another set of adjustments is required if the costs are first recorded as expenses.

ADJUSTMENTS AND ENTRIES IN THE FOLLOWING PERIOD

Unfortunately, adjustments to account balances made at the end of the preceding period may cause misstatements in the current period, unless additional intervention by the accountant is performed. Consider, for example, the first adjustment described in the chapter under the heading *Expense and Liability Adjustments*. Because the last utility bill received during the year considered services provided until December 15, the following adjusting entry was made to estimate for the last half of December:

Utility expense	$5,000	
Accrued utility payable		$5,000
To accrue unbilled utility liability, assuming expense is $10,000 per month		

The utility expense account is closed out at the end of the year; that is, the total balance in the account, including the $5,000 estimate made as an adjustment, is included in the income statement for the year just ended, and the utility expense account is set back to a zero balance so that the new expenses for the current year may be accumulated. However, the accrued utility payable account will still reflect its $5,000 credit balance in the current year.

When the first utility bill ($10,000) for the current year arrives on January 15, the journal clerk will follow standard operating procedure, and make the following entry:

Utility expense	$10,000	
Utility payable		$10,000
To record the utility bill received January 15		

However, half of this $10,000 relates to last year, and the other half to the current year. The journal clerk must follow standard operating procedure, even if the results are misleading.

Ongoing accounting systems are designed to be operated by clerks, without the frequent intervention of accountants. If the accountant did intervene in this case (an unlikely event), an entry might have been prepared as follows:

Utility expense	$5,000	
Accrued utility payable	5,000	
Utility payable		$5,000
To record the utility bill for the first half of January		

This entry does properly measure utility expense, and it does reflect the liability of $10,000. Unfortunately, it also requires the intervention of the accountant.

REVERSING ENTRIES FOR EXPENSE ACCRUALS

Reversing entries represent a second order adjustment made by the accountant as part of the normal closing process. Reversing entries are designed to correct expected future misstatements resulting from the application of standard operating procedure before the misstatements are recorded. For example, consider the following three journal entries:

Dec. 31	Utility expense	$ 5,000	
	Accrued utility payable		$ 5,000
	To accrue utility liability of period December 15—December 31		
31	Income summary	$120,000	
	Utility expense		$120,000
	To reflect expenses on income statement and close expense account		
Jan. 1	Accrued utility payable	$ 5,000	
	Utility expense		$ 5,000
	To reverse December 31 adjusting entry		

This last entry, a reversing entry, is made by the accountant as part of the normal year-end adjustments, in anticipation of the entry to be recorded by the journal clerk upon arrival of the utility bill. When the bill is received on January 15, the clerk will make the following entry:

Jan. 15	Utility expense	$10,000	
	Utility payable		$10,000
	To record utility bill of January 15		

The combination of the reversing entry and the regular entry made in accordance with standard operating procedure will produce the correct account balances, as reflected in the following set of ledger accounts:

Date		Explanation	Utility Expense (Dr.)	Utility Expense (Cr.)	Utility Payable (Dr.)	Utility Payable (Cr.)
Dec.	31	Adjusting	$ 5,000			$ 5,000
	31	Balance	$120,000			$5,000
	31	Closing		$120,000		
	31	Balance	0			$5,000
Jan.	1	Reversing		$5,000	$5,000	
	1	Balance		$5,000		0
	15	January 15—bill	$10,000			$10,000
	15	Balance	$ 5,000			$10,000

Thus, reversing entries are made in conjunction with other end-of-period adjustments in an effort to produce accounts with proper balances.

Reversal entries are applied to some, but not all, of the expense adjustments. In particular, adjustments that reclassify assets as expenses need not be reversed. Included in this category are reclassifications of inventory as cost of goods sold, the recognition of depreciation expense, and the transfer from prepaid expenses (rent, insurance) to expenses.

REVERSING ENTRIES FOR REVENUE ACCRUAL

Reversing entries are also appropriate for some end-of-year revenue accrual adjustments. Whenever the accountant makes an adjustment to recognize income or revenue that is earned but has not been collected, reversing entries are appropriate. That is, the end-of-year adjustment is made before the receipt of source documents evidencing completion of the earning process: a reversing entry will anticipate and correct the double-counting that occurs when the journal clerk records the revenue item upon receipt of the source documents in the current year. For example, consider the first example described above under the heading *Revenue and Asset Adjustment*. Here the fiscal year ends on September 30, but the semiannual interest on a $100,000, 8 percent loan is due on June 30 and December 31. At year-end, September 30, the following entry was made to recognize interest earned but not collected:

Accrued interest receivable	$2,000	
Interest revenue		$2,000
To accrue interest from July 1 to September 30		

The interest revenue account would then be closed out to include the $8,000 full year of interest ($100,000 × 8%) in the income statement and to set the interest revenue account back to zero so that it may accumulate fresh information for the new year.

Interest revenue	$8,000	
Income summary		$8,000
To reflect revenue in the income statement and close revenue account		

A reversing entry is then made by the accountant as part of the year-end adjustments as follows:

Interest revenue	$2,000	
Accrued interest receivable		$2,000
To reverse the September 30 adjusting entry		

When the December 31 interest check is received, the journal clerk will recognize the whole six-month collection ($100,000 × 8% × ½), $4,000, as income, even though the amount earned during the current year applies to the period October 1 to December 31, that is, $2,000. The clerk makes the following entry, in conformity with accounting sandard operating procedure:

Cash	$4,000	
Interest revenue		$4,000
To record the December 31 collection of interest		

The ledger accounts will reflect the correct balances, since the reversing entry anticipated the December 31 collection entry.

Date	*Explanation*	*Accrued Interest Receivable* (Dr.)	(Cr.)	*Interest Revenue* (Dr.)	(Cr.)
Sept. 30	Adjusting	$2,000			$2,000
30	Balance	$2,000			$8,000
30	Closing			$8,000	
30	Balance	0			0
Oct. 1	Reversing		$2,000	$2,000	
1	Balance	0		$2,000	
Dec. 31	Collection				$4,000
31	Balance	0			$2,000

Thus, the reversing entry, in conjunction with other end-of-period adjusting entries and the application of standard operating procedures for the journal entries, will produce correct account balances.

Reversal entries are applied to some, but not all, of the revenue adjustments. In particular, adjustments that transfer deferred revenue (a liability) into earned revenue, need not be reversed. For example, a magazine publisher may record prepaid subscriptions by crediting deferred subscription revenue. Year-end adjustments are as follows:

Deferred subscription revenue.	XXX	
Subscription revenue		XXX
To recognize portion of subscription earned		

This entry does not have to be reversed.

QUESTIONS

4-1 Describe the difference between an asset, expense and a loss.

4-2 Provide a synonym for the term "unexpired cost."

4-3 What are adjusting entries? Which combination of accounts generally are affected by adjusting entries?

4-4 Closing entries serve what purpose? Which accounts typically are closed?

4-5 Why are worksheets prepared as part of the closing cycle?

4-6 Will an increase in revenues only affect the income statement?

4-7 Which accounts are affected by the failure to recognize $100 in accrued but unpaid labor cost (wages)?

4-8 Which accounts are affected if $100 in earned interest revenue has not been received and, therefore, has not be journalized?

4-9 For each of the following items, indicate which accounts are debited and credited in recording end-of-period adjusting entries:

a. Insurance was purchased during the year and debited to prepaid insurance.
b. Supplies were purchased during the year and debited to supplies.
c. Rent received in advance from a tenant was credited to deferred revenue.
d. Advances from a customer were credited to a revenue account.

4-10 Define the net book value of an asset. Does this amount approximate the market value of the asset?

4-11 Define the term *depreciation*.

4-12 What information does a contra account report to the financial statement user?

4-13 Do all adjusting entries have an effect on the determination of net income? Explain.

4-14 What does the term "accrued" mean to an accountant?

4-15 What is unearned revenue?

4-16 Assume that the end-of-the-year adjustments ignored: (a) depreciation on equipment, and (b) accrued but unpaid property taxes. Which accounts will be misstated on the financial statements as a result of each error?

4-17 Distinguish between a trial balance and a balance sheet.

4-18 Explain the probable nature of each of the entries in the account shown below:

Insurance Expense

6/30	1,000	(a) 750	(b)	12/31
		250	(c)	12/31

EXERCISES

E4-1 Certain account balances taken from the ledger of Plum Co. prior to adjustments on December 31 are shown below:

	Debit	*Credit*
Prepaid insurance	$ 1,000	
Office supplies	500	
Unearned income		$2,000
Salaries expense	10,000	
Interest revenue		0

Information required for period-end adjustments is as follows:

a. The insurance policy was purchased on October 1 of the current year and covers a period of two years.
b. The inventory of supplies taken on December 31 revealed that $150 of supplies were on hand.
c. One-fourth of the unearned income has been earned as of December 31.
d. Salaries earned, but not paid, as of December 31, amounted to $200.
e. The company received a $1,000, sixty-day, 6 percent note receivable from a customer on December 1.

Required:

Prepare the necessary adjusting entries that should be made on December 31.

E4-2 Stabler Co. acquired a new machine on January 1, 19x2, for $11,000. The machine has an estimated life of five years, and it is anticipated that the residual value at the end of that time will be $1,000. The company uses the straight-line method of calculation depreciation.

Required:

a. Give the entries necessary to record the purchase of the machine and to record the depreciation expense at the end of 19x2.
b Show how the machine would be reported in the balance sheet at December 31, 19x4.

E4-3 The bookkeeper of Griffin Company made a number of errors during 19x8:

a. The company purchased a machine on January 1, 19x8, for $11,000. The machine had an estimated useful life of ten years, a $1,000 estimated residual value, and the company planned to use straight-line depreciation. The bookkeeper mistakenly debited the purchase to supplies expense.
b. The company received an advance payment of $1,000 for services to be rendered during 19x9. The bookkeeper credited this amount to revenue.
c. The companyy purchased supplies during the year for $500 and debited the amount to supplies inventory. At the end of the year, all of the supplies had been consumed, but the bookkeeper neglected to make the appropriate adjusting entry.
d. Wages earned during the last week of 19x8 but not payable until January 4, 19x9, amounted to $500. The bookkeeper failed to make the appropriate adjusting entry.

Indicate the effects of these errors by placing an O (overstate), U (understate), or N (no effect) in the chart below:

	Assets	*Liabilities*	*Owner's Equity*	*Revenues*	*Expenses*
(a)					
(b)					
(c)					
(d)					

E4-4 On April 1, 19x9, a company purchased office supplies for $1,200. The count of office supplies on hand on December 31, 19x9, totalled $300. Prepare the necessary adjusting entry at December 31 assuming that the purchase on April 1 was debited to office supplies. Prepare a second entry assuming that the April debit was to office supplies expense.

E4-5 Below is a list of accounts that might appear in the adjusted trial balance columns of a worksheet. The income statement columns and the balance sheet columns of a worksheet are shown to the right of the list of accounts. For each account listed, indicate with a check (✓) the normal account balance.

	Income Statement		*Balance Sheet*	
Account	*Debit*	*Credit*	*Debit*	*Credit*
1. Revenue				
2. Cash				
3. Accounts payable				
4. Equipment				
5. Salary expense				
6. Accumulated depreciation				
7. Capital stock				
8. Depreciation expense				
9. Accrued salaries payable				
10. Unearned revenue				
11. Prepaid insurance				
12. Retained earnings				
13. Insurance expense				

E4-6 Selected account balances for Smith Co. on December 31 prior to adjusting entries are shown below:

Revenue	$ 47,000
Unearned revenue	6,000
Prepaid insurance	4,000
Equipment	100,000
Accumulated depreciation	20,000
Salary expense	25,000
Supplies	4,000

Data for adjustments are as follows:

1. On June 30, a two-year insurance policy was purchased and debited to prepaid insurance.
2. Supplies on hand as of December 31 amounted to $500.
3. Accrued salaries on December 31 amounted to $700.
4. Depreciation expense on equipment for the year is computed to be $10,000.
5. The company received a $6,000 advance from a customer on September 1 and credited the amount to unearned revenue. As of December 31, one-half of this amount was earned.

Required:

a. Prepare the adjusting entries that should be made on December 31.
b. Prepare an income statement for the year ended December 31.

E4-7 On July 1, 19x8, Jones Co. accepted a $5,000, one-year, 8 percent note from Ames Co. in settlement of an overdue account receivable. Ames Co. paid the note plus the interest on June 30, 19x9. Prepare the necessary entries relating to the issuance and payment of this note and the adjusting entry on December 31, 19x8, on the books of Jones Co.

E4-8 The following four combinations of accounts are generally affected by adjusting entries:

1. Expenses and assets.
2. Expenses and liabilities.
3. Revenues and assets.
4. Revenues and liabilities.

Indicate the nature of each of the following adjustments by choosing the appropriate letter from the above list.

a. Recording depreciation on equipment.
b. Recording interest accrued on a notes receivable.
c. Recording salaries earned by employees but not paid as of the end of the year.
d. Warehouse space was rented to another company on June 30, and the tenant paid one year's rent in advance. The payment was credited to unearned revenue.
e. Office supplies purchased during the year were debited to an asset account. A year-end inventory revealed that a portion of the supplies was still on hand.

E4-9 Certain account balances of Hine Co. before and after adjustment are listed below. For each account, give the probable adjusting entry that caused the balance to change.

	Balance Before Adjustment	*Balance After Adjustment*
1. Prepaid rent	$ 1,200	$ 600
2. Interest receivable	0	50
3. Office supplies	0	400
4. Accumulated depreciation	3,000	4,000
5. Revenue	50,000	53,000
6. Wage expense	26,000	27,000
7. Interest expense	750	1,000

E4-10 Listed below are the balances in the adjusted trial balance columns of the worksheet for Carter Co. at the end of 19x6. Complete the worksheet by extending the amounts to the income statement and balance sheet columns.

Account	Adjust Trial Balance		Income Statement		Balance Sheet	
	Debit	Credit	Debit	Credit	Debit	Credit
Cash	$ 5,000					
Accounts receivable	10,000					
Prepaid insurance	1,000					
Equipment	50,000					
Accumulated depreciation		$ 15,000				
Accounts payable		6,000				
Notes payable		9,000				
Unearned revenue		5,000				
Capital stock		10,000				
Retained earnings		7,500				
Revenue		70,000				
Wage expense	40,000					
Insurance expense	500					
Rent expense	12,000					
Depreciation expense	5,000					
Interest revenue		500				
Interest receivable	500					
Wages payable		1,000				
	$124,000	$124,000				

E4-11 Copley Company paid $3,000 to acquire a twenty-four month insurance policy on its business property. The policy covered the period from July 1, 19x3, to June 30, 19x5. Copley uses a calendar year-end. Record the acquisition of the policy and any adjusting entries required on December 31, 19x3, 19x4, and 19x5, first assuming the policy was originally recorded as an expense and, second, assuming it was originally recorded as an asset.

E4-12 Van Horn Company acquired an automobile for use in its business that cost $7,600. The auto was acquired on April 2, 19x3, and is expected to have a useful life of three years, at the end of which it is expected to have a salvage value of $1,000. If the firm uses a March 31 year-end, complete the following depreciation schedule for this automobile, calculating depreciation using the straight-line method.

Date	Depreciation Expense	Accumulated Depreciation	Remaining Book Value
April 2, 19x3	0	0	$7,600
March 31, 19x4	________	________	________
March 31, 19x5	________	________	________
March 31, 19x6	________	________	________

E4-13 Listed below are the balances in the trial balance column of the worksheet for Keck Company at December 31, 19x9:

Account	Trial Balance Debit	Trial Balance Credit	Adjustments Debit	Adjustments Credit
Cash	$ 2,600			
Accounts receivable	4,050			
Prepaid rent	1,200			
Equipment	26,000			
Accumulated depreciation		$ 9,000		
Accounts payable		6,000		
Notes payable		2,000		
Owner's equity		7,900		
Revenue		41,000		
Salary expense	29,000			
Insurance expense	950			
Utilities expense	2,100			
	$65,900	$65,900		

Using the data given below, prepare the necessary adjustments in the adjustment columns to the worksheet:

a. Rent was prepaid on November 1, 19x9, for three months.
b. All of Keck's equipment has a ten-year life and was acquired less than five years ago. None was acquired in the current year. Only $1,000 is expected to be realized as salvage for all the equipment.
c. The notes payable balance represents a $2,000, three-year, 6 percent note, dated June 30, 19x9.
d. Wages totalling $1,000 were earned by employees up to December 31, 19x9, but unpaid at that date.
e. The insurance policy was a six-month accident policy dated February 1, 19x9. The firm elected not to renew it.

E4-14 Coleman, Incorporated purchased a machine on January 1, 19x0, for $10,000. Coleman will depreciate the machine a straight-line basis over a five year life, with no estimated salavage value. The company's fiscal year ends on June 30. Prepare a depreciation schedule showing the annual depreciation expense and the net book value of the asset for the years 19x0 through 19x4 inclusive.

PROBLEMS*

P4-1 Listed below are selected data concerning the operations of Aggie Co. during 19x9:

a. The company purchased a two-year insurance policy for $600 on April 1, 19x8, and the premium was debited to prepaid insurance.
b. The company purchased supplies during the year for $1,000 cash and debited supplies expense. The supplies on hand on December 31, amounted to $240.
c. Equipment was purchased on January 1, 19x4, for $20,000. The estimated life was ten years with zero residual value, and the straight-line method is used to compute depreciation.
d. Aggie rented a warehouse to another company on June 1 for $100 a month. The tenant paid one year's rent in advance at that time, and the amount was credited to deferred revenue.
e. The Aggie Co. received a $1,000 advance from a customer for future deliveries. The receipt was credited to a revenue account. As of December 31, $200 of products remained to be delivered to the customer.
f. The company borrowed $1,000 from the City National Bank on December 1 for ninety days with interest of 9 percent per year.
g. Income taxes for 19x9 are estimated to be $25,000.
h. Employee salaries for the week of December 26 were $1,000 to be paid on January 4.
i. The company rented office space to ABC Co. on September 1, 19x9, at a monthly rental of $200. The rent was to be paid by the last day of the month, but the December rent had not been received as of December 31.
j. Accrued interest on notes receivable at December 31 amounted to $180.

Required:

For each item, prepare the adjusting entry necessary at the end of the company's accounting period, December 31, 19x9.

***Note:** Problems marked with an asterisk relate to the Appendix.

P4-2 Listed below is information concerning the operations of the Watkins Company during 19x9:

a. Watkins Co. pays all salaries on the 15th of each month. Salary expense for a whole month is $8,000.
b. On June 30, the company paid $5,000 for license fees to the city and debited prepaid licenses, an asset. The licenses expire one year from date of purchase.
c. A truck was purchased on January 1, 19x5, for $6,000. Its estimated life is ten years and it has no salvage value. Depreciation is recorded using the straight-line method.
d. Watkins Co. purchased a five-year insurance policy on March 1, 19x7, and debited prepaid insurance at the time of purchase. The policy cost $10,000.
e. On January 1, 19x8, the company received an advance payment for services to be rendered over the next two full years. An unearned revenue account was credited at the time, and an adjusting entry was made on December 31, 19x8, transferring one-half of the amount to revenue. The amount of advance payment was $18,000.
f. Watkins Co. borrowed $20,000 for one year to finance operations on October 1, 19x9. The annual interest rate is 10 percent payable every April and September.
g. Purchased $500 worth of supplies during the year and debited an expense account. An inventory shows $150 worth of supplies left on December 31, 19x9.
h. Interest owed, but not paid, as of the end-of-year on bonds payable amounted to $4,000.
i. Watkins Co. rented office space on June 30 of this year from Mr. Lynn, a good friend of the president. They paid $4,000 for a full year's rent in advance on that date and debited rent expense.

Required:

Prepare the adjusting entries necessary at the end of the company's accounting period, December 31, 19x9.

P4-3 The ledger account balances after adjustment of Daniel Co. as of December 31, 19x9, as listed below. The balance of the retained earnings account has been intentionally omitted. All accounts reflect their normal balances.

Cash	$ 1,500
Accounts receivable	5,000
Prepaid insurance	500
Equipment	30,000
Accumulated depreciation	6,000
Accounts payable	3,000
Notes payable	1,000
Capital stock	10,000
Retained earnings	?
Revenue	40,000
Salary expense	21,000
Insurance expense	1,000
Rent expense	6,000
Other expense	5,000

Required:

a. Prepare the necessary closing entries.
b. Prepare an income statement and a balance sheet.

P4-4 The trial balance before adjustment of the Dole Co. at December 31, 19x9 is presented below:

Dole Co.
Trial Balance
December 31, 19x9

Account	Debit	Credit
Cash	$ 2,000	
Accounts receivable	5,000	
Supplies	3,000	
Prepaid insurance	1,000	
Equipment	20,000	
Accumulated depreciation		$ 8,000
Accounts payable		4,000
Deferred revenue		2,000
Capital stock		10,000
Retained earnings		4,000
Revenue		21,000
Wage expense	6,000	
Rent expense	9,000	
Miscellaneous expense	3,000	
	$49,000	$49,000

Additional data:

1. Accrued wages at December 31 amounted to $500.
2. A physical count indicated that $1,000 of supplies were on hand at December 31.
3. The balance in the prepaid insurance account resulted from a two-year insurance policy purchased on June 30, 19x9.
4. The equipment was purchased on January 1, 19x5, for $20,000. It had an estimated useful life of ten years, zero residual value, and straight-line depreciation was used.
5. One-half of the deferred revenues were earned as of December 31.

Required:

a. Prepare a worksheet.
b. Prepare an income statement and a balance sheet.
c. Prepare the necessary closing entries.

P4-5 The trial balance before adjustment of the Hart Co. at December 31, 19x9 is presented below:

Hart Co.
Trial Balance
December 31, 19x9

Account	Debit	Credit
Cash	$ 6,000	
Accounts receivable	7,500	
Supplies	600	
Prepaid rent	1,200	
Equipment	12,000	
Building	24,000	
Accumulated depreciation on building and equipment		$ 6,000
Accounts payable		4,000
Unearned revenue		400
Notes payable		1,000
Salaries payable		500
Capital stock		15,000
Retained earnings		13,000
Revenue		19,900
Insurance expense	4,000	
Salaries expense	2,000	
Miscellaneous expense	2,500	
	$59,800	$59,800

Additional data:

1. Depreciation on the buildings and equipment is calculated under the straight-line method. Estimated life of both is six years, with no residual value.
2. Rent for the year amounted to $1,200, which had been paid on January 1, 19x9, and debited to prepaid rent.
3. Exactly $500 of supplies were still on hand on December 31.
4. Annual interest on the note payable dated January 1, 19x9, is 10 percent. Interest has not been paid during 19x9.
5. One-half of the unearned revenues was earned during the year.

Required:

a. Prepare a worksheet to reflect appropriate adjustments.
b. Prepare an income statement and a balance sheet.
c. Prepare the necessary closing entries.

P4-6 Listed below are financial data extracted from the records of Boyd and Sons Service Company for calendar year 19x5:

a. Depreciation expense of $2,100 has not been recorded.
b. The supplies on hand account has a balance of $600. A count of supplies on hand shows only $200 actually on hand at year-end.
c. Utilities expense of $80 has been incurred but no formal bill had been received by year-end.
d. Rent expense for three months was prepaid on December 1, 19x5, totalling $1,500.
e. Wages of $900 have been earned by employees but unpaid at year-end.
f. Customers' fees totalling $1,000 have been received by the firm for services to be performed in January and February of next year. They were recorded as revenues.

Required:

Prepare general journal entries to record these adjustments.

P4-7 The Oil Company has completed one year of operations and has the following (normal) ledger balances before adjustments.

Accounts receivable	$ 3,000
Accounts payable	1,000
Cash	2,600
Equipment	8,000
Prepaid advertising	1,000
Prepaid rent	1,200
Notes payable	1,000
Sales	18,200
Wages expense	7,800
Utilities expense	800
Supplies expense	2,600
Owner's equity	6,800

The financial records of the firm disclose the following additional data:

1. All supplies acquired were recorded as supplies expense. Actually, $550 in supplies are still on hand at year-end.
2. The prepaid advertising relates to newspaper ads for October, November, and December, 19x3, the last three months of their year.
3. Prepaid rent was debited for three months rent paid in advance on December 1, 19x3.
4. Wages earned but unpaid to employees at year-end totalled $300.
5. The equipment account reflects the cost of two machine owned by the firm:

Machine	*Life*	*Cost*	*Salvage*
A	6	$3,200	$200
B	8	4,800	0

Depreciation for this year has not been recorded. The firm will use the straight-line method.

6. Sales include $400 in fees that have been received for services to be provided in the future.

Required:

a. Set up T-accounts and enter the unadjusted balances as shown above.
b. Prepare general journal entries to record the necessary adjusting entries.
c. Post the adjusting entries to the T-accounts.
d. Prepare an adjusted trial balance.

P4-8 The trial balance before adjustment of Coker Company at December 31, 19x6, is presented below:

Coker Company
Trial Balance
December 31, 19x6

Cash	$ 2,400	
Accounts receivable	1,800	
Supplies on hand	320	
Equipment	8,000	
Accounts payable		$ 3,520
Owner's equity		8,600
Sales		9,000
Wage expense	3,200	
Advertising expense	900	
Insurance expense	600	
Utilities expense	600	
Rent expense	3,300	
	$21,120	$21,120

An analysis of Coker's fiancial records disclose the following data:

1. December rent of $300 was unpaid due to oversight.
2. Straight-line depreciation of $1,200 for 19x6 is unrecorded.
3. Supplies on hand at December 31, 19x6, total only $100.
4. Revenues of $600 have been earned but are unrecorded at December 31, 19x6: invoices to customers will be mailed in January 19x7.
5. The $600 insurance premium was paid on June 27, 19x6, for a two-year fire insurance policy, expiring on the same date in 19x8.

Required:

a. Prepare a worksheet and enter the trial balance in the trial balance columns.
b. Enter all required adjustments on the worksheet.
c. Complete the worksheet by extending the balances from the adjusted trial balance column to the balance sheet and income statement columns.

P4-9* Refer back to P4-6. Prepare any reversing entries that should be made.

P4-10* Refer back to P4-7. Prepare any reversing entries that should be made.

P4-11* Refer back to P4-8. Prepare any reversing entries that should be made.

Learning Objectives

Chapter 5 discusses revenue recognition and preparation of a formal income statement. Studying this chapter should enable you to:

1. Discuss the meaning and methods of measuring business income.
2. Prepare the revenue section of an income statement.
3. Define realization and discuss alternative characteristics of the earning process that can indicate when realization occurs.
4. Calculate trade and cash discounts.
5. Contrast the multiple step and the single step form of an income statement.

5

The Income Statement: Revenues and Realization

INTRODUCTION

Businesses, like most organizations, prepare reports, or disseminate information, about the success or failure of their operations. The purpose of this reporting activity is to inform owners, creditors, and other interested parties about the organization and its accomplishments. Success can be measured in a variety of ways depending on the purpose of the evaluation. A baseball team, for example, may achieve success if it wins more games than its rivals. From another perspective, the baseball team may be evaluated on the profitability of its operations: Do the fans pay more for admission to see the team play than management pays the players and other suppliers of goods and services?

The investment of owners, the funds loaned by a bank, and the salaries of employees are examples of the financial interest that many individuals have in a business. The income statement is periodically prepared by accountants to report on the financial consequences of activities undertaken by a business within a certain period of time. If the enterprise has earned a profit, it has more resources available to it at the end of the period than were available at the beginning of the period. If a loss has been incurred, the converse is true, or the business consumed more resources in its operations than it generated during the period.

Profit and loss relate to business income, which is widely used as a measure of effectiveness and performance. However, there are alternative definitions of income.

BUSINESS INCOME

Economists have often viewed income as a measure of well-being relative to an enterprise. Income has been described as the maximum value that could be distributed to owners during a period and still leave the business as well off at the end of the period as it was at the start of the period. While conceptually appealing, the application of this definition becomes virtually impossible. Many assumptions must be made to measure how "well off" a business is at any point in time.

Another approach to income determination is to use a total venture concept. In this sense, the value of all investment inputs in a business venture are determined and accumulated over its life. At the end of the venture, the residual value, plus the value of all distributions made to owners are also accumulated. The difference between the inputs and the final value is deemed to be income. The total venture approach is very objective and accurate. However, income cannot be determined until the venture ends. Investors in most businesses require timely, ongoing feedback and could not wait for this type of information.

The Matching Concept

Accountants measure business income by *matching*, or relating, revenues and expenses for a specific time period. Since revenues and expenses are quantified by using historical data, the resulting income is deemed to be historical. Accounting income does not, necessarily, reflect current values or determinations of how well off a business is. It does provide for a timely, objective, periodic report.

Fundamentally, the accountant relizes, or isolates, revenue that relates to a specific time period. Normally, revenue realization follows a specific transaction with a customer of the organization. Once the revenues have been identified, the accountant determines the expenses that the business incurred to generate the revenues. The expenses and revenues are matched, or related, by the accountant. The difference between revenues and expenses is termed income or loss.

Accounting Income

When goods or services are sold by a business it receives an *inflow* as a part of the sale transaction. The form of the inflow is an asset, and it also increases the owner's claim through the recognition of revenue. The revenue is measured by the value of the asset received. The business entity also incurrs an expense which represents an *outflow* of cost associated with the product or service that was sold. Both revenues and expenses are valued by using the historical cost of specific assets received and given in the transaction.

Through a focus on revenues and expenses, accounting income produces a historical measure. The results are quantifiable and objective. The income statement is the reporting device used by accountants to disclose this information.

THE INCOME STATEMENT

The income statement provides a summary of revenues and expenses for a specific period of time. Revenue and expense items are grouped by type or by class to condense the report and to make it readable. Thus, a single line entitled "sales revenue" may be shown instead of 2,000 lines bearing such titles as "revenue from sale to Andy Barnes" and "revenue from sale to Betty Benett."

Although specific formats can vary among organizations, industries, or uses, a functional classification system is most popular. A functional system will isolate the expenses that relate to major activities. These normally include the cost of the product that was sold, the expenses incurred to sell (or market) the product, and the expense of administrating the organization. These classifications tend to follow major areas of interest to statement users.

An Example

Illustration 1 presents a classified income statement for the Morris Merchandising Company. The statement contains five major sections and several subsections. The major sections include the following:

1. *Sales.* The total revenue relating to primary operations of the business is reported in this section. Various deductions are considered in arriving at the net sales revenue (these are discussed later in this chapter).
2. *Cost of Goods Sold.* This is the expense the company incurred to purchase the goods that were sold during the period. It is deducted from net sales to determine the amount of gross margin on sales.
3. *Operating Expenses.* A variety of expenses that relating to the sales revenue are considered in this section. The expense items have been subclassified into cost of goods sold, selling expenses, and administrative expenses.
4. *Other Revenue and Expense.* The results of normal, ongoing operations are separated from revenue and expense items that relate to activities not directly associated with the principal operations of the firm.
5. *Earnings Per Share.* This is a required part of the income statement for most corporations. The goal is to provide additional user information by relating net income on a per share basis.

This chapter focuses on the sales or sales revenue section of the income statement, while the next chapter deals with the expense sections.

REVENUE REALIZATION

Business operations are based on a series of exchanges. Products and services are acquired, combined in a marketable form, and exchanged for other assets, or resources. For example, the Morris Merchandising Company acquired products, facilities, and personnel. These resources were initially valued at their cost to the firm.

Illustration 1
Morris Merchandising Company
Income Statement
For the Year Ended December 31, 19x0

Sales:			
Sales revenue		$412,900	
Less: Sales returns and allowances	$ 7,400		
Sales discounts	4,200	11,600	
Net sales			$401,300
Cost of goods sold			248,200
Gross margin on sales			$153,100
Operating expenses:			
Selling expenses—			
Sales salaries and commissions	$21,200		
Advertising	16,100		
Travel	5,200		
Telephone	2,100		
Supplies	900		
Depreciation on sales equipment	1,800		
Total selling expense		$ 47,300	
Administrative expenses:			
Salaries	$25,900		
Telephone	2,900		
Legal and professional fees	3,000		
Supplies	1,200		
Depreciation expense—building	5,000		
Depreciation expense—equipment	3,700		
Miscellaneous	400		
Total administrative expense		42,100	
Total operating expense			89,400
Net income from operations			$ 63,700
Other revenue:			
Rental income		$ 7,300	
Other expenses:			
Interest expense		5,100	2,200
Net income before taxes			$ 65,900
Income tax expense			26,400
Net income			$ 39,500
Earnings per share			$ 5.00

When the product was resold by the firm, the customers paid for the product and the service provided by the company. Thus, the customers paid for the combination of product, facility, and personnel. This combination is valued at the amount received by the firm in exchange for the resource given up. The acquisition value of the resources becomes an expense and the resale value is a revenue.

To the extent that revenue exceeds expense, income results. Income then suggests a positive market reaction to the activities of the firm. If expense exceeds revenue, a loss results and indicates that the market reacted in a negative way to the activities of the firm.

In determining periodic income, the accountant first identifies those revenue items that relate to the time period in question. This identification process is governed by the *realization principle.*

Revenue is realized, or recorded in the accounts and income statement, when an exchange has taken place and when the earning process is essentially complete. Realization provides the accountant with an objective means of determining when revenue should be included in the income statement.

Consider the following revenue-related situations in terms of the realization principle:

1. *Situation 1*—Goods or services are sold for $1,000 and the customer pays cash.

   Analysis—This is a common situation that clearly fits the constraints of the realization principle; an exchange has taken place and the earning process is complete. Revenue in the amount of $1,000 is recognized by the following entry:

Cash	$1,000	
Sales revenue		$1,000

2. *Situation 2*—Goods or services are sold for $1,200 on account.

   Analysis—In this situation a sale was made but cash was not received. Accounting practice treats this as a transaction, recognizing the account receivable as an asset. The other realization constraints have been met and the following entry is made:

Accounts receivable	$1,200	
Sales revenue		$1,200

3. *Situation 3*—A future service contract is sold to a customer for $800.

   Analysis—This situation does not meet the realization constraints. Although a transaction has taken place, the earning process is far from complete since the service has not been provided. The company has acquired cash and it has incurred a liability to provide a future service. The liability may be called "unearned revenue" and reported in the liabilities section of the balance sheet.

Cash	$800	
Unearned sales revenue		$800

Realization is an extremeley important accounting principle. It governs which transactions result in revenue attributable to a specific time period. The revenue items, in turn, lead to an identification of the periodic expenses through the matching concept. Revenue and expense together result in the periodic income or loss reported by a firm.

SALES

The sales, or sales revenue, section of the income statement sets out the revenue for the period that is related to normal, ongoing business operations. Nonrecurring or extraordinary items are disclosed in another part of the statement. (These are discussed later in the chapter.)

In most situations, a sale results in the immediate recognition of revenue. The accountant relies upon *source documents* to provide evidence of a sale and uses them as the basis for recording revenues. Source documents can include cash register summary tapes, receipts for credit sales, or special agreements between a buyer and seller.

Cash Sales

Sales result in an inflow of cash to the firm in exchange for the product or service provided. The cash inflow is used to value the revenue. If daily cash sales of $2,900 were made, the following entry is used to recognize the revenue:

Cash....................................	$2,900	
Sales revenue		$2,900

While an entry could be made to record each cash sale, there is no need for information in that much detail. Therefore, summary totals are normally recorded. Sometimes, management will use sales information about particular departments, locations, or products. To provide this information, the accountant can accumulate sales data in separate revenue accounts. For example, the previous sales of $2,900 could have come from three products and been records as follows:

Cash....................................	$2,900	
Sales revenue—Product A		$1,200
Sales revenue—Product B		800
Sales revenue—Product C		900

When the income statement is prepared, the three sales revenue accounts are merged into a single revenue item. However, by recording the sales data separately, the accountant was able to facilitate additional product information reporting at limited added cost.

Credit Sales

When credit sales are made, the firm receives a promise of payment from their customers. The promise of payment is termed an account receivable. The accountant must record the name of the customer who owes the firm money. However, there is no real need to differentiate revenue by customer name. Periodically, generally on a daily basis, the amount of the credit sales will be totalled and a summary entry will be made.

If a company had $3,300 of credit sales, the revenue would be recorded as follows:

Accounts receivable	$3,300	
Sales revenue		$3,300

Accounts receivable is an asset account reflecting the debts owed by customers. The accountant also maintains a set of subsidiary accounts, one for each customer, showing the individual amounts owed. The total of the subsidiary account balances equals the balance of the control, or summary, account—accounts receivable. The control account receivable appears in the general ledger. The relationship between the control and subsidiary accounts can be summarized as follows:

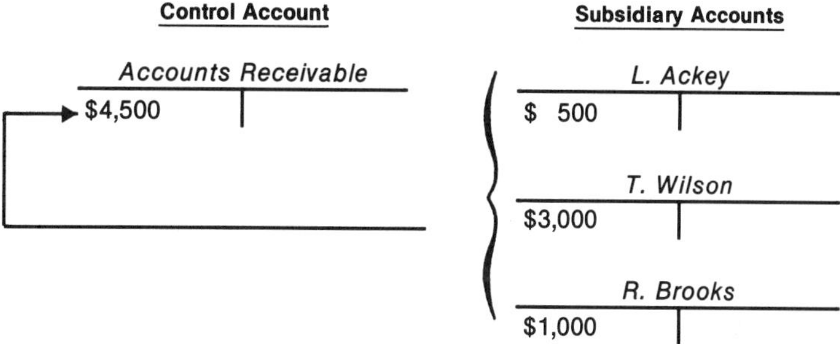

When transaction data is posted from the journal to the ledger, it must be posted once to the control account and once to the subsidiary account.

In the construction of an income statement, sales revenue is normally reduced by two types of items—returns and allowances, and discounts—to arrive at net sales revenue.

SALES RETURNS AND ALLOWANCES

Many businesses allow their customers to return damaged, defective, or unwanted items of merchandise. Depending upon the company's policy, such returns result in the firm's refunding cash to the customer, reducing the customer's account receivable balance, or issuing a credit allowance for future redemption. In all of these cases, the amount of revenue associated with the original sale should be reduced; to the extent that goods have been returned, revenue has not been earned.

One way to adjust revenue correctly is to reverse the original entry. For example, if the Dee Company sold $2,750 of merchandising on account, it would make the following entry:

Accounts receivable	$2,750	
Sales revenue		$2,750

If the customer subsequently returns $150 of the merchandise for credit, the Dee Company could make the following entry:

Sales revenue	$150	
Accounts receivable		$150

After the latter entry has been made, the balance of the sales revenue account is correctly stated at net sales of $2,600 ($2,750 credit less $150 debit).

The amount of returns and allowances is an extremely important type of management information. Excessive amounts of returns and allowances could indicate production or procurement problems relative to quality, extremely liberal return policies, a "too aggressive" sales force, or "problem" customers. To provide management with information concerning the volume of sales adjustments and returns, a separate account titled "sales returns and allowances" is generally used.

The *sales returns and allowances* account is used to accumulate the revenue reductions that result from customer returns and adjustments. The account is used as an offset (a contra account) against the sales revenue, or gross revenue, account to derive the amount of net revenue.

In the previous example of the Dee Fective Company, the entry to record the return would be:

Sales returns and allowances..............	$150	
Accounts receivable		$150

Sales returns and allowances will be deducted from sales revenue to derive the net sales revenue reported on the income statement.

SALES DISCOUNTS

Many times, especially in wholesale operations, customers will be quoted prices that are lower than the list or catalog prices of the selling firm. Also, customers can often secure an added discount or price reduction, either by paying cash or by paying within a specified time period. Reductions from list price are called *trade discounts* and prompt payment reductions are called *cash discounts*. Both must be considered in deriving the proper amount of sales revenue.

Trade Discounts

Trade discounts are reductions from a list price or a catalog price that are granted to a purchaser. The use of trade discount has certain advantages to the seller, including the following:

1. Catalogs can be printed at a suggested retail selling price. The trade discount can be used to reduce the catalog price for wholesale purchases.
2. Reprinting costs of the catalog prices can be saved by adjusting the amount of the trade discount instead of the list price.
3. Special sales situations, for quantities or types of products, can be priced without prepublishing a price structure for every possible circumstance.

The Robinson-Patman Act and other pieces of federal legislation impose limits on some types of special trade discounts.

Trade discounts are expressed as a percentage reduction of the list price. A 15 percent trade discount means that the actual sale price will be 85 percent (100% − 15%) of the list price. Frequently, several trade discounts will be given on a single purchase. The discounts may relate to several characteristics of the sale—quantity, type of product, type of customer—or they may relate to a single characteristic. Multiple discounts are treated in a cumulative fashion.

For example, if a company sold goods having a list price of $5,000 subject to trade discounts of 25, 20, and 10 percent, the actual sale price will be $2,700, computed as follows:

List price	$5,000
Less: 25%	1,250
	$3,750
Less: 20%	750
	$3,000
Less: 10%	300
Actual price	$2,700

Normal accounting practice is to deduct any applicable trade discounts and to bill customers for the net amount, or the actual sale price. Revenue will be realized at the net amount, and no separate disclosure of trade discounts is made in the income statement. Trade discounts are a part of the firm's pricing policy and, as such, the net sales price is the relevant information.

Cash Discounts

Many businesses will grant discounts for cash sales or for credit sales paid promptly. Cash discounts and credit terms are placed on the sales invoice to fully inform the customers and to avoid any misunderstandings. Generally, these terms are expressed as:

"n/20"—which means that the net amount of the sale is due no later than twenty days from the date of the sale.

"2/10, n/30"—which means that a 2 percent discount may be deducted from the net amount if payment is made within ten days of the date of sale and that if the discount is not taken, the net amount is due within thirty days of the date of the sale.

Cash discounts are normally offered because of industry practice or a desire to speed up customer payments and thus accelerate the cash flow for the firm. The discount terms will normally motivate purchasers to pay within the discount period. Purchasers can evaluate the discount in terms of an annual interest rate.

If a sale is subject to terms of 3/10, n/30, the purchaser will receive a 3 percent reduction up through the tenth day and no reduction from eleventh through the thirtieth day. Thus, by not paying within the discount period, the purchaser will lose 3 percent for withholding payment until the thirtieth day. This represents 3 percent for a twenty-day period ranging from day eleven through day thirty. There are roughly eighteen, twenty-day periods in a year (360 ÷ 20) and at the rate of 3 percent per period, these discount terms translate into an annual rate of 54 percent.

When discounts are taken, the revenue attributable to the sale should be reduced to reflect the cash actually received from the sale. This reduction is reflected in an account called sales discounts.

A company sold $15,000 of merchandise subject to terms of 2/10, n/30. At the time of the sale, the following entry would be made:

Accounts receivable	$15,000	
Sales revenue		$15,000

If the customer does not pay until the thirtieth day, the net amount—$15,000—must be remitted. The company would record this receipt as follows:

Cash	$15,000	
Accounts receivable		$15,000

However, if the customer pays within the discount period, $14,700 will be received by the company [$15,000 − (.02 × $15,000)]. Thus cash of $14,700 must be recorded, because it was received. Accounts receivable must be reduced by $15,000 since this debt was satisfied by the customer's payment. The difference is $300 and it represents a reduction in sales revenue because of a cash discount. To update this information, sales discounts is debited and subsequently used as an offset against revenue in the income statement. The entry appears as follows:

Cash	$14,700	
Sales discounts	300	
Accounts receivable		$15,000

Sales discounts will be reported on the income statement as a reduction in sales revenue to arrive at net sales. This information is included in the report to provide interested users with some indication of the cost of the firm's credit terms.

OTHER INCOME ELEMENTS

Most of the income statement is generally devoted to information concerning the primary normal, ongoing operations of the entity, as opposed to special or secondary items. This follows from an assumption that the ongoing operations provide the basis for the long-term success or failure of the enterprise. The results of ongoing operations are presented in the operating section of the income statement that ends with the calculation of net income from operations.

The next part of the statement is the nonoperating section, which presents other income and other expense. These items summarize revenues and expenses resulting from the secondary activities of the firm.

Other Revenue

The other revenue section of the income statement lists revenue, net of related expenses, resulting from nonoperating transactions. That is, the total received from these activities is reduced by expenses relating to them and the result is reported. This category often includes interest income, gains on sales of plant and equipment, and rental income. Several revenue and expense accounts may be summarized in a single disclosure of other revenue.

Other Expense

Like other revenue, other expense relates to nonoperating items. This section of the income statement summarizes expenses or losses incurred, net of any related revenue. Again, the total loss, less any related revenue is reported. Examples of other expenses include interest expense from financing operations and losses on the disposal of plant and equipment items.

Extraordinary Items

Sometimes, firms will add a section to the income statement after the other income and other expense section called *extraordinary gains or losses*. These are set out to inform statement users of highly unusual events that occurred during the period and influenced net income.

Accountants use a twofold test to determine if a transaction is extraordinary:

1. *Unusual Nature.* The event or transaction must be clearly abnormal and unrelated to the ordinary and typical activities of the entity.

2. *Infrequency of Occurrence.* The event or transaction should not be reasonably expected to recur in the future.

These criteria establish parameters on the types of items subject to classification as extraordinary.

When applying the unusual and infrequent criteria, both must be met and the environment in which the entity operates must be taken into account. For example, a hurricane loss for a company on the coast of Florida may not be considered extraordinary since hurricanes are not unusual in that geographical area. However, a hurricane loss for a company in Tennessee would be considered both unusual and infrequent for that environment and the loss would be an extraordinary item. Thus, the determination of whether an item is extraordinary must consider environmental factors such as geographic region, type of industry, etc. If a gain or loss meets one of the criteria but not the other, it is considered an ordinary item and is reported as part of other revenues or expenses.

AN EXAMPLE

To review the process of revenue realization and disclosure, consider the following transactions of Save-T Stores, Inc.:

1. Cash sales of $12,400 were made.
2. Credit sales of $18,200 subject to trade discounts of 20 and 10 percent were made.
3. $8,300 of the credit invoices were collected.
4. Credit sales of $9,800 were made and were invoiced with terms of 2/10, n/30.
   a. $5,200 of these invoices were paid within ten days.
   b. $4,600 of these invoices were paid after the discount period.
5. Merchandise that was sold for $800 cash was returned.
6. Rent of $1,000 on a vacant lot was collected.
7. Store equipment that cost $1,800 was deemed inappropriate and was resold one week later for $1,400.
8. Merchandise that cost $2,000 was destroyed in an uninsured fire.

Recording the Information

Journal entries for these transactions are presented in Illustration 2. The transaction numbers relate to the explanations presented as follows:

1. Cash sales meet the realization criteria and will lead to recording revenue.

Illustration 2
Recording Revenue Items

1.	Cash	$12,400	
	Sales revenue		$12,400
2.	Accounts receivable	13,104	
	Sales revenue		13,104
3.	Cash	8,300	
	Accounts receivable		8,300
4.	Accounts receivable	9,800	
	Sales revenue		9,800
4a.	Cash	5,096	
	Sales discounts	104	
	Accounts receivable		5,200
4b.	Cash	4,600	
	Accounts receivable		4,600
5.	Sales returns and allowances	800	
	Cash		800
6.	Cash	1,000	
	Rent revenue		1,000
7.	Cash	1,400	
	Loss on sale of equipment	400	
	Equipment		1,800
8.	Fire loss	2,000	
	Merchandise inventory		2,000

2. Revenue may also be realized on credit sales. The amount of the sale is deemed to be net of applicable trade discounts. In this case, that value is $13,104 [$18,200 − (.20 × $18,200) = $14,650 − (.10 × $14,560) = $13,104].

3. The collection of credit sales does not affect revenue. The collection transaction would be recorded as it does affect two asset accounts.

4. Credit sales again give rise to the realization of revenue. These sales may be recorded at their gross value and adjusted later for any cash discounts that are taken.

4a. Invoices paid within the discount period are reduced by 2 percent. Thus, the firm will receive $5,096 in cash ($5,200 − (.02 × $5,200)] as full payment. Sales discounts of $104 are recognized and will subsequently be used as a revenue reduction.

4b. Payments made after ten days are not subject to discount. Revenue is unaffected by this transaction.

5. Merchandise returns are set out in a special account. This entry will reduce sales revenue to the extent of the returned merchandise.

6. The receipt of rent gives rise to a revenue item. Since rental income is not a part of the firm's primary operations, it will be disclosed as other revenue.

7. The sale of store equipment also falls outside the normal oeprations. The resulting loss will be reported as another expense item. Other expenses relate to potentially recurring events that are not part of the primary business operations.

8. A fire loss is generally an extraordinary event. This loss will be reported as an extraordinary item.

Reporting the Results

The above transactions relate primarily to items of revenue for Save-T Stores, Inc. The partial income statement shown in Illustration 3 has omitted detail on the expense elements and focused on revenue.

Illustration 3
Save-T Stores, Inc.
Partial Income Statement
For the Year Ended December 31, 19x3

Sales:			
Sales revenue		$35,304	
Less: Sales returns and allowances	$800		
Sales discounts	104	904	
Net sales			$34,400
Cost of goods sold			XX
Gross margin on sales			$ XX
Operating expenses			XX
Net income from operations			$ XX
Other income:			
Rental income		$ 1,000	
Other expense:			
Loss on sale of equipment		400	600
Net income before taxes			$ XX
Income tax expense			XX
Net income before extraordinary items			XX
Extraordinary loss:			
Fire loss		$ 2,000	
Income tax effect		XX	XX
Net income			$ XX

The revenue elements included in the income statement were derived from the preceding transactions. The account balances resulting from these transactions provided the data for inclusion in the report.

FORMS OF THE INCOME STATEMENT

The purpose of the income statement is to convey meaningful economic information to users of the statement. To provide for consistency among firms and organizations, the income statement generally is laid out, or arranged in a predetermined form. However, the accountant does have the option to alter the statement to meet particular reporting needs.

The general format of the income statement follows the logic of computing net income; revenues, expenses, and income are reported in sequence. The statements illustrated in this chapter follow a *multiple-step form*. This multiple-step income statement has two main characteristics:

1. Primary and secondary operating results are separated and shown in different parts of the statement.
2. Cost of goods sold is deducted from net sales to display gross margin. This is an important figure because it shows how much of the sales dollars remain after paying for the goods that were sold. This is important information, particularly in terms of trends, for assessing the operations of the company.
3. Operating expenses are separated and classified by function, such as selling expense and administrative expense.

The *single-step income statement* uses revenues and expenses as major classifications but does not provide the detail found in the multiple-step form. Illustration 4 recasts the Morris Merchandising Company's income statement (Illustration 1) in a single-step format. Recognize that the amount of net income remains the same; only the amount of disclosure and the arrangement have changed.

Other variations of the income statement are prepared for special needs. A condensed income statement may be prepared by using just the major captions of the multiple-step statement and eliminating the subclassifications of the expense data. A divisionalized income statement will use multiple columns and separate income data by various segments of the organization. The accountant's judgment must be used to select the proper reporting format.

SUMMARY

There are various ways to define and measure business income. Accountants use a historical cost approach and relate revenues and expenses to derive periodic income for a business organization. Income is reported on the income statement, which most businesses must prepare regularly. The

Illustration 4
Morris Merchandising Company
Single-Step Income Statement
For the Year Ended December 31, 19x0

Sales revenue	$401,300
Other revenue	7,300
Total revenue	$408,600
Expenses:	
Cost of goods sold	$248,200
Selling expenses	47,300
Administrative expenses	42,100
Interest expense	5,100
Total expenses	$342,700
Net income before taxes	$ 65,900
Income tax expense	26,400
Net income	$ 39,500
Earnings per share	$ 5.00

income statement sets out a variety of revenue and expense information. The format of the statement depends on the final use for which it is intended.

Income measurement is based on matching revenues and expenses. Revenue is recognized on the income statement after it is deemed to be realized. Realization takes place when an exchange has occurred and the related earning process is essentially complete. The matching process identifies items of expense that are related to the revenues.

Sales revenue results from an organization selling a product or service. Revenue may be reduced if some of a customer's purchase is returned for credit. Trade discounts and cash discounts will also reduce the amount of net revenue during a period.

In the multiple-step form of the income statement, primary operating income is separated from the secondary operating income and expense elements. The goal of this disclosure is to provide users and analysts with additional information on the source of income. Extraordinary items, which are unusual and occur infrequently, are disclosed in another, separate section of the income statement.

In recent years, many business analysts have placed significant importance on the income statement and its contents. The information derived from this statement has profound effects on stock market prices, loan agreements, and employee wage settlements. All accountants, business managers, stockholders, and interested parties must be familiar with this statement and its contents.

Income determination begins with the realization process. Revenue, then, is a vital element in the process. This chapter provided the basis for revenue measurement. In the next chapter, the expense elements of income are considered.

KEY DEFINITIONS

Cash discounts—discount given to encourage early payment.

Control account—a general ledger account that summarizes information in subsidiary ledgers.

Extraordinary item—a gain or loss that resulted from an event that is unusual in nature and infrequent in occurrence given the environment in which the entity operates.

Multiple step form—a form of income statement that isolates the gross margin on sales and separates major operations from ancillary operations.

Realization principle—revenues should be recognized when the earning process is substantially complete and a transaction has taken place.

Sales returns and allowances—an account that summarizes the dollar amount of returns and adjustments to sales. It is a contra account to sales.

Single step form—a form of income statement that groups all revenues and expenses into single groups.

Source documents—written evidence that provides a basis for recording transactions.

Subsidiary account—an account that provides detail relating to the composition of a control account.

Trade discounts—discount from list price on purchased merchandise.

Appendix

Special Journals and Subsidiary Ledgers

INTRODUCTION

The accounting system must be effective and efficient to be of maximum service to an organization. An effective accounting system processes all data of accounting relevance into reports that are both useful and that conform with generally accepted accounting principles. Efficiency is concerned with the relationship between inputs and outputs; system efficiency relates to the manner in which tasks are performed and the methods employed to process data. Special journals and subsidiary ledgers can be integrated into the accounting data processing sequence to increase processing efficiency. Efficiency is greatly increased by using accounting software in a personal computer or mainframe. While the illustrations in the chapter relate to hand written records, the basic concepts and methods also apply to computerized systems.

SUBSIDIARY LEDGERS

Subsidiary ledgers which were illustrated in the chapter for accounts receivable, are books of secondary entry composed of a group of similar accounts. Subsidiary ledgers are designed to maintain detailed information about any general class of accounts. Subsidiary ledgers can be created to maintain detailed information on any asset, liability, owners' equity, revenue, or expense account. The listing of amounts owed to trade creditors would represent the accounts payable subsidiary ledger while a listing of stockholders' equity interests would represent the common stock subsidiary ledger. The subsidiary sales revenue ledger might maintain a separate accounts for each sales department, cash register, or general class of merchandise.

Subsidiary ledgers are linked to the general ledger through corresponding *control accounts*. A control account is established to represent each subsidiary ledger. The control account maintains a summary balance equal to the sum of the individual balances in the subsidiary ledger. Whenever a subsidiary ledger is established, one control account is substituted in the general ledger for many accounts. The general ledger is composed of control accounts that provide summary information used in preparing financial statements, while the subsidiary ledgers provide detailed information needed in day-to-day operations of the business.

SPECIAL JOURNALS

Special journals are books of original entry used to record information about a single type of recurring transaction. Sales journals, cash receipts journals, purchases journals, and cash disbursement journals are examples of special journals.

All transactions can be recorded in a general journal. However, general journals are organized so that each and every entry must be individually posted to the general ledger accounts. In contrast, special journals do not require that each and every entry be individually posted. Furthermore, special journals provide for a separation of duties so that several people can perform the journalizing task at one time. Task simplification through the use of special journals allows specialization, which in turn encourages greater speed and accuracy for greater control. The increased speed, accuracy, and control are each part of the increased efficiency associated with use of special journals and subsidiary ledgers.

Sales Journals

The simplest form of a sales journal only records transactions involving the sale of merchandise on account. This type of transaction is characterized by entries to two accounts:

1. A debit (increase) in accounts receivable.
2. A credit (increase) in sales revenue.

The design of a sales journal is shown in Illustration 1. Journal columns are used to record information on the date, invoice (sales slip) number, customer name, and dollar amount, all of which can be obtained from the sales slip. In nonelectronic accounting systems, sales clerks batch the sales slips and then transmit a batch to the accounting department, where entries are made in the appropriate columns of the sales journal. Advanced electronic systems can generate a sales journal entry automatically when the sales slip is created by the terminal at the point of sale.

Illustration 1
Sales Journal

Date	Invoice No.	Account Debited	Post. Ref.	Accounts Receivable—Dr. Sales Receivable—Cr.
6/1	213	Kaupp, Inc.	X	$ 295
6/2	214	Markell Company	X	1,025
6/2	215	Tiani & Minsley	X	65
6/2	216	R & R Construction	X	175
6/3	217	Kaupp, Inc.	X	950
6/3	218	R & R Construction	X	640
6/4	219	Frank Rogg	X	495
6/4	220	Tiani & Minsley	X	895
6/5	221	J. Knott, Inc.	X	1,200
6/5	222	Kaupp, Inc.	X	105
				$5,845

The "post. ref." (posting reference) column of the sales journal is used to reflect the posting activity that transcribes data from the journal to the ledger. Individual customer account numbers may be listed in the "post. ref." column as entries are posted to the individual customer's account. These numbers serve as a control reference to ensure that entries have been made to the correct account. Alternatively, an "X" or check mark may be placed in the "post. ref." column simply to indicate that a posting has occurred. Some electronic accounting systems automatically post credit sales to the customer's account when the sales slip is created by the terminal at the point of sale. In nonelectronic systems, the posting must be done as a separate operation.

Dollar amounts in the last column of the sales journal are periodically totalled, and the column total is posted to both the accounts receivable control account and to the sales revenue account. Individual transaction entries are not posted to these accounts, only the column totals. Thus, the credit to sales revenue will be reflected as one entry rather than as several entries.

While the accounts receivable control account will reflect the summarized debit, individual customer account balances must be maintained.

Information from the previous sales journal are posted to individual accounts in the accounts receivable subsidiary ledger. The total of these accounts equals the total in the accounts receivable account appearing in the general ledger. These relationships are shown in Illustration 2.

Information from a source document (sales invoice) is entered into the special sales journal. Individual account data from this journal is posted to

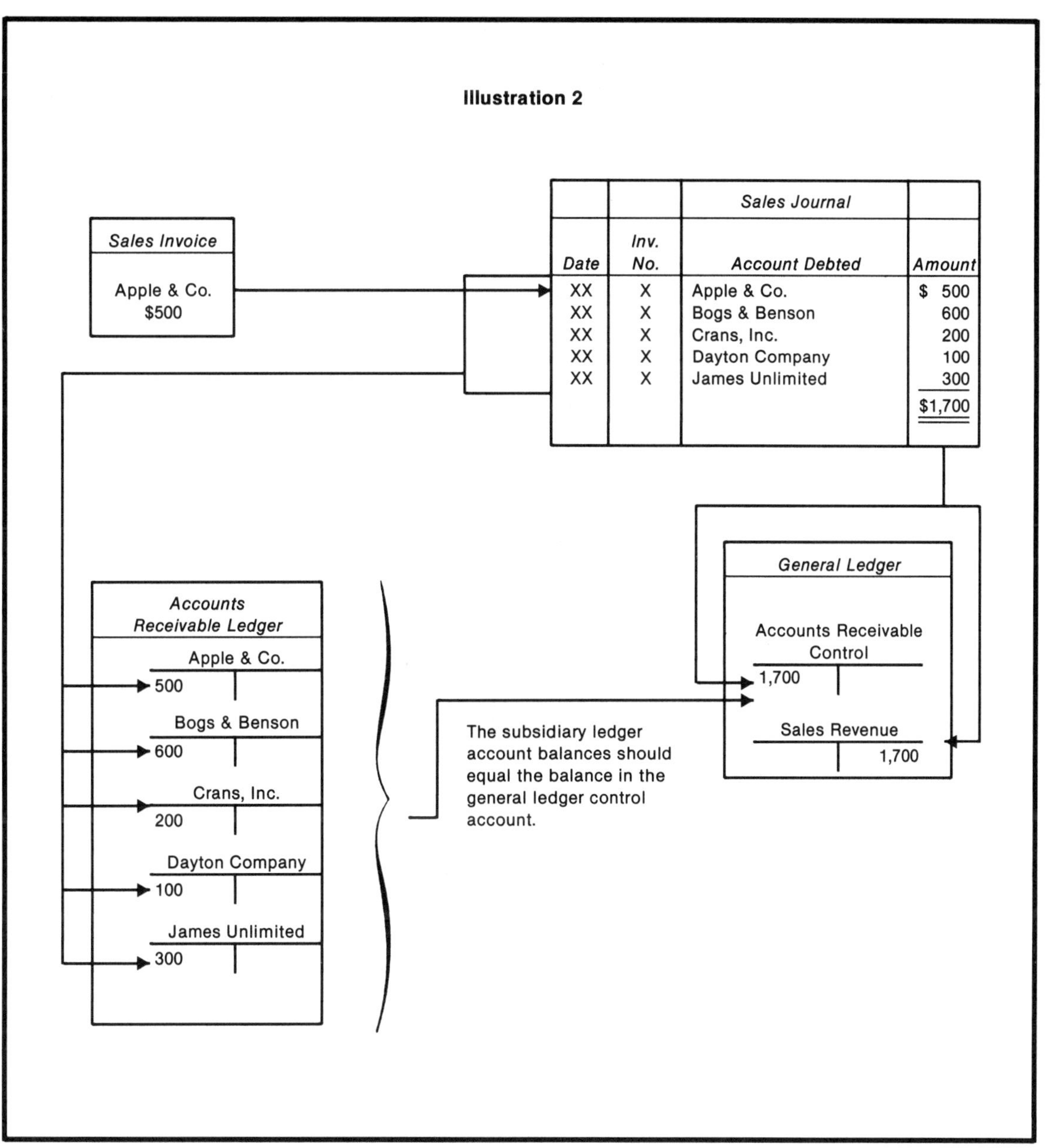
Illustration 2
Sales Invoice
Apple & Co.
$500
Sales Journal
Date
Inv. No.
Account Debted
Amount
XX X Apple & Co. $ 500
XX X Bogs & Benson 600
XX X Crans, Inc. 200
XX X Dayton Company 100
XX X James Unlimited 300
$1,700
General Ledger
Accounts Receivable Control
1,700
Sales Revenue
1,700
Accounts Receivable Ledger
Apple & Co.
500
Bogs & Benson
600
Crans, Inc.
200
Dayton Company
100
James Unlimited
300
The subsidiary ledger account balances should equal the balance in the general ledger control account.

corresponding accounts in the subsidairy accounts receivable ledger. Page totals from the sales journal are posted to the sales revenue and accounts receivable control accounts in the general ledger.

Cash Receipts Journal

The cash receipts journal is designed to expedite the process of recording cash receipt transactions. All cash receipts will result in a debit to, or an increase in, the account cash. The special journal provides for the more common types of cash receipt, including cash sales and the collection of accounts receivable. When a company uses a cash receipts journal, *all* cash receipts are recorded in this journal.

A cash receipts journal sample is shown in Illustration 3.

Illustration 3
Cash Receipts Journal

Date	Account/Explanation	Cash (Debit)	Sales Discount Debit	Sales Credit	Accounts Receivable Credit	*Sundry Credit* Account	Ref.	Amount
6/15	Markell Company	$1,025			$1,025			
	Sales	650		650				
	Kaupp, Inc.	103	2		105			
6/16	Sales	725		725				
6/17	Purchase return	50				Purchase return	644	$ 50
	Sales	810		810				
6/18	Notes receivable	1,000				Note Receivable	012	1,000
6/19	Sales	450		450				
		$4,813 (001)	2 (501)	$2,635 (500)	$1,130 (003)			$1,050

The recording process can best be explained by analyzing some selected transactions:

June 15 The Markell Company paid an account receivable resulting in a debit to cash and a credit to accounts receivable.

15 Cash sales are recorded by a debit to cash and a credit to sales.

15 Kaupp, Inc. paid an account receivable within the company's discount period and deducted $2 from their payment. The transaction is recorded by debiting cash and sales discounts and crediting accounts receivable.

June 17 Your company returned some merchandise that did not meet your specifications and the seller granted you a cash refund. The purchase account (account number 15) is credited and cash is debited. Because the special journal did not specifically provide for this transaction, the credit is entered in the sundry or miscellaneous column. The posting reference column shows the specific number of the account to be credited.

Periodically, the columns of the cash receipts journal are footed. The totals for sales, sales discounts, and cash are posted directly to the general ledger. The numbers appearing in brackets below the column total is the posting reference and shows the account number to which the column total was posted. Accounts receivable totals are posted to the general ledger control account, and specific accounts are credited in the subsidiary ledger. Sundry amounts are posted individually to the accounts involved in the general ledger and a separate posting reference column is established in these amounts.

Cash Disbursements Journal

Illustration 4 is an example of a cash disbursements journal. When this journal is used, all cash disbursements are made in this journal. As with the cash receipts journal, columns are established for the entry to cash, as well as, those accounts that frequently involve cash transactions. The journal shows the date of the transaction, the account or explanation, the check number,

Illustration 4
Cash Disbursements Journal

Date	Account/ Explanation	Check Number	Cash Credit	Accounts Payable	Wage Expense	Liabilities Expense	*Sundry Debit* Account	Ref.	Amount
6/3	Able Supply Co.	104	$ 500	$500					
6/5	Coastal Power Co.	105	150			$150			
6/5	Office Supply Co.	106	250	250					
6/15	Bob Smith	107	550		$ 550				
6/15	Bruce Swindle	108	650		650				
6/18	Bell Telephone	109	90			90			
6/20	City National Bank	110	425				Interest Expense	507	425
6/21	City Supply Co.	111	200	200					
6/25	Mobile Phone	112	75			75			
6/30	Bob Smith	113	550		550				
6/30	Bruce Swindle	114	650		650				
			$4,090	$950	$2,400	$315			$425
			(001)	(201)	(504)	(505)			

a credit column for cash and a debit column for each of the accounts that have frequent transactions during the month. In this simple illustration, columns were established for debits to accounts payable, wage expense, and utilities expense. The final columns in the journal are for sundry accounts (i.e., those accounts that do not have frequent transactions and, therefore, do not need a separate column for posting). The sundry columns show the name of the account, a reference for the account number from posting, and a dollar amount. The actual form may vary in practice and the journal is customized to meet the specific needs of the business.

The entries in the cash disbursements journal reflect the following transactions:

June	3	Paid $500 owed on account to Ace Supply Company.
	5	Paid the electric utility bill to Coastal Power.
	5	Paid $250 owed on account to Office Supply Co.
	15	Paid wages to Bob Smith ($550) and Bruce Swindle ($650).
	18	Paid the telephone bill of $90.
	20	Paid $425 of interest owed to City National Bank.
	21	Paid $200 owed to City Supply on account.
	25	Paid Mobile Phone Co. for month's charge of $75.
	30	Paid semi-monthly salaries to Bob Smith and Bruce Swindle.

Note that as with the cash receipts journal, the columns are totalled and the amounts posted to the respective ledger accounts as indicated by the account number in brackets below the column total. The accounts payable entries would also have to be posted to the individual subsidiary accounts. The sundry account, interest expense, is also posted individually.

Other Special Journals

Purchases journals are structured in a similar manner to the sales journal. The goal is to recognize that most purchase transactions require similar entries. The purchases journal normally provides for a credit to accounts payable and a debit to the purchases and/or supplies accounts.

Although some special journals and subsidiary ledgers are used more in practice than others, there is no set number or format that should be employed. The purpose of both special journals and subsidiary ledgers is to improve the efficiency of the recording process. In each particular organization, the accountant must decide which special journals and subsidiary ledgers fit the information flows and benefit the data processing effort.

The design of special journals and subsidiary ledgers is not fixed. Formats may be altered to fit any enterprise. While the format of special journals and subsidiary ledgers may vary from organization to organization, the ultimate purpose of these devices is to increase the efficiency of the accounting system.

QUESTIONS*

5-1 How does the economist measure income?

5-2 Describe the total venture concept of income measurement. Why is this concept not useful for periodic financial reporting?

5-3 Explain the matching concept.

5-4 Relate the terms "revenue" and "expense" to the conventional income determination process.

5-5 How is the accounting income measured?

5-6 What is meant by the realization principles?

5-7 Explain what is meant by the term, "sales returns and allowances." How are they reported in the financial statements?

5-8 Explain the difference between trade discount and cash discounts.

5-9 What is an extraordinary item? What are some examples of extraordinary items, and how are they reported in the income statement.

5-10 Describe the difference between the multiple-step and the single-step income statement. Will the net income figure be the same using the two different types of statement?

5-11 A company sells a product with a list price of $10,000 subject to a trade discount of 10 percent and terms of "2/10, n/30." What amount of revenue should be recorded on the sale, and how should the transaction be accounted for if the customer pays within the discount period?

5-12 Define the term "gross margin on sales."

5-13 What items of income might be reported on the income statement as "other income?"

5-14* How do special journals make the recording and posting process more efficient?

***Note:** Questions marked with an asterisk relate to the Appendix.

EXERCISES*

E5-1 Prepare the journal entries to record the following transactions for King Co.

a. Sold a product for $500 and the customer paid cash.
b. Sold a product to a customer for $600 on account.
c. Collected the account receivable from the customer, described in (b) above.
d. Received an advance payment of $300 from a customer for services to be performed in the future.

E5-2 The Jones Co. sold mechandise to a customer for $4,000 on January 15 with terms of "2/10, n/30." The customer returned a portion of the goods on January 17 with a cost of $500. The customer received credit from Jones Co. for these goods, which were damaged in shipment. On January 23, the customer paid Jones Co. the balance of the account receivable. Prepare the journal entries to record the above events, and show how the sales revenue from these transactions would be reflected in the income statement.

E5-3 The Longhorn Company sold merchandise with a list price of $1,000 on April 10. Trade discounts of 20 and 10 percent were allowed, and the credit terms were 2/10 n/30. On April 12, the customer requested and received an allowance for $200 (list price) of merchandise that had been destroyed in transit. The company received full payment from the customer on April 18.

Record all the entries required on the books of Longhorn Co.

***Note:** Exercises marked with an asterisk relate to the Appendix.

E5-4 The following account balances after adjustment were taken from the books of the Phillips Co. at December 31, 19x0:

Sales revenue	$50,000
Cost of goods sold	25,000
Rental revenue	2,000
Sales returns and allowances	3,000
Selling expenses	10,000
Administrative expenses	5,000
Interest expense	2,500
Income tax expense	3,000
Sales discounts	1,000

Required:

From the above information, prepare a single-step income statement.

E5-5 Refer to the information in E5-4 above and prepare a multiple-step income statement.

E5-6 A company sold merchandise with a list price of $20,000. The customer was granted trade discounts of 25, 20, and 10 percent, and the cash discount terms are 2/15, n/60. How much will the company receive if the account is paid within fifteen days? How much will the company receive if the account is paid after fifteen days?

E5-7 Listed below is selected information from the accounts of Richards Co. at December 1, 19x0.

Gross margin	$ 25,000
Sales revenues	200,000
Sales returns and allowances	5,000
Sales discounts	4,000

Compute the following:

a. Net sales.
b. Cost of goods sold.

E5-8 On October 1, the following entry was made to record the sale of merchandise on account:

Accounts receivable	1,000	
Sales revenue		1,000
To record a sale on which the terms were 2/10, n/60.		

Give the necessary journal entry if the customer paid on: (1) October 9, and (2) October 27.

E5-9 On April 1, 19x0, the Alexander Co. sold merchandise to a customer with a $10,000 list price. The terms of the sale provided trade discounts of 20 and 10 percent and a cash discount of 2/10, n/30. On April 5, the customer returned $100 (at list price) of the merchandise that had been damaged in transit. The remaining balance was paid by the customer on April 10. Prepare the journal entries required on the books of Alexander Co.

E5-10 Provide the missing amounts in the four income statements listed below.

	A	B	C	D
Sales revenue	$100,000	$100,000	$100,000	$100,000
Sales returns and allowances	5,000	6,000	6,000	6,000
Sales discounts	____	3,000	4,000	4,000
Net sales	92,000	____	____	90,000
Cost of goods sold	58,000	____	52,000	____
Gross margin on sales	____	____	____	22,000
Operating expenses	20,000	20,000	____	____
Net income from operations	____	____	13,000	2,000
Other revenues (expense)	(4,000)	5,000	0	2,000
Net income before extraordinary item	____	____	____	____
Extraordinary gain (loss)	(2,000)	0	5,000	____
Net income before taxes	____	____	____	____
Tax expense	4,000	2,000	____	0
Net income (loss	____	24,000	8,000	(5,000)

E5-11 Classify the following revenue items as: (a) operating income, expense, or loss, (b) other income, expense, or loss, or (c) extraordinary income or loss, for purposes of presentation on the income statement.

a. An uninsured fire loss.
b. Interest income to a bank.
c. Interest income to a shoe shop.
d. Gain on the sale of a machine recognized by a manufacturer who uses the machine in a trade or business.
e. Sale of a machine by the manufacturer of the machine who sells it as inventory.
f. Rental income recognized by a firm that rented a portion of an unused warehouse temporarily.
g. Income from sale of groceries in a supermarket.

E5-12 Prepare a partial income statement similar to Illustration 3, to report the following events for Hayes Manufacturing Company for the year ended March 31, 19x6:

a. Revenue from sales of manufactured goods—$78,520, sales returns and allowances—$2,650, and sales discounts—$610.
b. Interest income—$350.
c. Rental income from renting unneeded warehouse space—$2,000, related expenses—$240.
d. Sales of equipment at a loss—$300.
e. Loss from fire—$9,000, insurance recovery—$7,800.

E5-13 Brandon Company sold an item of inventory with a list price of $1,200 on November 1, 19x7. In each independent case below, determine: (a) the amount to be recorded as a sale, and (b) the appropriate amount of cash to be received.

Case	*Trade Discount*	*Credit Terms*	*Payment Date*
(a)	10%	2/10, n/30	November 9
(b)	10%, 10%	n/30	November 26
(c)	10%, 5%	2/15, n/30	November 18
(d)	30%	3/10, n/30	November 8
(e)	5%, 10%, 10%	n/30	November 30

E5-14 Gross billings for merchandise sold by Baker Company to customers last year amounted to $5,260,000, sales returns and allowances reduced the amounts owed by $160,000. How much were net sales last year for Baker Company?

E5-15 Management is considering a change in the discount terms offered by the firm. One proposal is to change the firm's credit terms from 2/10, n/60 to 2/10, n/30. If adopted, what effects will this change probably have on the firm's average collection and sales?

E5-16* Prepare a cash receipts journal for the Jackson Company to reflect the following events for the month of March. Then indicate the postings which would be made to the general journal at the end of March.

Mar.	5	Received $200 of interest revenue from an investment.
	9	John Jacob paid his account balance of $75.
	10	Cash sale of $110 was made.
	13	Alice Adams made a $100 payment on her account.
	15	Dividend income of $1,470 was received.
	17	Cash sale of $55 was made.
	20	Morris Martin paid $309 on his account.
	24	Pat Partin sent his remittance of $80.
	29	Cash sale of $103 was made.
	30	Sam Smith made a $30 payment on his account.

E5-17* The sales journal and the cash receipts journal of the Martin Paper Company are shown below. Make the necessary daily postings to the accounts receivable subsidiary ledger and determine the ending balance of each account for the month of August. Then post the necessary items to the general ledger.

Sales Journal

Date	*Invoice No.*	*Terms*	*Customer Account*	*Dr. A/R Cr. Sales*
8/1	801	n/30	Adam Alfred	97
8/6	802	n/30	Connie Carr	44
8/10	803	n/30	Elaine Ellis	123
8/11	804	n/30	Gary Gardner	85
8/13	805	n/30	Ivan Ingot	31
8/16	806	n/30	Karl Kernel	58
8/21	807	n/30	Norman Norton	200
8/23	808	n/30	Rita Reed	29
				667

Cash Receipts Journal

Date	*Account Credited*	*Dr. Cash*	*Cr. A/R*	*Cr. Sales*	*Cr. Sundry*
8/8	Adam Alfred	97	97		
8/13	Connie Carr	44	44		
8/19	Gary Gardner	85	85		
8/19	Interest Income	476			476
8/20	Karl Kernel	58	58		
8/23	Ivan Ingot	31	31		
8/28	Elaine Ellis	123	123		
8/30	Rita Reed	29	29		
8/30	Norman Norton	200	200		
8/30	Sales	75	—	75	
8/31	Balances	1,218	667	75	476

E5-18* Prepare a cash disbursements journal for the Dent Company for the month of April. Then make the required postings to the necessary ledgers.

Apr. 2 Paid the balance of $222 owed to the Adams Company.
4 Dividends of $3,000 were paid.
7 The account payable to Reed Store of $400 was paid, but the amount was reduced by a purchase discount of $40.
11 Raw materials were purchased for $642 in cash.
16 Paid salaries of $1,000.
22 Paid $101 to Supply Company to reduce the balance due.
29 A purchase discount of $14 reduced the amount paid the Static Company to $186.

Use the following column headings: cash credit, accounts payable, purchases, salaries, and sundry.

PROBLEMS*

P5-1 The following information was reflected in the accounts of Welker Co. on December 31, 19x0:

Sales revenue	$100,000
Sales discounts	1,000
Selling expenses	17,000
Administrative expenses	15,000
Interest expense	2,000
Sales returns and allowances	3,000
Rental revenue	4,000
Income tax expense	8,000
Fire loss (extraordinary item)	10,000
Cost of goods sold	38,000

Required:

Based on the above information, prepare a multiple-step income statement for Welker Co.

P5-2 The following list of transactions was selected from the records of Drexel Co. for the year ended December 31, 19x0.

1. Cash sales of $55,000 were made.
2. Credit sales of $40,000 were made subject to trade discounts of 20 and 10 percent with credit terms of 2/10, n/30.
3. One-half of the invoices from (2) were collected within ten days.
4. One-half of the invoices from (2) were collected after the discount period.
5. Rent of $1,200 on office space was collected. The rent was for the period from January 1 to December 31, 19x0.
6. Purchased merchandise for $40,000 cash.
7. Credit sales of $5,000 were made with credit terms of 2/10, n/30.
8. The customer from (7) requested and received an allowance of $500 on merchandise damaged in transit.
9. The customer from (7) paid the remainder of the account within the discount period.
10. Land that was purchased for $10,000 as a possible building site was sold for $11,000.
11. Equipment that cost $1,500 was destroyed in an uninsured fire one week after it was purchased. (Assume extraordinary.)

Required:

a. Prepare the journal entries to record the above transactions.
b. Prepare an income statement for the year ended December 31, 19x0, using multiple-step form (see Illustration 1) and assuming the following information:

Cost of goods sold	$42,000
Operating expenses	24,000
Income tax expense	10,000

P5-3 The following trial balance after adjustment taken from the ledger of the Moore Company at December 31, 19x6:

Moore Company
Trial Balance After Adjustment
December 31, 19x6

	Debits	Credits
Notes payable		$ 60,000
Retained earnings		52,200
Cash	$ 11,000	
Land	10,000	
Interest revenue		3,000
General administrative expenses	12,400	
Sales discounts	11,700	
Accounts receivable	45,200	
Common stock		175,000
Interest expense	6,000	
Inventory—December 31, 19x6	63,000	
Telephone—office	7,100	
Office and officers' salaries	95,000	
Accounts payable		9,000
Notes receivable	30,000	
Sales salaries and commissions	51,000	
Cost of goods sold	250,000	
Income tax expense	20,000	
Prepaid insurance	1,600	
Extraordinary loss	40,000	
Building and equipment	200,000	
Advertising	12,000	
Supplies expense	700	
Rental revenue		24,000
General selling expenses	23,000	
Sales		530,000
Accumulated depreciation		42,000
Interest payable		500
Sales returns and allowances	6,000	
	$895,700	$895,700

Required:

From the above data, prepare an income statement using: (a) the single-step form, and (b) the multiple-step form.

***Note:** Problems marked with an asterisk relate to the Appendix.

P5-4 Some account balances of the Hanson Corporation at December 31, 19x5, are presented below:

	Debit	Credit
Sales		$1,200,000
Sales returns and allowances	$ 20,000	
Flood loss (extraordinary item)	50,000	
Loss on sales of equipment	5,000	
Sales office salaries	25,000	
Salesmen's commissions	75,000	
Travel expense	15,000	
Interest revenue		6,000
Conventions and entertainment (selling)	11,000	
Telephone and telegraph—sales department	7,300	
Depreciation of sales equipment	3,400	
Cost of goods sold	592,000	
Miscellaneous selling expenses	2,100	
Officers' salaries	50,000	
Administrative salaries and wages	32,000	
Office supplies expense	3,300	
Telephone and telegraph—administration	2,500	
Depreciation of office furniture and equipment	2,700	
Miscellaneous office expenses	4,100	
Discounts on sales	31,000	
Rental income		12,000
Interest expense	9,000	
Income tax expense	135,000	
Merchandise inventory—December 31, 19x5	73,000	

Required:

a. Prepare an income statement for the year ended December 31, 19x5, using the mutiple-step form.
b. Prepare an income statement for the year ended December 31, 19x5, using the single-step form.

P5-5 The Kingsbery Co. had the following transactions for the year ended December 31, 19x3:

1. Cash sales of $100,000 were made.
2. Land, which was purchased for $25,000 as a possible building site, was sold for $28,000.
3. Cash sales of $35,000 were made.
4. Credit sales of $25,000 were made subject to trade discounts of 20 and 5 percent with credit terms 1/10, n/30.
5. A building in South America that cost $21,000 was totally destroyed by an earthquake one day after it was constructed. Unfortunately, the building was not insured.
6. All but $5,000 of the net sales in (4) were collected in less than ten days.
7. The rest of the credit sales were collected before the thirty days was up.
8. A company leased from Kingsbery the mineral royalties on the land in South America for $20,000 for the year of 19x3, and paid in cash.
9. Merchandise purchased for $40,000 on account.

Required:

a. Prepare journal entries to record the above transactions.
b. Prepare an income statement for the year ended December 31, 19x3, using the multiple-step form and assuming the following:

Cost of goods sold	$100,000
Administrative expense	19,000
Operating expenses	28,000
Selling expenses	14,000

P5-6 Morris Sales Company's account balances are shown below for the year ended December 31, 19x1:

Sales	$620,000
Sales returns and allowances	18,500
Sales discounts	7,400
Cost of goods sold	372,600
Sales salaries and commissions	71,000
Advertising expenses	18,000
Administrative salaries	38,000
Administrative supplies expenses	9,700
Miscellaneous administrative expenses	8,400
Interest income	2,000
Income tax expense	36,000

Required:

Prepare a single-step income statement for Morris Sales Company.

P5-7 A portion of the worksheet for Webb Company is shown below for calendar year 19x8.

	Income Statement		Balance Sheet	
	Debit	Credit	Debit	Credit
Owner's equity				$62,000
Sales		$108,000		
Sales returns and allowances	$ 2,600			
Sales discounts	1,050			
Cost of goods sold	42,500			
Wages expense	21,000			
Selling expenses	12,600			
Utilities expense	1,900			
Depreciation expense	16,200			
Loss on sale of equipment	800			
Loss on fire	5,000			

Required:

a. Prepare a single-step income statement for Webb Company for calendar year 19x8.
b. Prepare the necessary closing entries in general journal format.

P5-8 The unadjusted trial balance of Dill Service Company on December 31, 19x4 is shown below:

Dill Service Company
Trial Balance
December 31, 19x4

	Debit	Credit
Cash	$ 6,000	
Accounts receivable	8,200	
Supplies	14,200	
Prepaid insurance	1,200	
Equipment	16,500	
Accumulated depreciation		$ 3,200
Accounts payable		4,700
Owner's equity		20,100
Sales		103,000
Sales discounts	1,000	
Wage and salary expense	59,000	
Rental expense	12,000	
Insurance expense	1,800	
Utilities expense	2,100	
Advertising expense	9,000	
	$131,000	$131,000

These additional financial data are also available:

1. An inventory of supplies showed only $3,600 on hand at year-end.
2. Depreciation of $2,400 was unrecorded at year-end.
3. The insurance shown as prepaid on the trial balance was a twelve-month fire insurance policy dated April 1, 19x4.
4. Wages of $1,400 were earned by employees but not paid at year-end.

Required:

a. Prepare a worksheet for the Dill Company for December 31, 19x4.
b. From the income statement columns of the worksheet, prepare a multiple-step income statement in good form.

P5-9* Below are listed certain transactions of Sorrenson Sales Company for the month of June, 19x1.

June	1	Sold goods on credit to J.P. Nelson, $1,500, invoice no. 328, terms n/30.
	3	Sold merchandise on credit to Joe's Bar and Griss, $2,300, invoice no. 329, terms n/30.
	4	Cash sales of merchandise—$900.
	5	Sold merchandise to J.A. Baker, $1,300, invoice no. 330, terms n/30.
	7	Received payment in full on J.P. Nelson account.
	11	Received dividend of $35 on marketable securities.
	14	Received a check from Joe's Bar and Grill in full payment of account.
	17	Sold merchandise to T.W. Stark, $1,700, invoice no. 331, terms n/30.
	19	Received full payment from J.A. Baker.
	20	Sold merchandise to B.A. Spendler, $1,900, invoice no. 332, terms n/30.
	25	Cash sales of merchandise—$600.
	26	Received payment in full from B.A. Spendler.
	28	Received payment in full from T.W. Stark.
	30	Cash sales of merchandise—$3,200.

Required:

a. Prepare a sales journal and a cash receipts journal.
b. Open general ledger accounts for accounts receivable, cash, and sales.
c. Open subsidiary accounts receivable ledger accounts for the credit customers.
d. Enter the above transactions in the sales and cash receipts journals and post to the appropriate ledger accounts.

P5-10* Condor Company uses a cash receipts journal and a cash disbursements journal. Selected transactions during the month of April are listed below:

Apr.	1	Purchased merchandise on account from S. Klein—$600.
	2	Paid April rent—$500.
	3	Sold merchandise on credit to D. Gilman—$375.
	4	Sold merchandise on credit to W. Cox—$280.
	4	Received $200 rent for subleased office space.
	5	Paid $180 for advertisement in local newspaper.
	6	Received $105 dividend on marketable securities.
	8	Paid S. Klein $600 on account.
	9	Received payment in full from D. Gilman.
	10	Cash sales of merchandise—$6,250.
	11	Purchased merchandise on account from Main Supply Company—$7,100.
	12	Received payment in full from W. Cox.
	13	Paid $100 interest on loan from City National Bank.
	14	Sold merchandise on account to K. Telg—$625.
	15	Purchased equipment from Barton Brothers—$3,250 cash.
	17	Purchased merchandise for cash—$1,150.
	18	Cash sales of merchandise—$6,100.
	19	Sold a plot of land for $15,000 cash.
	24	Paid Main Supply Company $7,100 on account.
	27	Received payment in full from K. Telg.
	28	Cash sales of merchandise—$4,300.
	29	Paid salaries and wages—$6,750.

Required:

Prepare a cash receipts journal and a cash disbursements journal. Enter the above transactions in these journals as appropriate.

Learning Objectives

Chapter 6 discusses proper accounting for inventories and recognition of various expenses. Studying this chapter should enable you to:

1. Prepare a complete, detailed income statement.
2. Contrast the perpetual and periodic inventory systems.
3. Record inventory data.
4. Estimate uncollectable accounts receivable and bad debt expense.
5. Construct a retained earnings statement.

6

The Income Statement: Expenses

INTRODUCTION

Virtually all income-producing activity requires some consumption of resources. Accountants maintain that, to the extent these resources have an economic value, their cost must be included in the calculation of income. Therefore, revenue is reduced by related expenses for the cost of resources consumed or because the cost no longer has the future service potential to derive net income.

Business operations require a variety of expense items. The expenses related to operating a movie theater, for example, include employee salaries, film rentals, heat, power, maintenance, janitorial services, and the use of the building, its furnishings, and projection equipment. Some of these expense elements are more clearly identified and quantified than others.

If monthly income is to be calculated, the accountant can usually determine the salary, film rental, heat, power, and janitorial costs that were incurred during the month. These items were also consumed during the month, so they can be expensed. The use of the building, furnishings, and projection equipment also represents an expense to be charged against the month's operations. However, it is difficult to determine how much of the $2,000,000 cost of a theater building was used during a month. The accountant must determine which resources were consumed, the extent to which they were consumed, and their value as a part of the income determination process.

This chapter focuses on some major elements of expense as they relate to income measurement. Expenses must be properly measured and matched with reported revenues for income to be accurately determined.

COST OF GOODS SOLD

Income statements that follow a functional classification begin by isolating the expense of products sold during the period. In most manufacturing and merchandising operations, this cost of products sold is a significant expense item. As products are purchased or manufactured by a firm, their costs are accumulated in an *inventory* account. There are a variety of techniques available for determining the cost of inventory. Many of these are considered in Chapter 8. As inventory items are sold or consumed, their cost flows as an expense to the income statement and is reported as cost of goods sold.

Most businesses will begin a period with some quantity of merchandise on hand. This is termed the *beginning inventory*. Throughout the period, additional quantities of merchandise will be purchased (or manufactured) and added to the inventory.

The beginning inventory plus the purchases represents the amount of merchandise *available for sale* during the period. This is the amount of goods that the company could have sold during the period. Typically, sales will be less than the total quantity available and the firm will end the period with merchandise on hand, termed the *ending inventory*. Logically, the ending inventory of one period becomes the beginning inventory of the next period.

These relationships are used in calculating the cost of goods sold:

Cost of Beginning Inventory
\+ Cost of Purchases (net of returns)
= Cost of Goods Available for Sale
− Cost of Ending Inventory
= Cost of Goods Sold

Cost of goods sold results from deducting the ending inventory from the cost of goods available for sale; items available for sale will either be sold during the period or will remain at the end of the period.

If a firm began the period with an inventory valued at $125,000, purchased an additional $319,000 of merchandise during the period but returned $1,000 as damaged and ended the period with $98,000 of remaining inventory, its cost of goods sold is $345,000 calculated as follows:

Cost of beginning inventory		$125,000
Cost of purchases (net of returns)	+	318,000
Cost of goods available for sale	=	$443,000
Cost of ending inventory	−	98,000
Cost of goods sold	=	$345,000

Cost of goods sold is reported as an expense in the income statement. Ending inventory is an asset and will appear on the balance sheet. In this example, $98,000 is reported as the inventory value at the end of the period. It is also the beginning inventory value for the next accounting period.

Statement Presentation

The cost of goods sold calculation is often included in the income statement. This provides the reader with an overview of inventory and product cost flows during the period. Cost of goods sold is deducted from net sales revenue to determine the gross margin on sales.

Net sales		$1,945,000
Cost of goods sold:		
Beginning inventory	$ 113,000	
Purchases	1,206,000	
Cost of goods available for sale	$1,319,000	
Less: Ending inventory	152,000	
Cost of goods sold		1,167,000
Gross margin on sales		$ 778,000

The *gross margin* on sales is the difference between the net sales revenue and the cost of the merchandise that was sold during the period. It reflects the average markup applied to the merchandise to derive the sales price. In the preceding example, the gross margin in percentage terms was 40 percent of the selling price calculated as folows:

$$\text{Gross Margin Percentage} = \frac{\text{Gross Margin}}{\text{Net Sales Revenue}}$$

$$= \frac{\$\ 778{,}000}{\$1{,}945{,}000}$$

$$= .40 \text{ or } 40\%$$

Thus, 60 cents of each sales dollar generated by the firm was used to acquire the merchandise that was sold. The remaining 40 cents, or the gross margin, is available to provide for the operating and administrative expenses and for profit.

INVENTORY SYSTEMS

The cost of goods sold calculation is dependent upon the ending inventory and the purchases made during the period. There are two systems that can be used to record inventories—periodic and perpetual. A well-designed inventory system will provide for valuing the inventory and for effective inventory control.

Control ensures that proper valuations, measurements, and determinations have been made relative to the inventory. This ranges from monitoring inventory levels for decision-making purposes to verifying the existence of inventory items through periodic physical counts. Inventory controls require adequate records and information flows about inventory levels and certain physical safeguards relating to the custody of the items. Accounting systems focus on the information flows.

Periodic Inventory Method

Periodic inventory systems rely on periodic physical counts of merchandise to determine the ending inventory value. On a regular basis, usually annually, the inventory quantity is determined through actual observation. The number of units observed during the physical count is multiplied by the firm's purchase cost per unit to determine the inventory value. This value becomes the ending inventory and is used in calculating the cost of goods sold.

Under a periodic system, the inventory value is only available after the physical count. Many businesses that need inventory information for decision-making activities will supplement the accounting records with other inventory data such as: estimates of quantities sold, ordering models, and point-of-sale data accumulation. The annual physical count will serve to verify the inventory subsystem.

Perpetual Measurement

Perpetual inventory systems use physical counts to confirm the inventory balance. However, an ongoing, continuous determination of inventory quantity and value is maintained in the accounts. The inventory account is updated each time an item is purchased or sold. Perpetual inventory systems provide management with up-to-date information about quantities and costs throughout the period.

Obviously, a perpetual inventory system will involve more clerical effort and related cost than a periodic system. However, the perpetual data is usually used to support a variety of decision-making activities. Computers and other types of data processing equipment have been used extensively in maintaining perpetual inventory data.

RECORDING PERIODIC INVENTORY DATA

Since a running balance of inventory is not maintained under the periodic system, there is no need to change the inventory balance when an item is bought or sold. Instead, items bought for resale are recorded in a *purchases* account and accumulated in the account until financial statements are prepared. When items are sold, the sale is recorded, but there is no entry to reflect the reduction in inventory.

For example, if a company purchased $10,000 worth of merchandise on account and, subsequently, purchased $2,000 worth of merchandise for cash, the following entries would be made:

	Debit	Credit
Purchases	$10,000	
Accounts payable		$10,000
Purchases	2,000	
Cash		2,000

At times, goods are returned to the supplier because the wrong items were sent, they were defective, etc. When this occurs the purchases account is usually reduced through the use of a contra account called *purchase returns and allowances*. This is very similar to the sales returns and allowances discussed in the previous chapter. If goods purchased on account are returned, the entry would appear as follows:

Accounts payable	$500	
Purchases returns and allowances		$500

This contra account will reduce the purchases when calculating cost of goods sold in the income statement.

At the end of the year, the company must take a physical inventory and value it. The beginning inventory plus purchases, net of returns and allowances is added to obtain the goods available for sale and the ending inventory is deducted to determine cost of goods sold.

As was discussed in the previous chapter, frequently companies offer cash discounts as an incentive to get customers to pay early. When a company purchases merchandise for resale it will frequently be allowed a cash discount. If the company pays for the purchases within the discount period they will get the discount and it will reduce the cost of their purchases. Rather than reduce the purchases account directly, a contra account called *purchase discounts* is used. This contra account will allow management to track the amount of discounts they have taken. To illustrate the related entry, assume a company purchased $2,000 of merchandise with terms of 2/10, n/30. If the bill was paid within the discount period, the following entry would be made:

Accounts payable	$2,000	
Cash		$1,960
Purchase discounts....................		40

In the income statement, the two purchases contra accounts are usually netted against the purchases account and the net balance reflected as follows:

Sales—net..................................		$85,000
Cost of sales:		
Beginning inventory.........................	$10,000	
Purchases—net	60,000	
Goods available for sale......................	$70,000	
Less: Ending inventory	15,000	
Cost of goods sold		55,000
Gross margin on sale		$30,000

Adjusting Entries

When a periodic inventory system is used, the adjusting entry relative to ledger accounts, has four distinct objectives:

1. Remove the prior-period inventory from the accounts.
2. Place the current inventory in the accounts.
3. Remove any balance in the purchases and related accounts.
4. Isolate the cost of goods sold.

These objectives can be accomplished through the adjusting entry. The preceding example will lead to the following entry:

Inventory—December 31, 19x2	$15,000	
Cost of goods sold	55,000	
Inventory—December 31, 19x1		$10,000
Purchases		60,000

The ending inventory value (December 31, 19x2) is placed in the accounts by a debit. The prior-period inventory value (December 31, 19x1) is removed from the records by a credit. The purchases accounts are cleared (or closed) by crediting or debiting them for their balance. The difference between these debits and credits is reflected by a debit to cost of goods sold.

RECORDING PERPETUAL INVENTORY DATA

In perpetual systems, the inventory account is continually updated to record additions to or deletions from the merchandise inventory. Purchases are immediately reflected in the account balance by debiting (increasing) the inventory account and crediting accounts payable or cash, as appropriate. For example, if a firm purchased $15,000 of merchandise on account, the following entry would be made:

Inventory	$15,000	
Accounts payable		$15,000

A purchase return can be recorded as the reverse of this entry. Similarly, when a sale is made, the inventory account is immediately reduced to reflect the outflow of merchandise. The cost of the merchandise that was sold is moved from the inventory account to the cost of goods sold expense account where it is accumulated until year-end. At the end of the period, cost of goods sold will be used in the determination of income.

If a company sold merchandise costing $9,000, the following entry would be made:

Cost of goods sold	$9,000	
Inventory		$9,000

Therefore, at any given time, the perpetual system will provide an inventory account that contains the cost of the merchandise available for sale at that time. On a regular basis, a physical count should be taken to confirm the inventory balance.

At the end of the accounting period, the perpetual inventory account contains the ending inventory balance. The cost of goods sold account also contains the cost of merchandise sold during the period. Additional adjustments relative to these accounts are unnecessary.

In many product-related businesses, inventory is a significant item. It is essential for the accountant to use a system that will facilitate the accurate determination of cost of goods sold. This item of expense is extremely important in calculating periodic income. In selecting an inventory system, the accountant must weight the costs and benefits of the alternatives. Management uses of inventory data throughout the period and effective control over the items in inventory are factors to be considered.

OPERATING EXPENSES

After the gross margin on sales has been determined, the income statement sets forth operating expenses that relate to the reported revenues. Operating expenses are those elements of cost that were consumed during the period and were directly related to the production or distribution of the product or service that was sold. Administrative expenses and selling expenses may be set apart in separate subsections of the income statement.

Selling expense items normally include cost elements related to merchandising capacity and operations. Examples of these expenses include rent, depreciation of sales facilities and equipment, wages, and the cost of a credit policy. Most of these expenses will be recorded as they are incurred. Depreciation expense is a charge to reflect asset utilization. In accordance with accounting theory, depreciation is calculated using a reasonable and systematic method. Various depreciation techniques are discussed in Chapter 9.

Some operating expenses must be estimated by the accountant. These relate to situations where it is reasonable to expect that an expense has been incurred, but at the time the income statement is to be prepared, the exact amount of the expense is not determinable. Bad debt expense is an example of such a situation.

BAD DEBT EXPENSE

Companies offer their customers credit for a variety of reasons. One of these is to stimulate additional sales and, thus, additional profits. Credit policies will lead to some additional expenses for the firm.

When credit is extended, additional recordkeeping is necessitated. The firm must maintain information about who owes it money. Also, many organizations will establish credit departments to decide which customers should receive credit and what limits should be placed on their credit purchases. Both of these functions will have a cost and will comprise part of the expense of a credit policy.

When customers buy on credit, it is reasonable to expect that some of them will be unable or unwilling to pay their debts. In these cases, the seller must absorb the loss as a bad debt expense. Recognizing the expense is essential to maintain the integrity of the accounting records.

If the Watson Company purchased $17,000 of merchandise on account, the seller would recognize this promise to pay as an asset.

Accounts receivable—Watson Company	$17,000	
Sales revenue		$17,000

Subsequently, if the debt was not paid, the seller must remove the asset from the books and treat the $17,000 as an expense.

Bad debt expense	$17,000	
Accounts receivable—Watson Company		$17,000

Bad debt expense is another cost of a credit policy. In most cases, the profit resulting from additional sales will more than offset the expenses involved in granting customers credit. Organizations generally monitor their bad debt losses so that credit granting policies can be geared to acceptable levels of risk.

If credit is granted during an accounting period, it is reasonable to expect that some future bad debt losses will occur. At the end of the period, it may be impossible to determine which debts in particular will not be paid in the future. However, bad debts are an expense that relates to current sales revenue, revenue that resulted from the credit policy that has led to some bad debts. Therefore, the accountant must estimate future bad debt losses and include them as an expense in the current period so that the cause and effect relationship is reflected in the income statement.

ESTIMATING BAD DEBTS

Past experience is usually the basis for estimating bad debt losses. One widely used technique relates the estimate to sales volume. Another technique relates the estimate to the age of customer debt. Both methods are acceptable means of relating expected future losses to current income. However, the latter method usually provides better estimations although the bookkeeping costs are higher.

Sales Volume

Past experience and accounting data may reveal that bad debt losses follow in some constant or predictable relationship to the total dollar value of credit sales. In these cases, a percentage will be applied to the current sales revenue to derive an estimate of bad debt expense. Experience and knowledge of current business conditions enable management to make these estimates. Current sales are the base and set the parameters for the calculation.

The Markel Company has determined that about 1.4 percent of its past credit sales have resulted in uncollectable debts. During the current period, credit sales totalled $237,000. The firm will use $3,318 ($237,000 × .014) as an estimation of its current bad debt expense.

Age of Accounts

Sometimes, the amount of time that a debt has been outstanding will closely correlate with its probability of collection. Analysis of outstanding accounts receivable may be undertaken to provide an estimation of bad debt expense. Such an analysis is generally referred to as *aging the receivables.*

The aging process begins by classifying accounts into groups based on the length of time that they have been outstanding. The number of groups used will depend on previous experiences by the company. After the accounts have been grouped, percentages reflecting past experience will be applied to each group to determine the current amount of estimated bad debts.

The aging process is illustrated below:

	Age of Account			
Customer Balance	*1-30*	*31-90*	*91-180*	*Over 180*
Apple and Company	$ 390			
Bunt and Punt				$265
Clothier Limited		$ 120		
Etc.				
Zebra Stripe, Inc.			$ 225	
Total	$9,200	$7,300	2,500	$940

		Estimated Uncollectable	
Age Group	Total	Percentage	Amount
1-30 days	$9,200	2%	$ 184
31-90 days	7,300	5%	365
91-180 days	2,500	20%	500
Over 180 days	940	80%	752
Total			$1,801

In contrast, the sales volume method usually relies on current sales while the aging method applies to all outstanding receivables. Thus, aging tends to encompass more historic data than does percentage estimation. Either method is acceptable and both are used in practice.

RECORDING BAD DEBT ESTIMATIONS

At the end of an accounting period, the accountant must enter the estimated amount of bad debt expense in the accounts to properly match reveues and expenses. However, while the amount of bad debts can be estimated from prior experience, the specific customer accounts that will be uncollectable cannot be identified. Therefore, a contra account receivable account is used to facilitate reporting the desired information.

The contra account, *allowance for doubtful accounts*, is normally used to reflect bad debt estimations. This account will always be reported with the accounts receivable account and the net difference between the two will be disclosed as the receivable balance.

Assume that a company has made $102,000 of credit sales in its first year. These receivables have been directly entered in the accounts receivable account as follows:

Accounts receivable	$102,000	
Sales		$102,000

At the end of the accounting period, the company estimates that $4,500 of these accounts will be uncollectable. The following entry will be made:

Bad debt expense	$4,500	
Allowance for doubtful accounts		$4,500

The effect of this entry is to properly recognize an expense and to provide for the valuation of accounts receivable. The estimated expense of $4,500 will appear on the income statement and balance sheet will report accounts receivable as shown below:

Accounts receivable	$102,000	
Less: Allowance for doubtful accounts	4,500	$97,500

Recording Aged Information

When aging analysis is used, the result is an estimation of the total allowance balance to-date. To determine the amount of current expense, the difference between the current and prior allowance balances must be determined.

For example, assume that a company estimates from an aging schedule that the total allowance for doubtful accounts should be $28,300. If the prior balance in this account was $25,200, a current period expense of $3,100 ($28,300 − $25,200) will be recognized.

Bad debt expense	$3,100	
Allowance for doubtful accounts		$3,100

Bad Debts

When a specific account is deemed to be uncollectable and the allowance method has been used, the account is written off through the allowance account. If the Fox Company debt of $2,050 is uncollectable, the following entry will be made to remove this receivable from the books:

Allowance for doubtful accounts	$2,050	
Accounts receivable—Fox Company		$2,050

This entry reduces accounts receivable by the amount of the bad debt. When using an allowance account, bad debt expense was estimated in the period when the sale was made; an adjustment to the allowance account is all that must be recorded now. In the very unusual case where an account that has been written off as uncollectable is collected, the cash account is debited and the allowance for doubtful accounts is credited for the amount received.

ADMINISTRATIVE EXPENSES

Administrative expenses are normally set apart from selling expenses in the income statement. This is done to call attention to different types of expense elements. Selling expenses relate somewhat directly to the marketing of the product or service provided by the organization. By contrast, *administrative expenses* relate to the organization in general and to the cost incurred and consumed to provide for an administrative and supervisory capacity.

Examples of administrative expenses include the salaries of corporate officers and the supplies, equipment, personnel, and facilities to support their work. Most of these items will be directly recorded in expense accounts as they are incurred.

COMPLETING THE INCOME STATEMENT

Selling and administrative expenses are deducted from the gross margin on sales to derive the net income from operations. Operating income is adjusted for other revenue and expense provide net income before taxes. After taxes have been deducted, operating income after tax is presented. If the company has extraordinary gains or losses, these, along with their income tax affect, would be presented next and the total net income reported.

To enhance the usefulness of the income statement to stockholders, earnings per share must be calculated and reported on the face of the statement. Earnings per share relates the total reported income of a corporation to an individual by expressing earnings on the basis of the smallest unit of ownership interest—one share of stock.

Depending on the ownership and debt structure of a corporation, the earnings per share calculation can be quite simple or quite complex. In its simplest form, earnings per share involves dividing net income by the average number of outstanding shares of stock.

$$\text{Earnings Per Share} = \frac{\text{Net Income}}{\text{Average Number of Shares of Outstanding Stock}}$$

RETAINED EARNINGS STATEMENT

The income statement is often supplemented with an optional statement called the statement of retained earnings. This statement relates to corporations and the portion of owner's equity that results from earnings reinvested in the company. The statement explains increases and decreases in the retained earnings account during the period. Usually, net income and dividends are included in the statement and explain the changes. An example of such a statement is presented as follows:

Tiani Company, Inc.
Statement of Retained Earnings
For the Year Ended December 31, 19x3

Beginning retained earnings balance—	
January 1, 19x3	$190,250
Add: Net income—19x3	25,850
	$216,100
Less: Dividends paid—19x3	24,300
Ending retained earnings balance—	
December 31, 19x3	$191,800

An Example

The Harrison Company has been in existence for several years. During the current period, the following income related activities occured:

1. Net sales revenue was $118,500. All sales were made on credit.
2. Beginning inventory was $62,000. Purchases during the period were $14,000. A physical count revealed an ending inventory of $51,000.
3. Operating expenses during the year included sales salaries—$19,500, advertising—$2,800, promotional supplies—$1,800, and depreciation—$1,200.
4. Bad debts are estimated to be 1.6 percent of current sales.
5. Administrative expenses that were incurred during the year included: administratives salaries of $21,000 and supplies of $1,700.
6. The company is subject to a 50 percent federal and local tax rate on its earnings.
7. Since the firm is incorporated, all income or loss will be closed to retained earnings.

Recording the Information

Journal entries for these transactions are presented in Illustration 1. End-of-period closing entries are also shown for each transaction. The transaction numbers relate to the information given above and the explanations offered below.

1. Credit sales lead to a realization of revenue. Revenue will be closed to the income summary account.
2. Under a periodic inventory system, purchases are recorded as they are made. At the end of the period, the beginning inventory is removed from the accounts, the ending inventory is entered in the accounts and the purchases account is cleared through the adjustment process. The cost of goods sold is isolated.

Illustration 1
Recording Expense Items

	Original Entry			*Closing Entry*		
1.	Accounts receivable	$118,500		Sales revenue	$118,500	
	Sales revenue		$118,500	Income summary		$118,500
2.	Purchases	14,000		Inventory	51,000	
	Accounts payable		14,000	Cost of goods sold	25,000	
				Inventory		62,000
				Purchases		14,000
3.	Salary expense	19,500		Income summary	96,698	
	Advertising expense	2,800		Salary expense—sales		19,500
	Supplies expense	1,800		Advertising expense		2,800
	Cash		24,100	Supplies expense—sales		1,800
				Depreciation expense		1,200
	Depreciation expense	1,200		Cost of goods sold		25,000
	Accumulated depreciation		1,200	Bad debt expense		1,896
				Salary expense—		
4.	Bad debt expense	1,896		administrative		21,000
	Allowance for doubtful accounts		1,896	Supplies expense—		
				administrative		1,700
5.	Salary expense	21,000		Income tax expense		21,802
	Supplies expense	1,700				
	Cash		22,700			
6.	Income tax expense	21,802				
	Income tax payable		21,802			
7.				Income summary	21,802	
				Retained earnings		21,802

3. Salary, advertising, and supplies expenses are recognized as they are incurred. At the end of the period, depreciation expense is estimated and recorded. All of the expense accounts are closed to income summary.
4. The annual amount of bad debt expense results from an estimate based on past experience. In this case, the amount $1,896 resulted from applying 1.6 percent to the total sales revenue ($118,500 × .016). Bad debt expense is closed to the income summary account.
5. Administrative expenses are recorded in the appropriate expense accounts as they are incurred. These expense accounts are also closed to income summary.
6. Income taxes are levied on the firm's taxable income. In this case, taxable income is the difference between revenues and expenses—$43,604. By applying the 50 percent rate to the income, tax expense is determined. Like all expenses, income tax expense will be closed to the income summary account.
7. The balance in the income summary account is closed to retained earnings to complete the recording and the closing process.

Statement Presentation

The transactions considered above focus primarily on the expenses of the Harrison Company. The income statement shown in Illustration 2 shows the disclosure of this information. Earnings per share were calculated on the assumption that 10,000 shares of stock are outstanding.

SUMMARY

To properly compute income, accountants must identify and measure expenses related to the reported revenues. Expenses result from the sale or consumption of resources that had an acquisition cost to the firm. Some expense elements can be measured directly, others must be estimated.

Cost of goods sold is an expense item that represents the cost of products that were sold during the period. The calculation of cost of goods sold depends on the inventory system in use. A periodic inventory system accounts for purchases and relies on an ending physical count to calculate cost of goods sold. Perpetual inventory systems maintain a continuous balance and accumulate cost of goods sold data on an ongoing basis.

Operating expenses include all those costs that were consumed in selling activities and in providing for the administration of the organization. Bad debt expense results from uncollectable credit accounts. This expense item is usually considered to be part of the cost of maintaining a credit policy for customers of the firm.

Bad debt expense is usually estimated periodically based on the past experience of the firm. The estimations may be related to the total sales volume or to the age of the outstanding debts. A valuation or contra account is used to provide a reduction in the accounts receivable balance without specifically identifying the doubtful accounts.

Illustration 2
Harrison Company
Reporting Net Income Statement
For the Year Ended December 31, 19x9

Sales revenue			$118,500
Cost of goods sold:			
Beginning inventory—January 1, 19x9	$62,000		
Purchases during 19x9	14,000		
Cost of goods available for sale		$76,000	
Less: Ending inventory—December 31, 19x9		51,000	
Cost of goods sold			25,000
Gross margin on sales			$ 93,500
Operating expenses:			
Selling expenses—			
Salaries	$19,500		
Advertising	2,800		
Supplies	1,800		
Depreciation	1,200		
Bad debts	1,896		
Total selling expense		$27,196	
Administrative expenses:			
Salaries	$21,000		
Supplies	1,700		
Total administrative expense		22,700	
Total operating expenses			49,896
Net income from operations			$ 43,604
Income tax expense			21,802
Net income			$ 21,802
Earnings per share			$ 2.18

The income statement includes income tax effects and a calculation of earnings per share. The income statement is also used in preparing the optional retained earnings statement. The statement of retained earnings explains changes in this account during the period under consideration.

KEY DEFINITIONS

Aging receivables—a schedule of receivables by age used in estimating bad debt expense.
Bad debt expense—the cost of not collecting an account receivable.
Cost of goods available for sale—the cost of beginning inventory plus the cost of purchases during the period.
Cost of goods sold—the cost of materials purchased and sold to customers.

Earnings per share—income divided by shares of stock outstanding.

Inventory—goods held for resale of use in the business operations.

Periodic inventory system—a system that determines inventory values only periodically.

Perpetual inventory system—a system that determines the cost of inventory on a continuous basis.

Purchase returns and allowances—an account that summarizes the amount of materials purchased and returned or adjusted during the period. It is a contra purchases account.

Purchases—an account accumulating the cost of goods purchased for resale during the period.

QUESTIONS

6-1 How are expenses and assets related?

6-2 Why is it important for the accountant to determine the extent of consumption and the value of resources that a business consumes?

6-3 Many income statements include a section called cost of goods sold. What does cost of goods sold measure? How is it calculated?

6-4 The term gross margin is included in the income statement. What does it represent. Why is it set out for special attention?

6-5 A well-designed inventory system will provide the accountant with a value for the inventory. What else will the system provide?

6-6 Describe two major types of inventory systems, and identify their similarities and differences.

6-7 Why are two inventory systems available to the accountant? Would one system be sufficient for most business ventures?

6-8 Describe the objectives of the adjusting process when a periodic inventory system is used.

6-9 Explain the term operating expenses. Give three examples of items that probably would be operating expenses.

6-10 Why is bad debt expense considered part of the expense of a credit policy for the firm?

6-11 What happens if an overdue account is written-off as a bad debt and the customer subsequently pays?

6-12 Discuss two techniques for estimating bad debt expense.

6-13 If bad debt expense is estimated, will imprecision creep into the financial statements of a company?

6-14 What is the purpose of the retained earnings statement? Describe the basic structure of the statement.

EXERCISES

E6-1 The Taylor Clothing Company wishes to determine the amount of cost of goods sold at the end of the accounting period. The inventory at the start of the period was $250,000. During the period, the company purchased $125,000 of merchandise, and the ending inventory disclosed that $225,000 of stock was still on hand. What is the cost of goods sold for the period? What is the amount of inventory that will be disclosed on the balance sheet?

E6-2 The following three situations relate to different components involved in calculating cost of goods sold or inventory values. In each case, evaluate the data presented and complete the calculation.

a. Beginning inventory was $210,000. Inventory at the end of the period was $60,000 and cost of goods was reported to be $330,000. What is the value of purchases made during the period?
b. At the end of the accounting period, the income statement disclosed that cost of goods sold was $73,000, and the balance sheet reported an inventory value of $10,000. Management indicates that $51,000 of merchandise was purchased during the period. What was the beginning inventory?
c. A firm began the period with $13,000 of inventory. During the period, purchases totalled $18,000. Cost of goods sold expense is reported to be $14,500. What is the value of the ending inventory?

E6-3 If the beginning inventory and the ending inventory values are the same, then the firm's cost of goods sold must equal what amount? Similarly, if periodic purchases equal the ending inventory, then the cost of goods sold must equal what amount?

E6-4 The Mark Up Company recorded sales of $1,228,000 during the month of October. The cost of goods sold for October was $921,000. What was the gross margin on sales for the month. What was the gross margin percentage, and what does it mean?

E6-5 The income statement of Sampson Company reported that the gross margin on sales for the year was $273,000. The gross margin percentage for this company is 35 percent. What was the cost of goods sold for the Sampson Company for the year? What was the total annual sales revenue generated by this company?

E6-6 A firm had net sales of $587,500. At the beginning of the period, the inventory was $278,000, and at the end of the period the inventory was $252,000. Merchandise purchases during the period totalled $315,000. Construct in good form an income statement which reports the gross margin on sales for this company.

E6-7 The following transactions were made during a recent account period:

a. Merchandise of $208,000 was purchased on credit.
b. Sales totalling $302,000 were made. Cash sales accounted for $180,000 of the total, and the remainder were on credit.
c. Cash purchases of merchandise equalled $73,500.
d. Credit sales of $37,500 were made.
e. The merchandise purchased on credit in (a) was paid for in cash.
f. The merchandise inventory at the beginning of the period was $102,000, and at the end of the period it was $167,500.

Required:

Assuming that the company uses a periodic inventory system, give the journal entries that would have been made for each of the events described above. Prepare an income statement that reports the gross margin on sales.

E6-8 Using the information from E6-7, prepare the journal entries that would be made under the perpetual system.

E6-9 A company made purchases of $125,000, $250,000, and $375,000, respectively. At the start of the period, the inventory was $650,000, and at the end of the period, the inventory level had fallen to $550,000. Assuming that all of the purchases were made on credit, prepare journal entries to record these purchases (the company uses a periodic inventory system). Make the appropriate adjusting to close the purchase account at the end of the period and adjust the ending inventory balance.

E6-10 The Continual Corporation uses a perpetual inventory system. During the year of 19x4, the company made two purchases of $234,000 and $412,000, respectively. The inventory at the beginning of the period was $718,000 and cost of goods sold equalled $650,000. Assume that the purchases were made on credit. At the end of the period, what entries will be necessary to update the inventory account.

E6-11 The following three cases relate to estimations of uncollectable accounts receivable. In each case, make the appropriate journal entry to properly reflect the information in the accounts.

a. Amos Apple & Company estimates that $12,500 of this year's credit sales will be uncollectable.
b. Brown, Bear, and Son age accounts receivable. As a result of this process, they determine that the allowance for doubtful accounts should equal $48,000. The current credit balance in the account is $33,000.
c. C & D Company estimates that $2,500 of current sales will result in uncollectable accounts.

E6-12 Mitchell Corporation made sales of $410,000 during 19x9. The allowance for doubtful accounts currently has a credit balance of $16,200. Prepare appropriate journal entries to reflect the following events:

a. An account receivable from a prior year was determined to be uncollectable. It amounted to $1,700 and was written-off immediately.
b. Bad debt losses for the current year were estimated to be 2 percent of the current sales.
c. An account of $200, which was previously deemed to be uncollectable and written-off, was unexpectedly paid in full.

E6-13 The Key Company reported net income for the year 19x6 of $43,600. Retained earnings on January 1, 19x6, were $23,400. During the year, the firm paid dividends of $35,700. Prepare a retained earnings statement in good form for the Key Company.

E6-14 The Toe Towel Company makes the following information available:

Administrative expenses	$ 412,000
Beginning inventory—January 1, 19x9	112,000
Ending inventory—December 31, 19x9	100,000
Purchase during 19x9	815,000
Sales revenue	1,426,000
Selling expenses	318,000
Total outstanding shares of stock	10,000

Required:

Using this information, prepare an income statement for this company in good form. Make certain that the statement isolates the gross margin, net income from operations, net income, and earnings per share.

E6-15 Calculate the gross margin percentage for the following independent cases:

	A	*B*	*C*
Sales	$282,000	$192,000	$66,500
Sales returns and allowances	16,000	9,000	500
Sales discounts	3,000	2,000	0
Beginning inventory	47,000	31,000	6,000
Purchases	180,000	201,000	40,000
Purchases returns and allowances	6,000	11,000	0
Ending inventory	51,000	88,000	12,000

E6-16 Fill in the missing data in the following independent case situations:

	A	*B*	*C*
Sales	$100,000	$____	$200,000
Sales returns and allowances	1,000	3,000	____
Sales discounts	2,000	1,000	3,000
Net sales	____	____	196,000
Beginning inventory	____	35,000	____
Purchases	65,000	____	105,000
Purchases returns and allowances	1,000	0	2,000
Purchase discounts	1,000	1,000	0
Goods available for sale	90,000	____	170,000
Ending inventory	____	20,000	____
Cost of goods sold	60,000	____	____
Gross margin on sales	____	40,000	____
Gross margin percentage	____	40%	30%

E6-17 From the data below, prepare an aging of accounts receivable and make the necessary general journal entry to reflect your estimate of bad debts in the accounts:

Customer	*Receivable Amount*	*Age of Account*
A	$100	44
B	210	3
C	400	21
D	50	10
E	80	80
F	240	191
G	200	50
H	50	38
I	600	2
J	150	7

Estimated Uncollectable

Age Group	*Percentage*
1-30 days	1%
31-60 days	5%
61-90 days	12%
91-120 days	20%
over 121 days	80%

A $200 credit balance is in the allowance for doubtful accounts before the adjustment.

PROBLEMS

P6-1 The Light Company operates a retail lighting business in Wattville. Information about the company for the year of 19x8 is provided below:

1. During the year, total sales were $2,052,165. Of this amount, $425,745 were made for cash, and the remainder were made to regular customers who purchased on credit.
2. The company made several purchases during the year. Credit purchases amounted to $673,810 and $105,485 of merchandise was purchased for cash. Light Company uses the periodic inventory method.
3. Selling expenses for the year included: salaries—$78,340, wages—$104,480, rent—$26,745, and supplies—$35,700.
4. Depreciation on equipment owned by the company totalled $15,495 for the year.
5. Administrative expenses included the following items: salaries—$147,695, supplies—$4,890, and miscellaneous—$6,710.
6. On January 1, 19x8, the inventory was valued at $357,260, and at the end of the year, on December 31, 19x8, the inventory remaining equalled $298,750.
7. The company is subject to a combined 50 percent rate for federal, state, and local taxes.
8. The company has 20,000 shares of stock outstanding.

Required:

a. Prepare a set of summary journal entries to record the information given in items (1) through (5) above.
b. Prepare a complete set of inventory adjusting and all closing entries for this company.
c. Prepare an income statement for the Light Company for 19x8.

P6-2 During 19x5, the Johnson Corporation generated $147,260 of sales revenue. Of this amount, $102,620 of sales were made on account. The company began the year with an inventory at cost of $48,620. On December 31, 19x5, a physical count was made and the inventory cost was determined to be $50,700. During the year, the company made four major purchases of merchandise. All of the purchases were paid for in cash and were for the following amounts: January—$18,750, June—$17,580, August—$10,270, and November—$15,350.

Selling expenses, excluding depreciation and bad debt expense, were $14,270. Administrative expenses totalled $12,830. The annual depreciation charge was calculated to be $3,720. Bad debt expense was estimated to be 2 percent of current credit sales. The company is subject to a 40 percent income tax rate. Johnson has 1,000 shares of stock outstanding. At the beginning of the year, retained earnings were reported to be $43,820. During the year, dividends of $3.25 per share were declared and paid by the company.

Required:

a. Prepare an income statement for the Johnson Corporation for 19x5.
b. Prepare a retained earnings statement for the Johnson Corporation as of December 31, 19x5.

P6-3 The Walker Company is concerned about the adequacy of its allowance for doubtful accounts. Historically, the company has estimated bad debt expense as a percentage of sales volume. However, their accountant has suggested that an aging of accounts receivable could provide a better estimate. At the present time, allowance for doubtful accounts has a credit balance of $7,000.

The following information summarized from the financial records of the Walker Company. It was decided to base the percentage uncollectable on past experience.

	Past Experience		
Age Group	*Total Receivables*	*Total Collected*	*Outstanding Receivables*
1-30 days	$1,764,500	$1,746,855	$465,800
31-90 days	985,600	965,888	323,850
91-180 days	415,200	394,440	156,700
Over 180 days	158,300	66,486	12,400

Required:

Using this information, prepare an aging schedule for the current accounts receivable for the Walker Company. Determine the balance of the allowance for doubtful accounts. Prepare the journal entry that would be made to adjust the account balance to reflect the use of aging information. Discuss what effect this adjustment will have on current income for the company.

P6-4 The Brenner Company operates several wholesale outlets in the State of Nevada. Income-related information from the year of 19x7 has been summarized below. Although the company collected and summarized the information, none of it was entered into their accounting records.

1. Net sales revenue was $367,950. Of this amount, $312,400 was sold on credit, and the balance resulted from cash sales.
2. The company began the year with an inventory valued at $41,250. During the year, the company made several purchases for cash. Purchases for the year totalled $174,450. At the end of the year, a physical count of the inventory was taken. The ending inventory value was determined to be $53,675. The periodic inventory method was used.
3. Operating expenses incurred during the year included: salaries—$31,260, advertising—$2,750, rent—$12,675, supplies—$1,950, and depreciation—$2,975.
4. The company uses an estimating process to determine the current charge for uncollectable accounts. Based on past experience, the firm estimates uncollectables to be 2 percent of current credit sales.
5. Annual administrative expenses included the following items: salaries—$25,980, depreciation—$1,250, and supplies—$2,975. The firm is a corporation, and at the present time there are 1,000 shares of common stock outstanding. Because of its earnings, the company is subject to a combined 50 percent rate for federal and local taxes. All income or loss for the period will be closed to retained earnings. Beginning retained earnings balance for the year was $66,000.

Required:

a. Prepare summary journal entries to record all of the transaction information presented above.
b. Prepare adjusting closing entries for this information. Complete the process through closing the income summary account.
c. Prepare an income statement in good form for the Brenner Company.
d. Prepare a retained earnings statement for the company.

P6-5 The Wattsun Company merchandises imported desk and table lamps. During the year 19x8, 5,000 shares of the company's common stock were outstanding. The company uses a periodic inventory system to record information about the cost of the products it sells. At the end of the year, a physical count of the inventory is made and is used for control purposes and to value the ending inventory. The following information was taken from the general ledger on December 31, 19x8:

	Debit	*Credit*
Cash	$ 51,605	
Accounts receivable	102,750	
Allowance for doubtful accounts		$ 5,278
Inventory—January 1, 19x8	68,500	
Plant and equipment	278,790	
Accumulated depreciation—equipment		157,983
Accrued salaries payable		12,850
Accounts payable		53,575
Mortgage loan		125,000
Capital stock		100,000
Retained earnings—January 1, 19x8		32,854
Sales		587,325
Sales returns and allowances	11,125	
Selling expenses	183,230	
Administrative expenses	151,125	
Income tax expense	8,570	
Purchases	219,170	
	$1,074,865	$1,074,865

The company uses an estimating procedure to determine its provision for bad debts. Based on previous experience, the current provision is .8 percent of current net sales. The physical count resulted in a final inventory cost of $67,250.

Required:

a. Bad debt expense has not been recorded for the current year. Make the entry to record it on December 31, 19x8.
b. Make the necessary journal entries to record the ending inventory value and to close out the books for the year.
c. Construct an income statement for the Wattsun Company.
d. Prepare a retained earnings statement for the year. Assume that no dividends were paid.

P6-6 The unadjusted trial balance of the Helvering Company is shown below:

Helvering Company
Trial Balance
December 31, 19x4

	Debit	*Credit*
Cash	$ 3,000	
Accounts receivable	5,000	
Inventory—January 1, 19x4	18,000	
Prepaid insurance	1,200	
Supplies	1,100	
Machinery and equipment	8,000	
Accumulated depreciation		$ 2,600
Accounts payable		7,500
Helvering—capital		15,000
Sales		128,800
Sales returns and allowances	900	
Purchases	80,000	
Purchases returns and allowances		400
Wages expense	29,000	
Rental expense	7,000	
Miscellaneous expense	500	
Utilities expense	600	
	$154,300	$154,300

Adjustment data from Helvering's financial records are as follows:

1. Ending inventory at December 31 was $15,000.
2. Prepaid insurance was for a one-year fire insurance policy dated July 1, 19x4.
3. An inventory of supplies showed only $300 in supplies on hand at year-end.
4. Depreciation expense for the year is $1,300.
5. Wages of $900 have been earned by employees but have not been paid at December 31, 19x4.
6. Bad debts expense of $300 is estimated.

Required:

a. Prepare a worksheet for the Helvering Company.
b. Prepare a multiple-step income statement for the year ending December 31, 19x4.

P6-7 The Zinnie Wholesale Boutique sells high-fashion women's clothing. Beginning inventory had a cost of $2,000. Transactions for the month of July include the following involving inventory:

1. Purchased merchandise for $26,000 on account at terms 2/10, n/30.
2. Paid for merchandise within the discount period.
3. Sold merchandise costing $8,000 for $14,000 cash.
4. Sold merchandise costing $3,000 for $4,700 on account at terms n/30.
5. Sold merchandise costing $4,000 for $6,000 on account at terms 2/10, n/30.
6. Received payment for sale noted in (5) after the discount period.

Required:

Prepare the necessary journal entries to account for the above transactions assuming that:

a. The firm uses a periodic inventory system.
b. The firm uses a perpetual inventory system.

P6-8 Bimson Corporation's unadjusted trial balance at October 31, 19x8, the corporation's fiscal year-end is shown below:

Bimson Corporation
Trial Balance
October 31, 19x8

	Debit	*Credit*
Cash	$ 4,000	
Accounts receivable	8,000	
Inventory	10,000	
Equipment	9,000	
Accumulated depreciation		$ 3,000
Accounts payable		6,000
Common stock ($5 par)		5,000
Retained earnings		14,000
Sales		44,200
Sales discounts	1,000	
Cost of goods sold	25,000	
Salary expense	8,000	
Rental expense	7,200	
	$72,200	$72,200

Adjusting data are shown below:

1. The firm uses a perpetual inventory system.
2. Bad debts expense of $200 is estimated.
3. Depreciation is $1,000 per year.
4. Wages of $400 have been earned but not paid to employees as of October 31.

Required:

a. Prepare the necessary general journal entries to make the necessary adjustments.
b. Prepare a single step income statement for Bimson Corporation for the year ended October 31, 19x8.
c. Calculate earnings or loss per share assuming 1,000 shares of stock are outstanding during the year.
d. Prepare a retained earnings statement as of December 31, 19x8.
e. Make the necessary closing entries for Bimson Corporation.

Learning Objectives

Chapter 7 discusses proper accounting for cash investments and notes receivable. Studying this chapter should enable you to:

1. Describe the characteristics of current assets.
2. Discuss control procedures for cash.
3. Prepare a bank reconciliation statement.
4. Record the acquisition and disposition of temporary investments. Describe how temporary investments would be disclosed on a balance sheet.
5. Calculate the interest or discount associated with notes receivable.

7

Cash, Temporary Investments, and Receivables

INTRODUCTION

Cash is a fundamental financial resource. As the most common medium of exchange, it serves as the measurement standard for all other financial items. Because of this, cash measurement problems are minimal. However, cash is volatile—it can be lost, stolen, misplaced, or misused easily. Therefore, many accounting procedures relating to cash focus on areas of control and cash utilization. This chapter discusses the valuation, reporting, and control of the most liquid assets of an enterprise: cash, temporary investments, and short-term receivables.

CASH

All resources classified as cash must be negotiable and immediately available for use and exchange without any restrictions. The classification *cash* usually includes coin, currency, bank deposits, checks, and money orders. Some judgment must be used by the accountant in classifying items as cash. Technically, since banks retain the right to require notice prior to withdrawals, savings account deposits should not be classified as cash. As a practical matter, however, banks normally do not exercise this requirement, and savings deposits are generally reported as cash.

Cash that is restricted in any way is reported separately from the account *cash*. Usually, such items will be treated as a noncurrent asset and reported as funds held for some specific purpose. For example, cash that is set aside for redeeming outstanding bonds would be disclosed on the balance sheet as follows:

Noncurrent assets:
Funds for bond redemption $100,000

Control over the assets of a business is important to protect against loss, misappropriation, or inefficiency. Because of the volatility of cash, its control is fundamental to a good accounting system. The control of assets is based on a set of generally accepted concepts referred to as *internal control.* Internal control relates to policies, procedures, and activities designed to safeguard the assets of an enterprise and to promote their effective utilization.

CONTROL OF CASH

While there are various means of obtaining good internal control, the system should include at least the following characteristics:

1. A *plan of organization* that provides appropriate separation of functional responsibilities—those involved with receiving cash should be separate from those disbursing cash; those involved with handling cash should be separate from those recording cash.
2. A *system of authorization* and *recording* adequate to provide accounting control over assets, liabilities, revenues, and expenses—predetermined routines and procedures should be established; all flows of cash should be properly authorized, and the accounting system should be able to detect exceptions to these procedures.
3. *Sound practices* to be followed in all organizational functions involving resources—cash receipts should be deposited daily in a bank; cash on hand should be secured.
4. *Quality of personnel* should be commensurate with responsibilities—authority should match with responsibility; individual ability should be equivalent with the position held.

Control Procedures

Because cash is very transferable and not easily identified, it is very susceptible to misappropriation. Therefore, it is important to provide detailed controls over the receipt and disbursement of cash. The objectives of a system of cash control are to assure that all cash that should be collected is collected and properly recorded and that all disbursements are for valid business purposes and accounted for properly. While the specific procedures may vary depending on the characteristics of the entity, basic principles for controlling cash and cash transactions include the following:

1. Predetermined procedures for handling cash and recording cash transactions should be established.
2. Cash receipts should be deposited daily in a bank account and disbursements should be made by prenumbered checks.

3. All cash receipts and disbursements should be recorded immediately.
4. Separation of duties relating to the handling of cash and recording cash transactions and receiving cash and disbursing cash should be enforced.
5. Physical safeguards, such as cash registers, check protectors, and prenumbered business forms, should be used.
6. Disbursements should be made only for purposes authorized by a limited number of designated persons.
7. The responsibility for authorizing a disbursement and the responsibility for signing checks should be separated. All checks that are material in amount should require the signatures of two authorized persons.
8. Periodic audits should be made to determine that cash is being accounted for properly.

Specific methods of achieving good internal control must be developed for and adapted to a specific business enterprise. Also, the cost of each part of the control system must be weighed against the benefit derived from the control. Generally, only those procedures that provide for benefit in excess of their cost should be implemented. Cash control usually involves significant interaction with banks.

BANK CHECKING ACCOUNT

An important element of the cash control system is the requirement that daily cash receipts be deposited promptly and intact in a bank checking account. Checking accounts provide certain additional documentation about the receipt and disbursement of cash. When a bank deposit is made, the depositor details the information on a form provided by the bank. The deposit slip is usually prepared in duplicate, with one copy serving as the depositor's receipt for the transaction.

Disbursements from a checking account are authorized by checks. A check is a written legal instrument, signed by the maker, ordering the bank to pay a specified sum of money from the maker's account to the order of a person or entity designated on the check. Checks are normally printed bank forms that are sequentially numbered and contain the depositor's name, address, and account number. The sequential numbering can assist the accountant in determining that all checks have been recorded.

Banks provide their customers with periodic statements about the status of and changes in their accounts. These bank statements list deductions from the account (debits) and additions to the account (credits) that occurred during the period. The bank will usually return source documents along with the statement, including checks paid, deposit receipts, and memorandums relating to other account activities. A *debit memorandum* indicates that the account has been charged, or reduced, by the bank. This may result from account service charges, or from checks that were accepted by the bank as deposits but subsequently returned because of insufficient funds. A *credit memorandum* indicates that the account has been increased by the bank. For example, a bank may collect an outstanding note for the depositor and credit the amount to the depositor's account. A typical bank statement is shown in Illustration 1.

BANK RECONCILIATION

The cash balance shown on the bank statement normally will not equal the cash balance shown in the company's ledger account. The difference results from timing differences and/or errors in recording transactions by either the bank or the company. These differences can be classified into the following four types.

1. Amounts that have been added to the depositor's account by the bank but are not yet recorded by the depositor. Examples of these items are the proceeds of notes or drafts collected by the bank for the depositor.
2. Amounts that have been charged to the depositor's account by the bank but are not yet recorded by the depositor. Such items include bank service charges and NSF (not sufficient funds) checks returned to the bank.
3. Amounts that the depositor has added to his or her cash account but have not yet been added by the bank. This generally occurs when deposits are in transit at the date of the bank statement. The depositor will record the deposit when it is transmitted, but the bank will record it after it is received.
4. Amounts that the depositor has deducted from his or her cash account but have not yet been deducted by the bank. Normally, this results from checks issued by the depositor that have not yet been presented to the bank for payment.

As a part of the control process, a *bank reconciliation statement* should be prepared to explain differences between the cash balance in the ledger account and the cash balance on the bank statement. Control is enhanced, because the bank statement provides an independent record of the company's cash-related transactions. Reconciliation provides a mechanism for isolating errors made by the bank or the company in recording cash transactions and yields data necessary to adjust the company's cash records.

The bank reconciliation statement includes four distinct parts. The goal is to reconcile both the bank balance and the ledger balance to the correct cash balance at the end of the period. Accordingly, the bank balance is adjusted for additions and deductions by the depositor not shown on the bank statement, and the ledger balance is adjusted for additions and deductions by the bank not recorded in the books of the company. The bank reconciliation

Illustration 1
Bank Statement

City National Bank

Henderson Company
1217 Ring Street
Brian, TX 77840

Account Number	Page Number
02038001	1
5/31/x9	6/30/x9
From	To
Statement Period	

Date	*Debits*		*Deposits*	*Balance*
5/31				$1,116.08
6/1	100.00			1,016.08
6/3	50.00	425.00		541.08
6/6	181.00	163.20		196.88
6/8			1,432.62	1,628.50
6/12	145.00NF			1,483.50
6/14	274.36	191.17		1,017.97
6/15	371.15	22.60		624.22
	13.45	173.62		437.15
6/17			1,763.19	2,200.34
6/21	545.40	317.71		1,337.23
6/23	41.00	63.27		1,232.96
6/24			1,020.00CM	2,252.96
6/25	317.13	267.41		1,668.42
6/27	5.00SC	63.42		1,600.00

Beginning Balance	*No. of Credits*	*Total Credits*	*Ending Balance*
$1,116.08	3	$4,214.81	$1,600.00
	No. of Debits	*Total Debits*	*Code Explanation*
	20	$3,730.89	CC certified check CM credit memo NF nonsufficient funds LC late charges SC service charge XC certified check

usually is divided into two parts: one to reconcile the bank balance to the correct balance and one to reconcile the book balance to the correct balance. The form usually is as follows:

Balance per bank		XXX
Additions:		
Deposits in transit	XXX	
Bank errors understating balance	XXX	XXX
Deductions:		
Outstanding checks	XXX	
Bank errors overstating balance	XXX	XXX
Correct balance		XXX
Balance per books		XXX
Additions:		
Collections by bank	XXX	
Errors by company understating balance	XXX	XXX
Deductions:		
Charges by bank	XXX	
Errors by company overstating balance	XXX	XXX
Corrected balance		XXX

Notice that both reconciliations adjust to the correct balance. This is the amount that will be reported as cash in the balance sheet. When additions or deductions are made to the books, adjusting entries must be made to correct the book balance. For additions, the cash account will be debited and an appropriate account credited. If the bank collected a note for the company, the company would credit notes receivable and interest earned for any interest collected. Deductions will result in a credit to cash and a debit to the appropriate account. For example, if the deduction was for monthly account charges, the bank service charge expense account would be debited. If the deduction resulted from an NSF check, the debit would be to accounts receivable since the amount is still owed by the customer. Note that no adjustments are made for the adjustments to the bank balance. This is the banks responsibility. If the company discovers a bank error, it will inform the bank so that the bank may make a correction on its books.

An Example

A bank reconciliation for Henderson Company (see Illustration 1 for bank statement) is shown in Illustration 2. The City National Bank statement to the Henderson Company indicates a balance of $1,600 as of June 30, 19x9. On the same date, the company's ledger balance for cash in the bank was $1,757. The following additional data relate to information about the company's cash balance and are relevant in preparing a bank reconciliation statement:

1. Deposit mailed to the bank on June 30, but not recorded on the bank statement—$1,500.

Illustration 2
Henderson Company
Bank Reconciliation Statement
June 30, 19x9

Balance per bank statement—June 30		$1,600
Add: Deposit in transit	$1,500	
Check of Hinson Company incorrectly charged to Henderson account	100	1,600
		$3,200
Less: Outstanding checks (Nos. 527, 531, and 532)		600
Correct cash balance		$2,600
Balance per books—June 30		$1,757
Add: Note collected by the bank for the company		1,020
		$2,777
Less: Bank service charges	5	
NSF check—Smith Company	145	
Error in recording check no. 511	27	177
Correct cash balance		$2,600

2. Checks written during the month of June but not recorded by the bank as of June 30 (check 527 for $122.71, 531 for $167.19, and 532 for $310.10) total $600.
3. A credit memorandum included with the bank statement indicated that a note receivable of $1,000 plus $20 interest ($1,020 in total) had been collected by the bank and credited to the Henderson Company account.
4. A debit memorandum was forwarded by the bank and indicated that a check deposited by the Henderson Company (received from a customer) was being returned because of insufficient funds (NSF)—$145.
5. A debit memorandum was also included with the bank statement for service charges for the month of June—$5.
6. An examination of the cancelled checks returned by the bank revealed that a check written by the Hinson Company had been erroneously charged against the Henderson Company account—$100.
7. A comparison of the cancelled checks with the firm's accounting records indicated that check 511 for $41 to the Acme Supply Company had incorrectly recorded in the books as $14, indicating an error of $27.

The deposit made by the Henderson Company on June 30 should be a part of the cash balance. Because it was in transit when the bank statement was made, it was not included. Consequently, it is added to the balance per bank statement as a part of the reconciliation process. In certain situations, control procedures will require that a follow-up contact be made with the bank to ensure that the deposit was received.

A check prepared by the Hinson Company was erroneously charged against the Henderson Company account by the bank. To adjust for this error, $100—the amount of the check—is added to the balance reported by the bank. The bank should be notified promptly of the error.

Three checks were outstanding when the bank statement was prepared. Because they were not presented to the bank for payment, they have not been deducted from the Henderson Company account. They should be deducted from the bank balance to derive the proper cash balance. There is no reason to expect that all checks written by a company will be presented promptly for payment. Consequently, adjustments for the same outstanding check may be made for many periods. The first part of the Henderson Company reconciliation statement indicates that the correct cash balance is $2,600.

The bank reconciliation statement continues by focusing on the cash balance reported in the company's ledger on June 30. The bank statement notified the company that a note of $1,000 plus $20 interest was collected on its behalf by the bank and included in its account balance. This collection would be added to the reported cash balance since it had not previously been included by the firm. The bank also notified the company of three deductions from its cash balance.

Service charges during the month totalled $5. While these could be anticipated, service charges are usually not recorded until they are confirmed by notification from the bank. Henderson Company had previously deposited a check that it had received from the Smith Company. Deposits are accepted subject to collection of checks or other financial instruments. In this case, the check of the Smith Company was not supported by adequate funds and it was returned. Consequently, the $145 was not added to the account of the Henderson Company by the bank and should be deducted from the book balance. Finally, an error of $27 was made in recording check 511. This amount should be deducted from the bank balance to properly derive the cash balance. The second part of the reconciliation agrees with the first—that the adjusted cash balance is $2,600. Agreement does not assure correctness, but it does imply consistency.

The first part of the bank reconciliation dealt with adjustments to the balance reported by the bank. In cases where corrections are not automatic (such as deposits in transit), the bank should be notified to make the necessary adjustments. The second part of the reconciliation relates to the company's books. Adjustments and corrections here should be reflected in the cash account through an appropriate journal entry. In this case, four adjustment entries would be necessary.

Cash	$1,020	
Notes receivable		$1,000
Interest revenue...........................		20
To record the collection of an outstanding note plus interest		
Miscellaneous expense	$5	
Cash		$5
To record the payment of bank service charges for June		
Accounts receivable	$145	
Cash		$145
To record the return of an NSF check		
Accounts payable	$27	
Cash		$27
To record an error correction for recording payment to Acme Supply		

After the entries have been made, the cash balance in the ledger will be $2,600. This amount is in agreement with the balance derived in the bank reconciliation statement and would be reported as the cash in the bank on the balance sheet for June 30.

PETTY CASH

For control purposes, it is useful to have all cash disbursements made by check. However, it is impractical to issue checks for various small payments for items such as postage, miscellaneous supplies, and other minor expenditures. To allow such payments to be made in cash and at the same time to maintain control over these disbursements, many firms establish petty cash funds. A *petty cash fund* is a regulated quantity of cash under the control of an employee to be used for making minor payments.

The petty cash fund is established by cashing a check and placing the cash under the control of the employee who will have charge of the fund. As disbursements are made, the recipient is required to sign a voucher indicating the purpose and amount of the payment. Thus, at any time, the sum of the cash and the vouchers should equal the amount originally placed in the fund. Periodically, the fund is replenished by writing a check on the general bank account for the sum of the petty cash vouchers. The check is cashed and the proceeds are returned to the petty cash fund. When the petty cash fund is replenished, various expense accounts are debited (increased) as indicated by the vouchers and cash is credited (reduced). The fund is also replenished at the end of an accounting period so that the expenses reflected by the vouchers will be included in the financial statements.

To illustrate the use of a petty cash fund, assume that a company establishes a fund on January 1 by cashing a check for $500. The entry reflects the reclassification of cash within the firm:

Petty cash.................................	$ 500	
Cash		$ 500
To establish a petty cash fund		

Various disbursements are made by the cashier during January. The following list of disbursements is presented for reimbursement on January 25:

Postage	$ 70
Office supplies	180
Miscellaneous selling expenses	125
	$375
Cash on hand	125
	$500

The following entry would be made to record the reimbursement:

Postage expense	$ 70	
Office supplies expense	180	
Miscellaneous selling expense	125	
Cash		$375
To reimburse the petty cash fund		

Notice that no entry is made directly to the petty cash account at the time of reimbursement. The only entries to petty cash are on establishing the fund and on increasing or decreasing the amount of cash authorized for the fund.

The basic control over the petty cash fund is at the time of reimbursement, since all disbursements must be supported by vouchers. An additional control may be provided by periodic unannounced counts of the fund. When financial statements are prepared, the balance in the petty cash fund will be combined with other forms of cash and reported on the balance sheet as a single entry entitled "cash."

TEMPORARY INVESTMENTS

Businesses frequently have cash that is not currently needed in the operations of the organization. In such cases, it is economically wise for the firm to invest its cash and earn a return rather than leaving the balances idle and unproductive. In cases of a short-term cash surplus, temporary investments will be made. These *temporary investments* are normally in liquid securities that can easily be converted to cash, such as certificates of deposit, commercial paper, government securities, and corporate bonds and stock.

If the cash surplus is deemed to be other than temporary, a more permanent commitment of the resources will be made. The company will invest in growth, facilities, or another organization; the prospects of a quick conversion of these investments into cash is reduced. Consequently, for accounting and reporting purposes, a distinction is made between temporary investments and long-term investments. Temporary investments are shown as current assets, while long-term investments are included in the noncurrent asset section of the balance sheet.

For securities to be classified as temporary investments, they must satisfy the following two criteria.

1. The security must be readily marketable at a determinable price. Marketable means that a sales price is currently available on an organized securities exchange or that there is an established market for the security.
2. It is the intention of management to convert the securities into cash within one year (or the operating cycle of the business if it is longer than one year).

Long-term investments are those securities that do not meet the marketability criterion or that are acquired for some long-range objective such as exercising control over the operations of another company. Thus, a specific security that is readily marketable could be classified as either a temporary investment or a long-term investment depending on the intentions of management. Long-term investments are discussed in Chapter 9.

ACCOUNTING FOR TEMPORARY INVESTMENTS

The accountant primarily deals with three aspects of the temporary investment: acquisition, income, and valuation. Temporary investments are initially valued at their acquisition cost. This includes the purchase price of the security plus additional acquisition costs, such as broker's commissions. For example, assume that the Anderson Company purchased 100 shares of F and C Corporation common stock as a temporary investment. The stock was purchased at $48 per share plus a brokerage commission of $200. The following journal entry would be made by Anderson Company:

Temporary investments....................	$5,000	
Cash..................................		$5,000
To record the acquisition of 100 shares of F and C common stock		

Investment Income

Temporary investments are made to earn a return on otherwise idle cash. The return can be in the form of interest on bonds and notes and dividends on corporate stock. As it is earned, income from temporary investments is included in appropriate revenue accounts and recognized in the income statement. Measurement problems are the same as other assets earning a similar type of return.

As discussed in Chapter 4, interest revenue is earned with the passage of time and therefore must be recorded with an adjusting entry if the interest collection date and the end of the accounting period do not coincide. To illustrate this process, assume that the Anderson Company purchased $100,000 of Porter Comany 8 percent bonds on July 1 for $100,000 plus a $1,000 brokerage commission. The bonds pay interest annually on June 30. The purchase would be recorded by increasing (debiting) temporary investments and reducing (crediting) cash for $101,000. If the bonds are still held on December 31, the end of the company's accounting period, the following adjusting entry must be made to properly state income for the year:

Accrued interest receivable	$4,000*	
Interest revenue		$4,000
To recognize interest revenue earned on temporary investments		

*($100,000 × .08 × ½)

By contrast, common stock dividends are not earned until they are declared by the board of directors of the corporation. Normally, dividend income would be recognized when it is received by the firm. However, if a dividend is declared in one year, with payment to take place in the following accounting period, the revenue would be accrued and recognized in the period when the declaration was made.

Valuation of Investments

Many times, the market value of temporary investments will change during the accounting period when the investment is being held. If the market price exceeds the acquisition cost of the investment, no adjustment is made. No gains are recorded until they are realized through the act of sale. However, if the market price falls below the acquisition cost, an adjustment must be made. If the market price has declined, financial statements which report temporary investments at their acquisition cost could be misleading by implying a higher value for the securities than is realizable. In these cases, the value of the temporary investment will be lowered to the market value and a corresponding holding loss will be recognized. This valuation practice is known as the *lower of cost or market principle.*

Lower of cost or market is applied by comparing the total acquisition cost of all temporary investments with the total market value of these investments at the end of the accounting period. If the market value is lower than the cost, a loss is recognized, and the asset account temporary investments is reduced by the difference. Normally, the asset is reduced by means of a valuation or contra account, which is subsequently offset against the asset in the financial statements.

To illustrate this process, assume that the Derek Company had the following portfolio of temporary investments as of December 31:

	December 31, 19x9		
Security	*Cost*	*Market*	*Increase (Decrease)*
A............................	$10,000	$11,000	$1,000
B............................	7,000	4,000	(3,000)
C............................	5,000	3,000	(2,000)
Total	$22,000	$18,000	($4,000)

At the end of the year, the market value of these securities is less than their acquisition cost. Consequently, a loss of $4,000 will be recognized and the value of the securities will be reduced by that amount.

While the account, temporary investments, could be reduced directly, usually, a separate valuation account is used so that the historical cost of the investments is preserved in the resulting reports. In this case, the following journal entry would be made:

Loss on temporary investments	$4,000	
Allowance for decline in value of temporary investments.		$4,000
To value temporary investments at the lower of cost or market		

The reported loss will be included in the income statement for the period. The allowance account will be reported on the balance sheet as an offset against the historical cost balance for temporary investments as follows:

Current assets:		
Temporary investments	$22,000	
Less: Allowance for decline in value	4,000	$18,000

In subsequent accounting periods, increases in the value of temporary investment portfolio up to the amount of the original cost could be recognized by decreasing (debiting) the allowance account and increasing (crediting) a corresponding gain account. Because of the short-term nature of temporary investments, it is unlikely that offsetting gains will be recognized.

Disposition of Temporary Investments

When a temporary investment is sold, the gain or loss to be recognized on the sale is the difference between the original acquisition cost and the selling price. Previous valuation adjustments do not enter into the calculation. This follows the view that lower of cost or market is applied to the entire portfolio rather than to specific parts of the portfolio. However, if the whole portfolio of marketable securities is liquidated, the gain or loss will be determined with reference to the net book value of the portfolio.

If, in the previous example, security C was sold for $3,500, a loss of $1,500 would result and would be recognized through the following entry:

Cash	$3,500	
Loss on sale of temporary investments	1,500	
Temporary investments		$5,000
To record the sale of security C		

Accounting for the sale of temporary investments follows that procedure used for the sale of any other assets (except, of course, for inventory); the asset account is written down, the receipt is recognized, and any resulting gain or loss is reported.

RECEIVABLES

Receivables are claims held by the business against others for money or goods and services. Receivables are generated primarily from the sale of goods and services on credit, but they also result from transactions involving loans made to others, rentals, leases, or various types of refunds. Receivables that are collectable within one year or the normal operating cycle of the business are classified as current assets; all other receivables are listed as investments or other receivables in the noncurrent assets section of the balance sheet. Receivables which result from the sale of goods and services in the course of normal opeations are called *trade receivables*. Other types of receivables would be identified by the specific purpose of the transaction, such as loans to employees or interest on loans.

Trade receivables that are not supported by a written promissory note are normally short-term in duration (30 to 90 days) and do not have an explicit interest rate. As discussed in Chapter 5, many receivables bear an implicit interest in the terms of the invoice—such as 2/10, n/30 (2% discount if paid within 10 days but the net amount is due in 30 days).

In contrast, notes receivable are supported by a formal written promise to pay a certain sum (principal) of money at a fixed or determinable future time. Trade notes receivable are often used with goods and services with a high selling price or an extended payment period and for settling outstanding accounts receivable balances. Nontrade notes receivable may arise from transactions involving loans or the sale of noncurrent assets. Most notes provide for a specific interest rate to be charged for the period that the note is outstanding. Notes that do not specify a provision for interest are referred to as noninterest bearing and only the principal amount is due at maturity. Normally, an interest charge is implicitly provided in the terms of such a note. That is, the face amount of the note is higher than the cash value of a comparable transaction; the interest has been added.

Interest terms are usually specified in terms of an annual rate (for simplicity, interest will be calculated on the basis of 360 days per year) and is applied to the principal amount. Interest is calculated by the formula:

$$\text{Interest} = \text{Principal} \times \text{Rate} \times \text{Time}$$

Thus, the interest on a $2,000, 9 percent, ninety-day note would be computed as follows:

$$\text{Interest} = \$2{,}000 \times .09 \times 90 \div 360 = \$45$$

In this case, the amount due at the maturity of the note would be $2,045—the principal plus the interest. Terms specified by the creditor determine whether the computation of interest includes a day for the date that the note was originated and/or the date of replacement.

ACCOUNTING FOR NOTES RECEIVABLE

In the case of interest-bearing notes, the interest revenue accrues, or is earned, over the period of the note. When a note originates in one accounting period and matures in another, an adjusting entry must be made to properly reflect the interest earned during each period. When a note originates and matures in the same period, the interest revenue is recorded at maturity.

To illustrate, assume that on November 1, 19x9, Hawsey Company accepted a $2,000, 9 percent, ninety-day note from a customer in settlement of an open, or outstanding, account receivable. Hawsey Company would record the receipt of the note as follows:

Notes receivable	$2,000	
Accounts receivable		$2,000
To record the transfer of an open account to a note		

As discussed in Chapter 4, if the note extends beyond the end of an accounting period, an adjusting entry is necessary to record the interest revenue earned during the period and to record the interest receivable at the end of the period. If the Hawsey Company's accounting period ended on December 31, the following adjusting entry would be made:

Accrued interest receivable	$30	
Interest revenue		$30
(Calculated as $2,000 × .09 × 60 ÷ 360)		

The entry at the date of collection of the note and interest would be:[1]

Cash	$2,045	
Notes receivable		$2,000
Accrued interest receivable		30
Interest revenue		15
To record the collection of an interest-bearing note		

If the holder of the note is unable to collect from the maker at maturity, the note is termed *dishonored*. Since the holder still has a legal claim to the principal and interest, an entry should be made to record the dishonored note receivable at its maturity value. For example, if the note held by the Hawsey Company proved to be uncollectable, the following entry would be made on the maturity date:

---

[1] If the period of the note had not extended beyond the end of the period, no adjusting entry would have been made. The following entry would have been made on the collection date:

Cash	$2,045	
Notes receivable		$2,000
Interest revenue		45

Notes receivable—dishonored	$2,045	
Notes receivable		$2,000
Accrued interest receivable		30
Interest revenue		15
To record a dishonored note		

If the note is subsequently collected, the notes receivable—dishonored account is eliminated. If the note is ultimately determined to be uncollectable, the amount would be moved from notes receivable—dishonored and written-off against bad debt expense or allowance for doubtful accounts.

DISCOUNTING NOTES RECEIVABLE

A promissory note is a legally negotiable instrument that can be readily transferred between parties. For various reasons, a business may transfer a note receivable to a bank or other financial institution to obtain funds. The transfer is facilitated by the holder of the note endorsing it over to the bank. The process is similar to transferring a check by endorsement. The bank charges interest at a specified interest rate (referred to as the *discount rate*) for the use of its money on the maturity value of the note (principal plus interest). The bank will collect from the maker of the note at maturity. The proceeds received by the business are determined by deducting the amount of interest charged by the bank from the maturity value of the note.

Normally, notes transferred are endorsed with recourse. Recourse means that the endorser is liable to the bank if the maker of the note does not pay the bank at maturity. A contingent, or possible, liability results from discounting notes receivable, and it must be disclosed in the financial statements. A footnote is normally used to make the disclosure. The contingent liability is eliminated at the maturity of the note, when it is paid, or dishonored. If dishonored, the liability will become actual, rather than contingent.

When notes receivable are discounted, the payee receives proceeds calculated in the following manner:

1. Compute the maturity value of the note:

   Maturity Value = Principal + (principal × rate × time)

2. Compute the discount on the maturity value:

   Discount = Maturity Value × Discount Rate × Time to Maturity

3. Compute cash proceeds:

   Proceeds = Maturity Value − Discount

An Example

To illustrate the accounting procedures related to discounting, assume that the Hawsey Company discounted a $2,000, 9 percent, ninety-day note receivable at a bank after thirty days have elapsed at a 12 percent discount rate. The proceeds received by the Hawsey Company are computed as follows:

Maturity value	$2,045.00	[$2,000 + ($2,000 × .09 × 90 ÷ 360)]
Discount (bank interest)	40.90	($2,045 × .12 × 60 ÷ 360)
Proceeds	$2,004.10	

This process may be viewed as a set of financial transactions involving two loans. First, the Hawsey Company loaned $2,000 to a customer for ninety days at 9 percent interest. Subsequently, the Hawsey Company borrowed funds from the bank for sixty days at 12 percent interest. The difference between the initial note and the amount borrowed is the net proceeds received by the Hawsey Company.

When a note is discounted, the payee records the transaction by a debit (increase) to cash and a credit (decrease) to notes receivable. A balancing debit or credit will be made to interest expense or to interest revenue. The Hawsey Company would record the discounting as follows:

Cash	$2,004.10	
Notes receivable		$2,000.00
Interest revenue		4.10
To record discounting a ninety-day, 9 percent note for sixty days at 12 percent		

The interest revenue recorded at the time of discounting is actually the net difference between the interest revenue accrued on the note through maturity less the interest expense charged by the bank from the date of discount to maturity. In some cases (depending on the relationship between the interest rate on the note, the bank discount rate, and the time to maturity), the interest expense charged by the bank may exceed the accrued interest on the note. In these instances, the payee records the net interest on discounting the note. For example, if the Hawsey Company discounted the note on the same date, but the bank discount rate was 15 percent, the proceeds would be $1,993.88 and the transaction would be recorded as follows:

Cash	$1,993.88	
Interest expense	6.12	
Notes receivable		$2,000.00
To record discounting a ninety-day, 9 percent note for sixty days at 15 percent		

Because the payee of the note is contingently liable for the note a footnote disclosure would be made until the note matures. If the note is paid by the maker, the footnote would be removed. However, if the note is dishonored Hawsey Company must fulfill the liability, the following entry would be made:

Notes receivable—dishonored	$2,045	
Cash		$2,045
To record payment on a dishonored note		

SUMMARY

Cash, temporary investments, and receivables are fundamental financial resources of the firm. By its nature, cash is volatile and must be controlled to ensure its effective utilization and its security. Internal controls are an important part of the accounting system and relate to policies, procedures, and activities that are intended to safeguard assets and promote their effective utilization.

One control process requires all cash to be desposited in checking accounts and properly endorsed checks to be used for all disbursements. This action adds to the firm's system of control over cash. Periodically, the bank will report an account balance which, along with the balance shown in the firm's books, must be reconciled to derive the correct cash balance. As a part of the bank reconciliation process, items that should be brought to the attention of the bank will be found along with items that should be recorded in the books of the company. Notifications and adjusting entries should be made.

Many organizations will maintain an accessible supply of cash in a petty cash fund. The purpose of this fund is to pay for incidental items that require cash. The fund is limited to size and is controlled by periodic counts of the cash balance and the voucher receipts.

Temporary investments are made to earn a return on otherwise idle cash balances. The managerial intention is to convert these investments back to cash in the near future. Consequently, they are disclosed as a current asset rather than as a long-term investment. Income is recorded as earned and is accrued at the time of statement preparation. Many times, temporary investments are valued at the lower of cost or market to ensure conservatism in the financial statements.

Receivables represent claims against others that are due in the near future. They are reported as current assets on the balance sheet. Notes receivable represent a formal written document in support of the promise to pay. Notes normally are recorded at their principal amount, and interest is recognized as earned. Notes may be discounted, or sold, to a bank or other financial institution. In these cases, the original holder, or payee, usually is held liable for the payment until it is actually made.

KEY DEFINITIONS

Bank reconciliation—a work sheet that assists in reconciling the cash book balance and the bank balance.

Internal control—a system designed to protect assets and assure their efficient use.

Lower of cost or market—a valuation method that values assets at the lower of cost or market value as of the date of the financial statements.

Petty cash fund—a small quantity of money under the control of an employee to be used in making minor disbursements.

Temporary investments—readily marketable investments that management intends to hold for less than a year.

Trade receivables—receivables from customers resulting from sales or rendering of services.

QUESTIONS

7-1 Identify the individual accounts that may be grouped together on the financial statements under the caption cash.

7-2 Why is restricted cash reported separately from the account cash? What are the implications of failing to classify restricted cash separately?

7-3 What is meant by internal control? Why is this of concern to the accountant dealing with cash?

7-4 Identify the characteristics of a good internal control system. Give an example of each characteristic.

7-5 In what way can a bank checking account assist in providing internal control?

7-6 What is the purpose of a bank reconciliation? Describe the major sections of the reconciliation statement.

7-7 Discuss the nature of journal entries made as a result of completing a bank reconciliation statement.

7-8 For what purpose is a petty cash fund usually established? Describe the nature of controls used to monitor the petty cash fund.

7-9 Temporary investments are made for what purpose? Is there a difference in managerial intent between temporary investments and long-term investments?

7-10 Describe the valuation practice of lower of cost or market as applied to temporary investments. Explain the rationale for applying lower of cost or market to information that will appear on the financial statements.

7-11 Why are notes receivable sometimes discounted? Discounting has sometimes been equated to borrowing? Explain why this is true.

7-12 Is the bank reconciliation process different for business organizations and individual people? Discuss any major differences or similarities.

7-13 Alternatives are available to the accountant in valuing temporary investments. How can meaningful reports result if the information can be influenced by the accountant's judgment?

7-14 Notes and accounts receivable can be discounted, or sold, to financial intermediaries called factors. Explain how the factoring business can be profitable.

EXERCISES

E7-1 Several financial resources are listed below. Identify which ones would be classified as cash. Explain why items not classified as cash were so identified.

a. Coin and currency.
b. A promissory note.
c. Checks.
d. Funds restricted for paying employee bonuses.
e. Savings account deposits.

E7-2 A check is negotiable financial instrument. Identify how each of the following characteristics or features of a check contribute to internal control.

a. Sequential numbering.
b. Printed address of maker.
c. Numerical and written amount.
d. Name of bank.
e. Date.

E7-3 The general form of a bank reconciliation statement has four parts as shown below:

Balance per bank statement
Add: Type A items
Less: Type B items
Correct cash balance

Balance per books
Add: Type C items
Less: Type D items
Correct cash balance

Using the letters A through D, as appropriate, identify where each of the following items would appear in a reconciliation statement.

a. Deposit in transit.
b. Collection of a note by the bank.
c. Outstanding checks.
d. Service charges.
e. NSF check that was returned.
f. Debit memorandum.
g. Credit memorandum.

E7-4 Make the necessary journal entries to record the following petty cash activity:

a. Fund of $1,000 is established.
b. $100 is paid for postage.
c. $200 is paid for supplies.
d. The fund is reimbursed for $300, and vouchers for $100 and $200 are available.
e. The fund is permanently reduced to $500.

E7-5 Management of the Key Company decided to invest some surplus cash until it was needed later in the year. Make the necessary journal entries to record the events described below:

Jan.	15	Bought 100 shares of Lock Company common stock at $12 per share plus $40 brokerage commission.
	20	Received $10 (10 cents a share) as a dividend on the stock.
Feb.	1	Sold fifty shares at $11 per share. No brokerage commission was paid on the sale.

E7-6 The Vest Company has a portfolio of temporary investments. The original cost of these securities including brokerage commissions is as follows: Security G—$7,500, Security M—$20,000, Security C—$15,000. On December 31, the market values of these securities are calculated and used to determine the reported value of temporary investments. The company uses the lower of cost or market valuation method.

Determine the total value of marketable securities to be reported on the balance sheet in each case given below:

	Security		
Case	*G*	*M*	*C*
A	$6,000	$21,000	$13,000
B	5,000	18,000	20,000
C	7,500	19,000	16,000
D	7,000	18,000	14,000

E7-7 The Watson Printing Company accepted a $5,000, 12 percent, ninety-day note from one of its customers on June 1, 19x7.

a. Prepare the journal entries that Watson would make on June 1 to record the acceptance of the note and ninety days later to record its collection.
b. Assume that the Watson Printing Company's fiscal year ends on June 30, 19x7. Prepare the entries that would be made on June 1, June 30, and August 30 relative to this note.

E7-8 The Leaf Company accepted a $1,000, 6 percent, sixty-day note from Ted Bates on January 1. On February 1, the company discounted the note at Watt's s Bank and Trust Company. The bank charged an 8 percent discount rate. On March 1, Leaf was informed that Ted Bates had defaulted on the note. On April 1, Ted Bates settled with Leaf for the full value that was owed. Prepare the journal entries that Leaf Company would make on each date above.

E7-9 On November 1, several notes received from customers of AAA Company were discounted at the First Bank. The bank discount rate was 10 percent. Calculate the net proceeds paid by the bank for each note described below:

a. A $10,000, ninety-day note with 9 percent interest dated October 1.
b. A $4,000, 12 percent, 120-day note dated September 1.
c. A 10 percent, $1,000, sixty-day note dated November 1.

E7-10 Jones Company received a bank statement indicating a balance of $1,250. The company's books indicated a balance of $1,000.

a. Using the supplemental information shown below, prepare a bank reconciliation.
   1. Deposits in transit were $300.
   2. A $20 check for supplies had been erroneously recorded in the journal as $200 by the company.
   3. Checks totalling $400 were not cleared through the bank.
   4. Bank service charges were $30 for the month.

b. What journal entries should be made by the Jones Company?

E7-11 Determine the unknown data in each of the following independent situations using your knowledge of bank reconciliations, assuming that in each case the amounts do reconcile:

	A	*B*	*C*
Balance per books	$600	$14,170	$1,950
Balance per bank	937	13,650	____
Outstanding checks	____	755	640
NSF checks	110	300	220
Notes collected by bank	0	500	100
Bank service charge	10	25	10
Deposit in transit	60	____	370

E7-12 Calculate the proceeds to be received in discounting the following notes receivable:

	Terms of Note			*Discount*	
Note	*Principal*	*Term*	*Rate*	*Rate*	*Time to Maturity*
A	$3,000	90 days	10%	9%	60 days
B	500	60 days	6%	9%	30 days
C	8,000	180 days	8%	8%	30 days
D	1,000	60 days	9%	8%	45 days
E	700	120 days	6%	10%	60 days

E7-13 Record general journal entries for the following transactions involving a petty cash fund.

a. Created the fund for $100.
b. Increased the amount of the fund to $200.
c. Reimbursed the fund for the the following expenses:

Postage	$ 28
Freight fees	108
Supplies	21

d. Reimbursed the fund for the following expenses:

Postage	$ 31
Freight fees	68
Supplies	39

e. Reduced the fund balance to $150.

PROBLEMS

P7-1 The following independent situations relate to the cash controls of various businesses. In each situation, comment on the reasonableness of the procedures and their adequacy in providing internal control over cash. In cases where a control problem might exist, suggest procedures that could rectify the situation.

a. Able Company has expanded rapidly. No specific procedures for handling cash have been developed. "When a problem arises, we'll solve it then" says the president.
b. Because Baker Company is fairly small, the bookkeeper rotates his duties. About once every two weeks, he records cash receipts and disbursements.
c. The Denver Disbursing Company does not use prenumbered checks or a check protector to imprint the amount. The company feels that the bookkeeper has a distinctive handwriting.
d. Mildred Adams, president of a medium-sized firm, opposes any cash audits throughout the year. "Our buiness depends on our employees. To audit their cash would suggest that we don't trust them. We cannot afford to do this."
e. Frank's Bargain store is very concerned about cash controls. Bank deposits are made five times a day as a part of company policy.

P7-2 The Morris Company receives a monthly statement from the National Bank. On June 30, the bank reported a balance of $102,750. On the same date, the company's books showed a balance of $133,460. The following information relates to the reconciliation process:

1. A deposit of $23,000 was mailed to the bank on June 29. It does not appear on the bank statement.
2. A deposit of $11,000 was taken to the bank on June 30. It does not appear on the bank statement.
3. The bank statement included a credit memorandum for $2,200, resulting from the collection by the bank of a note receivable. The note was for $2,000 and provided for $200 interest at maturity.
4. A debit memorandum with the bank statement reported a $20 fee for collecting the note described in (3).
5. Twelve checks, totalling $1,730, were not included in the bank statement.
6. The bank notified the company a check for $300, included in a deposit, had been returned because of insufficient funds.
7. Check 619 included with the bank statement was made payable to Jones Company for supplies. The check had been incorrectly journalized by Morris as $210, but it was actually written for $21.
8. The bank statement showed that three checks written by the Marris Company had been deducted from the Morris Company account. The checks totalled $480.
9. The bank adjusted the account for service charges of $29 for the month.

Required:

a. Prepare a bank reconciliation statement for the company as of June 30.
b. After reviewing the reconciliation statement, prepare any appropriate journal entries for Morris Company. Should Morris take additional actions?

P7-3 The Zebra Company established a petty cash fund to provide a source of cash for small recurring expense items. Each disbursement from the fund required a voucher; vouchers were accumulated and recorded when the fund was replenished. Prepare the three general journal entries that would be made for the following petty cash activities during January:

Jan.	2	Petty cash fund of $300 is established.
	3	$30 paid for postage; $20 for office supplies.
	4	Shipping supplies of $40 were purchased.
	5	$10 paid for postage.
	6	$25 was paid for office supplies.
	9	The petty cash fund was replenished.
	10	$50 was spent for office supplies and $40 for shipping supplies.
	11	$20 paid for postage; a miscellaneous item of $10 was also paid.
	12	$15 was paid to the post office for special handling mail.
	13	Stationary costing $30 was purchased. $20 was paid for service on the office water cooler.
	16	The petty cash fund was replenished.

P7-4 On February 1, Johnson Company invested surplus cash in two temporary investments. The firm bought 100 shares of A Company stock for $5,000 and 100 shares of B Company stock for $4,000. Brokerage costs were $400 on the first purchase and $300 on the last.

B Company declared a dividend of $2 per share which was paid on March 1. The Johnson Company's fiscal year ends on March 31. On that date, A Company stock was selling for $40 per share and B Company stock for $30 per share.

On April 15, Johnson Company sold its stock in A Company for $60 per share and its B Company stock for $50 per share.

Required:

a. Prepare the journal entries that would be made by the Johnson Company on each of the dates identified above.
b. Show how temporary investments would be disclosed on the company's balance sheet on March 31.
c. If the stock in A Company and B Company was not sold on April 15, but held for another year when the market prices were $90 and $30 per share, respectively, how would they be reported and valued on the balance sheet?

P7-5 The Take Company accepted several notes from customers in exchange for food delivery equipment that they sell. Prepare the proper journal entries to record the transactions described below:

Jan.	10	Accepted a $2,000, 8 percent note from Albert Adams due in thirty days.
	15	Accepted a $5,000, 10 percent note from Buddy Baker due in thirty days.
Feb.	9	Collected Adams note plus interest.
	14	Collected Baker note plus interest.
Mar.	1	Accepted a $10,000, 6 percent note from Charles Case due in ninety days.
Apr.	30	Discounted the Charles Case note at the Jones Bank. The discount rate was 9 percent.
June	10	Jones Bank informed Take that Charles Case has defaulted on the note.
	15	The Charles Case note is deemed to be uncollectable.

P7-6 The tables shown below present information about a series of notes. Complete the missing information in each table:

Note	Date Originated	Period	Date Due	Interest Rate	Face Amount	Amount Received
A	March 1	30 days	March 31	?	$1,000	$1,005
B	April 1	60 days	?	12%	2,000	?
C	May 1	?	July 30	10	5,000	?
D	June 1	120 days	?	12	?	1,040

					Discount		
Note	Date Originated	Period	Interest Rate	Face Amount	Date	Rate	Proceeds
E	June 1	60 days	6%	$1,000	July 1	12%	?
F	July 1	120 days	10	2,000	July 31	5%	?
G	May 1	60 days	8	3,000	May 1	8%	?

P7-7 The Quantum Company has reported the following items in its cash account as of December 31, 19x6:

1. Cash balance in checking account—$6,947.
2. Cash balance in savings account—$1,000. The bank reserves the right to require thirty days notice of withdrawal, but has never required such notice for balances below $10,000.
3. Petty cash on hand for office use—$200.
4. Cash balances of $50 in each of six cash registers in its retail store.
5. Postage stamps costing $40.
6. A one-year bank certificate of deposit, costing $5,000, maturing two months after year-end and paying $300 in interest. The bank does not permit withdrawal of the funds prior to maturity.
7. $500 in cash are currently on deposit in a Mexican bank and are temporarily frozen (i.e., may not be withdrawn) because of a local legal dispute.
8. The firm has $8,000 in a fund for use in paying off a long-term liability that falls due in two years. The creditor required these funds to be accumulated in a "sinking" fund.

Required:

a. What is the correct balance of cash for the Quantum Company on December 31, 19x6?
b. What adjusting entry would be required to properly report these amounts?
c. How would the noncash items be classified on the balance sheet—current assets, noncurrent assets, or some other classification?

P7-8 On August 31 the cash account of the AAA Corporation totalled $680. On that date the bank statement received by the firm indicated a balance of $1,040. An analysis of the firm's cash records and the bank statement reveals the following:

1. Deposits in transit on August 31 total $290.
2. Outstanding checks on August 31 total $705.
3. The bank accidentally charged the firm's account with a $110 check drawn on the AA Corporation.
4. Service charges of $5 are shown on the bank statement but unrecorded on the books of the firm.
5. The bank has charge the firm's account for a $90 NSF check.
6. The bank statement also shows that the bank collected a note for the firm, totalling $140 in principal and $10 in interest, and has credited the account for those amounts.

Required:

a. Prepare a bank reconciliation as of August 31.
b. Make the necessary general journal entries to adjust the cash account to its appropriate balance.
c. What other actions shuld be taken in light of this reconciliation?

P7-9 The Ash Company finds itself with substantial amounts of cash on hand during certain times of the year, and normally invests these funds. The Ash Company had the following transactions involving temporary investments during the year.

1. Acquired 100 shares of Terminal, Inc. common stock at a total cost of $3,100.
2. Acquired 200 shares of Aileen, Inc. for $1,000.
3. Received $50 dividend from Terminal, Inc.
4. Acquired 100 shares of IBM for $25,000.
5. Sold the Terminal, Inc. stock for $3,600.
6. Sold the Aileen, Inc. stock for $900.
7. Received a dividend of $250.
8. Acquired 100 shares of Technology, Inc. for $6,000.

Required:

a. Prepare general journal entries to record these transactions.
b. The IBM stock has a fair market value of $23,800 and the Technology stock is worth $5,000 at year-end. Prepare any adjusting entries needed to value these temporary investments at lower of cost or market and show the balance sheet presentation of these items.

Learning Objectives

Chapter 8 presents accounting for inventory. Studying this chapter should enable you to:

1. Describe the differences in recordkeeping associated with use of the perpetual and periodic inventory systems, and define the abbreviation, FOB.
2. Determine inventory values that result from use of FIFO, LIFO, and other cost flow assumptions.
3. Relate inventory values to reported income.
4. Describe the lower of cost or market procedure.
5. Prepare estimates of inventoy values.

8

Inventory Measurement and Reporting

INTRODUCTION

Inventory is a significant component of current assets for most merchandising and many manufacturing businesses. In a merchandising firm, *inventory* generally includes all of the goods that are available for sale to customers in the normal course of business. Manufacturing organizations usually maintain three types of inventories: raw materials, partially completed production, and finished merchandise ready for sale to customers. In addition, all businesses normally hold quantities of supplies, such as office and maintenance supplies, for future use within the organization rather than for sale to customers.

Business inventories are maintained to provide continuity of operations. Merchandise inventories link the acquisition or manufacturing functions and the customer; customer demand can be satisfied with goods from inventory, thus averting delays that would result if customers had to wait for goods to be acquired or manufactured. While customer satisfaction can be increased by stocking large quantities of a variety of goods, the maintenance of such stocks requires a significant investment. Inventory management involves the balancing of opposing forces—increased inventories to satisfy demand and reduced inventories to minimize costs. Inventory accounting systems are designed to provide management with information needed to make intelligent decisions affecting inventory policy. In particular, management must be able to understand the physical flow of inventory items, the accounting flow of costs, and the relationship between inventory value and cost of goods sold.

The impact of inventories on the financial statements is not limited to the balance sheet. As noted in Chapter 6, inventory plays an important role in the measurement of income. Beginning inventory combines with net purchases to equal goods available for sale, most of which becomes cost of goods sold as shown in Illustration 1. Measurements of inventories at year-end not only affect the inventory account on the balance sheet, but also cost of goods sold, and, ultimately, net income. Because ending inventory in one year becomes beginning inventory in the next year, as shown by the arrows in Illustration 1, inventory balances relate to the income statements of a firm for two consecutive years. As a result, the proper determination of inventory has long been recognized by accountants as critical to both the balance sheet and the income statement.

The inventory measurement process involves two steps: first, the physical quantity of each inventory item must be determined and second, the physical quantity must be translated into dollar terms. The discussion in this chapter will focus on these two critical steps in measuring inventory for financial statement purposes.

PHYSICAL FLOWS

Most organizations acquire stocks of merchandise or raw materials from external suppliers. The acquisition process usually starts when the seller receives a *purchase order*. Purchase price, credit terms, and delivery schedules are determined by negotiation, and a firm contract is established. Typically, the inventory of a business includes only those items to which the firm has *legal title*. In most cases, delivery of merchandise is the critical event that indicates passage of title. Thus, the point of delivery is usually used in accounting to determine when a purchase has occurred.

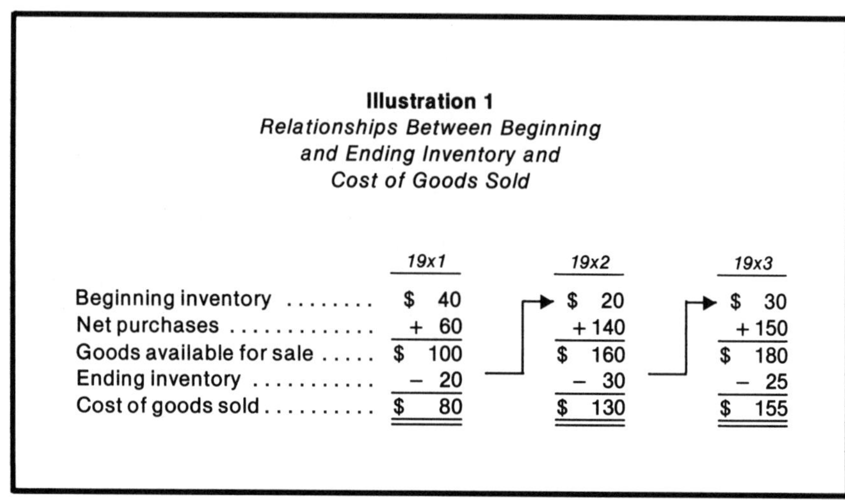

Illustration 1
Relationships Between Beginning and Ending Inventory and Cost of Goods Sold

	19x1	*19x2*	*19x3*
Beginning inventory	$ 40	$ 20	$ 30
Net purchases	+ 60	+ 140	+ 150
Goods available for sale	$ 100	$ 160	$ 180
Ending inventory	− 20	− 30	− 25
Cost of goods sold	$ 80	$ 130	$ 155

Provisions in the agreement between buyer and seller indicate when legal title has passed between them. Unless otherwise specified, the point of delivery hinges on who has responsibility for delivering the purchased goods. If the seller has this responsibility, the purchase does not occur until the goods are received. This condition is commonly referred to as "FOB destination," where FOB stands for "free on board." If the purchaser has the responsibility for delivery, termed "FOB shipping point," legal title passes as soon as the carrier picks up the goods from the seller.

Once the buyer gets title, the merchandise becomes part of the inventory balance and it remains in inventory until it is sold. Several accounting periods may elapse during that time, the physical counts of inventory stocks may be taken at the end of each period to validate the inventory levels. Physical counts and financial values are reconciled in the accounting inventory system. One of the two major systems is generally used to account for inventory. The appropriateness of a perpetual or a periodic system will depend on the organization, its inventory characteristics, and its information needs.

PERPETUAL INVENTORY SYSTEMS

Some companies desire data on the inventory balances at any moment in time. A *perpetual inventory system* facilitates this by providing a running count of the number of units and unit costs of each inventory item. At the heart of such systems are perpetual inventory cards or computer files. The file for an inventory item usually shows the units and dollar value of each purchase, each sale or transfer, and the balance on hand. The perpetual inventory file produces a timely update of inventory activity, including the beginning balance, purchases, sales (at cost), and the current balance. This continuous record is maintained for every transaction involving the inventory item, thus providing a complete activity history. A perpetual inventory card is shown in Illustration 2.

This file relates details concerning inventory activity of part A703, a leg assembly. A balance of 700 units was available at the beginning of the year. Issues of 200, 300, and 100 units were made on January 6, 10, and 15, respectively. An order for 1,000 units was placed on January 10 and received on January 17. An additional 200 units were shipped out on January 18; these units consisted of the remaining 100 units of the beginning balance and 100 units from the newest acquisition. Data about the four shipments during January would be determined from sales invoices, while information about the delivery would be obtained from a receiving report and supported by a copy of the purchase order.

Perpetual inventory records may be maintained manually, mechanically, or by means of a computer. Whatever the means, preparing such records is relatively costly, so they are usually reserved for situations where it is important to have continuous monitoring of inventory. Perpetual records can be used to monitor inventory balances and trigger the reorder procedure.

Illustration 2
Perpetual Inventory File

Part No.: A703	Weight	Class	Reorder Point	Reorder Quantity
Description: Leg Assembly	2.5 lbs.	A761	200	1,000

Date	Received (Purchased) Units	Received (Purchased) Unit Cost	Shipped (Sales) Units	Shipped (Sales) Unit Cost	Balance (Inventory) Units	Balance (Inventory) Unit Cost	Balance (Inventory) Total Cost
1/1	Balance				700	$5	$3,500
1/6			200	$5	500	5	2,500
1/10	Ordered	1,000					
			300	5	200	5	1,000
1/15			100	5	100	5	500
1/17	1,000	5.50			{ 100	5	
					1,000	5.50	6,000
1/18			100	5			
			100	5.50	900	5.50	4,950

For example, the illustrated file designates a reorder quantity; when the balance falls below this point, an inventory clerk or computer would initiate a purchase order.

Perpetual inventory files also represent subsidiary inventory accounts. That is, the sum of the balances on the individual perpetual inventory files will equal the balance in the inventory control account. Formal journal entries would reflect the same information as appeared on the perpetual inventory cards. A summary entry to reflect the four decreases in inventory that accompany transfers of goods to customers would appear as follows:

Cost of goods sold	$4,050	
Inventory		$4,050
To record issuance of 700 units @ $5 and 100 units @ $5.50		

A summary entry to reflect the acquisition of inventory would appear as follows:

Inventory	$5,500	
Accounts payable		$5,500
To record the acquisition of 1,000 units @ $5.50		

Periodic physical counts should be taken to verify the perpetual inventory records. Usually, an annual count will be made before the financial statements are prepared.

PERIODIC INVENTORY SYSTEMS

Periodic inventory systems do not require detailed records on specific inventory items. No ongoing count is kept of the actual usage of these items. Instead, *periodic inventory measurement* is based on physical counts of the goods on hand at the end of each period. The number of units on hand is multiplied by the purchase cost per unit (determined from the accounting records) to compute the total dollar value of the end of period inventory. Thus, the balance of goods on hand is not known until the last day of the period. The data in Illustration 2 would be recast as follows if a periodic system was used:

	Beginning Inventory	$3,500
+	Purchases	5,500
	Available for Sale	$9,000
−	Ending Inventory	4,950
	Cost of Goods Sold	$4,050

Once the ending inventory is physically counted and a total cost determined, the cost of goods sold can be calculated by subtracting the ending inventory from the cost of goods available for sale.

Remember that the journal entries used with a periodic inventory system differ from those used with a perpetual system. Purchases are recorded in separate account. Using the example data from above, the following entry would be made.

Purchases	$5,500	
Accounts payable		$5,500

The inventory account is not changed during the period and therefore it continually reflects the beginning inventory balance. At the end of the year, a physical count is taken, and the inventory account is adjusted via the process of adjusting journal entries as follows:

Inventory—ending	$4,950	
Cost of goods sold	4,050	
Purchases		$5,500
Inventory—beginning		3,500

THE VALUATION PROCESS

Inventory value is determined by multiplying the physical quantity of goods in inventory by a per unit dollar amount. Accountants generally value assets on the balance sheet at their cost to the firm, and inventory is no exception. In theoretical applications of the cost principle, the term *cost includes all expenditures incurred to bring an item to its existing condition and location.* Thus, in addition to the invoice price of the merchandise, inventory costs should include transportation charges, transit insurance costs, material handling, and assembly labor costs. Cost should be reduced for purchase discounts.

As a practical matter, many businesses use separate accounts to retain information on each element of cost. The invoice cost of inventory enters the inventory account in perpetual systems (or the purchases account in periodic systems) while accounts titled freight-in, transit insurance, materials handling, etc., collect information on other cost elements. These separate accounts provide management with information useful for control and decision-making purposes (e.g., should purchases be air-freighted or trucked-in). Often these costs are classified as expenses and are reported in the income statement for the period in which they were incurred. Thus, they may not always be included in the inventory as an asset because the bookkeeping cost of tracing such cost to inventory items is greater than the expected benefit of such tracings.

Although the concept of cost valuation is relatively simple, its application is not without complications. No difficulty exists if the cost of inventory items is constant. If forty units were sold and fifty units remained in inventory, the constant cost would be multiplied by the units to determine the cost of goods sold and the ending inventory value. However, if costs change during the period, the accountant must decide which cost to assign to which units. In a competitive economy, it is unusual for unit costs to remain constant over time.

To address changing prices, accountants have developed cost-flow methods and assumptions, including:

1. Specific identification.
2. Average cost.
3. First-in, first-out (FIFO).
4. Last-in, first-out (LIFO).

Each method assigns a different cost to a given physical quantity of goods under conditions of changing prices. The computation of inventory values using each of these methods is described and explained below. The objective of each method is to value the ending inventory and, as a consequence, the cost of goods sold.

Specific Identification

Accuracy is greatest if actual unit costs are accumulated and associated with specific units. *Specific identification* requires that a record is made of the acquisition cost of each inventory item by coding the cost on the item itself or by maintaining a perpetual record of items by serial number. As a sale is completed, the specific unit cost is identified with the specific unit sold and recorded as a cost of sales, thus excluding it from inventory.

For example, a car dealer might purchase an automobile and prepare an inventory card identifying it by the manufacturer's serial number. In addition to the cost, the card could list other useful sales information, such as optional equipment. If the car remains unsold at the inventory date, its cost is easily determinable for valuation purposes. When it is eventually sold, the cost of a specific automobile will become part of the cost of goods sold and the inventory card will be placed in a reference file.

In contrast to the above situation, a supermarket could not begin to maintain adequate records for the thousands of items it maintains in its inventory. Normally, the specific identification method is practical where:

1. A relatively few number of items are included in inventory.
2. The units are readily identifiable by a serial number or other unique characteristics.
3. Unit costs are high.

The expense of keeping detailed records must be evaluated in terms of benefits. Usually, minimum benefit results from extensive detail about low unit-cost items.

Average Cost Method

One cost-flow assumption that may be used in determining inventory cost is the average annual unit cost to the firm. The *average cost method* allocates the cost of goods available for sale between sales (cost of goods sold) and the ending inventory on a weighted average basis. Assume that there are ten units available for sale and that five different prices were paid for them ($70, 70, 60, 60, 50, 50, 40, 40, 30, 30) for a total cost of $500. If there are three units remaining in inventory, the pro rata distribution of cost would be:

$$\text{Inventory} = \tfrac{3}{10} \times \$500 = \$150$$
$$\text{Cost of Sales} = \tfrac{7}{10} \times \$500 = \$350$$

This result is usually achieved using the following computational process:

1. Average unit cost is:

$$\frac{\text{Cost of Goods Available for Sale}}{\text{Units Available for Sale}} = \frac{\$500}{10} = \$50$$

2. Total average cost is:

Cost of Sales (7 × $50)	=	$350
Ending Inventory (3 × $50)	=	150
Cost of Goods Available for Sale	=	$500

The average unit cost of $50 is a weighted average, since it is based on total cost and total units involved for the period.

Illustration 3 presents information about the inventory of the Redfern Corporation. If a periodic inventory system were used, inventory calculations would be made once a year. The average unit cost for the year would be calculated as follows:

Illustration 3
Redfern Corporation
Inventory Cost Information

Date		Units	Unit Cost	Total Cost
January	Beginning inventory	100	$5	$ 500
February	Purchase	50	7	350
June	Purchase	20	8	160
October	Purchase	30	9	270
	Available for sale	200		$1,280
	Sales (at cost)	50		A*
December	Inventory	150		B*

*The determination of unit cost and total sales cost is a function of the cost flow assumption.

$$\frac{\text{Cost of Goods Available for Sale}}{\text{Units Available for Sale}} = \frac{\$1{,}280}{200} = \$6.40$$

This result becomes part of the cost of goods sold calculation. During the year, fifty units were sold. Their value is as follows:

Average Unit Cost × Units Sold
= $6.40 × 50
= $320

The ending inventory is calculated as follows:

Goods available for sale	$1,280
Ending inventory—weighted average (150 units @ $6.40)	960
Cost of goods sold	$ 320

First-In, First-Out Method

The first-in, first-out, or *FIFO* method, makes the assumption that the first costs into the inventory (the oldest costs) are the first costs out of the inventory. Thus, the earliest costs incurred during the year are attached to the earliest units sold. Consequently, the ending inventory is priced at the most recent or latest unit costs paid by the firm. Some justification for using FIFO is that inventory values reported on the balance sheet should approximate current costs.

Many times, FIFO will approximate the actual flow of goods through the firm. The first units placed in stock are often the first units sold. However, the method is used to measure cost flows and is applicable regardless of the physical flow of goods. Thus, the cost-flow assumption, not the actual physical flow, determines the measurement method to be used.

In the Redfern Corporation example, FIFO assumes that the $5 units are sold first and the $9 units sold last. The inventory and cost of goods sold would be determined as follows:

Goods available for sale				$1,280
Ending inventory—FIFO:				
Units		*Cost*		
50	@	$5	$250	
50	@	7	350	
20	@	8	160	
30	@	9	270	1,030
Cost of goods sold				$ 250

Last-In, First-Out Method

The last-in, first-out, or *LIFO* method makes the cost-flow assumption that the units costs paid most recently (last) are the first ones to be attached to the goods sold. This supports the view that the cost of sales should be measured at the most recent costs paid during the period for purchases. This is the opposite view of FIFO. Even though the LIFO cost-flow assumption rarely reflects the physical flow of goods, it is a widely used method because it often results in a realistic matching of current inventory costs with sales revenue. In doing this, however, it does distort the balance sheet value of inventory, reporting the oldest costs as inventory value.

In the Redfern Corporation example, LIFO assumes that the costs associated with the latest acquisitions should be used to determine the cost of goods sold. Inventory and cost of goods sold would be calculated as follows:

Goods available for sale				$1,280
Ending inventory—LIFO:				
Units		*Cost*		
100	@	$5	$500	
50	@	7	350	850
Cost of goods sold				$ 430

COMPARISON OF COST FLOW ASSUMPTIONS

The four cost flow assumptions discussed above are all acceptable methods for valuing inventories. Firms can generally choose whichever method they prefer since all are generally accepted. However, they will produce different results whenever unit costs vary over time.

The Redfern Corporation example has shown that the cost-flow assumption will influence both the ending inventory and the cost of goods sold calculation. This impact will be carried through to the income statement and the balance sheet. Illustration 4 shows this effect for three of the methods.

Illustration 4
Redfern Corporation
Cost Flow Comparisons

	Partial Income Statements Using		
	Average Cost	*FIFO*	*LIFO*
Sales (50 units @ $12)	$ 600	$ 600	$ 600
Cost of goods sold:			
Beginning inventory	$ 500	$ 500	$ 500
Purchases	780	780	780
Available for sale	$1,280	$1,280	$1,280
Ending inventory*	960	1,030	850
Cost of goods sold	$ 320	$ 250	$ 430
Gross profit	$ 280	$ 350	$ 170

*Ending inventory will be reported as a current asset on the balance sheet.

Note that the FIFO method, in a period of *rising prices*, results in the highest net income. LIFO yields the lowest net income, while the average cost method falls in the middle. The differences in gross profit are equal to the differences in values assigned to ending inventory. That is, the FIFO cost of goods sold is $180 *lower* than the LIFO cost of foods sold, and the FIFO inventory is $180 *higher* than the LIFO inventory. Thus, the FIFO method defers some cost to future accounting periods. In this example, FIFO states the inventory at the most recent prices, which are higher, whereas the LIFO method includes the most recent costs in the cost of sales and prices the inventory at the older unit costs, which are lower. FIFO includes the more current costs of doing business on the balance sheet while LIFO tends to place these costs on the income statement. The average method tends to be in the middle of these extremes.

In periods of *falling prices*, the distinction between LIFO and FIFO will reverse. FIFO, using older, higher costs, will result in the lowest net income, while LIFO will yield a higher income amount.

COST FLOW IN PERPETUAL SYSTEMS

Perpetual inventory systems require a continuous determination of unit costs to facilitate updating the inventory records. The average cost method and the LIFO method can result in differences if a perpetual, instead of a periodic, system is used. Consider the following set of transactions.

Date	*Transaction*	*Units*	*Unit Cost*	*Total Cost*
Jan. 10	Purchase	50	$4	$200
12	Purchase	50	6	300
14	Sale 1	(60)		
17	Purchase	40	7	280
18	Sale 2	(20)		

Average Cost Method

The average cost method will generally produce different results under a perpetual system than under a periodic system. Because costs are determined currently on a perpetual system, the calculation of the average cost for or sale can consider only those costs incurred to-date.

Two rules govern the assignment of costs to inventory and goods sold under the average cost method for perpetual inventory systems:

1. A new average cost is calculated each time new units are purchased.
2. The cost of goods sold determined by multiplying the number of units sold by the current average cost per unit.

This method is frequently called the *moving' weighted average* method when applied to a perpetual inventory system.

The illustrated data would result in two calculations and different unit valuations for the two sales. These calculations and the results are shown in the perpetual inventory card shown in Illustration 5.

On January 12, a weighted average was taken, and the unit cost was revised up to $5 per unit (see calculation in footnote). Sales before this date would have been costed at $4 per unit. On the date of the next purchase, January 17, a new average is made and the per unit cost is revised to $6 per unit.

LIFO Method

The LIFO method of determining inventory cost will differ between the periodic and perpetual inventory systems. This results from LIFO values being based on the cost of the most recent acquisitions. Under a perpetual system, sales are valued at the most recent costs to the date of the sale, instead of the most recent costs *incurred during the year*.

The example data is used to show perpetual valuations in Illustration 6. The ending inventory is valued at $300 and the cost of goods sold is $480 (50 @ $6 + 10 @ $4 + 20 @ $7). If a periodic system were used, cost of goods sold would be 520 (40 @ $7 and 40 @ $6), and the ending inventory would be valued at $260 (50 @ $4 + 10 @ $6).

Illustration 5
Perpetual Inventory and Average Cost

Date	Received (Purchased)		Shipped (Sales)		Balance (Inventory)		
	Units	*Unit Cost*	*Units*	*Cost*	*Units*	*Unit Cost*	*Total Cost*
1/10	50	$4			50	$4	$200
1/12	50	6			100	5*	500
1/14			60	$5	40	5	200
1/17	40	7			80	6†	480
1/18			20	6	60	6	360

*Average Cost = Total Cost ÷ Total Units
= $500 ÷ 100
= $5

†Average Cost = Total Cost ÷ Total Units
= $480 ÷ $80
= $6

Although the inventory system can lead to differences when the LIFO and weighted average methods are used, FIFO will not differ under a periodic or a perpetual inventory system. Based on the earliest costs in the inventory, FIFO valuations will use the same data regardless of the inventory systems.

INVENTORY ON THE BALANCE SHEET

Merchandise inventory is reported in the current asset section of the balance sheet, typically after accounts receivable. As with all financial statement presentations, it is important to provide users with sufficient information. Consequently, balance sheet disclosures of inventory usually include a description of the cost flow assumption employed and the valuation method used. This information may be noted parenthetically or included in a footnote.

The following example extracts part of the balance sheet of the Redfern Corporation:

Illustration 6
Perpetual Inventory and LIFO

	Received (Purchased)		Shipped (Sales)		Balance (Inventory)		
Date	Units	Unit Cost	Units	Cost	Units	Unit Cost	Total Cost
1/10	50	$4			50	$4	$200
1/12	50	6			{50	4	
					50	6	500
1/14			50	$6			
			10	4	40	4	160
1/17	40	7			{40	4	
					40	7	440
1/18			20	7	{40	4	
					20	7	300

Redfern Corporation
Balance Sheet
January 31, 19x6

Assets

Current assets:		
Cash		$570
Accounts receivable	$129	
Less: Allowance for bad debts	19	110
Merchandise inventory		
(at cost using LIFO method).		300

If inventory is pledged as collateral for loans (or subject to other restrictions) that may have an impact on the decisions of financial statement users, full disclosure should be made.

LOWER OF COST OR MARKET

Most valuations reported on the balance sheet are based on the *historical cost* of the particular item. The inventory valuation methods discussed so far are based on the historical cost of the inventory items. However, accountants became concerned that a reduction in the *fair market value* of inventory below its *historical cost* (acquisition cost) to the firm could cause the financial statements to be misleading. Inventory could be valued on the balance sheet at a cost that exceeds its market value.

To respond to this concern, a *lower of cost or market convention* was developed as an alternative valuation technique. Lower of cost or market results in inventory reported on the balance sheet at the lower of its cost or fair market value. This leads to the recognition of losses at the time the loss occurs (value declines), instead of in later periods when the inventory is sold.

The adjustment is calculated by comparing the cost of individual items, groups of items, or the entire inventory, with the market price or replacement cost of those inventory items. Replacement cost is the amount that the firm must pay now to acquire similar goods. This process is shown below, comparing individual inventory items, which is the most common approach in practice.

Item	*Original Cost*	*Market Value*	*Number of Units in Ending Inventory*	*Total Cost*	*Total Market Value*	*Total Lower of Cost or Market*
A	.20	.25	1,000	$ 200	$ 250	$ 200
B	1.00	.80	100	100	80	80
C	5.00	6.00	200	1,000	1,200	1,000
D	4.00	3.00	300	1,200	900	900
E	6.00	8.00	100	600	800	600
Total lower of cost or market				$3,100		$2,780

In this case, inventory would be valued at $2,780 on the balance sheet. The difference between the cost ($3,100) and the lower of cost or market valuation ($2,780) would be reported on the income statement of separate cost item and identified as "loss from reduction of inventory to the lower of cost or market" ($320). As with other valuation methods, lower of cost or market provides a full accounting of all inventory costs; they are included in the balance sheet or reported on the income statement.

Lower of cost or market is defended on the grounds that it results in conservative financial statement presentations and is not unreasonably difficult to apply. It is commonly used in current financial accounting practice.

INVENTORY ESTIMATION

Periodic inventory systems are dependent on a physical count of the goods on hand to properly value the inventory. Physical counts are time-consuming and costly and often are taken only once a year to prepare the annual financial statements. However, many companies using periodic inventory systems need inventory data on an interim basis. Inventory valuation estimates can be made for these interim statements rather than making a physical count of all inventory. The most common estimating technique is the *gross profit method.*

This method makes use of the ratio of gross profit to sales:

$$\text{Gross Profit Ratio} = \text{Gross Profit} \div \text{Sales}$$

The basic assumption underlying the gross profit method is that the gross profit ratio of the immediately preceding period is a reasonable approximation of the current period's ratio. The estimated ratio is used to compute the total gross profit, given a level of total sales. The cost of sales and ending inventory are then calculated in that order.

To illustrate, assume that a firm's accounting records indicate the following account balances at the end of January:

	January	*Prior Year*
Sales	$200,000	$2,200,000
Purchases	125,000	
Beginning inventory	24,000	
Gross profit		660,000
Operating expenses	22,000	

These amounts can partially complete the following income statement:

Sales		$200,000
Cost of sales:		
Beginning inventory	$ 24,000	
Purchases	125,000	
Available for sale	$149,000	
Ending inventory	?	
Cost of sales		?
Gross profit		?
Operating expenses		$ 22,000
Net income		$?

Last year, the firm earned a gross profit of $660,000 on sales of $2,200,000. Consequently, the gross profit ratio is:

$$\text{Gross Profit Ratio} = \$660{,}000 \div \$2{,}200{,}000 = .30$$

By assuming that the gross profit ratio is consistent, current estimations may be made. The income statement will be completed as follows:

Sales		$200,000	
Cost of sales:			
Beginning inventory	$ 24,000		
Purchases	125,000		
Available for sale	$149,000		
Ending inventory	9,000 (3)		
Cost of sales		140,000	(2)
Gross profit		$ 60,000	(1)
Operating expenses		22,000	
Net income		$ 38,000	

These amounts were determined by the following steps:

1. Gross Profit = Gross Profit Ratio × Sales
   = .30 × $200,000
   = $60,000
2. Cost of Sales = Sales − Gross Profit
   = $200,000 − $60,000
   = $140,000
3. Inventory = Available for Sale − Cost of Sales
   = $149,000 − $140,000
   = $9,000

These calculations are estimates. If the gross profit percentage changes greatly, or if the inventory mix is composed of items with varying gross profit percentages, adjustments may be required to produce reliable estimates of the results of operations for the interim period.

SUMMARY

Inventories are important items on the financial statements of most firms. By virtue of their size in relation to total assets and their role in the measurement of net income, proper accounting for inventory is critical if the firm's financial statements are to be meaningful.

There are two aspects of inventory measurement: (1) determining the physical quantity, and (2) assigning a dollar value. Merchandise should be included in inventory only if the firm has legal title. The most common inventory system in use—the periodic system—determines inventory balances at year-end only, by taking a physical count and adjusting the account balance for items in transit. A perpetual inventory system maintains a continuous count of inventory on hand.

Inventory is valued at either its cost or the lower of its cost or market value. Because a specific identification of costs of units sold is often impractical, the assignment of costs goods sold may be made on the basis of several inventory cost-flow assumptions—weighted average, FIFO, and LIFO. The weighted average method assigns average costs to sales, while the FIFO method assigns the earliest incurred costs to goods sold and the LIFO method assigns the latest incurred costs to goods sold. These methods may be used with either periodic or perpetual inventory systems.

In accounting for a periodic inventory system, merchandise acquired during the year is recorded in a purchases account. No attempt is made to keep the inventory account balance current. A perpetual system maintains a current inventory account balance, increasing the account for purchases and decreasing it for the cost of goods sold as these events occur.

The balance sheet presentation of inventory requires full disclosure of all relevant information about the inventory, including valuation technique and flow assumptions. For interim financial statement purposes, firms using a periodic inventory system often estimate inventory balances using the gross profit method, instead of counting all units each month or quarter.

KEY DEFINITIONS

Average cost method—a cost flow method that determines the weighted average cost of items available for sale and assigns this cost to inventory and cost of goods sold.

FIFO cost method—a cost flow method that assigns the cost of the earliest goods available for sale to cost of goods sold.

Gross profit method—an inventory estimation method that determines the cost of inventory by applying recent gross profit ratio data to estimate cost of goods sold.

Inventory—goods that are available for sale to customers or for consumption in business operations.

LIFO cost method—a cost flow method that assigns the cost of the most recently acquired goods available for sale to the cost of goods sold.

Lower of cost or market—an inventory valuation method that values inventory at the lower of the inventory's cost or current replacement value.

Periodic inventory system—a system that determines inventory value only periodically either through a physical count of inventory or the use of an inventory estimation method.

Perpetual inventory system—a system that provides a running count of the number of units, unit costs, and total cost for each inventory item.

Specific identification—a cost flow method that specifically identifies inventory items and their specific cost.

QUESTIONS

8-1 What constitutes "inventory" for financial statement purposes?

8-2 Is the impact of the measurement of year-end inventory balances felt on the balance sheet, income statement, or both? Explain.

8-3 At what point in the process of purchasing merchandise are these goods considered inventory of the firm for financial statement purposes?

8-4 What do the terms "FOB shipping point" and "FOB destination" mean? What role do they play in inventory measurement?

8-5 Identify two steps in determining end-of-year inventory balances for accounting purposes?

8-6 Describe a perpetual inventory system.

8-7 What is a periodic inventory system?

8-8 What cost-flow methods are used to value inventory for financial statement purposes?

8-9 Relate the cost-flow assumption to the inventory valuation process.

8-10 List and describe the major cost-flow assumptions.

8-11 Which cost-flow assumption generally results in *higher* net income being reported during a period of consistently rising prices: FIFO, LIFO, or weighted average? Why?

8-12 For which of the following inventory cost-flow assumptions are identical costs assigned to ending inventory under periodic and perpetual inventory systems?

a. Specific identification.
b. Weighted average.
c. FIFO.
d. LIFO.

8-13 What information about inventories should be reported on the balance sheet?

8-14 Why do accountants abandon the historical cost principle in allowing ending inventory to be valued at lower cost or market?

8-15 If a periodic inventory system is used, and physical inventory is taken only annually, how can the firm prepare monthly or quarterly financial statements?

EXERCISES

E8-1 Which of the following items would be included in Bakely Corporation's inventory for June 30, 19x5?

a. One hundred units of part A106, ordered on June 21, 19x5, from a supplier, at terms FOB destination. Shipping documents show the units were shipped on June 29 and received July 7.
b. Two hundred units of part A200, ordered on June 28, 19x5, from a supplier at terms FOB shipping point. Shipping documents show the units were shipped on July 6 and received on July 19.
c. Three hundred units of Bakely Corporation's product, sold to customer at terms FOB shipping point. Bakely shipped the goods on June 29 and the goods were received by the customer on July 5.

E8-2 Anson Brothers uses a periodic inventory system. Give the journal entries necessary to adjust the balance in inventory and close the purchases account at year-end, given the following data:

Beginning inventory	$102,000
Purchases	400,000
Ending inventory	88,000

E8-3 A summary of perpetual inventory cards for Jake's Auto Service shows the following totals for the month:

Cost of Sales	$15,800
Purchases	16,200

Required:

Give the summary entries to record these totals in the firm's general journal.

E8-4 Which of the following costs are properly considered costs of inventory for a retail clothing store?

a. Cost of merchandise purchased from supplier.
b. Salesman's salary.
c. Freight cost in deliverying merchandise to retail store.
d. Insurance charge made by delivery firm for coverage of inventory in transit to retail outlet.
e. Materials handling costs.
f. President's salary.
g. Insurance on retail building.

E8-5 Assume the following data for the month:

Beginning Inventory and Purchases	Date	Unit Cost	Total Cost
100	June 1	$3.00	$ 300
200	June 19	3.20	640
300	June 26	3.50	1,050

Required:

a. Calculate the cost of goods sold if 400 units were sold, a periodic inventory system is used, and the FIFO inventory cost-flow assumption is used.
b. Calculate cost of goods sold under a perpetual inventory system assuming all sales were made on June 28.

E8-6 Calculate the weighted average cost of units in inventory for the following data, assuming no sales were made this month.

Date	Beginning Inventory and Purchases	Unit Cost	Total Cost
Aug. 1	200	$300	$60,000
Aug. 12	300	330	99,000
Aug. 26	100	100	35,000

E8-7 Determine the cost of goods sold and the cost of ending inventory for the firm data shown in E8-6, assuming the firm sells 270 units during the period and uses a weighted average cost-flow assumption and a periodic inventory system.

E8-8 Complete the blanks in the following perpetual inventory card assuming that the weighted average cost-flow assumption is in use.

	Purchases		Sales		Balance		
Date	Units	Cost	Units	Cost	Units	Unit Cost	Total Cost
Beginning					10	$3.00	$30.00
1/6	30	$4.00			40	____	____
1/8			5	____	35	____	____
1/9			15	____	20	____	____
1/10	20	4.25			40	____	____

E8-9 Calculate the cost of goods sold and ending inventory from the following data assuming that a periodic inventory system is in use and the following cost-flow assumptions are used: (a) LIFO, (b) FIFO, and (c) weighted average.

	Units	Unit Cost	Total Cost
Beginning inventory.	110	$3.00	$330
Sold—January 5.	70		
Purchased—January 8	200	4.00	800
Sold—January 9.	100		
Purchased—January 15	200	4.50	900
Sold—January 20.	150		
Purchased—January 27	100	4.80	480

E8-10 Repeat E8-9 assuming the company uses a perpetual inventory system.

E8-11 Fill in the blanks in the following perpetual inventory card assuming that the LIFO cost-flow assumption is used by this firm.

	Purchases		Sales		Balance		
Date	Units	Unit Cost	Units	Unit Cost	Units	Unit Costs	Total Costs
1/1					200	$3.00	$600
1/6			20	____	180	____	____
1/8	100	$3.25			____	____	____
					____	____	____
1/10			30	____	____	____	____
					____	____	____
1/18			70	____	____	____	____
			10	____	____	____	____

E8-12 Fill in the blanks for the cost of goods sold section of three income statements, given the data below.

	Firm X	*Firm Y*	*Firm Z*
Beginning inventory	$ 3,500	$175,000	$ 620,000
Purchases	______	600,000	1,380,000
Ending inventory....	5,000	______	260,000
Cost of goods sold ..	20,500	710,000	______

E8-13 Calculate the lower of cost or market valuation for the following independent cases.

Inventory Item	*Number of Units*	*Unit Cost*	*Unit Fair Market Value*
A	200	$ 1.10	$ 2.00
B	300	1.00	1.20
C	150	2.10	1.50
D	400	10.00	12.00
E	300	9.00	8.00
F	100	8.00	6.00

E8-14 Estimate ending inventory using the gross profit method. The firm's gross profit ratio is 30 percent and the following data are available:

Net purchases	$300,000
Sales	480,000
Beginning inventory	80,000

E8-15 In the following independent situations, calculate the lower of cost or market valuation for inventory, comparing individual inventory items, and give any general journal entries necessary to properly report the lower of cost or market valuation:

Case A:

Item	*Number of Units*	*Unit Cost*	*Unit Fair Market Value*
A	300	$3	$6
B	140	8	7
C	110	9	8

Case B:

Item	*Number of Units*	*Unit Cost*	*Unit Fair Market Value*
A	110	$ .60	$ .85
B	160	3.50	5.00
C	210	4.00	6.00

Case C:

Item	*Number of Units*	*Unit Cost*	*Unit Fair Market Value*
A	60	$1	$3.00
B	70	2	1.50
C	80	3	4.00

E8-16 Calculate ending inventory and cost of goods sold for the following perpetual inventory data, assuming a LIFO inventory flow assumption is used:

	Beginning Inventory and Purchases		
Date	*Units*	*Cost*	*Sales Units*
Dec. 1	100	$5	
7	400	6	
10			50
12			70
16	200	7	
21			500
28	50	8	

E8-17 Prepare the necessary general journal entries to account for the following transactions and to properly report inventory and cost of goods sold at year-end assuming: (1) a perpetual inventory system is used, and (2) a periodic inventory system is used.

a. Beginning inventory balance was $12,000.
b. Acquired inventory costing $2,500 on account.
c. Sold inventory costing $6,000 for $9,000 in cash.
d. Acquired inventory costing $15,000.
e. Sold inventory costing $3,000 for $4,500.

PROBLEMS

P8-1 The following data is taken from the financial records of Columbia Company for 19x1 and 19x2:

19x1:

a. Net sales......................	$180,000
b. Beginning inventory	21,000
c. Net purchases	158,000
d. Ending inventory	31,000
e. Operating expenses	29,000

19x2:

a. Net sales......................	$226,000
b. Net purchases	165,000
c. Ending inventory	30,000
d. Operating expenses	35,000

Required:

Prepare the income statements for Columbia Company for 19x1 and 19x2 in good form.

P8-2 The following financial data were abstracted from the records of Fern Company which uses a periodic inventory system:

Beginning inventory	$ 306,000
Purchases	1,140,000
Cash	261,000
Accounts receivable	300,000
Prepaid expenses	19,000
Allowance for bad debts	3,000
Ending inventory determined by physical count, valued at cost using LIFO	280,000

Required:

a. Give the necessary adjusting entries to account for inventory and cost of goods sold.
b. Prepare the current asset section of the balance sheet in good form for Fern Company, year 19x7.

P8-3 Flint is in the retail sporting goods business. During the current year, Flint had the following transactions for sailboats.

	Units	Unit Price
Beginning inventory	20	$395/ea.
Sold—January 6	10	
Purchased—February 7	40	429/ea.
Purchased—May 9	50	445/ea.
Sold—June 3	50	
Purchased—July 17	40	455/ea.
Sold—August 8	50	
Purchased—September 14	20	470/ea.

Required:

Calculate the cost of the ending inventory of sailboats, using these cost flow and system assumptions:

a. FIFO, periodic.
b. Weighted average, periodic.
c. LIFO, perpetual.

P8-4 Justin is a small wholesaler who currently deals in just two products, using a periodic inventory system. There are 350 units of product A and 350 units of product B on hand at year-end. Beginning inventories and purchases of these products during the year were as follows:

	Product A		Product B	
	Units	Unit Cost	Units	Unit Cost
Beginning inventory	100	$500	200	$260
Purchase one	200	520	300	240
Purchase two	500	550	400	230
Purchase three	200	570	200	220
Purchase four			100	200
Total	1,000		1,200	

Required:

a. Calculate cost of goods sold and ending inventory for product A and product B separately, using these cost flow assumptions:

   1. FIFO.
   2. Weighted average.
   3. LIFO.

b. What general conclusions can you draw about the relative effects of LIFO and FIFO on reported net income in a period of rising prices and a period of falling prices?

P8-5 Hornbeck Company uses a perpetual inventory system. The beginning balance, purchases, and sales for one of its products are given below:

	Flywheel—Type B			
Date	Transaction	Units	Unit Cost	Total Cost
Beginning balance		200	$3	$ 600
January 22	Sold	100		
February 14	Purchased	400	4	1,600
March 15	Sold	300		
May 9	Purchased	200	4	800
May 15	Sold	200		
July 22	Purchased	300	5	1,500
August 18......	Sold	200		
October 15	Purchased	200	6	1,200
November 18 ...	Sold	200		

Required:

a. Calculate cost of goods sold for this product using the: (1) FIFO, and (2) LIFO cost flow assumptions.
b. Recalculate the cost of goods sold assuming that a periodic inventory system was used.
c. Explain any differences you found in parts (a) and (b).

P8-6 Quentin Fabricating Company uses a perpetual inventory system to account for its inventory. Below is data from a perpetual inventory record for one of its products:

	Purchases		Sales		Balance		
Date	Units	Cost	Units	Unit Cost	Units	Unit Cost	Total Cost
Beginning inventory					200	$20	$4,000
3/16			80	____	120	____	____
4/8	120	$30			240	____	____
4/22			140	____	100	____	____
7/10	100	35			200	____	____
8/10			120	____	80	____	____
11/15	120	40			200	____	____

Required:

a. Fill in the blanks on the perpetual inventory record assuming a weighted average cost flow assumption is used.
b. Give the necessry general journal entries to account for these purchases and sales assuming that the sales price is $50 per unit.

P8-7 Bedly Company has three products in its wholesale inventory:

Product	Unit Cost	Unit Value	Units in Ending Inventory
X	$29	$26	3,000
Y	40	60	4,700
Z	59	80	2,600

Bedly uses a periodic inventory system to account for its inventory.

Required:

a. Calculate the lower of cost or market valuation for these items in inventory.
b. How will the accountant report the lower of cost or market adjustment on the financial statements?

P8-8 McGarity Enterprises is applying for a loan from a bank. The bank has asked the firm to present to it financial statements for the previous year and an income statement for the first two months of the current year. McGarity has received the approval of the bank to estimate inventory rather than incur the expense of taking a complete physical inventory for the two month income statement. McGarity's adjusted trial balance is given below as of February 28, 19x3:

	Debit	*Credit*
Cash	$ 2,100	
Accounts receivable	13,000	
Allowance for bad debts		$ 200
Merchandise inventory	23,000	
Prepaid expenses	300	
Equipment	18,000	
Accumulated depreciation		8,000
Furniture and fixtures	6,000	
Accumulated depreciation		600
Accounts payable		6,100
Notes payable (9%, due in 30 days)		10,000
McGarity—capital		36,450
Sales		29,000
Purchases	26,000	
Depreciation expense	500	
Selling expenses	200	
Salaries and wages	1,000	
Interest expense	150	
Other expenses	100	
	$90,350	$90,350

Required:

Prepare an income statement for the two months ended February 28, 19x3, using the gross profit method of estimating ending inventory for the two month period. Assume the gross profit ratio for McGarity was 42 percent in the previous year.

P8-9 Winston Sales Company had its retail outlet completely destroyed by fire. A balance sheet for the day of the fire is shown below:

	Debit	*Credit*
Cash	$ 2,400	
Accounts receivable	2,100	
Merchandise inventory—January 1, 19x8	11,000	
Prepaid insurance	200	
Supplies on hand	400	
Office furniture and fixtures	6,000	
Accumulated depreciation		1,400
Accounts payable		4,000
Capital stock		9,000
Retained earnings		5,100
Sales		64,000
Purchases	46,600	
Salaries expense	12,000	
Rent expenses	1,500	
Delivery expense	100	
Utilities expenses	1,200	
	$83,500	$83,500

The insurance company has asked Winston Sales to determine the cost of its inventory destroyed in the fire.

Required:

Using the gross profit method and agross profit percentage of 35 percent, estimate the amount of inventory on hand at March 9, 19x8.

P8-10 Earnhardt Company sells a single line of commercial solar heating units it purchases from a manufacturer. During the year, it has the following inventory transactions.

1. Beginning inventory was ten units costing $16,000 each.
2. Purchased twenty units for $16,500 each.
3. Sold nine units for $24,000 each.
4. Sold twelve units for $25,000 each.
5. Purchased ten units for $18,000 each.
6. Sold six units for $27,000 each.

Required:

Assuming all sales were for cash, calculate the cost of goods sold and ending inventory for Earnhardt Company, given that the firm uses:

a. Periodic inventory system and LIFO.
b. Periodic inventory system and FIFO.
c. Periodic inventory system and weighted average.
d. Perpectual inventory system and LIFO.
e. Perpetual inventory system and FIFO.
f. Perpetual inventory system and weighted average.

Learning Objectives

Chapter 9 presents proper accounting for long-lived assets and long-term investments. Studying this chapter should enable you to:

1. Define "noncurrent" and describe the major categories of noncurrent assets.
2. Determine the cost of assets acquired in a lump-sum purchase or in a trade-in transaction.
3. Prepare a noncurrent asset section of a balance sheet.
4. Calculate depreciation and amortization expense for full and partial years using different methods.
5. Record the sale and disposition of noncurrent assets.
6. Describe the financial statement presentation of long-term investments.

9

Noncurrent Assets

INTRODUCTION

Preceding chapters have discussed current assets and inventory. This chapter deals with all other assets, the noncurrent ones. These assets are also referred to as fixed assets or long-term assets because they have long lives and appear on several consecutive balance sheets of the firm. Major categories of noncurrent assets are land, plant and equipment, natural resources, intangible assets, long-term investments, and deferred assets. The investment in these types of assets depends on the nature of the business, but frequently is substantial.

A large public utility, such as an electric company, requires enormous investment in production facilities including generating plants, power lines, and maintenance equipment. A retailer may require a smaller percentage investment in noncurrent assets, and relatively higher investment in current assets, such as inventory. The investments of service businesses in long-lived assets varies widely, from the barber who rents his or her shop and has little investment in plant and equipment to the computer service bureau that owns its computers, and has a major investment.

This chapter is devoted primarily to the problems of accounting for plant and equipment. These assets are commonly held by almost all businesses and generally make up the most significant part of the noncurrent assets. Accounting problems relate to the nature of assets, the valuation methods used for financial statement presentations, the methods of matching the costs of long-lived assets with the revenues they help to generate, and the appropriate financial statement presentation for each class of noncurrent assets.

LAND

Land is unique among the tangible, long-lived, productive resources of an entity because it has an unlimited life. The major accounting problem involved with land is the measurement of the cost of land. The cost of an asset is defined as the cash or cash equivalent paid or incurred to acquire the asset and prepare it for its intended use. Items frequently included in the cost of land besides the purchase price are title insurance, legal fees, costs of recording the deed, and local taxes on the transfer.

Some special problems can arise in acquiring land. For example, if a firm acquires land for use as a parking lot that currently has a derelict building on it, what accounting treatment is given the building? Then, how do we account for the demolition of the building? As a general rule, the entire cost of the property is considered the cost of the land. In addition, the net cost (cost of demolition less any salvage receipts) of removing the building is treated as an additional cost of the land. In summary, the entire cost of acquiring the property and preparing it for its intended use is treated as the cost of the land.

Because land has an unlimited life, the accounting problem of measuring the expiration of the land's service potential and matching this expense with the revenues it helps to generate is solved easily. Since the land has unlimited service potential because of its unlimited life, none of the cost of the land is treated as an expense on the income statement. Consequently, the land account measures the cost of land acquired and is not reduced as the land is used. Likewise, the cost base is rarely adjusted upward regardless of the changing land values. Increases in potential market value of the land are not generally recorded in the accounts.

PLANT AND EQUIPMENT

Plant and equipment consists of the tangible, long-lived, productive assets that a firm will use in its operations. Common examples are buildings, machinery, office furniture and equipment, delivery trucks, and automobiles.

Three major problems in the accounting for plant and equipment are: (1) measurement of the cost, (2) measurement of cost expirations and allocation of the depreciation expense to the appropriate time periods, and (3) presentation on the financial statements. Plant and equipment items represent unexpired costs that will provide future benefits. When a machine is purchased for $500, the cost of the machine represents an unexpired resource of the firm. As the machine is used, its service potential is reduced by wear and age. The accountant must report the reduction in its service potential—the expiration of a part of the original cost of the machine—as an expense on the income statement. The expiration of part of the cost must then be reflected on both the balance sheet and income statement.

Maintenance cost must also be considered by the accountant. Distinctions exist between ordinary upkeep and major repairs and renovations. Treatments of these items will affect reported income and will provide the basis for valuing the asset.

Measurement of Cost of Plant and Equipment

The measurement of the cost of plant and equipment is similar to that of other assets. The original acquisition cost is defined as all reasonable and necessary expenditures to acquire the asset and place it in operating condition in the desired location at the appropriate time. By this definition, cost includes such expenditures as sales tax, transportation charges, handling charges, and installation charges. Allowable discounts should be deducted in arriving at the cost of an asset.

The materiality concept must be applied in the determination of asset costs. For example, if a machine is purchased and installed by the employees of the firm instead of paying someone outside the entity to install the machine, the cost of the machine should include the cost of the employees' time. The cost of the employees' time is based on the hourly rate and the appropriate portion of the cost of fringe benefits. If the employees take just a few minutes to install the machine, installation cost may be ignored since it is immaterial.

To illustrate these principles, suppose The Smith Manufacturing Company orders a new machine for the plant. The price is $8,000 but a cash discount of 5 percent is allowed if the amount due is paid within ten days. A 4 percent sales tax is added to the price of the machine. Freight charges are $27 and an outside firm is paid $75 to uncrate and install the machine. The cost of the machine is computed as follows regardless of whether the discount is actually taken:

Invoice price	$8,000
Sales tax	320
Freight	27
Installation charges	75
	$8,422
Less: 5% discount ($8,000 × .05)	400
Total cost	$8,022

The discount is deducted to get the cash equivalent cost of the machine. If the discount is not taken, the $400 would be charged to a financing cost such as interest expense.

Productive assets are sometimes acquired in a group by a lump-sum expenditure without a breakdown of the cost of each item. The total acquisition cost must then be allocated to the various assets on some systematic basis, usually on the basis of the relative fair market value of each asset. For example, suppose Jones Corporation acquires land and a building at a total price of $120,000. There is no indication in the agreement of how the total of $120,000 should be allocated to the two assets—land and building. This allocation is especially important because the building has a limited life, and a part of its cost will be charged as depreciation expense each period; the land has an unlimited life and none of its cost will be treated as an expense. To allocate the cost of $120,000 between the land and building, the relative fair market values of each asset must be determined. If the land is appraised at a value of $30,000 and the building is appraised at $95,000, we now have a basis for allocating the $120,000 between the two assets as follows:

Fair Market Values:

Land	$ 30,000
Building	95,000
Total fair market value	$125,000

Cost to be Allocated:

$120,000

Allocation to Land:

$$\frac{\text{Fair Market Value of Land}}{\text{Total Fair Market Value of Purchase}} \times \text{Cost to be Allocated} = \text{Cost Allocated to Land}$$

$$\frac{\$30,000}{\$125,000} \times \$120,000 = \$28,800$$

Allocation to Building:

$$\frac{\text{Fair Market Value of Building}}{\text{Total Fair Market Value of Purchase}} \times \text{Cost to be Allocated} = \text{Cost Allocated to Building}$$

$$\frac{\$95,000}{\$125,000} \times \$120,000 = \$91,200$$

The land would be debited for $28,800 and the building account is debited for $91,200. Note that the historical cost concept does not allow us to record these assets at their individual fair market values. They are recorded at their allocated portion of the total historical cost.

Sometimes productive long-lived assets are acquired in exchange for other assets or the firm's stock, but not cash. The accountant is faced with a problem of determining the cost of these assets so they may be properly recorded in the accounts and reported on financial statements. As a general rule, the cost of an asset acquired in an exchange is the fair market value of the asset given up, or the fair market value of the asset received, whichever is more readily valued. For example, if a corporation issues 1,000 shares of stock for land and the stock has recently sold for $15 per share, the land would reasonably be valued at $15,000. On the other hand, if the land is appraised at $22,000 and there have not been recent sales of the stock to establish its value, the land is properly recorded at $22,000.

Assets may be purchased that require additional expenditures before they are ready for use. If there are necessary expenditures to place the asset in operating condition, they are treated as part of the cost of the asset. These are especially common when used assets are acquired. For example, it may be necessary to incur expenditures to renovate and repair a building before it can be occupied by a new owner. These expenditures are treated as part of the cost of the building.

MEASURING COST EXPIRATIONS

Once the acquisition cost of an item of plant and equipment is determined, the next major accounting problem is measuring the cost expiration that occurs as a result of wear and age. The accountant faces this allocation problem: If a machine is acquired for $5,000 an will last five years, after which it will have no value, which year or years' net income should be charged with this $5,000 expense? It seems inequitable to charge the earnings of any one year with the full cost of the machine since it was used by the firm during all five years. Accountants will attempt to match an estimate of each year's cost expirations with the revenues that were generated. These cost expirations, resulting from reductions in asset's service lives caused by wear and age, are called *depreciation expense* on the income statement.

Calculating depreciation expense involves three factors:

1. Acquisition cost.
2. Service life.
3. Residual value.

The service life of a fixed asset is the time period over which the firm expects to use the asset. The service life is an estimate. If a firm plans to use an asset until it has no value, the service life would be the estimated useful life of the asset. Often, a firm plans to sell or trade in an asset before all its service potential is gone. For example, cars and trucks are often traded in while there is still some service potential. Under these circumstances, the service life would be the number of years the firm expects to keep the truck or car before it is traded.

Residual value of a fixed asset is the expected value of the asset at the end of its expected service life to the company. It represents that part of the asset's cost that is not expected to expire. The residual value of an asset is normally reduced for estimated disposition costs of the asset at the end of its service life. For example, if a building is expected to have a forty-year life with a salvage value of $4,000 at the end of its life and the costs of disposing of the building are expected to be $3,000, then its residual value is calculated to be $1,000 ($4,000 − $3,000).

The allocation of cost over time periods as depreciation expense lacks exactness. It is based on estimates of both the service life and the residual value of the asset. For example, assume The Ace Corporation purchases a delivery truck to be used in its business activity for $8,200. No one can know for certain just how long the delivery truck will be used, so an estimate must be made. Suppose management estimates that the truck will be used for four years. Next, an estimate must be made of the value (residual value) of the truck at the end of that four-year period. The estimate may take into consideration relevant information such as the "blue-book" value of a similar truck that is already four years old and projected supply and demand for used trucks. Assume that the residual value is estimated at $2,200.

If management decides to recognize an equal amount of depreciation expense each year, then it will allocate part of the asset's cost as depreciation expense, calculated as follows:

$$\frac{\text{Cost} - \text{Residual Value}}{\text{Estimated Service Life}} = \text{Annual Depreciation Expense}$$

$$\frac{\$8,200 - \$2,200}{4} = \underline{\underline{\$1,500}}$$

Note that changes in the estimate of residual value or service life can have a material impact on the calculation of annual depreciation expense.

The allocation of the cost of a fixed asset over its estimated service life is not an attempt to measure the market value of the asset. Depreciation is the allocation of part of the cost of an asset as a period expense over the time periods benefitted. The book value of the asset (cost minus total depreciation taken) may have no resemblance to the market value of the asset. As an extreme illustration, a building may, for a time, actually appreciate in market value because of its favorable location while it is being depreciated for accounting purposes. Depreciation is an attempt to match the expiring cost of an asset with the revenues derived from the asset. The cost is allocated over the period of time during which the service potential of the asset is used. It usually results in values quite different from an appraisal of fair market value.

DEPRECIATION ACCOUNTING AND REPORTING

Allocating the cost expiration of a long lived asset over the period of time it benefits the firm is accomplished by calculating depreciation expense. Once calculated, the depreciation expense is normally recorded as an adjusting entry at the end of the accounting period. It may also be recorded during the accounting period if there is a need to bring the account balances up-to-date. For example, if an asset is sold during the year, depreciation should be recorded up-to-date of sale. The entry to record depreciation expense is illustrated below:

Depreciation expense—auto	$500	
Accumulated depreciation—auto		$500

Note that the credit in this entry is to a contra asset account, entitled accumulated depreciation, rather than a direct reduction of the asset account. By this approach, the asset account continues to reflect the original cost of the asset and the contra account shows the cumulative effect of depreciation for all periods since the asset was placed into service.

The balance sheet presentation of fixed assets and their related accumulated depreciation is shown as follows:

Fixed assets:		
Equipment	$ 9,000	
Less: Accumulated depreciation	3,600	$ 5,400
Office furniture and fixtures	$ 1,800	
Less: Accumulated depreciation	600	1,200
Trucks	$15,000	
Less Accumulated depreciation	9,000	6,000
Total fixed assets		$12,600

Footnotes to the financial statements normally describe the accounting methods used to prepare the financial statements, and should describe the depreciation methods used to calculate depreciation expense.

DEPRECIATION METHODS

The estimate of annual depreciation expense may be calculated several ways. Each of the generally accepted techniques provides a systematic and rational method for allocating part of the cost of a long-lived asset to the periods benefitted. Each method makes a basic presumption about the rate at which the cost of the asset "expires," or should be recognized as an expense. In this chapter we discuss four depreciation methods:

1. Straight-line method.
2. Double-declining-balance method.
3. Sum-of-the-years'-digits method.
4. Units-of-production method.

The straight-line method assumes that the reduction in the service life of an asset occurs at an even, constant rate, and therefore charges each year that an asset is used with an equal amount of depreciation expense. The sum-of-the-years'-digits and double-declining-balance methods are referred to as accelerated methods. They hypothesize that an asset is more productive in its early years of use. Consequently, these methods charge higher depreciation expense to the earlier years of an asset's life, and lower amounts to the later years. This matches higher depreciation expense with higher revenues generated in the early, more productive years of the asset's life. The units-of-production method measures the life of an asset in output units or expected life in hours, instead of in an expected life in years.

Straight-Line Depreciation Method

The formula for *straight-line depreciation* is:

$$\frac{\text{Cost} - \text{Residual Value}}{\text{Useful Life}} = \text{Annual Depreciation Expense}$$

If a building is acquired at a cost of $80,000, and is expected to have a useful life of twenty years with no residual value at the end of the twenty years, the annual depreciation is computed as follows:

$$\frac{\$80,000 - 0}{20 \text{ Years}} = \$4,000 \text{ Per Year}$$

If this building is expected to have a residual value of $8,000 at the end of the twenty years, the annual depreciation would be computed as follows:

$$\frac{\$80,000 - \$8,000}{20 \text{ Years}} = \$3,600 \text{ Per Year}$$

Using this last example, the adjusting entry for the first year (and each year for 20 years) would be:

Depreciation expense—building	$3,600	
Accumulated depreciation—building		$3,600

The balance sheet at the end of the first year would contain the following information:

Plant and equipment:		
Building	$80,000	
Less: Accumulated depreciation	3,600	$76,400

Like all expense accounts, the depreciation expense account is closed at the end of the year. Thus, depreciation expense will have no balance after the closing entry has been made, but the accumulated depreciation account is not closed and will be carried forward to the next year. The depreciation expense on the income statement each year will be the current year's depreciation expense, but the asset contra account, accumulated depreciation, will include the total depreciation recognized on the asset over its life to-date and will be shown on the balance sheet.

For the building illustrated above, the entry to record depreciation for the second year would be the same as for the first year.

Depreciation expense on the income statement for the second year will be $3,600, the same as the first year. The relevant portion of the balance sheet for the second year will appear as follows:

Plant and equipment:		
Building	$80,000	
Less: Accumulated depreciation	7,200	$72,800

Although residual value is used in the calculation of the annual depreciation expense, it does not appear as a separate item on the balance sheet. It is assumed that the reader of the statements is interested in total cost and total accumulated depreciation, but not the exact calculations or estimates of residual value.

If the building is used for twenty years as estimated, the depreciation adjustment for the twenty-fifth year would be the same as for other years.

The income statement would include depreciation expense on the building of $3,600 and the balance sheet would be as follows:

Plant and equipment:		
Building	$80,000	
Less: Accumulated depreciation	72,000	$8,000

The book value of the building at this point—$8,000—is the residual value estimated at the time the building was acquired. Even if the building continues to be used, no additional depreciation expense would be taken. The building would be reported on the balance sheet at its residual value as shown above.

So far, this illustration has made the assumption that the business owns only one item of plant and equipment. When several items are owned, the balance sheet normally reports these items grouped together in a few asset classes, such as machinery, delivery equipment, office furniture and fixtures, land, and so on. This condenses the information into a more readable format for the financial statement user.

Double-Declining-Balance Depreciation Method

Accelerated depreciation methods recognize larger increments of cost in the earlier part of the asset life and smaller increments in the latter part of the life. *Double-declining-balance* is one of these accelerated methods.

Annual depreciation expense using the double-declining-balance method of depreciation is computed by the following formula:

$$\text{Book Value} \times \frac{2}{\text{Useful Life}} = \text{Annual Depreciation Expense}$$

The book value of an asset is the cost of the asset less the accumulated depreciation to-date. Book value and cost are the same at the date of acquisition, but the book value decreases each accounting period because of depreciation taken in prior periods.

Suppose a machine is purchased for $12,000, has an estimated service life of five years, and an estimated residual value of $2,000. Using the double-declining-balance method, how do we calculate depreciation expense?

Depreciation for the first year is computed as follows:

$$\$12{,}000 \times \frac{2}{5} = \$4{,}800$$

Depreciation for the second year is computed as follows:

$$(\$12{,}000 - \$4{,}800) \times \frac{2}{5} = \$2{,}880$$

Depreciation expense and the book value at the end of each year for this asset are shown below:

Year	Depreciation Expense	Book Value	Accumulated Depreciation
0		$12,000	
1	$4,800	7,200	$ 4,800
2	2,880	4,320	7,680
3	1,728	2,592	9,408
4	592	2,000	10,000
5		2,000	10,000

Note that the formula for calculating double-declining-balance depreciation does not consider the residual value of the asset in calculating the annual depreciation expense. But also note that the asset is not depreciated below its salvage value. For example, depreciation in year 4 in our example above is limited to $592, even though the formula would have calculated $1,037 in depreciation expense for that year. To take more depreciation than that would result in reporting the asset on the balance sheet below its salvage value. That would be inappropriate.

This depreciation method resulted from an income tax law that limits the annual depreciation expense to twice the depreciation expense that would be determined by the straight-line method, ignoring residual value. In effect, the double-declining-balance method uses a rate of depreciation that is double the straight-line rate. In our example of a machine with a five year life, the straight-line rate is 20 percent per year (100% ÷ 5 years). The double-declining-balance method uses twice the straight-line rate (2/5 or 40% in this example) but applies that rate to the book value, not original cost.

Sum-of-the-Years'-Digits Methods

The *sum-of-the-years'-digits method* of depreciation is another consistent approach to recognizing larger amounts of depreciation in early years and less in later years as compared with the straight-line method. Its formula is:

$$\text{(Cost} - \text{Residual Value)} \times \frac{\text{Year's Digit}}{\text{Sum-of-the-Years'-Digits}} = \text{Annual Depreciation Expense}$$

In this formula, the sum-of-the-years'-digits is the sum of the estimated life of the asset and each integer below that number, down to 1. For example, if the useful life of the asset is 5, the sum-of-the-years'-digits would be calculated as follows:

$$5 + 4 + 3 + 2 + 1 = 15$$

Since it would be rather time-consuming to calculate the sum-of-the-years'-digits for a building with a life of thirty years, the sum-of-the-years'-digits may be calculated using this formula:

$$n \left(\frac{n+1}{2}\right)$$

where n = estimated useful life.

For a useful life of five years, we could calculate the sum-of-the-years'-digits as follows:

$$5 \left(\frac{5+1}{2}\right) = 15$$

The numerator in the depreciation formula is the years of service life remaining. This number is the year's digit taken in declining order. Thus, for an asset with an estimated useful life of five years, the years' digits are 5, 4, 3, 2, and 1 in declining order. In year 1, the numerator of the fraction would be 5. In year 2, the numerator would be 4, and so on.

Using the same example as before, what is the depreciation expense for a machine with a cost of $12,000, a five-year estimated service life, and an estimated residual value of $2,000, using the sum-of-the-years'-digits method of depreciation?

Depreciation for the first year is computed as follows:

$$(\$12{,}000 - \$2{,}000) \times \frac{5}{15} = \$3{,}333 \text{ (rounded to nearest dollar)}$$

Depreciation for the second year is computed as follows:

$$(\$12{,}000 - \$2{,}000) \times \frac{4}{15} = \$2{,}667$$

The following table shows the depreciation expense for each of the five years along with accumulated depreciation and book value for each year.

Year	*Depreciation Expense*	*Accumulated Depreciation*	*Book Value*
0			$12,000
1	$3,333	$ 3,333	8,667
2	2,667	6,000	6,000
3	2,000	8,000	4,000
4	1,333	9,333	2,667
5	667	10,000	2,000

Both the double-declining-balance method and the sum-of-the-years'-digits method of depreciation are consistent ways to compute the larger amounts of depreciation during the early years than in the later years as compared with the straight-line depreciation method. The double-declining-balance method generally provides for faster depreciation than the sum-of-the-years'-digits method because mathematically it is more accelerated and because residual value is not considered in the double-declining-balance calculation, whereas the formula for the sum-of-the-years'-digits calculation does consider salvage values.

Many companies use accelerated depreciation for tax purposes because it gives higher depreciation expense and lower income taxes early in the life of the asset. Companies also use accelerated methods for assets that are subject to rapid technological change, such as computers. In this instance, the objective is to write-off most of the asset's cost early in its life, before it becomes obsolete.

Comparison of Methods Measuring Life in Years

Illustration 1 compares the depreciation calculation for the straight-line, double-declining-balance, and sum-of-the-years'-digits methods, using the example discussed previously: cost—$12,000, life—five years, and residual value—$2,000.

Illustration 1

Comparison of Depreciation Methods

Case: Asset with cost of $12,000, life of five years and estimated residual value of $2,000.

	Depreciation Expense	*Accumulated Depreciation*	*Book Value*
Straight Line Method:			
			$12,000
	$ 2,000	$ 2,000	10,000
	2,000	4,000	8,000
	2,000	6,000	6,000
	2,000	8,000	4,000
	2,000	10,000	2,000
	$10,000		
Double-Declining-Balance Method:			
			$12,000
	$ 4,800	$ 4,800	7,200
	2,880	7,680	4,320
	1,728	9,408	2,592
	592	10,000	2,000
		10,000	2,000
	$10,000		
Sum-of-the-Years'-Digits Method:			
			$12,000
	$ 3,333	$ 3,333	8,667
	2,667	6,000	6,000
	2,000	8,000	4,000
	1,333	9,333	2,667
	667	10,000	2,000
	$10,000		

In all three methods, a total of $10,000 in depreciation expense is allocated over the time periods. The difference occurs because of the timing of the cost allocation. The accelerated methods result in larger allocations of expense to earlier years and less to later years as compared to straight-line depreciation. This means that the income statement will include a larger depreciation expense and a smaller net income (compared to the straight-line method) during approximately the first half of the service life of an asset. The opposite is true during approximately the second half of the service life—depreciation expense will be lower and net income would be higher as compared with the straight-line method.

From the standpoint of the balance sheet, accelerated depreciation methods would result in a lower book value of the fixed assets and lower retained earnings during approximately the first half of the service life, as compared with the straight-line method.

The straight-line depreciation method is simple, rational, and systematic. Accelerated methods are appropriate when there is reason to allocate larger amounts of the cost to early years of the service life of the asset.

Units of Production

The *units-of-production method* measures the useful life of a productive machine in terms of the number of units the machine can produce during its life. The formula for units production depreciation expense is as follows:

$$\frac{\text{Cost} - \text{Residual Value}}{\text{Number of Units Machine Can Produce}} \times \text{Number of Units Produced This Year By This Machine} = \text{Annual Depreciation Expense}$$

The annual depreciation is based on utilization of the productive output potential of the machine.

For example, if a machine costs $9,000, has a $1,000 salvage value, an estimated useful productive capacity of 40,000 units, and actually produces 6,000 units this year, depreciation would be calculated as follows:

$$\frac{\$9{,}000 - \$1{,}000}{40{,}000 \text{ Units}} \times 6{,}000 \text{ Units} = \$1{,}200$$

The formula for calculating units of production depreciation expense is very similar to the formula for calculating straight-line depreciation, except estimated useful life is measured in terms of units of productive capacity instead of number of years. Note that it is also similar to straight-line depreciation in that it assigns the same amount of depreciation expense—20 cents per unit in the case above—to each unit produced. In addition to estimated units of production, other activity bases such as machine hours, miles, etc., may be used. The units of production method is normally adopted where the use of the asset is expected to vary from year-to-year.

Partial Year's Depreciation

If an asset is acquired or disposed during the year rather than at the beginning or end-of-the-year, depreciation must be calculcated for the partial year. One practical approach to this problem is to calculate depreciation to the nearest whole month. For example, if the straight-line depreciation expense would have been $2,400 for a whole year, and a machine is acquired on April 6 by a business using a calendar year, depreciation to the nearest whole month would count April (the asset was acquired in the first half of the month) and the fist partial year's depreciation is calculated as follows:

$$\frac{9}{12} \times 2{,}400 = \$1{,}800$$

Many firms have elected to use other methods to calculate partial year's depreciation. One way would be calculate one-half year's depreciation for all assets in the year they are acquired, and one-half year's depreciation in the year of disposal. Another way would be to calculate a full year's depreciation on assets acquired in the first half of the year, and none on assets acquired in the second half. Similarly, asset disposals in the second half of the year would have a full year's depreciation calculated, while none would be calculated on asset disposals in the first half. Although these "year-of-purchase, year-of-sale" conventions are much less exact than the nearest month method, the difference in total depreciation are unlikely to be material.

When accelerated depreciation methods are used, the calculation of partial depreciation follows the same logic. Also, annual depreciation charges are sometimes adjusted to reflect the inclusion of two partial years in the calculation. Assume that a company bought a machine for $18,000 on July 1, 19x6, and that the machine has no expected salvage value at the end of its life. If the sum-of-the-years'-digits method is used, annual depreciation for this asset is as follows:

Year	*Calculation*	*Depreciation*
1	$\frac{3}{6}$ × $18,000	$9,000
2	$\frac{2}{6}$ × $18,000	6,000
3	$\frac{1}{6}$ × $18,000	3,000

If the firm reports on a calender year basis, $4,500 of depreciation would be reported in 19x6. This is one-half of the first year depreciation on the machine. Depreciation of $7,500 would be reported in 19x7. This includes the remaining half of the first year depreciation added to one-half of the second year depreciation (½ × $9,000 + ½ × $6,000). Likewise, the depreciation expense recorded in 19x8 would be $4,500 calculated as follows:

$$(\tfrac{1}{2} \times \$6{,}000 + \tfrac{1}{2} \times \$3{,}000)$$

Consistency

An individual asset may be depreciated using any acceptable depreciation method. If three assets are acquired, each may be depreciation using a different method. Once a method is selected, however, that method should generally be used consistently throughout the life of the asset.

Maintenance

Periodically, repairs and other maintenance activities are undertaken to keep buildings, equipment, and other assets in proper operating condition. Usually, a certain amount of recurring service is necessary for all facilities. Those expenditures that provide for normal operating repairs and maintenance are called *revenue expenditures* and are treated as an expense and charged to income immediately.

For example, the annual cost of maintaining a manufacturing plant is $14,200, which includes the necessary materials and labor. Because of its annual nature, the maintenance is related to activities of the current period. This cost would be recorded as an expense.

Maintenance expense	$14,200	
Cash		$14,200

Capital expenditures are maintenance and repair activities will alter or improve a facility. These expenditures generally increase the useful life of an asset or improve its operating efficiency. In the case of improvement, the benefit of the maintenance activity may extend for several periods in the future. It would not be appropriate to write-off this cost by charging it to expense immediately. Instead, the cost is treated as a capital improvement and is recorded as an asset. The asset may be depreciated over its expected useful life as would any other resource owned by the organization.

For example, suppose a company decides to replace the wiring in its manufacturing plant with a new system costing $45,600. If the new wiring system does more than replace regular recurring wear and tear, it should be treated as an asset and recorded as such. In this case, the expenditure would probably be included in the total cost of the plant and depreciated as it is used in the future.

Plant	$45,600	
Cash		$45,600

DISPOSITION OF PLANT AND EQUIPMENT

The disposition of plant and equipment may occur through sale, trade-in on another asset, or scrapping the asset. No matter which takes place, the results of the disposition should be reflected in the accounting records of the firm. The first step in accounting for the disposition of an asset is to bring the depreciation on the asset up-to-date by recording depreciation for a partial year, if necessary. This ensures that the appropriate amount of depreciation expense is recorded and that the accumulated depreciation account is current.

If the asset is sold, and depreciation has been recorded up to the date of sale (as we will assume in the remaining examples), the next step is to account for the sale itself. For purposes of illustration, assume the sale of the machine used in previous examples: cost—$12,000, life—five years, and salvage value—$2,000. If this machine is depreciated using the straight-line method and sold at the end of year 2 for $8,500 cash, we would make the following calculations:

Cost	$12,000
Less: Accumulated depreciation	4,000
Book value	$ 8,000

Because the cash received exceeds the book value of the asset sold, a gain of $500 is recognized on the sale:

Cash received	$8,500
Book value	8,000
Gain	$ 500

The journal entry to record the sale of the machine for $8,500 cash is as follows:

Cash	$8,500	
Accumulated depreciation machine	4,000	
Machine		$12,000
Gain on sale of machine		500

If the machine had been sold for less than its book value, a loss would be recognized. For example, if the machine were sold for $7,000, a loss of $1,000 would be recognized by the following entry:

Cash	$7,000	
Accumulated depreciation machine	4,000	
Loss on sale of machine	1,000	
Machine		$12,000

The purpose of the journal entry is to:

1. Record the amount of assets received (cash, accounts receivable, and notes receivable are examples).
2. Remove the cost of the asset sold from the asset account.
3. Remove the accumulated depreciation.
4. Recognize a gain or loss, if any.

Accounting for a trade-in requires recognition of the newly acquired asset as well as an entry for the disposition of the old assets. The cost of an asset includes all reasonable and necessary expenditures to acquire the asset and place it in operating condition in the desired location at the appropriate time. In a trade-in, the cost basis of the new asset is measured by the fair market value of the assets given or the assets received, whichever is more readily determined. Frequently, it is easier to establish the fair market value of the asset received in trade-in situations because the asset is usually new and its value more readily determined.

Suppose a machine originally acquired for $80,000 with accumulated depreciation of $60,000 is traded for a machine with a fair market value of $100,000. The firm is allowed a trade-in allowance of $15,000 on the old machine, reducing the cash required to $85,000.

This is the general journal entry made to record the trade-in:

Machinery (new)	$100,000	
Accumulated depreciation	60,000	
Loss on disposition of assets	5,000	
Cash		$85,000
Machinery (old)		80,000

The purpose of the entry is to:

1. Record the new machine at its fair market value (the most easily determinable)—$100,000.
2. Remove the cost of the old machine—$80,000.
3. Remove the accumulated depreciation on the old machine—$60,000.
4. Record the payment of $85,000 cash.
5. Record the loss of $5,000 as the difference between the book value of the machine ($20,000) given and the fair market value of the old machine—the trade-in allowance ($15,000).

If the fair market value of the old machine had been equal to its book value, no gain or loss would be recognized.

When the fair market value of the asset acquired is greater than the cash paid plus the book value of the asset traded, the transaction involves a gain. Under current GAAP, the gain will be recognized only if the exchange involves dissimilar assets. In this circumstance, the company is disposing of a particular type of asset and realization of the gain is assumed. For example, assume in the previous example that the fair value of the new asset was $110,000, that the new asset was a stamping machine, and the old asset was a truck. A trade-in allowance of $95,000 was given on the truck. Since dissimilar assets were traded, the gain is realized and should be recognized as follows:

Machinery (new)	$110,000	
Accumulated depreciation	60,000	
Cash		$85,000
Machinery (old)		80,000
Gain on the sale		5,000

If similar assets were involved, both the old and new assets were trucks, the gain is not recognized because it has not been realized in the sense that the company still owns a truck (i.e., the same type of asset). The entry in this case would be as follows:

Machinery (new)	$105,000	
Accumulated depreciation	60,000	
Cash		$85,000
Machinery (old)		80,000

Notice that the new asset value is adjusted (decreased) for the amount of the gain. No gain is reported in the current year's income statement, however, future depreciation expense will be $5,000 less.

The following summarizes accounting for asset exchanges:

Loss involved: Recognize the loss in all cases.

Gain involved: Dissimilar assets—recognize the gain and value the new asset at its market value, if known, or at the market value of the traded asset plus any cash paid.
Similar assets—do not recognize the gain, value the new asset at the book value of the asset traded plus any cash paid.

If a depreciable asset is scrapped, or abandoned, a loss is recognized in the amount of the book value. If the book value is zero, there would be no gain or loss. Assume a machine costing $12,000 has accumuted depreciation of $10,000. If the machine is abandoned, a loss of the book value (i.e., $2,000) is recognized by the following entry:

Accumulated depreciation—machine	$10,000	
Loss on abandonment of fixed asset	2,000	
Machine		$12,000

The recognition of losses on asset dispositions may be viewed as simply allocating additional asset expirations as expenses (though called losses) to the income statement, suggesting that insufficient depreciation was taken in the past.

NATURAL RESOURCES

Natural resources are those assets of the firm such as timber, coal, and oil. Like land, they are provided by nature—unlike land, their service potential expires when they are exhausted. Accounting for natural resources involves problems of determining the cost of the natural resource (i.e., separating the cost of the land from that of the resource and accounting for the extraction of the natural resource and allocating its cost to the periods benefitted), called *depletion*.

The accounting records of the firm must separate the cost of minerals, which will be extracted and whose cost expiration should be recorded as depletion expense, from the land that bears the resources, which will not be expensed. As noted earlier, if the purchase contract fails to specify how this division is to be made, accountants normally allocate a lump-sum purchase price between land and a natural resource on the basis of their relative fair market values. If $400,000 is paid for timberland and timber, and ¾ of the value of the property is attributable to the land and ¼ attributable to the timber, the following entry would be made:

Land	$300,000	
Timber	100,000	
Cash		$400,000

As the resource is used, the accounting records should report the cost expiration associated with the mining or cutting. For examples, if one-half of the timber is cut and sold during the first year after acquisition, the following entry would be made to record the depletion expense:

Cost of timber land	$50,000	
Timber		$50,000

Note that the asset account, timber, is reduced directly rather than indirectly through a contra asset account as with depreciation of plant and equipment. From a theoretical standpoint, the credit could be to either timber or accumulated depletion—timber. Conventionally, the asset account is reduced directly.

Depletion is almost always calculated on a unit of production basis, assigning and equal amount of depletion expense (cost expiration) to each unit mined or harvested.

INTANGIBLE ASSETS

Intangible assets are noncurrent rights or privileges acquired or developed by a firm to which costs may be assigned. Common examples of intangible assets are patents, franchises, copyrights, and goodwill. The primary problems in accounting for intangible assets are the same as for natural resources—accounting for the cost of the asset and determining the appropriate cost expiration.

A patent is the exclusive right to produce and sell an item. A copyright is the exclusive right to print and sell a literary or musical creation, such as a book, play, song, or symphony. Both are granted by the government to encourage creativity. A franchise is an exclusive right to market a product or service within a specified geographical region. Many motels and fast-food restaurants are franchises, acquired by contract with the creator of the product or service.

Intangible assets are recorded at the cost of the asset. Cost is defined as all the necessary and customary expenditures to acquire the asset and have it ready for use in the entity. If a patent is purchased, the asset patents is measured at the entire cost, or expenditure, to acquire the patent. This definition would include any legal fees involved in acquiring the patent or defending its integrity in court.

Goodwill poses some rather thorny problems for accountants. Goodwill is a purchased intangible asset. It has been described as a master valuation account for a business—that additional cost of acquiring a business above the fair market value of its physical assets, attributable to its potential to earn an unusually high rate of return because of location, reputation, or a combination of other factors. Although some accountants argue that goodwill is imaginary and should not be recognized, it is recognized only when purchased in the acquisition of a business and valued as the excess of the total purchase price of the business over that value directly attributable to the physical and other intangible assets of the firm. In other words, it is a residual value. If $400,000 is paid for a business, and the fair market value of its identifiable assets is $350,000, goodwill would be valued at $50,000. See Chapter 15 for an extended discussion of goodwill that is associated with the purchase price of a business.

The cost expiration associated with the reduction in the service life of intangible assets is recognized and called *amortization* or amortization expense. Amortization of intangible assets is the same as depreciation of plant and equipment. Amortization is usually calculated on a straight-line basis over the expected useful life of the asset. If a patent has a maximum legal life of seventeen years, but is expected to benefit a firm for only ten years, and it cost $100,000, the following entry would be made:

Amortization of patent	$10,000	
Patent		$10,000

Note again that the asset account is usually reduced directly rather than through a contra account.

Intangible assets are reported on the balance sheet at their net amount. For example, at the end of the first year, the patent recorded above would be reported as follows on the balance sheet:

Intangible assets:	
Patents	$90,000

Again, goodwill poses problems for accountants. How long does goodwill remain an asset? Does the cost of goodwill expire, and if so, how fast? The Accounting Principles Board requires that goodwill be amortized over its estimated useful life. This period of time may not exceed forty years in the board's opinion. Many firms—uncertain as to how long goodwill lasts—simply amortize the cost over forty years.

RESEARCH AND DEVELOPMENT

Many companies have research and development centers where scientists conduct experiments to develop new products or methods of manufacturing. These efforts frequently result in a patent.

The research effort needed to develop a patent may take many years and may or may not be successful. Frequently, as the research is being conducted, scientists and management may not be able to assess the probability of success. A problem arises concerning how to account for the cost of this research. If the research costs are deferred in an asset account, assets may be overstated because the project may not be successful. Such treatment would mislead stockholders and others into thinking the company has a significant asset when in fact the research costs were unproductive. Because of the great deal of uncertainty concerning the ultimate outcome of research and development efforts, the FASB decided that it would be best to write-off all research and development costs in the year incurred by charging them to research and development expense.

LONG-TERM INVESTMENTS

Marketable securities were defined in Chapter 7 as investments in securities (e.g., stocks, bonds) for which there is a ready market and the securities are not held in order to control or influence another firm, or for some other long-term benefit. Securities held for some long-term benefit or for which there is no ready market are classified in accounting as long-term investments. This is a noncurrent category on the balance sheet. Other assets of an investment nature that management intends to hold for long-term benefit should also be reported as a long-term investment. For example, if the firm invests in land with the intention of possibly developing the land several years in the future, that land should be reported as a long-term investment.

Long-term investments usually are recorded and reported in accordance with the historical cost principle. For example, if a firm acquires stock for $3,200,000, and pays $32,000 in brokerage fees and $6,000 additional transfer costs, the purchase would be recorded as follows:

Long-term investment in stock	$3,238,000	
Cash		$3,238,000

The exact content of financial statement disclosures for long-term investments in common stock depends upon the relative size of the stockholding, the purpose for making the investment, and the nature of the business being conducted. Further discussion of accounting for long-term investments in corporate common stock is found in Chapter 15. A company may also invest in bonds as a long-term investment. Bonds are long-term loans to another company evidenced by a certificate. Bonds are traded similar to stock. Accounting for investments in bonds is discussed in Chapter 11.

DEFERRED CHARGES

Deferred charges sometimes appear on a balance sheet as noncurrent assets. *Deferred charges* are prepaid expenses that are long-term; they cannot appropriately be included in the current assets. An example of a deferred charge would be organization costs. These are costs incurred to organize a business. Obviously, these costs will benefit the business as long as it functions and they therefore cannot be classified as current assets. Deferred charges should be recognized as expenses as they benefit the firm. This asset expiration is normally recognized by reducing the asset account and debiting an appropriate expense.

SUMMARY

Noncurrent assets are also called fixed or long-term assets. The primary problems in accounting for noncurrent assets are measuring the cost of the assets, measuring their cost expiration, matching the expired cost with revenues, and accounting for the ultimate disposal of the assets.

The historical cost principle is used to value noncurrent assets at acquisition. All reasonable and necessary expenditures incurred to acquire, install, and prepare the assets for use become part of the cost of the assets. Adjustment entries are made to reflect the expiration of the service potential through age, wear, use, or consumption, but the name for the expired costs, depreiation, depletion, or amortization, depends upon whether the asset is classified as plant and equipment, natural resources, or intangibles and deferred charges. Several systematic depreciation methods are currently in use, including the straight-line method, the sum-of-the-years'-digits method, and the double-declining-balance method, and the units of production method. Depletion usually is calculated under the units of production method. Amortization is calculated under the straight-line method. Disposal of noncurrent assets includes sales, trade-ins, or abandonment, and gains or losses on disposal usually are reflected in the income statement for the year of disposal. Accounting for trade-ins, deferred charges, and long-term investments was also discussed.

KEY DEFINITIONS

Amortization—the process of allocating the cost of an intangible asset to the periods benefitted.

Deferred charges—long-term prepaid expenses.

Depletion—the process of allocating the cost of a natural resource to the periods benefitted.

Depreciation—a process of allocating the cost of a fixed asset to the periods benefitted.

Double-declining-balance method—a depreciation method that allocates the depreciable cost of a fixed asset the periods benefitted on an accelerated basis. The rate (twice the straight-line rate) is applied to the book value of the asset.

Intangible asset—a long lived asset without tangible or physical qualities.

Residual value—the value an asset is expected to have at the end of its service life of the company.

Straight-line method—a depreciation method that allocates the depreciable cost of an asset equally to the periods benefitted.

Sum-of-the-years'-digits method—an accelerated depreciation method that allocates the cost of an asset to each period on the basis of a fraction where the numerator is the year in the asset's useful life, in descending order, and the denominator is the sum of the individual digits in the asset's life.

Units-of-production method—a depreciation method that allocates the depreciable cost of an asset to the years benefitted on a straight-line basis using units of production rather than years of useful life.

QUESTIONS

9-1 What are noncurrent assets?

9-2 List the major classes of noncurrent assets.

9-3 How do accountants value noncurrent assets at the time of their acquisition for balance sheet purposes?

9-4 How is land unique from most other long-lived, noncurrent assets? What is the accounting impact of this difference?

9-5 If several assets are purchased for a single price, how should the total price paid be allocated to the various individual assets?

9-6 Why should the lump-sum purchase price of a group of assets be allocated to the individual assets?

9-7 How should a long-lived asset be valued if it is acquired in an exchange for assets other than cash?

9-8 Does the balance sheet presentation of plant and equipment reflect their fair market value?

9-9 Why do accountants recognize depreciation expense for part of a year?

9-10 What three factors must be known or estimated to calculate depreciation expense?

9-11 What is the residual value of an asset?

9-12 Identify the elements used in both the calculation of straight-line depreciation and units-of-production depreciation.

9-13 What does the account accumulated depreciation measure?

9-14 Why are the double-declining-balance and sum-of-the-years'-digits methods of depreciation called accelerated depreciation methods?

9-15 Is depreciation expense related to depletion expense? Explain.

9-16 Distinguish between tangible and intangible assets.

9-17 How do accountants calculate the cost expiration associated with the reduction in the service life of an intangible asset?

9-18 Describe the difference between marketable securities and long-term investments.

9-19 Define deferred charge.

EXERCISES

E9-1 Classify the following as current assets or noncurrent assets:

a. Cash.
b. Rent prepaid for five years.
c. Treasury bills maturing in ninety-one days held as a temporary investment.
d. Land and building used in manufacturing.
e. Stock in a company that supplies parts.
f. Patents to a process developed by the firm.
g. Inventory.
h. Coal in a coal mine operated by the firm.

E9-2 Consider the following data:

Purchase price of land and building	$225,000
Cost to demolish building	32,000
Cost of constructing new building on land ...	72,000

Determine: (a) the cost of the land, and (b) the cost of the building.

E9-3 Five machines of varying sizes are purchased for a bargain $27,000. Estimates of their individual fair market values are as follows:

Machine A =	$ 5,000
Machine B =	5,000
Machine C =	6,600
Machine D =	9,000
Machine E =	12,400

What cost is allocated to each machine?

E9-4 Calculate the first full year straight-line depreciation expense for a machine acquired on January 2 of the current year for $6,000. The machine is estimated to have a residual value of $500 and a useful life of five years. Give the entry to record the depreciation.

E9-5 Calculate the depreciation expense to the nearest whole month for a truck purchased on March 28 by a calendar year business for $8,000, using an estimated residual value of $2,000, a useful life of three years, and the straight-line method.

E9-6 Calculate depreciation expense for each year on a truck purchased for $8,000 with a residual value of $500 and an estimated useful life of five years, using the sum-of-the-years'-digits method.

E9-7 Calculate depreciation expense for the second full year in the life of a machine acquired for $40,000 with a residual value of $4,000 and an estimated life of eight years, using the double-declining-balance method.

E9-8 Calculate and compare the depreciation expense for each complete year in the life of an automobile with a cost of $8,000, a residual value of $2,000, and a life of three years, using the straight-line and double-declining-balance methods.

E9-9 A machine is estimated to be able to produce 40,000 units during its productive life, costs $16,000, and has no estimated residual value. Calculate the depreciation expense for the machine if it produces 2,940 units this year.

E9-10 Prepare a journal entry necessary to record the sale of a machine that originally cost $6,200, has depreciation recorded to-date of $4,800, and is sold for $1,500.

E9-11 For each of the following items indicate whether it is a capital or revenue expenditure:

a. Cost of putting a new roof on a building.
b. Cost of a tune-up on a truck.
c. Cost of painting a building.
d. Cost of a replacement motor for a machine. The motor will increase the rate of production on the machine.
e. Cost of overhauling the transmission on a truck.
f. Cost of rearranging a plant layout to make it more efficient.

E9-12 Singleton Company traded an old asset for a new one. The cost of the old asset was $50,000 and it had a book value of $10,000. The new asset had a fair market value of $75,000. Give the entry to record the exchange assuming the assets were dissimilar and the following amount of cash was paid:

a. $60,000
b. $70,000

E9-13 Work E9-12 assuming the assets exchanged were similar.

E9-14 Prepare the journal entries necessary to account for the trade-in of an automobile. The old automobile originally cost $4,200, the new automobile has a fair market value of $7,000, the accumulated depreciation on the old automobile to-date is $3,700, and $6,600 cash is required along with the old automobile.

E9-15 A coal mine is estimated to contain 1,500,000 tons of coal reserves and the cost allocated to the reserves is $6,000,000.

Required:

a. Prepare a journal entry to record depletion expense on 125,000 tons of ore removed and sold during the year.
b. Present the balance sheet disclosure of the coal mine at the end of the year.

E9-16 Classify the following investments of a manufacturing firm as temporary or long-term investments:

a. Land that management intends to hold as an investment for appreciation in value.
b. Common stock of a firm listed on the New York Stock Exchange that management plans to sell when the price goes up.
c. Common stock of a local corporation for which there is no established market.
d. Common stock of a supplier that is acquired to insure a constant supply.
e. A two-year note evidencing a loan to a valuable customer who is in temporary financial difficulty.
f. Land in a developing tract that management expects will appreciate rapidly and they will soon sell.
g. Bonds acquired to earn interest on excess funds available in the business.
h. Stock of a subsidiary corporation.

E9-17 The following events are associated with patents of the Ross Development Co.

a. Purchased a patent costing a total of $120,000. Estimated life is eight years.
b. Purchased a patent for $160,000. This patent is estimated to have a ten-year useful life to the firm.
c. Amortized the cost of both patents for one full year and give the journal entry.

Required:

Show how these patents wold be shown in the balance sheet at year-end.

E9-18 The Token Company sold some of its fixed assets during 19x7. The original cost of the fixed assets was $750,000, and the allowance for accumulated depreciation at the date of sale was $600,000. The proceeds from the sale fo the fixed assets were $210,000. Prepare the journal entry to record the sale of the fixed assets by the Token Company.

E9-19 On February 1, 19x7, the Reflection Corporation purchased a parcel of land as a factory site for $50,000. An old building on the property was demolished, and construction began on a new building that was completed on November 1, 19x7. Costs incurred during this period are listed below:

Demolition of old building	$ 4,000
Architect's fees	10,000
Legal fees for title investigation and purchase contract	2,000
Construction costs	500,000

(Salvaged materials resulting from the demolition of the old building were sold for $1,000.)

Reflection Corporation would report the value of the land and the value of the new building at what amounts on their year-end financial statements.

E9-20 On July 1, 19x6, the Carol Corporation purchased factory equipment for $25,000. Salvage value was estimated to be $1,000. The equipment will be depreciated over ten years using the double-declining-balance method. Counting the year of acquisition as one-half year, calculate the amount of depreciation expense that the Carol Corporation should record in for 19x6 and 19x7.

E9-21 On December 1, 19x6, the Hobart Company acquired a new delivery truck in exchange for an old delivery truck that it had acquired in 19x3. The old truck was purchased for $7,000 and had a book value of $2,800. On the date of the exchange, the old truck had a market value of $3,000. In addition, Hobart paid $3,500 cash for the new truck, which had a list price of $8,000. Prepare the journal entry to record this exchange.

PROBLEMS

P9-1 The Retsin Company engaged in the following transactions involving noncurrent assets during the year:

a. Retsin purchased twenty acres of land for $40,000, paid $2,200 in expenses associated with the purchase and $1,600 to have the land prepared for construction.
b. Retsin incurred $20,000 in costs to purchase rights to a patented process. Additional attorney's fees to close the transaction were $3,000.
c. Retsin purchased an earth mover for $26,000. Additional sales taxes on the purchase were $1,030.
d. Retsin abandoned as worthless a truck that had originally cost $11,000 but had a related accumulated depreciation account balance of $9,600. Depreciation for the partial year up to the date of abandonment has not been recorded and is $600.
e. Retsin paid $6,000 to a firm going out of business to acquire an automobile and a truck. The automobile and the truck each had a fair market value of $4,000.

Required:

Prepare general journal entries necessary to record these transactions.

P9-2 Moscowitz and Sons is trading in a printing press for a larger, newer model on September 28, 19x7. The old press was purchased on January 6, 19x1, for $27,000. It was estimated to have a $2,000 salvage value and a useful life of ten years. Straight-line depreciation was used by the firm. The new press has a market value of $68,000, and a $6,000 trade-in allowance is given for the old press.

Required:

a. Give the entry to bring the depreciation up-to-date on the old machine, assuming the firm takes a half-year depreciation on assets in the year of purchase or sale.
b. Give the entry necessary to account for the trade-in.

E9-3 Corbin and Company has the following land, plant, and equipment account balances in 19x5. Depreciation is determined to the nearest half-year.

Item	*Date of Purchase*	*Cost*	*Life*	*Residual Value*
Automobile	1/6/x3	$ 3,600	4 years	$ 600
Office equipment	1/3/x3	9,000	8 years	1,000
Printing press	1/3/x3	13,000	6 years	0
Building	6/28/x3	48,000	30 years	3,000
Land	6/28/x3	10,000		

Required:

a. Calculate depreciation expense for Corbin and Company for 19x5, assuming the building is depreciated using the straight-line method and the double-declining-balance method is used for all other depreciable assets.
b. Give the entries to record depreciation expense.
c. Show the balance sheet presentation of these assets at year-end, December 31, 19x5.

P9-4 Lohman Enterprises acquired an air-conditioning unit this year, paying $18,000 for the unit on September 23, 19x2. Management estimates that the unit has a useful life of ten years and will have no residual value thereafter.

Required:

Calculate straight-line depreciation expense for 19x2 on this air-conditioning unit, based on: (a) the nearest whole month, and (b) the half year "year-of-purchase, year-of-sale" alternative.

P9-5 Reynard Clothiers has remodeled its shop, installing movable clothing racks costing $17,500. The racks are chrome plated and estimated to have a useful life of five years and a residual value of $2,500. They were installed during the second week of the firm's fiscal year.

Required:

Construct a depreciation schedule for these racks showing annual depreciation for each of the five years of its expected life, using the straight-line method, the sum-of-the-years'-digits method and the double-declining-balance method.

P9-6 Rothchild Industries produces corduroy cloth for the apparel industry. The production process is completed in two steps, utilizing two different machines, A and B. Machine A cost $26,000 and has an estimated productive capacity of 1,600,000 yards of cloth. Machine B cost $39,000 and has an estimated productive life of 12,000 machine hours.

Required:

Calculate depreciation expense for 19x3, assuming that machine A produced 243,000 yards of cloth in 19x3 and machine B operated 2,120 hours. Neither machine is expected to have residual value at the end of its life.

P9-7 Hamm Company is curtailing its operations due to a reduction in the demand for its product. To carry out this process, Hamm disposed of the following equipment during 19x4:

Item	*Date of Acquisition*	*Cost*	*Depreciation Method*	*Life*	*Accumulated Depreciation*	*Residual Value*	*Date of Disposition*	*Sales Price*
Leather cutter	1/5/x1	$2,200	Straight-line	5 years	$1,200	200	6/20/x4	Abandoned
Wood Roller	1/5/x1	3,800	Straight-line	6 years	1,800	200	8/26/x4	$ 600
Truck	4/3/x1	5,600	Straight-line	3 years	4,200	1,400	9/3/x4	1,000
Packing machine	1/6/x3	3,000	Double-declining-balance	5 years	1,200	500	12/20/x4	1,500

Required:

Present general journal entries to account for these dispositions during 19x4. Assume the firm uses the nearest half of a year method of recognizing depreciation expense on dispositions during the year.

P9-8 The Greenbriar Coal Company has the following intangible assets and natural resources during 19x8:

Patent on Coal Extraction Process:
Cost—$150,000, Life—12 years, year of development—19x5.

Coal in Lucky Dollar Coal Mine:
Cost—$220,000, total coal at time of discovery—800,000 tons, coal removed and sold in 19x8—136,000 tons.

Coal in Greenbriar Coal Mine:
Cost—$60,000, total coal at time of discovery—1,200,000 tons, coal removed and sold in 19x8—155,000 tons.

Required:

Give the adjusting entries needed at year-end to record depletion expense and patent amortization.

P9-9 The following accounts are found in the general ledger of Simpson, Inc., before year-end adjustment, December 31, 19x7:

Delivery equipment	$25,000
Machinery	45,000
Building	60,000
Land	60,000
Patents	30,000
Goodwill	20,000
Accumulated depreciation—delivery equipment	0
Accumulated depreciation—machinery	18,000
Accumulated depreciation—building	10,000

Additional data about these assets are shown below:

Asset	Date of Acquisition	Depreciation or Amortization Method	Salvage	Life, in Years
Delivery equipment	7/6/x7	Double-declining-balance	$5,000	3
Machinery	1/3/x6	Double-declining-balance	5,000	5
Building	1/8/x2	Straight-line	0	30
Patents	1/8/x2	Straight-line	0	10
Goodwill	1/8/x2	Straight-line	0	10

Required:

a. Prepare general journal adjusting entries to bring these accounts up-to-date on December 31, 19x7, Simpson's year-end.
b. Prepare the long-term asset section of the balance sheet.

P9-10 The Lightfoot Company acquired a new delivery truck on April 3, 19x4, paying the amounts shown here:

List price	$8,000
Options	1,300
Taxes	460
	$9,760
Less: Dealer discount	(1,000)
	$8,760

In addition, the firm added storage racks and decorative lettering to the truck. Costs of these additions were $420 for the racks and $120 for the lettering. All of this work was completed on April 10, 19x4.

Required:

a. Present general journal entries necessary to reflect these activities.
b. Prepare a four-year depreciation schedule using the sum-of-the-years'-digits method assuming a life of four years and a salvage value of $1,300.
c. Give the general journal entry needed to record the trade-in of this truck on April 12, 19x7, on a new truck costing $10,600, given a $4,000 trade-in allowance on the old truck. Remember to bring depreciation up-to-date.

P9-11 During the current year, R. Smith Co. traded an old asset for a new one. The old asset had a cost of $90,000 and a book value of $20,000. The new asset had a fair market value of $160,000. Give the entry to record the exchange under each of the following conditions:

a. $150,000 cash was paid and:
   1. the assets were similar
   2. the assets were dissimilar
b. $130,000 cash was paid and:
   1. The assets were similar
   2. the assets were dissimilar

Learning Objectives

Chapter 10 presents the proper accounting for current liabilities. Studying this chapter should enable you to:

1. Identify the characteristics of liabilities and describe their financial statement disclosure.
2. Present procedures for efficient liability management.
3. Describe the accounting and reporting of deferred revenue.
4. Specify journal entries and financial statement disclosures related to payroll costs and liabilities.
5. Calculate the effects of purchase discount on accounts payable.
6. Determine interest expense and describe disclosure of related liabilities.
7. Calculate future values and present values.

10

Current Liabilities and Time Value of Money

INTRODUCTION

Creditors are one of the most important sources of economic resources for businesses. They provide a firm with the use of goods, services, or direct loans of cash. Claims by creditors of the business are called *liabilities*. They are probable future sacrifices of economic benefits that arise from present obligations to transfer assets or provide services as a result of a past transaction or event. A broad variety of transactions may give rise to liabilities. Direct loans of cash from banks or other sources are common transactions that cause the recognition of liabilities. Credit may also be extended by suppliers who allow the firm to pay for goods or services after the date of purchase. The very nature of some transactions automatically generates a liability. For example, employees are rarely paid at the end of each workday. To avoid the time and expense of drawing daily payroll checks, employees ordinarily are paid weekly, biweekly, or monthly. Because each employee extends services to the business for which he or she will be compensated on payday, he or she is a creditor for that period of time.

CHARACTERISTICS OF LIABILITIES

The following characteristics of liabilities deserve particular notice: the presence of a specific obligation that is measureable or definite in amount and that calls for satisfaction on or before specific future dates.

Specific Obligation

By its very nature, a liability is an obligation of the firm. All legally enforceable obligations constitute accounting liabilities. However, the accounting definition of liability is broader than the legal concept. Liabilities include all future obligations for assets or services that arise from past events or transactions and can be measured or closely estimated in monetary terms.

Most liabilities require the payment of cash to satisfy an obligation. Some liabilities, however, require the provision of specific goods or services to satisfy an obligation. Advances from customers, for example, are called *deferred revenues*. They represent the value of goods or services that the firm is obligated to provide. Even though they do not require the payment of cash, deferred revenues are properly classified as liabilities because they represent an obligation of the firm.

Definite Obligation

The amount of a future obligation must be known or subject to reasonable estimation before it can be classified as an accounting liability. A bank note indicates exactly how much principal and interest must be paid on the loan. An invoice indicates exactly how much the firm must pay for the purchase of goods. The exact amount of some liabilities may not be known, however. For example, the extent of liability to perform under warranty contracts is unknown at the time of the sale of merchandise. Although the firm knows that some warranty claims will be made, it does not know exactly how many or what the cost of those claims will be. If the firm can estimate the amount of future warranty claims, this reasonably definite amount should be recorded as a liability. If the uncertainty of the amount the liability is great or if there is material uncertainty as to the existence of the liability, no liability should be recorded.

For example, a lawsuit may impose substantial liabilities to pay damages if the suit is lost, but no liability at all if it is won. Such liabilities are called *contingent liabilities*. They are potential future obligations which existence will be resolved when one or more future events occur. Contingent liabilities are recorded when it is probable that the future event will occur and when reasonable estimates of the liability can be made. When these two conditions are not met, the contingent liability, if material, is usually disclosed in a footnote. The footnote to the financial statements describe the nature of the contingent liability in order to provide the financial statement user with information about the possible liability.

Specific Due Date

Almost all liabilities require satisfaction on or by a specific date. This date is usually specified in a contract, by a law, or as a matter of business custom. For example, the contract between a lender and borrower usually specifies when the borrower must repay the loan. Tax laws indicate exactly when taxes must be paid. Business custom in a particular industry may determine when a supplier is paid for goods purchased. Some liabilities, however, do not have specific due dates. For example, deferred income taxes, discussed in Chapter 11, may have indeterminate due dates. Nonetheless, they are generally classified as liabilities for lack of a better classification.

CLASSIFICATION OF LIABILITIES

The proper measurement and reporting of liabilities helps the financial statement user to evaluate the financial position of the firm. Of particular importance in assessing the impact of a liability on the firm is the date on which the obligation must be satisfied; this is called the *maturity* date. A great deal of confusion would exist if those liabilities, which must be paid within one week, are combined with long-term liabilities, which may not be repaid for several years. To aid the financial statement user in assessing the impact of liabilities with greatly varying maturity dates, all liabilities are divided into two separate balance sheet classifications: current liabilities and long-term liabilities.

Current liabilities are obligations of the firm that must be satisfied within one year or one operating cycle, whichever is longer. Also, it must be reasonable to expect them to be satisfied by the use of current assets or by the incurrence of additional current liabilities. All other liabilities are classified as long-term liabilities. This classification system produces a balance sheet presentation of liabilities that highlights the impact of differences in maturity dates.

This chapter discusses the measurement and reporting problems of current liabilities, including accounts payable, notes payable, payroll liabilities, accrued liabilities, and deferred revenues. In addition, the second part of this chapter will describe important concepts in the measurement of all liabilities: compound interest and present value. Chapter 11 completes the presentation of liabilities with a discussion of long-term liabilities.

OBJECTIVES IN ACCOUNTING FOR CURRENT LIABILITIES

There are two broad objectives in accounting for current liabilities: to provide for the efficient internal management of current liabilities and their costs and to provide relevant information about current liabilities for financial statement users.

EFFICIENT INTERNAL MANAGEMENT

The efficient internal management of current liabilities is aimed at controlling the costs of using short-term credit and establishing a system of internal controls over the payments made to satisfy current liabilities.

Costs of Credit

If management is to evaluate alternative sources of funds properly, it must have accurate information about differences in costs. The cost of using borrowed funds is the interest charged by the creditor. Interest rates for current liabilities vary widely. Some current liabilities have no cost, while others bear extremely high rates of interest. For example, there is no interest cost associated with paying employees weekly instead of daily. Nor is there any interest expense associated with trade credit, as long as payments are made within the discount period. If the firm fails to pay within the discount period, however, the cost of using trade credit may become very high. For example, if merchandise costing $1,000 is purchased at terms of 2/10, n/30, the firm gets a 2 percent discount if it pays for the merchandise within ten days of the invoice date. Otherwise, the firm must pay the full $1,000 instead of only $980 [$1,000 − ($1,000 × 0.02)]. The 2 percent discount expressed as an annual rate of interest for the use of the credit for an additional twenty days is very high—approximately 36 percent.[1] The rates of interest charged by banks or other commercial lending institutions vary.

Timely Payment

Providing management with information about the relative cost of using credit in various forms is an important function of the accountant. After management has considered costs and established liability policies, the accountant plays an active role in implementing these policies. Trade credit poses a special problem for the firm. Many businesses elect to make all payments within the discount period to avoid the high rates of interest associated with the use of trade credit beyond the discount period. If the payment is delayed, the discount is lost. To insure that discounts are taken, many firms file invoice that require payment in a "tickler file" by discount payment date instead of by vendor's name. All invoices that require payment on a particular day to get the discount are kept in the same file. The use of tickler files reduces the chance that discounts may be accidentally lost.

Some firms also modify their accounting systems to highlight the amount of discounts lost. As we noted in Chapter 5, a purchase normally is recorded at cost:

Purchases	$1,000	
Accounts payable		$1,000

If a discount of 2 percent is taken, the entry to record the payment is:

Accounts payable	$1,000	
Cash		$980
Purchase discounts		20

[1] Two percent (rate for using money for 20 days) times eighteen (approximate number of 20-day periods in a year) equals 36 percent. The difference between paying on the tenth day and the thirtieth day is twenty days. The cost of holding funds for this period is 2 percent, thus the 36 percent annual rate.

But if the discount is lost, this accounting system fails to note this additional interest cost:

Accounts payable	$1,000	
Cash		$1,000

By recording the purchase "net of discount," the accountant creates the vehicle for highlighting lost discounts. Consider these entries to record a purchase, a payment within the discount period, and a payment after the discount period:

Purchase recorded "net of discount:"

Purchases	$980	
Accounts payable		$ 980

Payment within discount period:

Accounts payable	980	
Cash		980

Payment after the discount period:

Accounts payable	980	
Purchases discounts lost	20	
Cash		1,000

Management is continually advised about the consequences of failure to adhere to their discount policy. Since this method separates interest charges from the purchase price of merchandise, it is also theoretically more acceptable. It does not group these dissimilar items together under one label.

INFORMATION FOR FINANCIAL STATEMENT USERS

Two questions are posed by the objective of providing relevant information about current liabilities for external financial statement users: how do we measure current liabilities, and how do we report them on the balance sheet?

The Measurement Issue

To answer the measurement question, current liabilities are initially measured and recorded in accordance with the cost principle. Thereafter all liabilities should, in theory, be reported on the balance sheet as the current cash equivalent amount of the liability, which is often called the present value of the liability. This means that the liability should be reported at the amount for which the liability could paid off, or liquidated, on the balance sheet date. A valuation problem is created when the initial cost valuation of the liability differs from the amount that must be paid at maturity. If the obligation, for example, could be satisfied for $1,000 today or $1,050, ninety days from today, such a valuation problem would be created for a balance sheet that had to be prepared thirty days from today. An implicit interest charge explains the difference in these two values. In the case of current liabilities, however, this valuation problem rarely exists because of the short time period involved before payment of the liability. Generally, the initial cost value placed on a current liability is also the amount that must be repaid later. As a result, accountants run into few valuation problems in valuing current liabilities. Where the problem does arise, it is resolved using present-value techniques. The concepts of compound interest and present value will be discussed at the end of this chapter. Their importance in valuing liabilities will be discussed in the context of long-term liabilities in Chapter 11 where they are more applicable.

The Reporting Issue

The question of how to report current liabilities should be answered in terms of the information needs of the financial statement users. How do users evaluate the impact of current liabilities? Financial statement users perceive the relationship between current assets and current liabilities to be an important measure of the ability of the firm to meet its financial obligations. The term *liquidity* refers to the ability of the firm to pay current debts when they become due. The proper classification of liabilities as either current or long-term provides important information about liquidity to financial statement users. The primary reporting problems in reporting liabilities lie in proper classification of an item as a liability and then in proper classification as a current or long-term liability.

There are two major measures of liquidity that financial statement users calculate to help them assess the relationship between current assets and current liabilities. One measure of this relationship is *working capital*, which is defined as the difference between total current assets and total current liabilities. This relationship may also be expressed as a ratio, commonly called the *current ratio*. It is calculated as current assets divided by current liabilities. Illustration 1 shows the calculation of these two measures.

A $300,000 working capital balance tells the financial statement user that the firm has $300,000 more in current resources to meet current obligations than it requires. Viewed another way, this is the amount of current assets that is available for investment or other purposes without impairing the ability of the firm to pay its current liabilities. Expressed as a ratio, the firm has 2.5 times as many resources to meet current obligations as it has current obligations. Improper classification of current liabilities could mislead the financial statement user by causing him or her to calculate working capital or the current ratio incorrectly. To avoid this error, special care should be taken to classify liabilities appropriately.

Not only should the accountant properly identify and classify all of the liabilities of the firm, but the financial statements should also disclose all relevant details about the current liabilities of the firm that a financial statement user would need to evaluate the impact of the liability on the firm. Due dates, rates of interest, and other relevant information should be presented parenthetically or in footnotes to the financial statements.

Illustration 1
Calculation of Liquidity

Working Capital Calculation

Total current assets		$500,000
Less: Total current liabilities	–	200,000
Working capital		$300,000

Current Ratio Calculation

$$\frac{\text{Total current assets}}{\text{Total current liabilities}} = \frac{\$500{,}000}{\$200{,}000} = 2.5$$

TYPES OF CURRENT LIABILITIES

Accounts Payable

Accounts payable are claims against the firm that generally arise from the purchase of merchandise or supplies on account. An account payable is less formal than a note payable. Generally, no legal debt instrument signed by the parties supports the debt. Instead, the purchase order, invoices, and shipping documents serve as evidence that merchandise was shipped and received by the firm. Two ways of recording the incurrence and payment of accounts payable have been described in this chapter. One involved recording the liability at the full amount of the purchase price. The more theoretically accurate method recorded the liability "net of discount." If the discount was not taken, the additional amount to be paid was reported as "purchases discounts lost." This system more accurately characterizes the interest element as purchases discounts lost and reports the liability at the amount for which it may be satisfied on the day it is incurred.

Notes Payable

A note is a legal debt instrument representing a written promise to pay a stated sum at one or more dates in the future. A note usually provides for the payment of interest. Notes are more formal evidences of obligations than accounts payable. They are legal evidence of the debt and are more easily processed in court in the event of a controversy over the obligation. For these reasons, traditional accounting practice separates classifications for short-term notes payable and accounts payable. The current liability section of the balance sheet should reflect all notes payable that are due within one year, including that portion of the longer term liabilities that are currently falling due.

The party promising to pay the amount of the note is called the *maker* of the note; the party to be paid is called the *payee*. If a note requires the maker to pay interest for the extension of credit, the note is called an *interest-*

bearing note. If the note requires payment of its face amount and no more, the note is called a *noninterest-bearing note*. The accounting treatment for interest-bearing notes differs from noninterest-bearing notes.

Interest-Bearing Notes

The interest terms on interest-bearing notes are always stated as annual rates of interest. The amount of interest to be paid on a short-term note can be calculated by using this formula:

$$\text{Principal} \times \text{Rate} \times \text{Time} = \text{Interest}$$

For example, interest would be calculated on a $1,000, ninety-day note charging 6 percent interest per year as follows:

$$\$1{,}000 \times .06 \times 90 \div 360^{2} = \$15$$

Because this was only a ninety-day note and the interest rate is stated as a rate per year, the time element in the formula adjusts for the actual part of a year the money was used.

When merchandise is purchased and a note is given for the purchase, the maker of the note should record it is follows:

Purchases (or inventory)	$1,000	
Notes payable		$1,000
Gave Ace, Inc. thirty-day, 6 percent note dated June 15, 19x8		

Note that the liability is recorded at its principal or face amount, which corresponds to the cost of the purchases. When the note is paid on July 15, $5 of interest ($\$1{,}000 \times .06 \times 30 \div 360 = \$5$) is also due and would be recorded as follows:

Notes payable	$1,000	
Interest expense	5	
Cash		$1,005

Interest expense is incurred over the period of the note, even though it does not have to be paid until the time specified in the note. Therefore, when the accounting period ends during the term of the note, an adjusting entry must accrue the interest expense that has been incurred but has not yet been paid. This accrual is required to match interest expense with the revenues that the interest expense helps to generate. If the firm's fiscal year ends on June 30, the note given Ace, Inc. in the previous illustrations would require this entry:

---

[2] Interest will be calculated on a 360-day year.

Interest expense	$2.50	
Interest payable		$2.50
Adjusting entry to accrue interest expense on Ace, Inc., note ($1,000 × .06 × 15 ÷ 360 = $2.50)		

When this note is paid on July 15, the entry to record the payment would be as follows:

Notes payable............................	$1,000.00	
Interest payable	2.50	
Interest expense..........................	2.50	
Cash..................................		$1,005.00
Paid Ace, Inc. note, recognized $2.50 in additional interest expense ($1,000 × .06 × 15 ÷ 360 = $2.50)		

Noninterest-Bearing Notes

A noninterest-bearing note is one that requires that the maker pay only the principal, or face amount, of the note. There are actually two types of noninterest bearing notes: discounted notes and true noninterest-bearing notes. A *discounted note* is a note on which interest is subtracted from the principal amount of the note in advance. For example, if a $1,000, sixty-day note is drawn by the maker for a bank loan in the form of a noninterest-bearing note with 6 percent interest on the face discounted, the maker would only receive $990—$10 in interest would be taken in advance. The maker would record the note as follows:

Cash	$990	
Discount on notes payable	10	
Notes payable		$1,000
Borrowed from First State Bank on discounted sixty-day note due March 3 ($1,000 × .06 × 60 ÷ 360 = $10)		

The discount on notes payable account is a contra-liability account. If a balance sheet were prepared on the day this note was made, it would report the note under current liabilities as follows:

Notes payable	$1,000	
Less: Discount on notes payable	10	$990

Payment of the note on March 3 would be recorded as follows:

Notes payable	$1,000	
Interest expense	10	
Discount on notes payable		$ 10
Cash		1,000

Describing a discounted note as noninterest-bearing is misleading. Although no interest is charged above the face of the note, the maker does pay interest, and at a higher rate than the stated discount rate of interest. In the preceding example, the stated rate of interest used in discounting was 6 percent. But note that the effective interest rate is actually 6.06 percent, because $10 in interest was paid for the use of only $990—not $1,000—for sixty days.

Rate of discount .... 6% %
Effective rate of interest:

Interest ÷ Principal	=	Rate for 60 days
$10 ÷ $990	=	1.01%
Annual Rate	=	(6 × Rate for 60 days)
Annual Rate	=	$(6 \times 1.0\dot{1}\%)$

A true noninterest-bearing note is one on which no interest is charged or discounted. Even in this case, professional standards do require that interest be imputed on the note. This means that a portion of the note payable must be recognized and treated as interest, even though none is provided in the note itself.

PAYROLL LIABILITIES

Wages and salaries are frequently the largest single expense incurred by a firm. Accurate accounting for wages and salaries is extremely important. Errors in accounting for wages certainly would destroy employees' confidence in the firm. In addition, employers are legally obligated to withhold certain taxes from the pay of employees, as well as other deductions if the employee consents. The law also requires that employers pay certain payroll taxes. Consequently, accurate accounting for payrolls, payroll deductions from employees, and payroll taxes for the employer, is essential if the firm is to meet its obligations to employees and to the government.

When an employee is hired by the firm, certain information about the employee is gathered for the company's payroll records: the employee's full name; the employee's address; social security number (for proper crediting of social security taxes to the employee's account with the Social Security Administration), number of withholding exemptions claimed for purposes of income taxes to be withheld; the classification of the job to be performed and rate of pay; other deductions to be made by the employer such as union dues, U.S. savings bonds, life or health insurance premiums, pension contributions, and other information that may be helpful to the firm. From this information and a record of the time worked by employees, the accountant prepares the payroll. An understanding of payroll accounting requires a brief review of the various deductions withheld from employees' paychecks and the payroll taxes assessed on the employer.

Payroll Deductions

The most common payroll deductions from employees paychecks are federal and, sometimes, state income taxes, and FICA (social security) taxes. Employers are required by law to withold and remit periodically to the government income taxes out of each employee's paycheck. In this fashion employees pay their income tax gradually throughout the year instead of in one lump sum at the end of the year. The amount of the payroll deduction for income taxes is determined by reference to a set of tables published by the Internal Revenue Service. Withholdings are based on the amount of the employee's pay for the period covered (weekly, monthly, etc.) and the number of withholding exemptions claimed by the employee. The withheld taxes must be remitted to the government by the employer. During the time between withholding money from the employees' paychecks and sending it to the government, a liability to pay these amounts must be recorded on the employer's books.

Under the terms of the Federal Insurance Contribution Act, employers or their family members who are qualified, receive pension benefits at retirement and other benefits such as Medicare and Survivors and Disability Insurance. To receive these benefits, employees must meet the specific requirements of the law and make contributions to pay for the benefits. The contributions are withheld from each covered employee's paycheck. The employer is required to match this amount, paying a sum equal to that withheld from the employee's wage as an additional payroll expense.

Many other payroll deductions are frequently withheld from employee's pay. A contract with a union may require the employer to withhold union dues from the employee's check and periodically pay them to the union. The employee may elect to take advantage of pension plans, life or health insurance plans, stock purchase plans, or other fringe benefits that require him or her to bear some cost of the benefits. These amounts are usually withheld periodically. The employee may also elect to become involved in savings plans. He or she may have a specific sum withheld from his or her paycheck and directly deposited with a private savings institution or invested in U.S. savings bonds.

The entry to record wage and salary expenses and related liabilities for employee deductions is illustrated as follows:

Wage and salary expense	$20,000	
Liability for federal income taxes withheld		$ 3,500
Liability for state income taxes withheld		500
Liability for FICA taxes withheld		1,170
Liability for pension contributions withheld		500
Wages payable		14,330

Each of the liability accounts would be debited when the employer sends the withheld funds to the government as follows:

Liability for federal income taxes withheld	$ 3,500	
Liability for state income taxes withheld	500	
Liability for FICA taxes withheld	1,170	
Cash		$ 5,170
(Paid employee withholdings to government at Federal Reserve Bank in Atlanta)		
Liability for pension contributions withheld	500	
Cash		500
(Paid employee withholdings for pensions to pension trust)		
Wages payable	14,330	
Cash		14,330

Employer Payroll Taxes

In addition to the taxes that must be withheld from the paychecks of employees, the law imposes certain additional taxes on the employer. The employer must pay the Social Security Administration a sum equal to the FICA taxes withheld from employees' paychecks. In accordance with the terms of the Federal Unemployment Tax Act (FUTA), employers are required to pay a tax on wages paid each employee each year to the federal government to support a program of federal unemployment insurance. The tax rate may vary from year-to-year and it is only on wages up to a preset limit. Recently the federal rate has been .6 percent on wages up to $7,000. Furthermore, each state operates an unemployment compensation program and charges a tax on wages up to the same preset limit as the federal tax. Each of these taxes is imposed on the employer—not withheld from the wages of employees[3]—and is a tax expense to be recognized by the firm.

For example, assume that the federal unemployment tax rate is .6 percent and the state rate is 5.4 percent both in wages up to $7,000. Continuing the example from above, assume that $5,000 of the wages paid was to employees who had already earned $7,000 during the year. The entry to record the payroll tax expense would be as follows:

Payroll tax expense	$2,070	
FICA taxes payable........................		$1,170
FUTA taxes payable ($15,000 × .6%)		90
State unemployment taxes payable ($15,000 × 5.4%)		810

The liability accounts for payroll taxes would be debited when payments of taxes are made to the federal and state governments.

ACCRUED LIABILITIES

Accrued liabilities result from end-of-period accounting adjustments for the acquisition of goods or services that remain unpaid. Full disclosure re-

[3] Except in some states.

quires that these liabilities be reported on the balance sheet and that related expenses be recognized on the income statement. As a result, the accountant must search for unrecorded business transactions and recognize accrued liabilities. As discussed in Chapter 4, this recognition takes the form of an adjusting entry made at year-end. Common accrued liabilities include wages payable, income taxes payable, and property taxes payable. The Hornblower Corporation would make the following entry to accrue $105,000 in federal income taxes, which are properly the expense of calendar year 19x8 but not payable until May 15, 19x9.

Income tax expense	$105,000	
Income taxes payable		$105,000
Accrued income tax expense for 19x8		

DEFERRED REVENUES

When advances are received from clients or customers, the standard entry is similar to the following entry for rental income:

Cash	$1,200	
Rental income		$1,200

Care must be made to ensure that all receipts recorded in this manner have been earned by year-end. For example, if the entry just illustrated related to cash received on October 1, 19x5, for twelve months rental paid in advance, financial statements prepared on December 31, 19x5, would also fail to show that the firm has a current liability to perform under the rental contract. An adjusting entry would recognize the deferred revenue and reduce the revenue account:

Rental income	$900	
Deferred rental income....................		$900

Financial statements will now report $300 in earned rental income and $900 in deferred rents to be earned in the next accounting period.

THE TIME VALUE OF MONEY: COMPOUND INTEREST AND PRESENT VALUE

Given the opportunity to receive $1 today or $1 in one year, most people choose to receive $1 today. They do so because they have a *time preference for money*. Money has time preference, or value, because its early possession opens opportunities for investment or early consumption. For example, $1 invested at 6 percent simple interest per year is worth $1.06 at the end of one year. Clearly, $1.06 received at the end of one year is preferable to $1 received at the end of one year. If consumption rather than investment is the individual's objective, $1 received today would be preferable to $1 to be received at the end of one year, if all other factors are unchanged, because it allows immediate instead of postponed consumption. As a result of the time preference for money, money may be said to have *time value*.

The concept of the time value of money is very important in accounting. It is used by the accountant to calculate the amount of periodic payments needed to repay debt, the recorded value of noninterest-bearing notes, the recorded value of assets acquired for debt, and many other value measurements. Measuring the time value of money requires that an interest rate be known. The rate would be what the company would have to pay if it borrowed the money from a bank, called the *incremental borrowing rate*. The rate could also be the rate of interest that the company would earn by investing money, called the *earning rate*.

After determining the appropriate rate, the accountant is now able to calculate the time value of a specific amount of money. Two kinds of problems can be solved: (1) we can take a sum of money today and determine its value at some future point in time, or (2) we can take a sum of money in the *future* and determine its value today. In the first kind of problem, we calculate the future *amount* of money. For example, we can calculate the future amount that would be available at the end of four years, assuming that $100 was invested in a bank at 6 percent interest. In the second kind of problem, we calculate the *present value* of money. This, for example, would allow an accountant to determine how much must be invested in a bank at 6 percent interest to have $100 available in four years. The remainder of this discussion will demonstrate the techniques for calculating the future amount and present value of money.

FUTURE AMOUNT AND COMPOUND INTEREST

Compound interest extends the concept of simple interest beyond one year. Using compound interest, accountants can evaluate decisions that extend two, four, or more years into the future. For example, an accountant with a 10 percent time value of money and an opportunity to receive $100 now or some money in three years could calculate the indifference values as $100 now or $110 a year from now; $100 now or $121 two years from now; or $100 now and $133 three years from now. To determine the second- and third-year amounts, consider each year as a separate proposition. For example, at the end of the first year, the future value would be $110. At the end of the second year, the future amount would be 10 percent more than $110, or $121. At the end of the third year, $133 (rounded to the nearest whole dollar). The first year's interest would amount to $10, the second year's interest would amount to an additional $11, and the third year's interest would be an additional $12. In other words, each year's interest is calculated on both the interest from prior years and the original $100. Calculating interest on interest is called *compounding*.

A simple formula can be used to determine the future amount for any number of future years in return for $1 given up initially at any rate of interest. Let r represent the decimal equivalent of the rate of interest and let n represent the number of years before payoff. The amount an individual would require in return for an initial $1 given up for n years at r rate of interest is equal to \$1 times $(1.0 + r)^n$. Applying the formula to the previous example of a three-year indifference situation and a 10 percent rate of interest, the payoff at the end of three years equals \$1 times $(1.0 + .10)^3$, or \$1.33 (rounded). Since the initial investment was \$100 and not \$1, the payoff is calculated by multiplying the \$100 by the results determined from the formula, or \$133. The initial investment is commonly called *principal* and is abbreviated as *P*. The compound interest formula to yield some future value for any amount, *P*, for *n* years at *r* rate of interest is $P(1.0 + r)^n$.

For any given *n* and *r*, the compound interest formula will produce only one answer, thus allowing a compound interest table to be drawn. Table 10-1 is a compound interest table. To use Table 10-1, select the desired interest rate in one of the columns. Next select a row that corresponds to the number of periods during which the compounding is to occur. Then find the intersection of the row and the column to find the compounded value of principal and interest for \$1 for that rate and period of time. For example, the value of \$1 to be invested for five years at 6 percent interest is \$1.3382; for six years at 8 percent interest is \$1.5869. For original amounts other than \$1, simply multiply the principal by the factor from the table.

If the accountant is attempting to calculate the future amount of several deposits to a bank account, the procedures just described are followed; each deposit is treated separately. For example, if \$100 is deposited on the first day of the year, \$200 in year 2, and \$300 in year 3, the accumulated balance of the account compounded annually at 6 percent interest is calculated in this fashion:

$$[\$100(1.06)]^3 + [\$200(1.06)]^2 + [\$300(1.06)] = \$661.82$$

This problem could be alternatively solved by using Table 10-1 as follows:

Amount		*Future Amount Factor n Periods at 6%*		*Total*
\$100	×	1.1910 where $n = 3$	=	\$119.10
\$200	×	1.1236 where $n = 2$	=	\$224.72
\$300	×	1.0600 where $n = 1$	=	\$318.00
				\$661.82

If the stream of payments is an *annuity*, a great deal of simplification is possible. An annuity is a series of equal sums of money to be received or paid at regular intervals. The payment or receipt may occur at either the beginning or the end of the period, but compound interest applies only to sums covered by the full period; that is, no interest accrues on principal invested at the end of the period or withdrawn at the beginning of the period. A table can be constructed to display the growth of an annuity, much as compound interest tables display the growth of a single amount. Table 10-2 parallels the compound interest Table 10-1. For example, consider the following situation.

One thousand dollars are deposited in a savings account at the end of each year for four years. If the account pays 6 percent interest compounded annually, what is the balance of the account at the end of the fourth year? Deposits such as these, where the investment is made at the end of the year, would result in $1,000 accruing interest for three years, another $1,000 accruing interest for two years, and another $1,000 for one year. The final deposit would not accrue interest since it was made at the end of the year. If we go to the 6 percent column, fourth row in Table 10-2 and find the factor 4.37462, which represents the future amount of an annuity of $1. Finally, to find the balance at the end of the fourth year, multiply the factor by the principal: 4.37462 × $1,000 = $4,374.12.

DISCOUNTED PRESENT VALUE

Compound interest allows us to calculate the future unknown amount of some currently known amount of money. The original problem can be reversed by asking, "How much would we be willing to pay now in order to receive $106 one year from today or $112.36 two years from today, assuming a 6 percent rate of interest?" Based on our prior calculation, we know that the amount would be $100. What we have done, however, is to discount some future amount back to its present value—hence the name discounted present value.

Discounted present value is the amount of current cash that is equivalent to some specified amount of cash to be received or given in some specified future period. Calculation of a discounted present value requires data on the amount of the future flow, the date of the flow, and the interest rate. For example, we can readily calculate that $100 is the discounted present value of $106 one year from today and $112.36 two years from today, assuming a 6 percent rate of interest compounded annually. A formula for discounted present value can be easily calculated, since it is nothing more than the reciprocal of the compound interest formula. That is, for compound interest we were willing to pay out $1 now in order to receive $1 multiplied by $(1.0 + r)^n$ at some future date. Under the present-value assumption, we would be willing to receive $1 in the future only if the amount that we had to pay out now were $1 multiplied by $1 \div (1 + r)^n$. For example, consider the following. How much would you be willing to pay now (discounted present value) in order to receive $100 (P) in three years ($n = 3$) if the rate of interest we require is 10 percent (r)? The terms in the brackets equal 0.751.

$$P\left[\frac{1}{(1 + 0.1)^3}\right]$$

To find the discounted present value of $100, multiply $100 times 0.751; the answer is $75.10.

For any given n and r, the discounted present value formula will produce only one answer, thus allowing a precalculation of present-value tables. Table 10-3 is a present value table. To use Table 10-3, select an interest rate, next select a row corresponding to the number of future periods that will pass before the future flows will occur. Then find the intersection of the row and the column to find the discounted present value of $1 for that rate and period of time. For example, the discounted present value of $1 to be received in five years at 6 percent interest is $0.74726; in six years at 8 percent interest it is $0.63017. If the principal were some amount other than $1, simply multiply the principal by the factor found in the table. Table 10-3 can be used to determine the present value of a stream of cash flows simply by multiplying the appropriate factors from the table by the corresponding amount of cash flow for each year. For example, if the amount to be received at the end of one year equals $100, at the end of two years equals $200, and at the end of three years equals $300, what is the discounted present value of this flow of cash, given a 6 percent rate? Using Table 10-3, the solution to this problem is as follows:

Amount		*Future Amount Factor n Periods at 6%*		*Total*
$100	×	0.9434 where $n = 1$	=	$ 94.34
$200	×	0.8900 where $n = 2$	=	$178.00
$300	×	0.8396 where $n = 3$	=	$251.88
				$524.22

If the stream of payments is an *annuity*, the calculation is once again simplified. Table 10-4 gives the present value of an annuity of $1 per period. The factors shown in Table 10-4 illustrate the algebraic summation of the present-value factors (previously shown in Table 10-3) for the appropriate interest rate and number of periods. The date of valuation of the annuity is the beginning of the first period and is constructed to answer questions such as: "What single sum must be deposited in a fund on the first of every year to permit five annual withdrawals of $1,000 each, beginning on the last day of each year, assuming that the fund pays 6 percent interest compounded annually?" To find the answer, look at Table 10-4, row five ($n = 5$), in the 6 percent interest column, for the factor 4.21236. Multiplying this factor by $1,000 produces the answer to the problem, $4,212.36. This is the amount that would have to be deposited at the beginning of the first year to provide constant payments of $1,000 each at the end of the next five years. Notice that each factor in each column of Table 10-4 is a vertical accumulation of preceding factors from Table 10-3.

Table 10-1
Future Value Amount of $1.00

Periods	Interest 6%	8%	10%	11%	12%	15%	18%
1	1.06000	1.08000	1.10000	1.11000	1.12000	1.15000	1.18000
2	1.12360	1.16640	1.21000	1.23210	1.25440	1.32250	1.39240
3	1.19102	1.25971	1.33100	1.36763	1.40493	1.52087	1.64303
4	1.26248	1.36049	1.46410	1.51807	1.57352	1.74901	1.93878
5	1.33823	1.46933	1.61051	1.68506	1.76234	2.01136	2.28776
6	1.41852	1.58687	1.77156	1.87041	1.97382	2.31306	2.69955
7	1.50363	1.71382	1.94872	2.07616	2.21068	2.66002	3.18547
8	1.59385	1.85093	2.14359	2.30454	2.47596	3.05902	3.75886
9	1.68948	1.99900	2.35795	2.55804	2.77308	3.51788	4.43545
10	1.79085	2.15892	2.59374	2.83942	3.10585	4.04556	5.23384
11	1.89830	2.33164	2.85312	3.15176	3.47855	4.65239	6.17593
12	2.01220	2.51817	3.13843	3.49845	3.89598	5.35025	7.28759
13	2.13293	2.71962	3.45227	3.88328	4.36349	6.15279	8.59936
14	2.26090	2.93719	3.79750	4.31044	4.88711	7.07571	10.14724
15	2.39656	3.17217	4.17725	4.78459	5.47357	8.13706	11.97375
16	2.54035	3.42594	4.59497	5.31089	6.13039	9.35762	14.12902
17	2.69277	3.70002	5.05447	5.89509	6.86604	10.76126	16.67225
18	2.85434	3.99602	5.55992	6.54355	7.68997	12.37545	19.67325
19	3.02560	4.31570	6.11591	7.26334	8.61276	14.23177	23.21444
20	3.20714	4.66096	6.72750	8.06231	9.64629	16.36654	27.39303
21	3.39956	5.03383	7.40025	8.94917	10.80385	18.82152	32.32378
22	3.60354	5.43654	8.14027	9.93357	12.10031	21.64475	38.14206
23	3.81975	5.87146	8.95430	11.02627	13.55235	24.89146	45.00763
24	4.04893	6.34118	9.84973	12.23916	15.17863	28.62518	53.10901
25	4.29187	6.84848	10.83471	13.58546	17.00006	32.91895	62.66863
26	4.54938	7.39635	11.91818	15.07986	19.04007	37.85680	73.94898
27	4.82235	7.98806	13.10999	16.73865	21.32488	43.53531	87.25980
28	5.11169	8.62711	14.42099	18.57990	23.83387	50.06561	102.96656
29	5.41839	9.31727	15.86309	20.62369	26.74993	57.57545	121.50054
30	5.74349	10.06266	17.44940	22.89230	29.95992	66.21177	143.37064
31	6.08810	10.86767	19.19434	25.41045	33.55511	76.14354	169.17735
32	6.45339	11.73708	21.11378	28.20560	37.58173	87.56507	199.62928
33	6.84059	12.67605	23.22515	31.30821	42.09153	100.69983	235.56255
34	7.25103	13.69013	25.54767	34.75212	47.14252	115.80480	277.96381
35	7.68609	14.78534	28.10244	38.57485	52.79962	133.17552	327.99729
36	8.14725	15.96817	30.91268	42.81808	59.13557	153.15185	387.03680
37	8.63609	17.24563	34.00395	47.52807	66.23184	176.12463	456.70343
38	9.15425	18.62528	37.40434	52.75616	74.17966	202.54332	538.91004
39	9.70351	20.11530	41.14478	58.55934	83.08122	232.92482	635.91385
40	10.28572	21.72452	45.25926	65.00087	93.05097	267.86355	750.37834
41	10.90286	23.46248	49.78518	72.15096	104.21709	308.04308	855.44645
42	11.55703	25.33948	54.76370	80.08757	116.72314	354.24954	1044.82681
43	12.25045	27.36664	60.24007	88.89720	130.72991	407.38697	1232.89563
44	12.98548	29.55597	66.26408	98.67589	146.41750	468.49502	1454.81685
45	13.76461	31.92045	72.89048	109.53024	163.98760	538.76927	1716.68388
46	14.59049	34.47409	80.17953	121.57857	183.66612	619.58466	2025.68698
47	15.46592	37.23201	88.19749	134.95221	205.70605	712.52236	2390.31063
48	16.39387	40.21057	97.01723	149.79695	230.39078	819.40071	2820.56655
49	17.37750	43.42742	106.71896	166.27462	258.03767	942.31082	3328.26853
50	18.42015	46.90161	117.39085	184.56483	289.00219	1083.65744	3927.35686
51	19.52536	50.65374	129.12994	204.86696	323.68245	1246.20606	4634.28109
52	20.69689	54.70604	142.04293	227.40232	362.52435	1433.13697	5468.45169
53	21.93870	59.08252	156.24723	252.41658	406.02727	1648.10751	6452.77300
54	23.25502	63.80913	171.87195	280.18240	454.75054	1895.32364	7614.27214
55	24.65032	68.91386	189.05914	311.00247	509.32061	2179.62218	8984.84112
56	26.12934	74.42696	207.96506	345.21274	570.43908	2506.56551	10602.11252
57	27.69710	80.38112	228.76156	383.18614	638.89177	2882.55034	12510.49278
58	29.35893	86.81161	251.63772	425.33661	715.55878	3314.93289	14762.38148
59	31.12046	93.75654	276.80149	472.12364	801.42583	3812.17282	17419.61014
60	32.98769	101.25706	304.48164	524.05724	897.59693	4383.99875	20555.13997

Table 10-2
Future Value Annuity of $1.00

Periods	6%	8%	10%	11%	12%	15%	18%
1	1.00000	1.00000	1.00000	1.00000	1.00000	1.00000	1.00000
2	2.06000	2.08000	2.10000	2.11000	2.12000	2.15000	2.18000
3	3.18360	3.24640	3.31000	3.34210	3.37440	3.47250	3.57240
4	4.37462	4.50611	4.64100	4.70973	4.77933	4.99337	5.21543
5	5.63709	5.86660	6.10510	6.22780	6.35285	6.74238	7.15421
6	6.97532	7.33593	7.71561	7.91286	8.11519	8.75374	9.44197
7	8.39384	8.92280	9.48717	9.78327	10.08901	11.06680	12.14152
8	9.89747	10.63663	11.43589	11.85943	12.29969	13.72682	15.32700
9	11.49132	12.48756	13.57948	14.16397	14.77566	16.78584	19.08585
10	13.18079	14.48656	15.93742	16.72201	17.54874	20.30372	23.52131
11	14.97164	16.64549	18.53117	19.56143	20.65458	24.34928	28.75514
12	16.86994	18.97713	21.38428	22.71319	24.13313	29.00167	34.93107
13	18.88214	21.49530	24.52271	26.21164	28.02911	34.35192	42.21866
14	21.01507	24.21492	27.97498	30.09492	32.39260	40.50471	50.81802
15	23.27597	27.15211	31.77248	34.40536	37.27971	47.58041	60.96527
16	25.67253	30.32428	35.94973	39.18995	42.74328	55.71747	72.93901
17	28.21288	33.75023	40.54470	44.50084	48.88367	65.07509	87.06804
18	30.90565	37.45024	45.59917	50.39594	55.74971	75.83636	103.74028
19	33.75999	41.44626	51.15909	56.93949	63.43968	88.21181	123.41353
20	36.78559	45.76196	57.27500	64.20283	72.05244	102.44358	146.62797
21	39.99273	50.42292	64.00250	72.26514	81.69874	118.81012	174.02100
22	43.39229	55.45676	71.40275	81.21431	92.50258	137.63164	206.34479
23	46.99583	60.89330	79.54302	91.14788	104.60289	159.27638	244.48685
24	50.81558	66.76476	88.49733	102.17415	118.15524	184.16784	289.49448
25	54.86451	73.10594	98.34706	114.41331	133.33387	212.79302	342.60349
26	59.15638	79.95442	109.18177	127.99877	150.33393	245.71197	405.27211
27	63.70577	87.35077	121.09994	143.07864	169.37401	283.56877	479.22109
28	68.52811	95.33883	134.20994	159.81729	190.69889	327.10408	566.48089
29	73.63980	103.96594	148.63093	178.39719	214.58275	377.16969	669.44745
30	79.05819	113.28321	164.49402	199.02088	241.33268	434.74515	790.94799
31	84.80168	123.34587	181.94342	221.91317	271.29261	500.95692	934.31863
32	90.88978	134.21354	201.13777	247.32362	304.84772	577.10046	1103.49598
33	97.34316	145.95062	222.25154	275.52922	342.42945	664.66552	1303.12526
34	104.18375	158.62667	245.47670	306.83744	384.52098	765.36535	1538.68781
35	111.43478	172.31680	271.02437	341.58955	431.66350	881.17016	1816.65161
36	119.12087	187.10215	299.12681	380.16441	484.46312	1014.34568	2144.64890
37	127.26812	203.07032	330.03949	422.98249	543.59869	1167.49753	2531.68570
38	135.90421	220.31595	364.04343	470.51056	609.83053	1343.62216	2988.38913
39	145.05846	238.94122	401.44778	523.26673	684.01020	1546.16549	3527.29918
40	154.76197	259.05652	442.59256	581.82607	767.09142	1779.09031	4163.21303
41	165.04768	280.78104	487.85181	646.82693	860.14239	2046.95385	4913.59137
42	175.95054	304.24352	537.63699	718.97790	964.35948	2354.99693	5799.03782
43	187.50758	329.58301	592.40069	799.06547	1081.08262	2709.24647	6843.86463
44	199.75803	356.94965	652.64076	887.96267	1211.81253	3116.63344	8076.76026
45	212.74351	386.50562	718.90484	986.63856	1358.23003	3585.12846	9531.57711
46	226.50812	418.42607	791.79532	1096.16880	1522.21764	4123.89773	11248.26098
47	241.09861	452.90015	871.97485	1217.74737	1705.88375	4743.48239	13273.94796
48	256.56453	490.13216	960.17234	1352.69958	1911.58980	5456.00475	15664.25859
49	272.95840	530.34274	1057.18957	1502.49653	2141.98058	6275.40546	18484.82514
50	290.33590	573.77016	1163.90853	1668.77115	2400.01825	7217.71628	21813.09367
51	308.75606	620.67177	1281.29938	1853.33598	2689.02044	8301.37372	25740.45053
52	328.28142	671.32551	1410.42932	2058.20294	3012.70289	9547.57978	30374.73162
53	348.97831	726.03155	1552.47225	2285.60526	3375.22724	10980.71674	35843.18331
54	370.91701	785.11408	1708.71948	2538.02184	3781.25451	12628.82425	42295.95631
55	394.17203	848.92320	1880.59142	2818.20424	4236.00505	14524.14789	49910.22844
56	418.82235	917.83706	2069.65057	3129.20671	4745.32565	16703.77008	58895.06957
57	444.95169	992.26402	2277.61562	3474.41944	5315.76473	19210.33559	69497.18209
58	472.64879	1072.64514	2506.37719	3857.60558	5954.65650	22092.88593	82007.67486
59	502.00772	1159.45676	2758.01490	4282.94220	6670.21528	25407.81882	96770.05634
60	533.12818	1253.21330	3034.81640	4755.06584	7471.64111	29219.99164	114189.66648

Table 10-3
Present Value of $1.00

	Interest						
Periods	*6%*	*8%*	*10%*	*11%*	*12%*	*15%*	*18%*
1	0.94340	0.92593	0.90909	0.90090	0.89286	0.86957	0.84746
2	0.89000	0.85734	0.82645	0.81162	0.79719	0.75614	0.71818
3	0.83962	0.79383	0.75131	0.73119	0.71178	0.65752	0.60863
4	0.79209	0.73503	0.68301	0.65873	0.63552	0.57175	0.51579
5	0.74726	0.68058	0.62092	0.59345	0.56743	0.49718	0.43711
6	0.70496	0.63017	0.56447	0.53464	0.50663	0.43233	0.37043
7	0.66506	0.58349	0.51316	0.48166	0.45235	0.37594	0.31393
8	0.62741	0.54027	0.46651	0.43393	0.40388	0.32690	0.26604
9	0.59190	0.50025	0.42410	0.39092	0.36061	0.28426	0.22546
10	0.55839	0.46319	0.38554	0.35218	0.32197	0.24718	0.19106
11	0.52679	0.42888	0.35049	0.31728	0.28748	0.21494	0.16192
12	0.49697	0.39711	0.31863	0.28584	0.25668	0.18691	0.13722
13	0.46884	0.36770	0.28966	0.25751	0.22917	0.16253	0.11629
14	0.44230	0.34046	0.26333	0.23199	0.20462	0.14133	0.09855
15	0.41727	0.31524	0.23939	0.20900	0.18270	0.12289	0.08352
16	0.39365	0.29189	0.21763	0.18829	0.16312	0.10686	0.07078
17	0.37136	0.27027	0.19784	0.16963	0.14564	0.09293	0.05998
18	0.35034	0.25025	0.17986	0.15282	0.13004	0.08081	0.05083
19	0.33051	0.23171	0.16351	0.13768	0.11611	0.07027	0.04308
20	0.31180	0.21455	0.14864	0.12403	0.10367	0.06110	0.03651
21	0.29416	0.19866	0.13513	0.11174	0.09256	0.05313	0.03094
22	0.27751	0.18394	0.12285	0.10067	0.08264	0.04620	0.02622
23	0.26180	0.17032	0.11168	0.09069	0.07379	0.04017	0.02222
24	0.24698	0.15770	0.10153	0.08170	0.06588	0.03493	0.01883
25	0.23300	0.14602	0.09230	0.07361	0.05882	0.03038	0.01596
26	0.21981	0.13520	0.08391	0.06631	0.05252	0.02642	0.01352
27	0.20737	0.12519	0.07628	0.05974	0.04689	0.02297	0.01146
28	0.19563	0.11591	0.06934	0.05382	0.04187	0.01997	0.00971
29	0.18456	0.10733	0.06304	0.04849	0.03738	0.01737	0.00823
30	0.17411	0.09938	0.05731	0.04368	0.03338	0.01510	0.00697
31	0.16425	0.09202	0.05210	0.03935	0.02980	0.01313	0.00591
32	0.15496	0.08520	0.04736	0.03545	0.02661	0.01142	0.00501
33	0.14619	0.07889	0.04306	0.03194	0.02376	0.00993	0.00425
34	0.13791	0.07305	0.03914	0.02878	0.02121	0.00864	0.00360
35	0.13011	0.06763	0.03558	0.02592	0.01894	0.00751	0.00305
36	0.12274	0.06262	0.03235	0.02335	0.01691	0.00653	0.00258
37	0.11579	0.05799	0.02941	0.02104	0.01510	0.00568	0.00219
38	0.10924	0.05369	0.02673	0.01896	0.01348	0.00494	0.00186
39	0.10306	0.04971	0.02430	0.01708	0.01204	0.00429	0.00157
40	0.09722	0.04603	0.02209	0.01538	0.01075	0.00373	0.00133
41	0.09172	0.04262	0.02009	0.01386	0.00960	0.00325	0.00113
42	0.08653	0.03946	0.01826	0.01249	0.00857	0.00282	0.00096
43	0.08163	0.03654	0.01660	0.01125	0.00765	0.00245	0.00081
44	0.07701	0.03383	0.01509	0.01013	0.00683	0.00213	0.00069
45	0.07265	0.03133	0.01372	0.00913	0.00610	0.00186	0.00058
46	0.06854	0.02901	0.01247	0.00823	0.00544	0.00161	0.00049
47	0.06466	0.02686	0.01134	0.00741	0.00486	0.00140	0.00042
48	0.06100	0.02487	0.01031	0.00668	0.00434	0.00122	0.00035
49	0.05755	0.02303	0.00937	0.00601	0.00388	0.00106	0.00030
50	0.05429	0.02132	0.00852	0.00542	0.00346	0.00092	0.00025
51	0.05122	0.01974	0.00774	0.00488	0.00309	0.00080	0.00022
52	0.04832	0.01828	0.00704	0.00440	0.00276	0.00070	0.00018
53	0.04558	0.01693	0.00640	0.00396	0.00246	0.00061	0.00015
54	0.04300	0.01567	0.00582	0.00357	0.00220	0.00053	0.00013
55	0.04057	0.01451	0.00529	0.00322	0.00196	0.00046	0.00011
56	0.03827	0.01344	0.00481	0.00290	0.00175	0.00040	0.00009
57	0.03610	0.01244	0.00437	0.00261	0.00157	0.00035	0.00008
58	0.03406	0.01152	0.00397	0.00235	0.00140	0.00030	0.00007
59	0.03213	0.01067	0.00361	0.00212	0.00125	0.00026	0.00006
60	0.03031	0.00988	0.00328	0.00191	0.00111	0.00023	0.00005

Table 10-4
Present Value of Annuity of $1.00

	Interest						
Periods	*6%*	*8%*	*10%*	*11%*	*12%*	*15%*	*18%*
1	0.94340	0.92593	0.90909	0.90090	0.89286	0.86957	0.84746
2	1.83339	1.78326	1.73554	1.71252	1.69005	1.62571	1.56564
3	2.67301	2.57710	2.48685	2.44371	2.40183	2.28323	2.17427
4	3.46511	3.31213	3.16987	3.10245	3.03735	2.85498	2.69006
5	4.21236	3.99271	3.79079	3.69590	3.60478	3.35216	3.12717
6	4.91732	4.62288	4.35526	4.23054	4.11141	3.78448	3.49760
7	5.58238	5.20637	4.86842	4.71220	4.56376	4.16042	3.81153
8	6.20979	5.74664	5.33493	5.14612	4.96764	4.48732	4.07757
9	6.80169	6.24689	5.75902	5.53705	5.32825	4.77158	4.30302
10	7.36009	6.71008	6.14457	5.88923	5.65022	5.01877	4.49409
11	7.88687	7.13896	6.49506	6.20652	5.93770	5.23371	4.65601
12	8.38384	7.53608	6.81369	6.49236	6.19437	5.42062	4.79322
13	8.85268	7.90378	7.10336	6.74987	6.42355	5.58315	4.90951
14	9.29498	8.24424	7.36669	6.98187	6.62817	5.72448	5.00806
15	9.71225	8.55948	7.60608	7.19087	6.81086	5.84737	5.09158
16	10.10590	8.85137	7.82371	7.37916	6.97399	5.95423	5.16235
17	10.47726	9.12164	8.02155	7.54879	7.11963	6.04716	5.22233
18	10.82760	9.37189	8.20141	7.70162	7.24967	6.12797	5.27316
19	11.15812	9.60360	8.36492	7.83929	7.36578	6.19823	5.31624
20	11.46992	9.81815	8.51356	7.96333	7.46944	6.25933	5.35275
21	11.76408	10.01680	8.64869	8.07507	7.56200	6.31246	5.38368
22	12.04158	10.20074	8.77154	8.17574	7.64465	6.35866	5.40990
23	12.30338	10.37106	8.88322	8.26643	7.71843	6.39884	5.43212
24	12.55036	10.52876	8.98474	8.34814	7.78432	6.43377	5.45095
25	12.78336	10.67478	9.07704	8.42174	7.84314	6.46415	5.46691
26	13.00317	10.80998	9.16095	8.48806	7.89566	6.49056	5.48043
27	13.21053	10.93516	9.23722	8.54780	7.94255	6.51353	5.49189
28	13.40616	11.05108	9.30657	8.60162	7.98442	6.53351	5.50160
29	13.59072	11.15841	9.36961	8.65011	8.02181	6.55088	5.50983
30	13.76483	11.25778	9.42691	8.69379	8.05518	6.56598	5.51681
31	13.92909	11.34980	9.47901	8.73315	8.08499	6.57911	5.52272
32	14.08404	11.43500	9.52638	8.76860	8.11159	6.59053	5.52773
33	14.23023	11.51389	9.56943	8.80054	8.13535	6.60046	5.53197
34	14.36814	11.58693	9.60857	8.82932	8.15656	6.60910	5.53557
35	14.49825	11.65457	9.64416	8.85524	8.17550	6.61661	5.53862
36	14.62099	11.71719	9.67651	8.87859	8.19241	6.62314	5.54120
37	14.73678	11.77518	9.70592	8.89963	8.20751	6.62881	5.54339
38	14.84602	11.82887	9.73265	8.91859	8.22099	6.63375	5.54525
39	14.94907	11.87858	9.75696	8.93567	8.23303	6.63805	5.54682
40	15.04630	11.92461	9.77905	8.95105	8.24378	6.64178	5.54815
41	15.13802	11.96723	9.79914	8.96491	8.25337	6.64502	5.54928
42	15.22454	12.00670	9.81740	8.97740	8.26194	6.64785	5.55024
43	15.30617	12.04324	9.83400	8.98865	8.26959	6.65030	5.55105
44	15.38318	12.07707	9.84909	8.99878	8.27642	6.65244	5.55174
45	15.45583	12.10840	9.86281	9.00791	8.28252	6.65429	5.55232
46	15.52437	12.13741	9.87528	9.01614	8.28796	6.65591	5.55281
47	15.58903	12.16427	9.88662	9.02355	8.29282	6.65731	5.55323
48	15.65003	12.18914	9.89693	9.03022	8.29716	6.65853	5.55359
49	15.70757	12.21216	9.90630	9.03624	8.30104	6.65959	5.55389
50	15.76186	12.23348	9.91481	9.04165	8.30450	6.66051	5.55414
51	15.81308	12.25323	9.92256	9.04653	8.30759	6.66132	5.55436
52	15.86139	12.27151	9.92960	9.05093	8.31035	6.66201	5.55454
53	15.90697	12.28843	9.93600	9.05489	8.31281	6.66262	5.55469
54	15.94998	12.30410	9.94182	9.05846	8.31501	6.66315	5.55483
55	15.99054	12.31861	9.94711	9.06168	8.31697	6.66361	5.55494
56	16.02881	12.33205	9.95191	9.06457	8.31872	6.66401	5.55503
57	16.06492	12.34449	9.95629	9.06718	8.32029	6.66435	5.55511
58	16.09898	12.35601	9.96026	9.06954	8.32169	6.66466	5.55518
59	16.13111	12.36668	9.96387	9.07165	8.32294	6.66492	5.55524
60	16.16143	12.37655	9.96716	9.07356	8.32405	6.66515	5.55529

SUMMARY

This chapter considered the major accounting problems of current liabilities. A liability is an obligation to convey specific assets or perform specific services of definite or measurable amount on or by specific future dates. Once having determined that an obligation is a liability, its classification as a current liability or a long-term liability is critical to the proper interpretation of the balance sheet. Failure to classify current liabilities properly can obscure the calculation of working capital and the current ratio, two liquidity measures used by financial statement users to determine the ability of the firm to meet its obligations.

The primary objectives in accounting for current liabilities are promoting efficient internal management of current liabilities, minimizing their costs, and providing information for financial statement users. Efficiency is accomplished by providing management with the information it needs to establish policies for the use of current liabilities, by implementing these policies, and by establishing controls over disbursements of cash. Cost information is perhaps the most critical in establishing policies about current liabilities. By using tickler files for accounts payable and recording purchases net of discount to highlight discounts lost, the accountant can help to insure that management policies are fully implemented.

Providing information to financial statement users requires that the current liabilities of the firm—accounts payable, notes payable, payroll liabilities, accrued liabilities, and deferred revenues—be accounted for in accordance with generally accepted principles. Current liabilities should be initially recorded at cost and thereafter reported at their present values.

The chapter also presented compound interest and discounting techniques. An investment in an interest bearing account will grow to a larger amount in the future, this is called its compound value. A future amount that is due can be settled for less today because a lesser amount can be set aside in an interest drawing account and the principle plus the interest earned will meet the future payment. The amount that would have to be invested today is called the present value. Compound amounts and present values can also be applied to a recurring stream of payments called an annuity.

KEY DEFINITIONS

Contingent liability—potential future obligations whose existence will be resolved when one or more future events occur.

Current liability—a liability that will be paid out of existing current assets or require the creation of another current liability within one year or operating cycle.

Current ratio—current assets divided by current liabilities.

Deferred revenues—revenues that have been collected in advance but have not yet been earned.

Discounted note—a note on which the interest is deducted from the principal in advance.

Interest-bearing note—a promissory note that has a stated rate of interest.

Liabilities—probable future sacrifices of economic benefits that arise from present obligations to transfer assets or provide services as a result of a past transaction or event.

Liquidity—the ability of a company to pay current debts as they mature.

Noninterest-bearing note—a promissory note that does not have an interest rate.

Working capital—current assets less current liabilities.

QUESTIONS

10-1 List and describe three characteristics of all liabilities.

10-2 Identify the differences between current and long-term liabilities.

10-3 Define the term deferred revenue.

10-4 Under what major caption on the balance sheet should deferred revenue be disclosed?

10-5 Why are liabilities classified as current or long-term?

10-6 How and why is working capital determined?

10-7 The current ratio is composed of which elements?

10-8 What is a tickler file and what function does it serve?

10-9 How do accountants measure current liabilities?

10-10 Specify the objectives in accounting for current liabilities.

10-11 What are the advantages in reporting purchases net of discounts?

10-12 List some common payroll deductions.

10-13 Distinguish between payroll deductions and payroll taxes.

10-14 Why are payroll deductions a current liability?

10-15 When is a long-term liability reclassified as a current liability?

10-16 Distinguish between stated and effective interest rates.

10-17 What is a contingent liability and how is it reported in the financial statements?

EXERCISES

E10-1 Calculate the approximate effective annual rate of interest incurred by a firm that purchases $2,000 in merchandise and fails to take a discount of 3/15, n/30.

E10-2 Calculate the amount of working capital and the current ratio for a firm with $400,000 in current assets and $260,000 in current liabilities.

E10-3 How much interest is charged on a 6 percent, $15,000 interest-bearing note for 150 days?

E10-4 Prepare the necessary entries to account for the issuance and payment of a discounted noninterest-bearing note of $1,000, discounted for ninety days at 9 percent interest.

E10-5 Prepare journal entries to account for the following events, assuming purchases are recorded at gross:

a. Purchased merchandise on account for $5,000 at terms 2/10, n/30.
b. Paid half of the liability within the discount period.
c. Paid the remaining liability in thirty days.

E10-6 Prepare journal entries to account for the transactions in E10-5; assume that the purchases are recorded net of discount.

E10-7 What adjusting entry will accrue interest expense on a ninety-day, 8 percent, interest-bearing note of $2,000, if the year-end date is thirty days before the maturity date of the note?

E10-8 Record the issuance and payment of a $700, sixty-day, noninterest-bearing note discounted at 6 percent.

E10-9 Record employees' wages given the following:

Gross wages	$9,000.00
Less:	
Federal income taxes	1,000.00
State income taxes	200.00
Union dues	80.00
Employee FICA taxes	526.50
Employer taxes:	
FUTA	45.00
State unemployment	135.00
FICA taxes	526.50

E10-10 A partial list of assets and liabilities for the Jones Company on December 31 is shown below:

Current Assets:	
Cash	$ 40,000
Accounts receivable	120,000
Inventory	180,000
Liabilities:	
Accounts payable	60,000
Accrued liabilities	10,000
Notes payable (due in 30 days)	100,000
Long-term liabilities	200,000

Determine the following as of December 31:

a. Working capital.
b. Current ratio.
c. Determine the current ratio assuming that all of the cash was used to pay accounts payable.

E10-11 On November 1, a firm received a check for $1,000 from a client for payment of six months' service in advance. How should receipt of this payment be recorded? What adjusting entry is needed on December 31?

E10-12 During August, the G&S Department Store had total credit sales of $100,000. This amount includes $5,000 sales tax, which must be remitted by September 15. Will the current liability section of a balance sheet dated August 31 reflect an item related to these events?

E10-13 On December 31, Watts Company issued a one-year noninterest-bearing note with a face value of $1,000 to acquire some production supplies. This was recorded as follows:

Purchases	$1,000	
Notes payable		$1,000

If the cash value of supplies is $900, what adjusting entry should be made on December 31?

E10-14 A payroll for the XYZ Company required $10,000 in salaries of which $3,000 was withheld for income taxes. FICA taxes amounted to 13 percent of salaries, half of which is borne by the employer. FUTA taxes are fully borne by the employer: the state receives 5.4 percent and the federal government receives 0.6 percent. No payments on this payroll or on payroll taxes have been made by year-end. Present the current liability section of the balance sheet at year-end.

E10-15 Prepare the general journal entries to record the following transactions and any adjusting entries needed at year-end, April 30, 19x5:

a. Issued a discounted $1,000, ninety-day note to a bank on March 16, 19x5. Proceeds of the note were $985.
b. Issued a 6 percent, thirty-day, $200 note to a supplier on March 20, 19x5.
c. Issued a 9 percent, ninety-day, $1,000 note to another supplier on April 15, 19x5.
d. Paid the 6 percent, thirty-day, $200 note on time.

E10-16 The following general ledger accounts are found in the RHD Corporation's general ledger after adjusting entries have been posted. Prepare the current liability section of the firm's balance sheet:

Accounts payable	$ 32,000
Notes payable (due in 6 months)	9,000
Discount on notes payable	600
Bonds payable (due in 18 years)	150,000
Accrued wages payable	2,700
Accrued interest payable	12,000
Deferred rental income	400
Liability for federal income taxes withheld	1,800
Liability for state income taxes withheld	300
FICA taxes payable	180
FUTA taxes payable	80

E10-17 Present general journal entries to record the following transactions assuming purchases are recorded net of discount.

a. Purchased $600 in merchandise on account at terms 2/15, n/30.
b. Purchases $1,500 in merchandise on account at terms 3/15, n/60.
c. Paid purchase (a) within the discount period.
d. Paid purchase (b) fifty-seven days after the purchase date.

E10-18 Bruce Swindle is saving to buy a new sports car. Bruce is planning to put $2,500 in a savings account paying 8 percent interest each year for the next seven years. How much would he have at the end of seven years?

E10-19 Ray Chandler is developing a savings plan to save for his child's college education. Over the next five years he plans to deposit the following sums into an account paying 6 percent.

Year	
1	$2,000
2	2,500
3	3,000
4	3,500
5	4,000

How much would he have accumulated at the end of five years?

E10-20 Randy Swad Co. is selling a piece of land. The purchaser has offered to pay cash of $15,000 now or make the following payments at the end of the years indicated:

Year	
1	$ 2,000
5	5,000
10	25,000

If Swad Co. can earn 10 percent of its money, which alternative should it take?

E10-21 Determine the present value of a twenty year annuity of $1,000 at 6 percent and 10 percent interest rate.

E10-22 B. Smith Co. just purchased a piece of machinery in exchange for a noninterest-bearing note. The note calls for payment of $50,000 five years from now. B. Smith Co. wants to record the transaction but it does not know the current market value of the machine. If the company's incremental borrowing rate is 10 percent, at what amount should the machine be recorded?

PROBLEMS

P10-1 Marsha Donaldson is considering an investment in Bilge, Inc. Among other factors, she is evaluating the following data:

Current assets:		
Cash		$ 35,000
Accounts receivable	$128,000	
Less: Allowance for bad debts	13,000	115,000
Marketable securities (market value and cost)		10,000
Inventory		35,000
Prepaid expenses		500
Current liabilities:		
Accounts payable		108,000
Notes payable		60,000
Interest payable		8,000
Liabilities for payroll deductions		5,000

Required:

a. Calculate the current ratio and working capital.
b. Evaluate the impact of this firm's current liabilities and make a recommendation to Ms. Donaldson.
c. Demonstrate the effect of accidentally classifying $20,000 in current liabilities as long-term on the current ratio and working capital balance of Bilge, Inc. Assume the error has already been made in the preceding data.

P10-2 The fiscal year for the Hemp Company ends on November 30. Hemp borrowed $500 from each of two banks and a stockholder on November 1, giving the following notes:

	Note 1	*Note 2*	*Note 3*
Face amount	$500	$500	$500
Interest rate	8%	—	—
Discount rate	—	8%	—
Term of loan	90 days	180 days	1 year
Lender...........	Bank	Bank	Stockholder

Required:

a. Record the borrowing of the money.
b. Record the accrual of interest on November 30.
c. Record the payment of the notes.

P10-3 Baxter, Inc. has the following transactions involving accounts payable:

1. Purchased merchandise, 2/10, n/30, for $1,500.
2. Purchased merchandise, 3/15, n/30, for $1,800.
3. Paid for first purchase within discount period.
4. Paid for second purchase thirty days after the purchase.

Required:

a. Record these transactions assuming that purchases are recorded at the gross amount.
b. Record these transactions assuming that purchases are recorded net of discount.

P10-4 The Weeks Company incurs $3,000 in wage expense this month. Assume this is the first month of the year and that the federal income tax withholding rate is in aggregate 15 percent and the state income tax withholding rate is 3 percent. FICA is 7.5 percent each and the employer's pension cost is 5 percent. The FUTA tax rate is 0.6 percent while state unempoyment is 5.4 percent.

Required:

a. Record the wage expense and payroll tax expense.
b. Record the payment of payroll liabilities incurred.
c. Determine the total cost to the Weeks Company of employing its workers for one month.

P10-5 Reproduced below is a portion of the trial balance for Horn, Inc.:

	Debit	*Credit*
Accounts payable		$66,000
Purchase discounts lost	$ 42	
FICA taxes payable		200
FUTA taxes payable.............		40
State unemployment taxes payable		120
Notes payable		8,000
Discounts on notes payable	180	

Additional data:

1. Wages of $3,000 are owed employees as of December 31, year-end for Horn. No FUTA or state unemployment taxes are recognized because all employees have already earned above the $7,000 limit this year.
2. The notes payable account results from one ninety-day note discounted at 9 percent by the bank on November 1.
3. Estimated federal income taxes for Horn are $13,000. Estimated state income taxes for Horn are $3,000.
4. FICA tax rate is 15 percent, split between employee and employer.

Required:

a. Make the necessary adjusting entries.
b. Produce the current liability section of the balance sheet for Horn, Inc.

(**Note:** Federal withholding rate is 20 percent.)

P10-6 The following transactions involving current liabilities occurred during the current fiscal year of the North Company:

Jan.	10	Purchased merchandise for $25,000 before a 2 percent discount from the supplier. Both purchases and accounts payable are recorded net of discounts.
	19	Paid $15,300 on January 10 invoice. The invoice was billed at $15,612.
	31	Paid balance of January 10 invoice after discount period.
Apr.	1	Issued a one-year note to settle a March 27 invoice for $5,000. This invoice had been recorded net of the 2 percent discount, or $4,900. The note was recorded at a face value of $5,300 ($5,000 plus 6% interest).
Dec.	31	Wages for December were $8,000 before the following withholdings:

Income taxes	$940
FICA, 5 percent	400
Union dues	175

The payroll taxes are recorded at the end of each month. December wages are subject to a 5.4 percent state unemployment tax and a 0.6 percent federal unemployment tax, all other withholdings and payroll taxes have been paid.

Dec.	31	The company has sold service contracts on its products. Deferred service contract revenue was credited on the receipt of customer payments and totals $37,000. Realized revenue from the service cntracts for the current fiscal year is $5,300.
	31	Interest expense on the April 1 note is recognized.

Required:

a. Prepare general journal entries.
b. Prepare the current liability section of the balance sheet dated December 31.

P10-7 The Boston Company's monthly payroll for November is as follows:

Officers' salaries	$15,000
Sales salaries	32,000
Clerical salaries	12,000
Total payroll	$59,000

Other data include the following:

Wages subject to FICA tax	$16,000
Wages subject to FUTA tax	3,000
Federal income taxes withheld	8,700
State income taxes withheld	3,000
Voluntary deduction:	
Pension contributions withheld	600
Payroll deductions for U.S. savings bonds	450
FICA tax rate	7.5%
FUTA tax rate	.6%
State unemployment rate	5.4%

Required:

Prepare the general journal entries to record the:

a. Accrual of the November wages and related liabilities.
b. Accrual of related employer's taxes.
c. Payment of liabilities to employees and appropriate state, federal, and pension agencies.

P10-8 The Art Mart frequently acquires supplies from Gordon Art Distributors, a wholesaler. The following transactions took place between these two firms:

a. Mart purchased supplies costing $1,200 from Gordon on terms 2/15, n/30.
b. Mart paid the amount due Gordon thirteen days later. But financial problems were developing for Mart.
c. Mart purchased $2,000 in supplies from Gordon on terms 2/15, n/30.
d. Forty days later, Gordon agrees to accept a ninety-day, 9 percent note in satisfaction of the $2,000 debt.
e. Fifteen days later both Mart and Gordon's fiscal years end.
f. Mart pays Gordon the full amount of the note and interest.

Required:

Prepare the general journal entries needed to account for these transactions, including any adjusting entries needed at year-end for both Mart and Gordon. Assume Mart records purchases net of discount.

P10-9 Below is the trial balance before adjustments for the Iris Sales Company.

	Debit	*Credit*
Cash	$ 2,000	
Accounts receivable	7,000	
Inventory	16,000	
Notes receivable	3,000	
Supplies	900	
Furniture and fixtures	18,000	
Accumulated depreciation		$ 6,000
Accounts payable		1,200
Notes payable		6,000
Discount on notes payable	90	
Liability for federal income taxes withheld		800
Liability for pension contributions withheld		360
FICA taxes payable		180
Bonds payable		10,000
Owner's equity		9,750
Sales		89,000
Sales discounts	1,200	
Purchases (net of discounts)	41,000	
Purchases discounts lost	250	
Wage and salary expense	22,000	
Payroll tax expense	2,500	
Utilities expense	350	
Rental expense	9,000	
	$123,290	$123,290

An analysis of the firm's financial records yields the following data:

1. Bad debts of 1 percent of the current accounts receivable balance are anticipated.
2. Ending inventory is $18,000.
3. Supplies of $600 have been used this year.
4. The assets being depreciated have a six-year useful life with no expected salvage value. Straight-line depreciation is used.
5. The note payable is a discounted bank loan for ninety-days dated December 1.
6. The bookkeeper failed to record the employer's FICA taxes on the December payroll of $180.
7. Bond interest expense of $900 is unpaid.

Required:

a. Prepare adjusting general journal entries.
b. Prepare a balance sheet for the Iris Sales Company.
c. Calculate the current ratio for the firm as of December 31, 19x4.

P10-10 McKenzie Co. is purchasing a machine and the seller has provided several payment options as follows:

1. Cash now of $35,000.
2. Five year annuity payment of $10,000 per year.
3. A deferred payment plan where $25,000 will be paid after three years and $30,000 will be paid at the end of five years.

If McKenzie's incremental borrowing rate is 10 percent, which alternative should it select?

P10-11 Determine the future value of each of the following streams of investments assuming an 8 percent interest rate:

1. Invest $3,000 annually for twelve years.
2. Invest $1,000 annually for twenty-five years.
3. Invest $5,000 each five years for a period of twenty-five years.
4. Invest $40,000 now and $50,000 five years from now. What is the value in ten years?
5. Invest $1,000 each year in years one through five and $2,000 per year in years six through ten. What is the value at the end of ten years?

P10-12 Chip Co. has to make a payment to an executive under a deferred compensation plan. Under the plan, the executive will receive $20,000 per year for five years starting ten years from the current date. If the relevant interest rate is 8 percent, what is the present value of the deferred compensation?

P10-13 Tiger Co. has borrowed money under a plan that calls for an annual payment of interest in the amount of $600. In addition, principal of $10,000 will be paid ten years from now. If Tiger's incremental borrowing rate is 10 percent, what is the present value of the obligation?

P10-14 Hebert Co. is currently involved in a patent infringement suit. The company's attorney estimates that the company will win the case and collect $100,000 one year from now. The company being sued has offered an out-of-court settlement that involves paying $10,000 per year for ten years plus lump sum payments of $20,000 five years from now and $40,000 ten years from now. Assume Hebert can earn 8 percent interest on its funds, the company is sure it will win the case and collect the $100,000. Should it accept the out-of-court settlement?

Learning Objectives

Chapter 11 presents accounting for long-term debt such as bonds, leases, pensions, and deferred income. Studying this chapter should enable you to:

1. Describe the measurement and reporting objectives in accounting for long-term liabilities.
2. Discuss the generally accepted accounting treatment for bonds payable and interest expense.
3. Identify accounting problems and their resolution for lease and pension liabilities.
4. Present financial statement disclosures for deferred taxes.

11

Long-Term Liabilities

INTRODUCTON

Long-term liabilities are obligations of the firm that will not require satisfaction for a period of at least one year or one operating cycle, whichever is longer. Long-term liabilities are usually incurred to meet the long-term financing needs of the firm, such as the acquisition of buildings, equipment, a new subsidiary, or new product lines from another firm. Frequently long-term liabilities are secured, which means that creditors are granted the right to seize specific assets in satisfaction of the debt if a debtor is unable to repay. Security is provided in a *mortgage contract*, which legally establishes the rights and duties of both parties to the lending transaction. It usually specifies which property may be seized if the debtor firm cannot meet its obligations. If a long-term liability is unsecured, the creditors of the firm do not have special rights or privileges in the event of default. Their rights are no greater than other creditors of the firm. Consequently, weaker firms may have difficulty borrowing on unsecured liabilities, or they must pay a higher rate of interest to compensate the lender for the additional risk.

Several types of long-term liabilities are commonly found on balance sheets. Long-term notes and bonds are the most common debt instruments used in long-term borrowing. In addition, a firm may incur long-term liabilities in connection with lease contracts, pension plans, or deferred income taxes. All of these obligations are reported on the balance sheet under the separate heading "long-term liabilities." Disclosure of long-term liabilities clearly distinguishes them from current liabilities, thus indicating the nature and amounts that must be satisfied in the more distant future as opposed to debts that must be satisfied in the near future.

WHY INCUR LONG-TERM DEBT?

There are several reasons why the majority of businesses choose to acquire some of their operating funds by incurring long-term liabilities instead of by selling additional shares of common stock or other ownership interests. The major advantages of long-term liabilities lie in the basic distinction between the rights and duties of creditors and owners and in the differing income tax treatment of interest and dividends. Creditors have preference over owners in the event of the dissolution of the business. Creditors must be completely repaid before owners can receive anything if business is discontinued. In addition, creditors must be paid the interest prescribed in the note or bond, while profit distributions received by owners depends in part on how profitable the firm has been. Consequently, new enterprises or weaker firms find it difficult to raise funds by selling stock: thus they raise funds by borrowing on notes or bonds because of the protection and privileges accorded creditors. At times, general economic conditions are so poor that even stronger firms have difficulty selling new issues of stock and must raise needed funds through long-term debt.

Even the strongest and most successful firms choose to raise funds by long-term borrowing, since creditors do not normally acquire the rights of owners. Current owners will not dilute their control of the firm if needed funds are borrowed. In addition, the cost of using borrowed funds is interest, a fixed amount (rate) determined by negotiation upon issuing the bond or note. The interest rate on a particular debt does not change over the life of the debt. If the firm has an extraordinarily profitable year, the amount paid creditors is no higher than in poor years, leaving the bulk of the profits to be divided among the current owners of the business. Using debt with fixed costs to fund business operations is referred to as *leverage*.

Leverage allows a company to use its owner's equity as a base for borrowing money. As long as the company can earn more than the cost of borrowed funds, the excess earnings accrue to the owners as additional profits. For example, assume a company begins operations with the owner investing $100,000. If the business earns $20,000 per year in net income, the return on the owner's investment is 20 percent, calculated as follows:

$$\frac{\text{Net Income}}{\text{Investment}} = \frac{\$20{,}000}{\$100{,}000} = 20\%\ \text{Return}$$

Suppose the business is very successful and the owner wants to double the size of the company and that doubling the investment in assets will also double the net income. This could be accomplished by the owner investing an additional $100,000 or by borrowing the amount needed. If the owner invests the additional funds, his or her return will remain at 20 percent:

$$\frac{\text{Net Income}}{\text{Investment}} = \frac{\$40{,}000}{\$100{,}000} = 20\%\ \text{Return}$$

On the other hand, assume the owner borrows $100,000 at 12 percent interest. Now the return to the owner increases to 28 percent without any additional financial risk to the owner:

$$\frac{\text{Net Income} - \text{Interest}}{\text{Investment}} = \frac{\$40{,}000 - \$12{,}000}{\$100{,}000} = 28\%\ \text{Return}$$

Thus, by leveraging the owner's original investment, the return increased by 8 percent.

The benefits of leverage are heightened by the income tax treatment of interest. While distributions of profits, such as dividends to owners, create no income tax savings to the firm, the payment of interest is tax deductible. Consequently, the cost of borrowing is considerably less than it initially seems to be. For example, if the company is in a 35 percent income tax bracket, it will pay $12,000 interest per year. But the effective cost of using that $100,000 is actually less than $12,000, because the company saved $4,200 by deducting the interest as an expense for federal income tax purposes. As shown, the net cost of using these borrowed funds was only $7,800 per year, or 7.8 percent—not 12 percent.

Annual interest expense	$12,000	
Less: Taxes saved by interest deduction (interest deduction × tax rate) ($12,000 × .35 = $4,200)	4,200	
Net cost of using borrowed funds	$ 7,800	
Effective after-tax rate of interest ($7,800 ÷ $100,000)		7.8%

However, the fixed costs of borrowing must be paid in less successful years as well as in profitable years. When a firm generates only small profits, the interest costs can consume the bulk of the earnings. In years with losses, interest payments may consume funds needed for operations. Leverage increases business risk, since inability to pay the interest may force the business into bankruptcy. Leverage generally increases the earnings available to the owners of the business in highly profitable years while reducing them in less successful years.

The benefits and risks of leverage are available to all business organizations, regardless of their form—proprietorship, partnership, or corporation. Because most large businesses are incorporated, however, the remainder of our discussion of long-term liabilities will be directed to corporations, although it would be equally applicable to other forms of business.

BONDS PAYABLE

A *bond* is a written unconditional promise to pay the holder of the bond the *principal* or face value of the bond at *maturity date* and interest on the face value of the bond at a specified rate on specified dates. Most bonds carry a face value, sometimes called *par value*, of $1,000. While maturity dates vary greatly, terms of twenty-five to thirty years are common for corporate bonds. The rate of interest paid on the bond is called *nominal* or *coupon rate* and is a fixed percentage of the face value of the bond. Interest is normally paid semiannually.

When a company issues bonds, it normally sells the entire bond issue to an *underwriter*. An underwriter is an investment firm (or, for large bond issues, a syndication of several investment firms) that sells the individual bonds to investors. Because there may be several thousand geographically dispersed individual bondholders for any one bond issue, the issuing company selects a *trustee*, who serves as representative for the individual bondholders. The rights of the bondholders are specified in a *bond indenture agreement*, and the trustee insures that the company lives up to the terms of the agreement. If the terms are violated, the trustee will take whatever action is necessary to protect the bondholders, including foreclosure.

Since a bond is a legal contract between a borrower and a lender, an almost infinite variety of contracts is possible. Normally, bond types are differentiated on the basis of their security, interest payment, or duration. The accounting procedures focus on the economic substance of the bond transaction. Consequently, two bond issues would be recorded in the same manner, even if one is secured by a mortgage against the buildings and the other is unsecured.

ACCOUNTING FOR BONDS PAYABLE

Several complex factors interact in determining the amount that investors will pay for newly issued bonds. Investors must assess the risk associated with investing in the bonds of a particular firm. If the investment is perceived as being fairly risky, a higher interest rate may be required to sell the bonds. In addition, the *market rate of interest* must be determined by the investor. This is the rate of interest at which willing borrowers and willing lenders would agree to borrow and lend at a given level of risk. The market rate of interest fluctuates daily as a function of the supply of and demand for loanable funds.

When a corporation issues bonds, it must obtain the approval of its stockholders to the major features of the bond issue in advance of its issuance. Weeks or even months before the bonds are sold, the indenture agreement must be drawn up and bond certificates must be printed. Consequently, the rate of interest that is paid on the bonds must be determined well in advance of the day on which they are first available for sale. As a result, the nominal rate of interest printed on the bond certificates may differ from the actual market rate of interest for an investment with that level of risk. Since the interest paid on the bonds is fixed and cannot be changed, the issuance price is adjusted to convert the nominal rate into the current market rate of interest.

BONDS ISSUED AT FACE VALUE

Bonds are issued at face value when the contract rate printed on the bonds are perceived by investors as being approximately equal to the market rate of interest for the risk level involved. If the Smith Corporation sells $1,000,000 of 10 percent, ten-year bonds, paying interest semiannually, and receives $1,000,000 in proceeds from the sale, the entry to record the sale of these bonds at face value would be:

Cash	$1,000,000	
Bonds payable		$1,000,000
Sold $1,000,000, 10 percent, ten-year bonds payable at face value on December 31, 19x5		

If the Smith Corporation makes the semiannual interest payments on June 30 and December 31 of each year, one-half of annual bond interest will be paid on each date and recorded as follows:

Bond interest expense	$50,000	
Cash		$50,000
Paid semiannual bond interest expense ($1,000,000 × 10% × ½) on June 30, 19x6		
Bond interest expense	50,000	
Cash		50,000
Paid semiannual bond interest expense ($1,000,000 × 10% × ½) on June 30, 19x6		

When the Smith Corporation prepares financial statements at the end of its accounting period on December 31, 19x6, the financial statements would report the following with respect to this issue of bonds:

Income statement:		
Bond interest expense	$100,000	
Balance sheet:		
Long-term liabilities—		
Bonds payable, 10%, due December 31, 19y5		$1,000,000

At the maturity date, the Smith Corporation would record the retirement of this bond issue as follows:

Bonds payable	$1,000,000	
Cash		$1,000,000
Retired bond issue at maturity		

DETERMINING BOND ISSUE PRICE

Frequently, the sale price of the bond must be adjusted from its face value because the interest rate is normally fixed in the bond contract and cannot be changed. Given a fixed annual interest, an adjustment in the sale price will effectively adjust the effective yield of the bond. The following example, which ignores the time value of money, provides a simple illustration this concept. If a company issues a $10,000 bond at a 10 percent face or coupon rate of interest, the bondholders will receive $1,000 per year in interest. Since the interest rate is established in the bond contract, the $1,000 must be paid each year and cannot be adjusted. If the bonds sell for face value, the yield (effective interest rate) on the bonds will be 10 percent:

$$\frac{\text{Interest}}{\text{Proceeds}} = \frac{\$1{,}000}{\$10{,}000} = 10\%$$

However, if on the date of issue, the market rate of interest was 11 percent, purchasers would not be willing to buy the bonds at face value because they could buy other bonds that yield an 11 percent return. The purchasers would be willing to pay only $9,091 because this would give them the 11 percent market rate:

$$\frac{\text{Interest}}{\text{Proceeds}} = \frac{\$1{,}000}{\$9{,}091} = 11\%$$

Likewise, if the market rate of interest fell to 9 percent, the issuer would not be willing to sell the bonds for $10,000 because the interest rate would be higher than the market rate. In this case, the issuer would want an issue price of $11,111 to yield the market rate of interest:

$$\frac{\text{Interest}}{\text{Proceeds}} = \frac{\$1{,}000}{\$11{,}111} = 9\%$$

While the above example ignores the time value of money, it does illustrate how the issue price will affect the effective yield on the bonds. Bonds are sold at a discount when the market rate is above the stated rate of interest and at a premium when the market rate is lower than the stated rate. Thus, the discount and premium represent adjustments to the interest rate on the bonds. For this reason, when the discount or premium are amortized, it is done through the interest expense account to properly reflect the correct amount of interest on the bonds.

While the above example ignored the time value of money, it is an important factor when actually determining the issue price for a bond. A bond represents two forms of future cash payments. The first, a lump-sum payment, is the payment of principle at the maturity date of the bonds. The second, an annuity, is the annual interest payments on the bonds. To determine the issue price of a bond, the principle, a lump-sum payment, is discounted using the present value of a dollar table (Table 10-3) and the interest payments, the annuity, are discounted to the present using the present value of an annuity table (Table 10-4).

To illustrate, assume a company has registered a $100,000, 10 percent, ten-year bond to be issued on January 1, 19x1. Assume the interest is paid annualy on December 31. The market rate of interest on the date of issuance is 12 percent. The issue price of the bond is the discounted value (at 12%) of the future cash payments as follows:

PV of principle (lump-sum payment):	
$100,000 × .32197* =	$32,197
PV of interest payments (annuity):	
$ 10,000 × 5.65022** =	56,502
Issue price	$88,699

*PV factor at 10 percent for ten years from Table 10-3
**PV factor for 12 percent at ten years from Table 10-4

In order for this bond to yield the 12 percent market rate of interest, it would sell at a $11,301 discount. Similar calculations are made when the market rate of interest is below the face rate. The present value of the bond would be greater than the face amount and the bond will sell at a premium.

BONDS ISSUED AT A DISCOUNT

To illustrate the treatment of discounts, assume Jay Corporation were selling $1,000,000, 10 percent, ten-year bonds, and the market rate of interest had risen to 11 percent on the date of issue, investors would expect to pay less than $1,000,000 for the bonds. If investors bid $941,103[1] for the bonds, the corporation's effective interest rate would be 11 percent.

The Jay Corporation would record the sale of these bonds on January 1, 19x6, by making this entry:

Cash	$941,103	
Discount on bonds payable	58,897	
Bonds payable		$1,000,000
Sold $1,000,000, 10 percent, ten-year bonds payable at a discount of January 1, 19x6.		

[1] Present value calculated as follows:

PV of principle:	
$1,000,000 × .35218* =	$352,180
PV of interest:	
$ 100,000 × 5.88923** =	588,923
Issue price	$941,103

*PV factor at 11 percent for ten years from Table 10-3
**PV factor at 11 percent for ten years from Table 10-4

Note that the face amount of the bonds payable is credited to the bonds payable account. The discount, which is the difference between the principal amount of the liability and the actual proceeds of the sale of the bonds, is recorded in a separate discount on bonds payable account. This account is reported as a contra liability. A balance sheet produced on January 1, 19x6, would report bonds as follows:

Balance sheet:		
Long-term liabilities:		
Bonds payable, 10%, due		
December 31, 19x5	$1,000,000	
Less: Discount on bonds payable	58,897	$941,103

In this way the financial statement user is given all relevant information about the bonds, including the principal amount of the bonds that must be repaid at maturity. The objective of reporting the bonds at the current cash equivalent is accomplished by subtracting the unamortized discount from the principal amount of the bonds payable at maturity.

As noted earlier, the effect of a discount is to increase the effective rate of interest that the corporation must pay for the use of the borrowed funds. This additional interest expense is reflected in the income statement by the process of amortizing the discount in accordance with the matching principle. That is, the additional interest expense is recognized periodically over the life of the bond issue by matching the revenues earned through the use of borrowed funds with this additional cost of those funds.

There are two methods for calculating the amount of premium or discount to be amortized each interest payment period: the straight-line method of amortization and the effective-interest method of amortization. The straight-line method is a simple method that amortizes an equal amount of discount each period. It is, however, theoretically less acceptable than the more complex effective-interest method.[2] The effective-interest method accelerates amortization so that more discount is reclassified as expense earlier in the life of the bond issue than late in its life.

Straight-Line Amortization

Under the straight-line method of amortizing bond discount, the total amount of discount is amortized equally over the life of the bond. In the case of the Jay Corporation, the amount amortized each interest payment period would be calculated as follows:

[2] Methods other than the effective interest method may be used only if the results are not materially different from those that would result from using the effective interest method.

Amount of discount to be amortized		$58,897
Number of interest periods—		
10-year bonds, interest paid annually		10
Amount to be amortized each		
interest period	$58,897 ÷ 10 =	5,890

Each interest payment date the following entry would be made to pay the interest and amortize the discount.

Interest expense	$105,890	
Discount on bonds payable		$ 5,890
Cash		100,000

Effective-Interest Amortization

The effective-interest method provides discount amortization such that reported interest expense equals the effective-interest rate. The calculation is based on the carrying value of the bonds. Carrying value is the face amount adjusted for unamortized discount or premium. A partial amortization table for Jay Corporation is shown below:

Jay Corporation
Amortization Schedule—Interest Method

Year	*Bond Carrying Value**	×	*Effective Interest Rate*	=	*Annual Interest Expense*	–	*Cash Interest Payment*	=	*Discount Amortization*
1	$941,103		.11		$103,521		$100,000		$3,521
2	944,624		.11		$103,909		100,000		3,909
3	948,533		.11		$104,339		100,000		4,339
4	952,872		.11		$104,816		100,000		4,816
5	957,688		.11		$105,346		100,000		5,346

*Bond carrying value equals the face amount of the bonds less unamortized discount. As discount is amortized each year, the bond carrying value increases.

The carrying value of the bond at the end of each year actually represents the present value of the bond on that date, given the market rate of interest at the date of issuance. The Jay Corporation would record the payment of the first year's interest as follows:

Bond interest expense	$103,521	
Discount on bonds payable		$ 3,521
Cash		100,000
Paid annual interest December 31, 19x6		

Financial statements prepared on December 31, 19x6, would report:

Income statement:		
Bond interest expense	$ 103,521	
Balance sheet:		
Long-term liabilities—		
Bonds payable, 10%, due		
December 31, 19x5	1,000,000	
Less: Discount on bonds payable	55,376	$944,624

The amortization of bond discount properly reflects the additional cost of selling bonds at a discount by increasing the firm's interest expense. Also note that the amortization of discount reduces the balance in the discount on bonds payable account, thereby increasing net present value of the liability, as reported on the balance sheet, from $941,103 to $944,624. By the bond maturity date, the discount on bonds payable account will have a zero balance (it will be fully amortized), and the liability's reported net present value will be $1,000,000—the exact amount due on that date.

BONDS ISSUED AT A PREMIUM

If the market rate of interest on the bond issue date is lower than the face interest provided, the bonds will sell for an amount greater than par value. Like discounts, the premium that investors will pay equates the bond's effective interest rate to the current market rate of interest. For example, if the market rate of interest is 8 percent, investors would bid $1,134,198[3] for the Jay Corporation's $1,000,000, 10 percent, ten-year bonds. The Jay Corporation would record the issuance of $1,000,000, 10 percent, ten-year bonds at $134,188 premium on January 1 in this entry:

Cash	$1,134,198	
Premium on bonds payable		$ 134,198
Bonds payable		1,000,000

A premium reduces the effective interest rate. To record the payment of annual interest, the bond premium is amortized, thus reducing bond interest expense. The amount of premium amortized each period is calculated under the straight-line method in the same fashion as was discount amortization:

Amount of discount to be amortized		$134,198
Number of interest periods— 10-year bonds, paying interest annually		10
Amount to be amortized each interest period	$134,198 ÷ 10 =	13,420

The Jay Corporation would record the first year's interest payment as follows:

Bond interest expense	$86,580	
Premium on bonds payable	13,420	
Cash		$100,000

---

[3] Present value calculated as follows:

PV of principle:	
$1,000,000 × .46319 =	$ 463,190
PV of interest:	
$ 100,000 × 6.71008 =	671,008
Issue price	$1,134,198

The Jay Corporation's financial statements prepared on December 31, 19x6, would report bonds and bond transactions as follows:

Income statement:		
Bond interest expense	$ 86,580	
Balance sheet:		
Long-term liabilities—		
Bonds payable, 10%, due		
December 31, 19x5.	1,000,000	
Add: Premium on bonds payable	120,778	$1,120,778

The effective interest method would have the following amortization schedule for the first five years:

Jay Corporation
Amortization Schedule—Interest Method

Year	*Bond Carrying Value*	×	*Effective Interest Rate*	=	*Annual Interest Expense*	−	*Cash Interest Payment*	=	*Premium Amortization*
1	$1,134,198		.08		$90,736		$100,000		$ 9,264
2	1,124,934		.08		$89,995		100,000		10,005
3	1,114,929		.08		$89,194		100,000		10,806
4	1,104,123		.08		$88,330		100,000		11,670
5	1,092,453		.08		$87,396		100,000		12,604

Note that the interest expense decreases each year because the carrying value of the bond is decreasing. The entry in the first year to record the interest payment and premium amorotization would be:

Interest interest	$90,736	
Premium on bonds payable	9,264	
Cash		$100,000

BONDS ISSUED AFTER DATE ON BOND CERTIFICATE

Although bonds may be dated January 1, they are likely to be sold after January 1. This may be caused by actions of investors, underwriters, or issuers. Potential investors or underwriters may be reluctant to purchase bonds on the stated date. Alternately, the corporation may voluntarily withhold the bonds for a short while in hopes that the market rate of interest will fall, thus reducing its future interest expense. When bonds are issued after their initiation date, two problems result. The amortization of premium or discount must be adjusted to reflect the fact that the bonds will not be outstanding for their full term, and the measurement of bond interest expense for the first interest period must reflect the "shortness" of the first period.

The Amortization Problem

Bonds issued after the date printed on the certificates actually span a period shorter than the stated life. For example, bonds dated January 1, 19x6, maturing December 31, 19y5, and actually sold on March 1, 19x6, are outstanding only for 118 months instead of the anticipated 120 months. In accordance with the matching principles, amortization of premium or discount should occur within the time period over which the bonds are actually outstanding. For example, on March 1, 19x6, the Northwestern Corporation issued $1,000,000, 8 percent, ten-year bonds dated January 1, 19x6, at a discount of $20,060. The discount amortization would be calculated as follows:

Amount of discount to be amortized		$20,060
Number of months outstanding		118
Amount to be amortized each month	$20,060 ÷ 118 =	170

The Northwest Corporation would record semiannual June 30 and December 31 interest payments for 19x6 in these entries:

Bond interest expense	$40,680	
Discount on bonds payable ($170 × 4)		$ 680
Cash ($1,000,000 × .08 × ½)		40,000
Paid semiannual bond interest and amortized four months discount at $170 per month		
Bond interest expense	41,020	
Discount on bonds payable ($170 × 6)		1,020
Cash		$40,000
Paid semiannual bond interest and amortized six months discount at $170 per month		

Interest for the Short First Period

When bonds are sold between interest payment dates, interest expense for that period should be less than if the bonds had been outstanding for the full period. Keeping records of the exact bond sales dates on large issues could be an extremely time-consuming task. Therefore, investment bankers established an alternate mechanism: the buyer of a bond customarily pays the fair market value of the bond *plus accrued interest*. The bond issuer receives an amount equal to the interest the investor has not earned for that interest period. On the first interest payment date, that "prepaid" amount is returned to the investor in addition to the interest that has been earned.

For example, on March 1, 19x6, the Northwest Corporation issues $1,000,000, 10 percent, ten-year bonds, dated January 1, 19x6, at par. Investors will pay Northwest $1,000,000 plus the two months interest for the period between January 1 and March 1, or $16,667 ($1,000,000 × 10% × $\frac{2}{12}$). On the next semiannual interest payment date, Northwest will pay $50,000 interest to bondholders. Only $33,333 will be actual payments of interest; the other $16,667 will *simply be a return* of amounts paid by the bondholders. The sale of the Northwest Corporation's bonds and the payment of interest would be recorded in these entries:

Cash	$1,016,667	
Bonds payable		$1,000,000
Bond interest payable		16,667
To record the March 1, 19x6, sale of $1,000,000, 6 percent bonds dated January 1, 19x6, at par plus accrued interest		
Bond interest expense	33,333	
Bond interest payable	16,667	
Cash		50,000
Paid semiannual bond interest June 30, 19x6		

The interest collected for the two month's prior to issuance should be credited to an interest payable account since it is an amount owed to bondholders.

ACCRUED BOND INTEREST EXPENSE

When bond interest payment periods differ from the corporation's accounting period, an adjusting entry is required to measure bond interest expense for the year correctly. For example, if the Mesa Corporation, a calendar year corporation, issues $1,000,000, 10 percent, ten-year bonds on the face date, April 1, 19x6, at a $20,000 discount, the entry to record semiannual interest on September 30 would be:

Bond interest expense	$51,000	
Discount on bonds payable		$ 1,000
Cash		50,000
Payment of semiannual bond interest and amortization of bond discount—September 30, 19x6		

On December 31 of this year and each year thereafter, the following adjusting entry must be made to measure bond interest expense for the year correctly:

Bond interest expense	$25,500	
Discount on bonds payable		$ 500
Bond interest payable		25,000
Accrual of three months' bond interest expense and amortization of discount—December 31, 19x6		

When this interest is actually paid on March 31, 19x7, the entry will be:

Bond interest expense	$25,500	
Bond interest payable	25,000	
Discount on bonds payable		$ 500
Cash		50,000
Payment of current and accrued bond interest and amortization of discount—March 31, 19x7		

INVESTMENT IN BONDS

Accounting for investments in bonds is very similar to the accounting for the issuer. One difference is that discounts and premiums are not isolated in separate accounts. The investment account is debited for the net cost of the investment. Any discount or premium amortization is charged directly to the investment account. Assume on January 1, 19x1, Swad Co. invested in $100,000 of Sami Co. bonds. The bonds have a remaining life of five years and cost Swad Co. $98,000. Assume the stated rate of interest is 8 percent and that interest is paid semiannually on June 30 and December 31. The entry to record the purchase is:

Investment in bonds	$98,000	
Cash		$98,000

An investor will amortize premiums and discounts only when the bond is held as a long-term investment. If it is a short-term investment only the cash interest received will be recorded.

If we assume Swad Co. bought the bonds as a long-term investment and that the company uses the straight-line amortization method, the entries for the collection of interest and the amortization of the $2,000 discount will be:

Cash ($100,000 × .08 × ½)	$4,000	
Investment in bonds ($2,000 ÷ 10)	200	
Interest earned		$4,200

Note that the amortization directly increases the investment account. The discount is amortized over the ten remaining interest periods.

The investor may also use the effective interest method. In this case, an amortization schedule similar to that used by the issuer is employed. The only difference is that the interest expense will now be interest revenue and the cash interest paid will become cash interest received.

Accounting problems relating to purchases of bonds between interest dates are treated conceptually the same way as with the issuer. The only difference is that now an interest receivable account will be used and the investor will be paying the cash.

NOTES PAYABLE

Instead of selling bonds to hundreds or thousands of bondholders, funds can often be borrowed from banks, insurance companies, or other financial institutions. These loans are usually evidenced by notes maturing in two to ten years or more. Notes are especially common when firms need funds for a relatively short period of time (less than 5 years) or when bond interest rates are unfavorable. Borrowing on long-term notes allows the firm to avoid the costs of dealing with thousands of bondholders and trustees, and it avoids the necessity of registering bonds with the SEC.

Notes are accounted for in the same fashion as bonds. Much of the complexity of accounting for bond transactions is eliminated in the case of notes payable by the common practice of issuing notes at par and dating the notes on the date the funds are actually borrowed. The common entries for notes payable transactions are illustrated here for the Regency Corporation on the issuance of a $500,000, 9 percent, two-year note, paying interest annually:

Cash	$500,000	
Notes payable		$500,000
Issued two-year, 9 percent note to First National Bank—January 1, 19x6		
Interest expense	45,000	
Cash		45,000
Paid one year's interest on First National Bank note—December 31, 19x6		
Interest expense	45,000	
Cash		45,000
Paid one year's interest on First National Bank note—December 31, 19x7		
Notes payable	500,000	
Cash		500,000
Repaid First National Bank note at maturity—December 31, 19x7		

Accrual entries are needed for notes with interest dates that do not coincide with the corporate year-end.

LEASE LIABILITIES

The popularity of leasing equipment and buildings has grown rapidly. No large immediate outflow of cash is necessary if assets are leased. The growth of leasing has caused a heated controvesy over the measurement of lease liabilities. Under what circumstances does a lease agreement give rise to a liability? When and how is this liability measured?

To answer these questions, accountants have divided leases into two classifications. *Operating leases* are generally cancellable and the lessor usually retains all or most of the incidents of ownership (such as paying property taxes, insuring the asset, and making repairs). *Financing leases* are characterized by long-term, noncancellable contracts that may cover the approximate life of the asset and impose the rights and responsibilities of ownership on the lessee. Financing leases are considered, in substance, to be purchases in which the lessee is allowed to pay for the asset in installments. Indeed, many financing leases provide that the lessee may purchase the asset at the end-of-lease period for only a nominal price.

If the lease is an operating lease, no long-term liability arises. This method of leasing is sometimes referred to as off-balance sheet-financing. Rental payments under the lease are recorded in this simple entry:

Rental expense	$5,000	
Cash		$5,000

A lease is usually considered a financing type lease if one of the following four conditions are met in the noncancellable lease contract:

1. The lessee gets title to the property at the end of the lease.
2. The lease contains a bargain purchase option (i.e., the lessee has the right to purchase the property at a nominal amount at the end of the lease term.
3. The lease term is for 75 percent or more of the useful life of the asset.
4. The present value of the lease payments is 90 percent or more of the fair market value of the asset.

These criteria were developed to determine when a lease agreement is in substance a purchase and therefore, should be reported as a financing lease rather than an operating lease.

If the lease is considered a financing lease, most accountants believe that a long-term liability is incurred and that the lease transaction should be accounted for as if it were a purchase transaction. If the Southwest Corporation entered into a financing lease for a machine that could be purchased for $20,000 and agreed to pay $5,000 per year for five years (the estimated life of the equipment), the lease would be recorded in this entry:

Machinery	$20,000	
Deferred lease cost	5,000	
Lease liability		$25,000
Recorded five-year financing lease of machinery		

The machinery is recorded at its current fair market value and difference between the total lease liability and the fair market value of the equipment would be recorded as a deferred financing lease cost. Each year part of the deferred cost would be amortized, thus increasing interest expense. The machine would also be depreciated. Depreciation, amortization, and the rental payment would be recorded as follows:

Lease liability	$5,000	
Cash		$5,000
Paid one year's rental of machinery		
Depreciation expense	4,000	
Interest expense	1,000	
Deferred lease cost		1,000
Accumulated depreciation		4,000
To reclassify expired cost as expenses		

The effect of this accounting treatment is to: (1) record the lease as a purchase, (2) recognize that the difference between the fair market value of the leased assets and the total lease liability is interest, (3) recognize interest expense over the life of the lease by amortizing the financing lease discount, and (4) record the lease liability and report it on the balance sheet.

RECLASSIFYING THE CURRENT PORTION OF LONG-TERM DEBT

Generally, the significant determining question in classifying a liability as current or long-term is "by when must the liability be satisfied." If satisfaction is required within one year or one operating cycle, whichever is longer, the liability is usually classified as current. A secondary criterion for the current classification is that the debt must be satisfied by expending current assets. Under these general rules, the character of a liability (or part of a liability) could change from one year to the next. For example, if the Research Corporation, a calendar year corporation, borrows money on an eighteen-month note on December 31, 19x6, the balance sheet for that date would report the note as a long-term liability. On the balance sheet prepared on December 31, 19x7, the note would be reclassified and reported as a current liability, because at that point in time satisfaction is due within less than one year. However, if the note is to be repaid out of funds deposited in a sinking fund or from other noncurrent resources, the note will not meet the requirements for reclassification as current liabilities in the year of maturity. Therefore, the note should remain classified under long-term liabilities. Parenthetically or in a footnote, the accountant should indicate that the note is to mature within the upcoming year.

A related issue concerns refinancing short-term debt. In some cases, long series of short-term debt are used to finance an operation. Accordingly, it might not be appropriate to classify these obligations as current liabilities. Short-term debt may be excluded from current liabilities if two conditions are met: (1) there is intent to refinance the obligations, and (2) there is a demonstrated ability to consummate the refinancing.

OTHER SIGNIFICANT LIABILITIES

In addition to the liabilities discussed previously, companies may also have significant liabilities for pensions and deferred taxes. Most companies have a pension plan for their employees which is offered as a fringe benefit. The plan is usually conducted through an insurance company where the company makes payments to the insurance company which invests the funds and ultimately makes payments to the retirees. Frequently, the company has not paid the full amount owed to the plan and a liability must be recorded. For some companies this can be a large liability.

Most public companies have deferred tax liabilities. This results from accounting for income tax expense. When preparing an income statement, the accountant uses generally accepted accounting principles (GAAP) whereas when the tax return is prepared, the accountant must use tax rules. Frequently there are differences in the timing of revenue and expense items for accounting and tax purposes. For example, assume a company sells a piece of land at a gain and will collect the sale price over a four year period. When preparing the financial statements, GAAP requires that the total gain be recognized in the year of sale. However, tax laws allow the company to treat the sale as an installment sale and the gain is recognized over the four year collection period. In this case, accounting income will be larger than taxable income in the first year. The income statement reflects income tax expense based on the tax rate times accounting income. However, the tax return reflects a tax liability based on the tax rate times the reported lower taxable income. Thus, the recorded tax expense is greater than the actual tax that has to be paid in the first year. The difference between the expense and the liability is reflected as a deferred tax. This amount will be paid in future years when the gain is recognized for tax purposes. Deferred tax liabilities are a significant liability for most companies.

Accounting for pensions and deferred taxes is very complex. While they are mentioned here to let you know that they frequently are significant liabilities, the detailed accounting for these is deferred to more advanced accounting texts.

ADEQUATE DISCLOSURE

Adequate disclosure requires enough information to be presented so that financial statement users can intelligently assess the effect of the liability on the firm. This information is presented either parenthetically in the body of the balance sheet or in footnotes to the financial statements. Generally, this information should include amounts authorized to be borrowed, due date or dates, interest rate, property mortgaged or pledged, and any other significant characteristics of the liability or indenture agreements that might be useful to the financial statement reader.

SUMMARY

Chapter 11 considered the accounting problems associated with long-term liabilities. Long-term liabilities are defined as the obligations of the firm that do not require satisfaction for a period of one year or one operating cycle, whichever is longer. Because the rights and duties of creditors and owners differ, acquiring funds by incurring long-term liabilities can be easier and more advantageous for many firms than selling additional stock. Common long-term liabilities include bonds payable, notes payable, lease liabilities, pension liabilities, and deferred income taxes.

Bonds payable are accounted for at the exchange price at which they are issued. Thereafter they are reported at the net present value of the liability. Reporting them at their net present value may require amortization of premium or discount, which reduces or increases the interest expense of the firm. Issuance of the bonds after the date printed on the bond certificates requires that the rate of amortization be adjusted and that the expense of the firm for the short period be reduced.

Many of these problems in accounting for bonds are eliminated in accounting for notes payable. Notes are generally issued at par on the date of the note. Accounting for long-term lease liabilities, pension liabilities, and deferred taxes involves different problems than accounting for notes or bonds. Long-term liabilities are recognized in lease transactions only if the lease is a financing lease and not an operating lease. Long-term liabilities are recognized in pension transactions only if the pension plan is underfunded. Deferred tax liabilities arise whenever the time for recognizing income or expense differs for income tax and financial accounting purposes.

KEY DEFINITIONS

Discount—issuing bonds at a sale price below the face value to reflect a market rate of interest that is greater than the face rate.

Effective-interest amortization—a method of premium and discount amortization that adjusts interest expense to reflect the actual rate on the bond.

Financing leases—long-term leases that are in substance a purchase of the leased property.

Leverage—using equity to borrow funds that are expected to earn more than the cost of the borrowing.

Long-term liabilities—obligations that will be paid in more than one year or operating cycle.

Operating leases—short-term leases where the lessee does not acquire an equity interest in the property.

Premium—issuing bonds at a sale price greater than the face value to reflect a market rate of interest that is less than the face rate.

Straight-line amortization—a method of amortizing premiums and discounts that charges an equal expense to each period over the life of the bond.

QUESTIONS

11-1 What is a long-term liability?

11-2 List the relative advantages of raising money through issuing bonds rather than through issuing stock.

11-3 Define the word leverage and explain how leverage can be favorable for stockholders.

11-4 Under what circumstances are bonds sold at par, at a discount, or at a premium?

11-5 How should bonds payable be disclosed in the balance sheet?

11-6 Over what period is bond discount or bond premium amortized?

11-7 How is the issue price of a bond determined?

11-8 Distinguish between an operating lease and a financial lease.

11-9 What is a nominal rate of interest associated with a bond?

11-10 What accounting problems are posed by bonds issued after the date printed on the bond certificate? How do accountants solve those problems?

11-11 When would a corporation recognize accrued bond interest expense associated with one of its own bonds?

11-12 When should long-term liabilities be reclassified as current liabilities?

11-13 Why do deferred tax liabilities arise?

EXERCISES

E11-1 ABC Company has outstanding $5 million, 8 percent bonds as of December 31 of the current year. These ten-year bonds are due in five years and six months. The unamortized premium on these bonds was $137,500 at July 1 of the current year. Prepare the journal entry to record the interest accrual and the amortization for the six months ended December 31.

E11-2 Can Company issued $100,000, 5 percent, twenty-year bonds at 98 on June 1, 19x6. The interest is payable on June 1 and December 1. Make the journal entries for the following:

a. The issuance of the bonds on June 1, 19x6.
b. Interest payments and amortization for 19x6.
c. Adjusting entries for year-end on December 31, 19x6.

E11-3 State whether the bond is sold at par, at a discount, or at a premium for each of the following cases:

a. The effective rate of interest is 6 percent and the stated rate is 5¾ percent.
b. The 6 percent, $1,000 maturity-value bond sold at 100.
c. The coupon rate is 6 percent but the bond yields 5½ percent.
d. The nominal rate is 4 percent and the market rate is 6.7 percent.
e. A 4 percent bond is sold at 101.

E11-4 Irwin Co. is planning to issue $50,000 of ten year 8 percent bonds with interest payable annually at the end of each year. What will be the issue price if the market rate of interest is 10 percent on the date of issuance?

E11-5 G. Jackson Company is planning to issue $500,000 of 12 percent, five-year bonds on January 1, 19x2. Interest on the bonds is payable each December 31. What will be the issue price of the bonds if the market rate of interest is 11 percent on the date of issue?

E11-6 If bonds are issued initially at a discount and the straight-line method of amortization is used for the discount, interest expense in the earlier years will be:

a. Greater than if the effective interest method were used.
b. The same as if the effective interest method were used.
c. Less than if the effective interest method were used.
d. Less than the amount of the interest payments.

Explain your answer.

E11-7 The Fox Corporation issued $20,000,000 par value 5 percent bonds at 105 on March 1, 19x6, plus accrued interest of $166,667 from January 1, 19x6. Maturity date of the bonds is June 30, 19x9. Interest is paid by the Fox Corporation on June 30 and December 31 annually. The premium is amortized at year-end, December 31. Prepare all entries for 19x6 related to the Fox Corporation bonds.

E11-8 Marco Corporation issued $200,000 par value 7 percent bonds on April 1, 19x6, at 102½. Interest is payable on March 31 and September 30 each year. These bonds mature in ten years. Prepare journal entries for the following dates (use the straight-line amortization method):

a. April 1, 19x6, to record the bond sale.
b. September 30, 19x6, to pay the interest and amortize the premium.
c. December 31, 19x6, to accrue interest and amortize premium.
d. At the date of maturity to pay interest, amortize premium, and retire bonds.

E11-9 Dee Corporation sold Zee Corporation $100,000 par value 10 percent bonds. The bonds are due in ten years and pay interest on March 1 and September 1. Zee Corporation purchased the bonds for $97,000 on September 1. Prepare the first complete year's journal entries for Dee and Zee Corporations. Assume straight-line amortization and closing of the books on December 31.

E11-10 On January 1, 19x0, Strawser Co. signed a five-year, noncancellable lease with Leasing, Inc. for a piece of equipment. The lease contract required an annual rental of $2,000 payable at the beginning of each year starting with January 1, 19x0. It was estimated that the equipment would have a useful life of ten years, and Strawser Co. was given the option to purchase the equipment at the end of the lease period for $1. Assume that the lease is considered a financing lease, that the equipment could be purchased for $8,500 cash on January 1, 19x0, and that the management of Strawser Co. estimates a zero salvage value and uses straight-line depreciation. Prepare for Strawser Co. those sections of the balance sheet dated December 31, 19x0, relating to the lease.

E11-11 Tummins Company entered into a contract on July 1, 19x5, to lease a mini-computer. The computer originally cost the lessor $9,000 and has an estimated useful life of twelve years. Tummins Company has signed a two-year lease, agreeing to pay $2,750 per year. The lessor remains responsible for repairs and maintenance. Is this lease a financing lease or an operating lease? What entries should be made to report the lease payment of $2,750 on July 1, 19x5, and at year-end, December 31, 19x5, assuming that Tummins always uses straight-line depreciation?

PROBLEMS

P11-1 On April 1, 19x6, Duggs Corporation issued $100,000 par value bonds for $97,291.40. The bonds have a nominal interest rate of 5 percent and mature April 1, 19x9. Interest is payable on April 1 and October 1. The bonds were issued to yield 6 percent.

Required:

a. Prepare an amortization table using the straight-line method.
b. Show the balance sheet presentation of these bonds for Duggs Corporation on December 31, 19x6.

P11-2 The Cook Company prepared the following interest and amortization schedule for its ten-year bond issue.

Date	Cash	Interest Expense	Amount Amortized	Bond Book Value
1/1/x6				$104,491
19x6	$ 2,500	$ 2,090	$ 410	104,081
19x7	2,500	2,082	418	103,663
19x8	2,500	2,073	427	103,236
19x9	2,500	2,065	435	102,801
19x0	2,500	2,056	444	102,357
19x1	2,500	2,047	453	101,904
19x2	2,500	2,038	462	101,442
19x3	2,500	2,029	471	100,971
19x4	2,500	2,019	481	100,490
19x5	2,500	2,010	490	100,000
	$25,000	$20,509	$4,491	

Required:

a. Were the bonds issued at a discount or a premium?
b. Was the straight-line method of amortization used?
c. Prepare the journal entry to record the bond issuance on January 1, 19x6.
d. Prepare the necessary journal entries for 19x1.
e. Prepare the necessary journal entries for December 31, 19x5, recording the repayment of the bond.

P11-3 The 19x6 balance sheet of Dean Company included the following accounts:

Six percent bonds payable, maturing on December 31, 19x9	$100,000
Discount on bonds payable	3,000

Required:

a. Compute the annual interest expense assuming straight-line amortization is used.
b. How would the accounts appear in the December 31, 19x8, balance sheet?

P11-4 Company A issued $200,000 par value at 6 percent bonds on January 1, 19x6. These ten-year bonds pay interest semiannually on June 30 and December 31. The bonds were sold at 120. Company C issued $200,000 par value 4 percent, ten-year bonds on January 1, 19x6. Interest is payable semiannually on June 30 and December 31. The bonds were sold at 80.

Required:

a. Prepare all the journal entries necessary for the two companies for 19x6.
b. Show both balance sheet presentations of these bonds as of December 31, 19x6.

P11-5 Ruth Perkins formed Perkins Soda Ash Corporation on January 1, 19x5. The corporation engaged in the following transactions.

1. Sold on April 1 $2 million in twenty-year bonds, dated April 1, 19x5, paying 9 percent interest, for $2,060,000 net.
2. Entered into a lease for heavy equipment on June 1. The lease is for two years requiring payments of $30,000 per year on June 1, 19x5, and 19x6. The lessor guaranteed to make all repairs required and to make all required insurance and property tax payments, when due. The life of the equipment was estimated to be twelve years.
3. Entered into a lease for ten heavy trucks on September 1. The lease was for the estimated useful life of the trucks—four years—requiring payments on September 1, 19x5, and each September 1 for the term of the lease thereafter, of $50,000. Perkins assumed all ownership responsibilities for the trucks and the lease was noncancellable. Estimated current purchase price for the trucks is $190,000.
4. Made the first semiannual interest payment on the bonds on October 1.

Required:

a. Prepare the general journal entries necessary to record these transactions. Amortize bond premium or discount with each interest payment.
b. Prepare the adjusting entries required to adjust these accounts on December 31, 19x5.
c. Prepare the long-term liability section of Perkins' balance sheet as of December 31, 19x5.

P11-6 T. Dickens Co. issued $150,000 of 10 percent bonds on January 1, 19x2. The bonds pay interest each December 31. The ten year bonds were issued to yield an 11 percent interest rate.

Required:

a. Determine the issue price of the bonds.
b. Prepare an effective interest amortization table for the first three years of the bond life.
c. Prepare the journal entries that would be necessary for the first two years of the bonds life.
d. Show how the bonds would appear on the balance sheet at the end of the third year.

P11-7 Trapnell Co. issued $250,000 of 10 percent, fifteen year bonds on January 1, 19x2. The bonds pay interest each December 31. The market rate of interest on the date of issue was 8 percent.

Required:

a. Determine the issue price of the bonds.
b. Prepare an effective interest amortization table for the first three years.
c. Prepare any journal entries that would be necessary in 19x2.
d. Prove that the carrying value of the bonds at the end of three years is approximately equal to their present value using the market rate of interest on the date of issue.

P11-8 Camelback Corporation had the following transactions dealing with long-term liabilities during 19x8:

1. Issued $400,000 of ten-year, 7 percent bonds for $396,000 on January 1, 19x8. The bonds pay interest on June 30 and December 31.
2. Paid $6,000 annual lease payment on heavy equipment. The lease contract is a one-year renewable lease, providing for the lessor to retain major incidents of ownership.
3. Paid semiannual interest on bonds. Management elects to amortize any premium or discount related to bonds semiannually along with bond interest payments. Straight-line amortization is used.
4. Renewed a 270-day, $10,000 note with a bank, paying $800 in interest.
5. Paid semiannual interest on bonds and amortized premium or discount.

Required:

a. Give the general journal entries to record these transactions.
b. Prepare the long-term liability section of Camelback Corporation's balance sheet at December 31, 19x8.

P11-9 Below is the unadjusted trial balance for Pima Sales Company, Inc.

Trial Balance
December 31, 19x8

	Debit	*Credit*
Cash	$ 60,000	
Accounts receivable	26,000	
Inventory	60,000	
Prepaid expenses	4,000	
Deferred lease cost	4,000	
Equipment, furniture, and fixtures	306,000	
Accumulated depreciation		$125,000
Accounts payable		15,000
Notes payable		5,000
Bonds payable		102,000
Financing lease liability		20,000
Owner's equity		116,000
Sales		600,000
Cost of goods sold	380,000	
Salary expense	80,000	
Rental expense	36,000	
Interest expense	19,000	
Utilities expense	8,000	
	$983,000	$983,000

Data needed for liability adjustments are as follows:

1. The note payable is a one-year, 6 percent note due on March 1, 19x9.
2. Bonds payable are ten-year, 9 percent bonds issued June 30, 19x8, paying interest on December 31 and June 30. Interest payable on December 31 had been recorded, but the premium has not been amortized (straight-line).
3. The financing lease is a six-year lease requiring $5,000 in lease payments each December 31. While these amounts were properly handled in the previous two years, this year, on the hectic last day of the year, a new bookkeeper recorded the lease payment as rental expense. The equipment would have cost $24,000 to purchase and depreciation was properly recorded.

Required:

a. Give the adjusting general journal entries necessary to record the adjustments.
b. Prepare an income statement and balance sheet for Pima Sales Company, Inc.

Learning Objectives

Chapter 12 discusses proper accounting for the equity section of a corporation. The Appendix discusses accounting for alternative forms of business organizations. Studying this chapter should enable you to:

1. List characteristics of business that are related to the form of organization (proprietorship, partnership, and corporation).
2. Present journal entries for stock issues, treasury stock repurchases, dividends, and closing entries to transfer earnings to retained earnings.
3. Prepare a balance sheet presentation for corporate owners' equity.
4. Prepare a statement of changes in retained earnings.

12

Accounting for Owner's Equity

INTRODUCTION

The owners' equity in the firm is reported in the owners' equity section of the balance sheet. This section of the balance sheet will vary, both in form and content, depending on the form or organization selected by the business. If the business is a sole proprietorship, there is only one owner whose equity must be accounted for. In a partnership, there are multiple owners, each of whose equity must be accounted for separately. In the corporate form of business, the reporting of the stockholders' equity varies significantly from either sole proprietorships or partnerships. All the principal differences in the financial reports of sole proprietorships, partnerships, or corporations lie in the reporting of owners' equity. The remainder of the balance sheet and the income statements of sole proprietorships, partnerships, and corporations are otherwise identical in form. Consequently, a discussion of the differences in accounting for these various forms of business organization is basically a discussion of the owners' equity section of the balance sheet. In this chapter, we consider the more complex reporting problems of corporate stockholders' equity. The Appendix presents accounting for proprietorships and partnerships.

CORPORATIONS

The corporate form of organization is a common form selected by most major businesses. Although some corporations are enormous in size, such as General Motors, the corporate form of business has advantages that lend its use to even small businesses like cafes or drug stores. There are more sole proprietorships or partnerships than corporations in the United States, but the corporation is clearly the dominant business form in this country, in terms of total assets and total revenues. Consequently, an understanding of the special accounting problems encountered in the corporate form is essential to the student of accounting. This part will discuss the characteristics of a corporation, the reporting of stockholders' equity on the corporation's balance sheet, the method of accounting for the issuance, repurchase, and reissuance of corporate stock, and the accounting and reporting problems of dividends and retained earnings.

CHARACTERISTICS OF A CORPORATION

A *corporation* is a separate, distinct legal entity. It has a separate legal existence, quite apart from that of its shareholders, who are the owners of the corporation. If a sole proprietorship or partnership is sued, it is the sole proprietor or partners who are liable for the damages that must be paid in the event the suit is lost. In the case of a suit against a corporation, however, only the corporation is liable for damages—not its stockholders. As a separate legal entity, a corporation may buy or sell property, sue or be sued, and enter into a wide variety of contracts with other parties. The existence of a corporation as a separate entity provides the corporate form of organization with most of the advantages that make its use appealing to businesses of all sizes.

Corporations acquire their legal existence by securing a *charter of incorporation* from a state or the federal government. This is accomplished by filing an *application for charter* with the appropriate government official. Since the federal government charters only a few kinds of corporations, such as banks and savings and loan associations, the appropriate official is usually the Secretary of State in the state of incorporation. The application for charter usually includes the names of the original stockholders, the name and address of the corporation, a statement of the purpose for which the corporation is formed, and a complete description of the kinds of stock the corporation is authorized to issue. After the legal requirements of the state of incorporation are met, the new corporation is granted a charter. At the first stockholders meeting, the stockholders adopt a set of by-laws which govern the operation of the corporation and select a board of directors. The board of directors has the formal authority to oversee the operations of the corporation on behalf of the stockholders. The board of directors selects the officers of the corporation who have the day-to-day responsibility of mananging the business of the corporation.

Because corporations are separate legal entities, they have the following characteristics.

Limited Liability

Shareholders of a corporation are not responsible for the actions or debts of their corporation. Creditors must look to the assets of the corporation alone to satisfy debts. In contrast, sole proprietorships and partnerships provide unlimited liability, holding sole proprietors and partners accountable for the actions and debts of their businesses.

Continuity of Life

The life of the corporation is determined by the laws in the state of incorporation or by its charter. In most states, corporations are allowed to be incorporated into perpetuity, or to renew their charters after a maximum life, which effectively allows perpetual incorporation. The life of the business is unaffected by the death, insanity, or other legal incapacity of a shareholder. The sale of shares of stock has no effect on the life of the corporation. In contrast, sole proprietorships and partnerships are ended by any of these events and must be reorganized if the business is to continue.

Centralization of Management

The authority to bind the corporation to contracts is vested solely in the hands of the officers and board of directors of the corporation. Shareholders do not have this authority. As a result, shareholders are relieved of the burden of investigating the integrity of fellow shareholders and can rely on professional management to operate the business. The absence of the partnership's mutual agency may prove a substantial advantage where many capital providers are required to fund a business operation.

Ease of Transferability of Ownership Interests

The stock owned by shareholders, evidenced by stock certificates, represents the ownership rights of each stockholder. To transfer these ownership rights, all the stockholder must do is sell the stock. These transactions can be effected easily by simply endorsing the stock certificates over to the buyer. In contrast, the sale of a partnership interest is a much more complex process, requiring special legal documents to effect the sale and new partnership agreements if the new partner is acceptable to other partners.

ADVANTAGES AND DISADVANTAGES OF THE CORPORATE FORM

The corporate form of organization provides its owners with many unique advantages that are unavailable to either sole proprietors or partners. Each of the major characteristics noted above provides strong incentive to select the corporate form. Limited liability protects the stockholder from the personal consequences of business operations. All the shareholder can lose is what he or she has invested in the stock of the corporation. Continuity of life helps to insure the stability of the business, regardless of what may happen to shareholders or officers. Centralization of management vests in professional management the right to bind the corporation to contracts, protecting shareholders from the misdeeds of other shareholders. Ease of transferability-of-ownership interests attracts small as well as large investors who wish to be able to change their investments as business conditions change.

The result of these advantages is the ability of corporations to raise the massive amounts of investment capital required by capital-intensive industries such as the automobile industry or the steel industry. The characteristics of the corporate form of organization allow thousands or even millions of individuals to pool their investment dollars and build the giant business that dominate American and world business.

There are some disadvantages of the corporate form that should be considered, too. The primary disadvantage of the corporate form lies in its federal and state income tax treatment. Corporations are taxable entities and paying federal income taxes on taxable income. In addition, dividends paid to shareholders are also taxable income to the shareholders. The resulting double taxation of corporate earnings can substantially increase the tax burden of a business if it selects the corporate form of organization. Most states also tax corporate income and dividends. Note that sole proprietorships and partnerships do not pay taxes at the business level. The owners are taxed on this income only once, as income on their individual income tax returns.

Another disadvantage of the corporate form of organization is its inflexibility. As a creature of the state, corporations are required to meet the requirements of state law. Periodic stockholders meetings are required, as well as meetings of the board of directors. Some states even require that the meetings be held in the state of incorporation. In addition, regular reports are usually required to be filed with the state government regarding the operation of the corporation. Many major business decisions require action by the board of directors and, in many instances, the stockholders. These and other requirements of state law not only contribute to inflexibility but also generate additional expenses that must be borne by the corporation. Because of this inflexibility, formality, and the income tax consequences of the corporate form, many businesses do not elect to incorporate.

ACCOUNTING FOR STOCKHOLDERS' EQUITY

All of the principal differences found in reporting for corporations, sole proprietorships, or partnerships lie in the reporting of owners' equity. In sole proprietorships or partnerships, each owner of the business is provided with a capital account that measures at year-end the claim of each owner against the book value of the assets of the firm. This method of accounting for and reporting owners' equity is unwieldly and impractical for corporations for seveal reasons. Corporations may have thousands or even millions of shareholders. The exact makeup of the shareholder group changes constantly as shares of stock are bought and sold. In addition, the relative claims of stockholders against the assets of the corporation may differ if more than one class of stock is issued by the corporation. For example, the claims of common stockholders may differ substantially from the claims of preferred stockholders. Instead of accounting for stockholders' equity as a direct dollar measure of the claim of each shareholder, stockholders' equity is accounted for and reported by source. Illustration 1 demonstrates the reporting of stockholders equity by source.

Reporting stockholders' equity by source is not only a practical solution to the problem of reporting the diverse equity interests of a large, ever-changing group of stockholders, but it also clearly reports the *minimum legal capital* of the corporation. Minimum legal capital is the amount of original invested capital that the law does not allow to be impaired by the payment of dividends. Originally, the concept was designed to provide creditors with assurance that shareholders would not pay all of the assets out in dividends, leaving nothing to satisfy creditors' claims. A *par value* was established for stock and printed on the stock certificate. This establishes the amount of minimum *legal capital* per share of stock. For example, if 1,000 shares of stock with $10 par value are issued, the minimum legal capital of the corporation is $10,000. Thus, legal capital is a function of the number of shares of stock outstanding and the par value.

Illustration 1
Stockholders' Equity

Contributed capital:		
Preferred stock, $100 par value, 6 percent cumulative and nonparticipating, 10,000 shares authorized, 1,000 shares issued and outstanding		$ 100,000
Common stock, $100 par value, 100,000 shares authorized, 10,000 shares issued, 100 shares held as treasury stock		1,000,000
Additional contributed capital from preferred stockholders		20,000
Additional contributed capital from common stockholders		230,000
Contributed capital from plant-site donation		40,000
Contributed capital from treasury stock transactions		14,000
Total contributed capital		$1,404,000
Retained earnings:		
Appropriated retained earnings for plant expansion	$100,000	
Unappropriated retained earnings	606,000	
Total retained earnings		706,000
Total		$2,110,000
Less: Cost of treasury stock		9,000
Total stockholders' equity		$2,101,000

The concept of a par value has proven very confusing to investors and has been largely unsuccessful in protecting creditors. Some naive investors may think that par value is a measure of fair market value, which it clearly is not. The corporation could dissipate its assets by unsuccessful operations or invest in equipment with resale values only a fraction of their original cost. In either instance, the concept of par value fails to provide creditors with assurance that funds are available to meet their demands. Many states now allow corporations to issue *no-par-value stock*. Where no-par-value stock is issued, the minimum legal capital is either a stated amount set by the corporation called stated value, or the full amount paid for the stock at issuance, depending on state laws.

All state laws now forbid the original issuance of stock at a *discount*, that is, below the amount of minimum legal capital per share. Stock may be issued at a *premium*, however, which is an amount above par or stated value. When it is issued at a premium, the amount above par or stated value is reported in a separate account. In Illustration 1, the premium on common stock is reported as additional contributed capital from common stockholders. In so doing, the amount of minimum legal capital is separately reported to provide information to creditors and investors.

TYPES OF STOCK

When an investor acquires stock of a coporation, he or she acquires a bundle of rights and privileges in exchange for his or her investment. One corporation may issue several different kinds of stock, each kind of stock granting to investors different rights. If only one class of stock is issued, it is called *common stock*. If more than one class of stock is issued, one class is common stock and the other class or classes are usually called *preferred stock*. Preferred stockholders usually receive certain dividend and liquidation preferences that common stockholders do not receive. Dividends are periodic earning distributions made by the company. By contrast, liquidation proceeds result from the partial or total dissolution of the company.

Common Stock

The common stockholder is the residual equity holder of the corporation. Only after preferred stockholders are paid their dividends does the common stockholder receive dividends. Only after creditors and preferred stockholders have been satisfied does the common stockholder receive anything in the liquidation of the corporation. However, the common stockholders' dividends are not subject to fixed limits as is the usual case with preferred stock. Consequently, if the corporation is very successful, the common stockholders receive the greatest benefits, in higher dividends and appreciation in stock values. In addition, almost all common stock is voting stock. In effect, the common stockholders control the corporation by electing the members of the board of directors.

Preferred Stock

Preferred stockholders receive rights and privileges that may differ from those of common stockholders in several ways. The most common preference given preferred stockholders is *current dividend preference*. Preferred stockholders must receive their stated current dividends before common stockholders may be paid a dividend. Dividend rates for preferred stock are stated as an annual dollar amount per share or a percentage of par value per share. For example, the preferred stock in Illustration 1 is 6 percent, $100 par value preferred stock. This means that each share of preferred stock must be paid $6 in dividends during the year before common stockholders may be paid any dividends.

Notice that the payment of dividends—even preferred—is discretionary on the part of the board of directors. No liability to pay dividends exists unless the board of directors declares the dividend. If the stock has *cumulative dividend preferences*, dividends that are not declared in prior years must be paid in later years before common stockholders may receive dividends. If dividends are not declared on cumulative preferred stock, the unpaid dividends are called *dividends in arrears*. For example, if 6 percent, $100 par value cumulative preferred stock is two years in arrears in dividend payments, the corporation must declare and pay all dividends in arrears plus the current dividend before common stockholders may be paid a dividend. In the absence of cumulative-dividend preference, preferred stockholders need to be paid only the current dividend before common stockholders can receive dividends as shown in Illustration 2. Note that in case A, where preferred is noncumulative, preferred can expect a maximum annual dividend of $6,000. In the first year only $1,000 of dividends were declared and it went to preferred shareholders. In this year, they received $5,000 less than the stated dividend rate. Since the preferred on noncumulative, they do not have a future right to dividends not paid in any one year. In years two through four, when dividend declarations exceeded the preferred dividend, preferred shareholders received only their dividend for that year and the remaining declared dividends went to common shareholders.

Contrast case A to case B where the preferred is cumulative. Now any dividends not paid to preferred in any year must be made up in subsequent years before common shareholders can receive any dividends. For example, in the second year, preferred shareholders are entitled to receive $5,000 of dividends in arrears from year one, plus the current dividend of $6,000, before any distributions can be made to common stock. Since only $7,000 is distributed, it will all go to preferred stock and dividends of $4,000 ($5,000 + $6,000 − $7,000) remain in arrears. In year three, dividends of $13,000 are distributed. Preferred shareholders are entitled to the first $11,000 ($4,000 arrears + $6,000 current). Since $13,000 of dividends were declared, the $2,000 excess goes to common stock. In year four, there are no dividends in arrears and preferred will only receive its current dividend of $6,000; the remaining declared dividends go to common.

Illustration 2

Comparison of Cumulative and Noncumulative Dividend Preference

Assumptions: Preferred stock is 6 percent, $100 par value, 1,000 shares outstanding; common stock is $10 par, $1,000 shares outstanding

Case A—Noncumulative

Year	Total Dividends Declared	Dividends Paid To: Noncumulative Preferred Stock	Common Stock
1	$ 1,000	$1,000	$ 0
2	7,000	6,000	1,000
3	13,000	6,000	7,000
4	19,000	6,000	13,000

Case B—Cumulative

Year	Total Dividends Declared	Dividends Paid To: Cumulative Preferred Stock	Common Stock
1	$ 1,000	$ 1,000	$ 0
2	7,000	7,000	0
3	13,000	11,000	2,000
4	19,000	6,000	13,000

One additional form of dividend preference that can be given preferred stock is *participating dividend preference*. Normally, the dividends paid to preferred stockholders are limited to their stated dividend rate. In rare instances, preferred stock may be given the opportunity to participate in additional dividends that are paid beyond their stated dividend rate. While participation features vary greatly, they usually require that the common stockholders receive the same percentage of par value in dividends as the preferred stockholders before preferred stockholders are allowed to share in any additional dividends. For example, if participating preferred stock is 6 percent, $100 par value, and the corporation's common stock is $10 par value, the corporation must declare sufficient dividends to pay the preferred-stock $6 dividend and a 60 cents dividend per share of common stock ($10 par value × 6% preferred-stock dividend rate) before the preferred stockholders participate in additional dividends. The rate of participation can be unlimited, that is, *fully participating*, or limited to a maximum dividend, that is, *partially participating*. The exact manner in which common and preferred shareholders share in dividends is established in the corporate charter in the description of the various securities and varies from corporation to corporation. In the case of fully participating preferred stock, the two shareholder groups usually share in dividends by each receiving an equal percentage of par or stated value as shown in Illustration 3.

Following established priorities, the preferred stock is first allocated dividends up to the established 6 percent rate (step 1). Next, the common shareholders are allocated an equal rate of dividend on their investment (step 2). The remainder is allocated so that both common and preferred stockholders earn the same rate on the par value of their investment (step 3). When complete, each has earned 9 percent calculated as follows:

	Number of Shares	×	*Par Value*	=	*Legal Capital*	÷	*Dividend*	=	*Rate*
Common	50,000		$ 10		$ 500,000		30,000		6%
Preferred	10,000		100		1,000,000		60,000		6%

If the preferred is also cumulative, step 1 would include any dividends in arrears as well as the current dividend. In step 2, common shareholders are entitled only to the current dividend rate. For example, assume the same facts as in Illustration 3 plus assume dividends are in arrears $15,000 on preferred. The dividends would be distributed as follows:

	Preferred	*Common*	*Dividends Remaining*
			$135,000
1. Preferred stock:			
Arrears	$15,000		120,000
Current (6%)	60,000		60,000
2. Common stock:			
Current (6%)		$30,000	30,000
3. Participation	(⅔) 20,000	(⅓) 10,000	
Total	$95,000	$40,000	

Preferred stock may have other preferences in addition to dividend preferences. Almost all preferred stock is granted *liquidation preference.* In the event the corporation is liquidated, the preferred stockholders must receive a predetermined amount—usually at or slightly above par or stated value. Preferred stock may also carry a *conversion privilege,* which allows the investor to exchange the preferred stock for a predetermined amount of common stock in the same corporation. It should be noted, however, that preferred stock is rarely voting stock. Preferred stockholders rarely acquire a direct voice in the management of the corporation.

ISSUANCE OF STOCK

When a corporation issues stock in exchange for cash, the cash account is debited for the proceeds of the sale, and the amount of minimum legal capital is credited to the common stock or preferred stock account, depending

Illustration 3
Dividends Paid to Fully
Participating Preferred Stockholders

Assumptions: Preferred stock is 6 percent, $100 par value, fully participating, 10,000 shares outstanding. Common stock is $10 par value, 50,000 shares outstanding. Dividends declared total $135,000.

	Dividends to Preferred Stock	*Dividends to Common Stock*	*Dividends Remaining to be Allocated*
			$135,000
1. Current dividends to preferred stock (6% × $100 × 10,000 shares)	$60,000		75,000
2. Prorata dividend to common stock (6% × $10 × 50,000 shares)		$30,000	45,000
3. Participating dividends	(2/3)* 30,000	(1/3)* 15,000	0
Total	$90,000	$45,000	

*Calculated as follows:

Total preferred par value = ($100 × 10,000 = $1,000,000)	$1,000,000
Total common par value = ($10 × 50,000 = $500,000)	500,000
Total par value	$1,500,000

Part allocated to preferred stock:

$$\frac{\$1,000,000}{\$1,500,000} \times \$45,000 = \$30,000$$

Part allocated to preferred stock:

$$\frac{\$500,000}{\$1,500,000} \times \$45,000 = \$15,000$$

on the type of stock issued. If the stock has an assigned par value, this is the amount that is credited to the stock account. If the stock has a stated value determined by the corporation, this amount is credited to the stock account. In either instance, any excess proceeds above par or stated value are credited to an account entitled, for example, additional contributed capital from common (preferred) stockholders. If the stock is issued in a state in which all original proceeds from the sale of no-par-value stock are considered minimum legal capital, the entire proceeds are credited to the stock account.

Issuing par value stock:

Cash	$180,000	
Common stock—par		$100,000
Preferred stock—par		25,000
Additional contributed capital from common stockholders		50,000
Additional contributed capital from preferred stockholders		5,000
Issued 100,000 shares of $1 par value common stock at $1.50 per share and 1,000 shares of $25 par value preferred stock at $30 per share.		

Issuing no-par-value share with stated value assigned:

Cash	$180,000	
Common stock—stated value		$100,000
Preferred stock—stated value		25,000
Additional contributed capital from common stockholders		50,000
Additional contributed capital from preferred stockholders		5,000
Issued 100,000 shares of no-par-value common stock with $1 stated value at $1.50 per share and 1,000 shares of no-par-value preferred stock with $25 stated value at $30 per share.		

Issuing no-par-value share without assigned stated value:

Cash	$180,000	
Common stock		$150,000
Preferred stock		30,000
Issued 100,000 shares of no-par-value common stock with at $1.50 per share and 1,000 shares of no-par-value preferred stock at $30 per share.		

Instead of issuing stock for cash, corporations may issue stock to individuals for performing services for the corporation or to suppliers in exchange for equipment or other assets. In these instances, the assets received should be recorded at the fair market value of the stock issued or the asset received, whichever is more clearly determinable. When the fair market value of the stock cannot be determined, the assets should be valued at their estimated fair market value. For example, if a corporation acquires machinery for the issuance of 1,000 shares of common stock with a fair market value of $15 and par value of $10, the entry would be as follows:

Machinery	$15,000	
Common stock		$10,000
Additional contributed capital from common stockholders		5,000

Sometimes corporations sell stock on credit, taking installment payments for stock and issuing the stock after it is fully paid. Stock sold on credit terms is called *subscribed stock*. Assume a corporation receives subscriptions to 1,000 shares of $5 par value at $10 per share and that $1,000 cash is paid at the time of the subscription. The following entry would be made:

Cash	$1,000	
Subscriptions receivable, common stock	9,000	
Common stock subscribed		$5,000
Additional contributed capital from common stockholders		5,000

Subscriptions receivable is an asset, just as are other receivables, and the resulting common stock subscribed and additional contributed capital accounts are owners' equity items that reflect the increased claim of the stockholders against the assets of the corporation. Note that since the stock has not been issued, a common stock subscribed account is credited rather than the regular common stock account. The subscribed account would appear immediately below common stock in the equity section of a balance sheet. When the stock is fully paid and the shares are issued, these entries are made:

Cash	$9,000	
Subscriptions receivable—common stock		$9,000
Common stock subscribed	5,000	
Common stock		5,000

TREASURY STOCK TRANSACTIONS

When a corporation buys its own stock that previously has been issued, the stock is called *treasury stock*. Corporations frequently reacquire their own shares to eliminate dissident minority shareholders, to acquire stock needed in employee stock bonus plans or executive stock options, to acquire shares to be used in acquiring other businesses, or to influence the market price of the stock. While treasury stock is technically still issued but no longer outstanding, treasury stock is not allowed to vote, nor are dividends paid on treasury stock. The purchase of treasury stock effectively reduces the stockholders' equity as shown earlier in Illustration 1. Treasury stock is most frequently valued at the cost to reacquire the stock. For example, if a corporation purchases 100 shares of its own common stock for $3,000, it records the purchase as follows:

Treasury stock	$3,000	
Cash		$3,000

Again note that the treasury stock account reduces stockholders' equity. It would be reported on the balance sheet in this manner:

Stockholders' Equity

Contributed capital:	
Common stock, par value $10, 100,00 shares authorized and issued, of which 100 are in the treasury	$1,000,000
Additional contributed capital from common stockholders	100,000
Retained earnings:	
Unappropriated retained earnings	3,000,000
Total	$4,100,000
Less: Cost of treasury stock	3,000
Total stockholders' equity	$3,097,000

When treasury stock is later sold, it could be sold for its cost, or above or below its cost. If the stock is sold above its cost, the profit on the sale is treated as additional contributed capital—not as gain reported on the income statement. Sale of the treasury stock, acquired for $3,000 at the higher price of $4,000 is recorded as follows:

Cash	$4,000	
Treasury stock		$3,000
Contributed capital from treasury stock transactions		$1,000

If treasury stock is sold for less than its cost, the loss on the transaction is treated as a reduction in stockholders' equity. The contributed capital from treasury stock transactions account is debited for as much of the loss as its account balance is sufficient to absorb. Any remainder may be debited to retained earnings. If the balance of the contributed capital from treasury stock transactions account is in excess of $1,000, the following entry would be made for sale of the stock for $2,000:

Cash	$2,000	
Contributed capital from treasury stock transactions	1,000	
Treasury stock		$3,000
Sold treasury stock costing $3,000 for $2,000		

If the balance of the contributed capital from treasury stock transactions account is $600, the following entry would be made:

Cash	$2,000	
Contributed capital from treasury stock transactions	600	
Retained earnings	400	
Treasury stock		$3,000

State laws normally prohibit purchases of treasury stock unless the corporation has a retained earnings balance at least equal to the cost of the treasury stock. Some states also require the appropriation of retained earnings, a subject described in more detail below. This continues to give some assurance to creditors that stockholders will not be able to remove the cushion provided by legal capital by having the company own itself.

OTHER SOURCES OF CONTRIBUTED CAPITAL

Contributed capital may come from sources other than shareholders. For example, a city may donate land to a corporation in an effort to get the corporation to locate a plant in the city. These or other capital contributions made to a corporation by nonstockholders are reported on the balance sheet under a descriptive title that indicates the source of the capital contributed. The assets contributed are valued at their fair market value and entered in the books of the firm so that accounting control can be established over the assets, and the balance sheet can report the nature of this capital contribution. For example, if a city contributed land valued at $50,000 to a corporation, the entry to record the contribution would be:

Land	$50,000	
Contributed capital from plant-site donation		$50,000

ACCOUNTING FOR RETAINED EARNINGS

The *retained earnings* account of the firm reflects the net result of its lifetime profits and losses, reduced by dividends declared during its life. Many studies have emphasized the importance of retained earnings as a source of capital to finance the growth and expansion of businesses. Retained earnings are normally the last major source of capital reported in the stockholders' equity section of the balance sheet. In the closing process, the income summary and the dividend accounts are closed to retained earnings in this entry:

Income summary	$500,000	
Retained earnings		$400,000
Dividends		100,000
To close income summary and dividends account to retained earnings		

Retained earnings may be reported on the balance sheet as either unrestricted retained earnings or as retained earnings restricted for some special purpose. Retained earnings become restricted or appropriated by action of the board of directors. By appropriating retained earnings, the board of directors hopes to convey to shareholders information regarding the intended use of assets generated by these earnings and to explain why these assets were not paid out to shareholders in dividends. In addition, state laws may require the appropriation of retained earnings for the cost of treasury stock.

If a corporation has issued bonds, the bond indenture agreement may require the corporation to appropriate retained earnings. Presumably, unappropriated retained earnings are not earmarked for specific projects. However, it must be remembered that retained earnings represents a claim against all assets in general and none in particular. An appropriation in no way assures that cash or other liquid resources are or will be available when needed.

To place a restriction on retained earnings merely requires the action of the board of directors to that effect. An appropriation of $300,000 in retained earnings for plant expansion would be recorded in this entry:

Retained earnings	$300,000	
Retained earnings appropriated for plant expansion		$300,000

Statement of Retained Earnings

To fully disclose all relevant financial data, many corporations present a *statement of retained earnings*, sometimes called a statement of changes in retained earnings. The function of the retained earnings statement is to summarize all changes in retained earnings during the year. A retained earnings statement is shown in Illustration 4.

Prior-Period Adjustments

A large group of accountants has consistently sought to have all items that were nonrecurring or extraordinary in nature reported as changes in retained earnings. Thus, they would appear on the retained earnings statement rather than the income statement. However, the extraordinary items

Illustration 4
The Kenya Corporation
Statement of Retained Earnings
For the Year Ended December 31, 19x5

Retained earnings balance—January 1, 19x5	$114,000
Prior-period adjustment: Decrease in 19x3 federal income tax liability	12,000
Adjusted retained earnings balance—January 1, 19x5	$126,000
Add: Net income—19x5	91,000
Balance	$217,000
Less: Dividends declared in 19x5	30,000
Retained earnings balance—December 31, 19x5	$187,000

should be separated from the results of normal, recurring operations on the income statement (see Chapter 6). *Prior-period adjustments* result from corrections of errors in previous year's financial statements. Since the net result of these errors is part of retained earnings, prior-period adjustments are shown as an adjustment to the beginning balance of retained earnings (see Illustration 4).

Prior-period adjustments will be quite rare in practice. Nevertheless, users and preparers of financial statements should be aware of the potential to adjust the beginning balance of retained eranings.

ACCOUNTING FOR DIVIDENDS

Dividends are a distribution of the earnings of a corporation to its shareholders. The term dividend usually refers to a distribution of cash. The terms *property dividends* or *dividend in kind* refer to a distribution of assets other than cash. Before dividends may be paid to any shareholder, the board of directors must declare the dividend. It is important to note that no liability to pay dividends exists until they are declared by the board of directors. A typical declaration announcement would read as follows:

> "The board of directors of Caddo Corporation today declared a quarterly dividend of $1 per share on the common stock, to be paid to shareholders of record on March 15, 19x5, payable on April 10, 19x5."

Three important dates are referred to in this announcement. The *date of declaration* is the day on which the board of directors declares the dividend and the corporation incurs the liability to make the dividend payment. This entry would be made:

Dividends (retained earnings)	$50,000	
Common dividend payable		$50,000

In this entry, the dividends account is increased (or the retained earnings account is directly reduced) and the liability to pay the dividend is recognized. The second date referred to in the announcement is the *date of record*. This is the date on which the shareholder records of the corporation are consulted to determine who will receive the dividends declared. A shareholder's name must appear in the corporation's records, that is, he or she must be a "shareholder of record" on this date before he or she is entitled to receive the dividend. No accounting entries are made on this date. On the *date of payment*, which may follow the date of record by a month or more in order to give the corporation an opportunity to prepare checks, the dividend is paid and this entry is made:

Common dividend payable	$50,000	
Cash......................................		$50,000

Both assets and shareholders' equity have been reduced for the payment of the dividend.

In determining whether to declare and pay dividends to shareholders, the board of directors must consider many factors. Initially, they must decide if they are able to pay dividends. That is, do they have sufficient cash and retained earnings? Both are required before a dividend could legally and wisely be declared. More difficult considerations lie beyond these two essential ones. Does the corporation believe its business will prosper in the upcoming period, or does it need to retain its earnings? Does the business plan to expand or to invest in new equipment that will require extensive capital? Will the corporation suffer from some unforeseen event that will require large amounts of capital, such as a natural calamity like a flood or fire, or a lawsuit? Because of these and other considerations, corporations rarely pay all their earnings out in dividends to shareholders. Indeed, many corporations pay no dividends at all.

Stock Dividends

A *stock dividend* is a distribution of additional shares of stock in a corporation to the shareholders of the corporation. In effect, the corporation gives its shareholders additional evidence of their continuing interest in the corporation. A stock dividend accomplishes two things. First, it may relieve the corporation of shareholder pressure for the payment of cash dividends, which the board of directors may feel it is unwise to pay. Note that when cash dividends are paid, both assets and shareholders' equity are reduced. The distribution of a stock dividend does not reduce cash or total stockholders' equity. Second, the stock dividend causes a transfer of retained earnings to contributed capital. This permits the company to distribute additional shares of stock to existing stockholders. Each stockholder's proportionate interest in the firm remains the same. The entries to record a stock dividend of 500 shares of $5 par value common stock with a fair market value of $25:

Stock dividends (retained earnings)	$12,500	
Common stock dividend distributable		$ 2,500
Additional contributed capital from common stockholders		10,000
Declared a 500 share common stock dividend		
Common stock dividend distributable	2,500	
Common stock		2,500
Distributed common stock dividend		

Notice that the effect of the stock dividend is to ultimately reduce retained earnings by an amount equal to the fair market value of the stock dividend declared and to transfer these amounts to contributed capital. At the time of the declaration of the stock dividend, a contributed capital account entitled common stock dividend distributable is credited with the minimum legal capital for the stock to be distributed. While the title of the account suggests that it is a liability account, the account is a contributed capital account belonging in the stockholders' equity section of the balance sheet. It is not a liability since its settlement will not require the distribution of assets.

This process of transferring retained earnings to contributed capital is frequently referred to as *capitalizing* retained earnings. It is important to note that this process does not increase or reduce stockholders' equity; it merely rearranges the nature of that equity as shown in Illustration 5. This may eliminate some pressure on a company to distribute cash dividends.

The stock dividend in Illustration 5 would be referred to as a 5 percent stock dividend, because the amount of the distribution totalled 5 percent of the outstanding stock (500 ÷ 10,000 = 5%). Each shareholder who owned 100 shares would receive five additional shares. But if assets and stockholders' equity remain unchanged as a result of the stock dividend, what has the shareholder really received? From the corporation he or she receives only additional evidence of his or her same interest in the corporation. If the a stockholder owned 20 percent of the outstanding common stock of the corporation before the distribution, he or she would still own 20 percent of the outstanding common stock afterward.

Illustration 5

Effect of a Common Stock Dividend

Assumption: A 500 share, common stock dividend with total fair market value of $25 per share is distributed on $5 par value common stock.

Stockholders' Equity Before Stock Dividend

Contributed capital:	
Common stock (10,000 shares)	$ 50,000
Additional contributed capital	16,000
Retained earnings	80,000
Total stockholders' equity	$146,000

Stockholders' Equity After Stock Dividend

Contributed capital:	
Common stock (10,500 shares)	$ 52,500
Additional contributed capital	26,000
Retained earnings	67,500
Total stockholders' equity	$146,000

In the previous example, a small percentage stock dividend was declared. In this situation, it is assumed that the dividend declaration will have little or no effect on the market price of the stock and, therefore, the entry was valued at the market value of the stock on the dividend declaration date. However, in some cases a company may declare a large dividend, such as a 50 percent dividend. In this case, the stock dividend distribution would have a material impact on the market value of the stock and market value would not be appropriate for valuing the transaction. GAAP requires that when a stock dividend is large, 20 to 25 percent or more of outstanding stock, the entry be recorded at par value instead of market value. This position is taken because the company would not know what exact impact the large dividend would have on the market value. For large stock dividends, the stock dividend distributable account would be credited for the par value of the stock and no additional contributed capital would be recorded.

Stock Splits

Corporations frequently have a range of prices within which they prefer their stock to trade. If the price per share grows too large, it discourages small investors from purchasing it. Corporations normally prefer that publicly held stock be widely distributed among as many shareholders as possible. This stabilizes the price of the stock, preventing wild fluctuations. To keep the price of the stock low and affordable to the average investor, a corporation may effect a stock split. A *stock split* occurs when the corporation calls all of its stock in and issues two or more shares for each share that was previously outstanding, reducing the par or stated value of the stock accordingly. For example, if stock selling at $125 per share has a par value of $20 per share and is split 2 for 1, the corporation calls all $20 par shares in and issues two $10 par shares for each $20 par share.

A stock split has no effect on total stockholders' equity or on the balances of contributed capital and retained earnings accounts. Since the only effect of a stock split is to reduce the par value of the shares and increase the number of shares outstanding, no accounting entries are required. However, a memorandum, or parenthetical, entry would be made providing details of the split. Normally, the corporation would record the details of the stock split in the corporate records and adjust the description of the stock on the balance sheet.

ADEQUATE DISCLOSURE

The stockholders' equity section of the balance sheet can be long and very complex. To make it easy for shareholders, creditors, and potential investors to understand the items in the stockholders' equity section, it is important that all relevant information regarding the sources of equity capital be presented, either parenthetically or in footnotes to the statements. The various classes of stock issued by the corporation should be fully described, including the number of share authorized, issued, outstanding, and in the treasury, as well as the par or stated value. The preferences granted to preferred stock should be clearly described, although lengthy descriptions are usually placed in footnotes rather than made parenthetically in the body of the balance sheet. Other items should be described in sufficient detail to allow a knowledgeable creditor or investor to understand the item and to judge its impact.

SUMMARY

The corporate form of organization is the dominant business form in the United States and the world. A corporation is a separate legal entity with the characteristics of limited liability, continuity of life, centralization of management, and ease of transferability of ownership interests. These characteristics provide the corporation with significant advantages over other forms of business. These may, in part, be offset by the disadvantages of double taxation, organizational rigidity, and numerous legal requirements imposed by the state of incorporation.

Stockholders are the owners of the corporation. Many corporations issue more than one class of stock, providing owners with different rights and privileges. If only one class of stock is issued, it is called common stock. If more than one class of stock is issued, one class is common stock and the other are usually called preferred stock, providing preferred stockholders with one or more special rights or privileges.

Corporate accounting differs from the accounting for sole proprietorships or partnerships principally in accounting for owners' equity. Instead of accounting for the equity of each owner in the book value of the firm's assets, corporate owners' equity is accounted for by source—common stockholders, preferred stockholders, gains on treasury stock transactions, capital contributed by nonstockholders, retained earnings, and other sources. The financial statements prepared for corporations may also include a retained earnings statement, summarizing the changes in retained earnings during the accounting period. Because of the complexity of corporate accounting, it is especially critical that accountants make extra effort to ensure that sufficient disclosure of corporate events is made in the body of the financial statements or in their footnotes to allow financial statement users to interpret the statements.

KEY DEFINITIONS

Arrears—dividends on preferred stock that have not been paid in previous years.

Capitalizing—shifting retained earnings to contributed capital through stock dividends.

Common stock—the basic class of stock which represents non-preferred ownership interests.

Corporation—a separate, distinct legal entity.

Cumulative—a preferred stock feature that requires that any dividends in arrears be paid before distributions to common shareholders.

Dividends—distributions of profits to shareholders.

Large stock dividend—a stock dividend of greater than 20 to 25 percent of the outstanding stock.

Legal capital—the minimum capital that must be maintained in a corporation to protect creditors; normally it is the par value times the number of shares outstanding.

Par value—a minimum value assigned to shares of stock by the state in which the company is incorporated.

Participation—a preferred stock feature that allow it to share in dividend distributions above the stated dividend rate.

Preferred stock—a stock which has preferences over common stock.

Prior-period adjustment—an adjustment to retained earnings resulting from an error in a prior year's financial statements.

Property dividends—distribution of noncash dividends to shareholders.

Stock dividend—a dividend paid in additional shares of the company's stock.

Stock split—an exchange of shares of stock for the same company's stock at a different par value.

Subscribed stock—stock under contract for sale.

Treasury stock—a company's previously outstanding stock that has been repurchased by the company.

Appendix

Proprietorships and Partnerships

PART I: SOLE PROPRIETORSHIPS

Any business owned by only one person is a sole proprietorship. Accounting for and reporting the owner's equity in a sole proprietorship is relatively simple, because all changes in the residual equity of the firm affect only one owner. A sole proprietorship requires only two accounts: a capital account and a drawing account. The capital account is usually entitled using the name of the sole owner of the business. For example, John Smith's shoe repair business would use a capital account, entitled John Smith—capital, or John Smith—owner's equity. The capital account is debited or credited for all transactions directly affecting owner's equity, except owner withdrawals from the firm. For example, the capital account is credited for investments that the owner makes. The capital account is also debited or credited for profits or losses in closing the accounts at the end of the accounting period.

The drawing account is also usually entitled using the owner's name, such as John Smith—drawing, or John Smith—withdrawals. The drawing account is debited for the market value of assets that are withdrawn from the business by the owner. Neither common law nor tax recognize a sole proprietor as an employee of his own business, because he would be hiring himself. Therefore, the drawing account is used to record all payments made to the owner—even regular weekly or monthly checks—instead of a salary account. The drawing account is closed directly to the capital account of the proprietor at the end of the accounting period. The capital account at that point in time reflects the claim of the owner against the book value of the assets of the business—the net result of the investments and withdrawals plus or minus the results of business transactions, all measured on the basis of historical costs.

The following transactions and entries illustrate the accounting for owner's equity in sole proprietorships:

January 1, 19x1—John Smith invests $5,000 in a shoe repair business:

Cash	$5,000	
John Smith—capital		$5,000
Initial investment by owner		

January 31, 19x1—John draws his monthly $500 check to meet living expenses:

John Smith—withdrawals	$500	
Cash		$500
Regular monthly withdrawal by owner		

November 15, 19x1—John withdraws typewriter from business for personal use.
Typewriter cost $300 and has $30 accumulated depreciation and a market value of 270.

John Smith—withdrawals	$270	
Accumulated depreciation—office equipment	30	
Office equipment		$300
Withdrew typewriter		

December 31, 19x1—At the end of the year, after closing revenue and expense accounts, assume the following balances remain:

	Debit	*Credit*
Income summary		$12,000
John Smith—withdrawals	$6,270	
John Smith—capital		5,000

To complete the closing process, the following entries would be made:

Income summary	$12,000	
John Smith—capital		$12,000
Closed income summary account		
John Smith—capital	6,270	
John Smith—withdrawals		6,270
Closed withdrawals account		

The owner's equity section of John Smith Shoe Repair Service's balance sheet dated December 31, 19x1, would be reported as follows:

Owner's Equity

John Smith—capital (January 1, 19x1)	$ 5,000
Add: Net income for 19x1	12,000
Total	$17,000
Less: John Smith—withdrawals for 19x1	6,270
John Smith—capital (December 31, 19x1)	$10,730

In keeping with the adequate disclosure concept, the owner's equity section of the balance sheet details those changes in owner's equity resulting from business transactions reported on the income statement and separately reports other changes to owner's equity, such as withdrawals and additional investments.

PART II: PARTNERSHIPS

A *partnership* is defined by the Uniform Partnership Act as "an association of two or more persons who carry on as co-owners of a business for profit." All of the elements in this definition are required before a partnership is recognized. If only one person is the owner of a business, it is not a partnership. The term "persons" should be viewed in a broad sense, however. Thus, corporations, estates, or trusts may be partners in a partnership. The relationship of the partners must be that of co-owners. Therefore, no partnership exists if the relationship between, for example, the two people who run a plumbing company is an employer-employee relationship or an agent-principal relationship. At the same time, there must be an intent to carry on a business and divide profits. Simple co-ownership of property does not create a partnership.

Partnership accounting is very similar to the accounting for sole proprietorships. Because there are multiple owners in a partnership, however, there must be a capital account and a withdrawals account for each partner. In addition, some means of dividing the profit or loss of the partnership among the partners must be determined, and the result of this division must be reflected in the capital accounts of the partners. Further complications in partnership accounting are caused by the withdrawal of a partner or by the complete liquidation of the partnership. Before illustrating the proper treatment of these accounting problems, it will be useful to examine the legal characteristics of a partnership. Business executives frequently ask accountants to help them decide whether to operate a business as a partnership or as a corporation. An understanding of the characteristics of a partnership is critical to that decision.

LEGAL CHARACTERISTICS

The partnership form of organization has four significant legal characteristics: (1) voluntary contractual association, (2) limited life, (3) mutual agency, and (4) unlimited liability.

Voluntary Contractual Association

A partnership results from partners voluntarily entering into a contract to form and operate a partnership. A partner may not be forced into a partnership. Because of the mutual agency and unlimited liability of each partner, great care is required in selecting partners. Consequently, the law requires that each partner *voluntarily* contract with others to form the partnership. The contract may be written or oral. Because of the significance of the partnership relationship, legal advisors strongly urge that it be written and that it provide a set of operating rules covering all situations on which there may be future disagreement. For example, the contract should establish the formula for dividing profits and losses among the partners, rules for making major business decisions, and rules for dividing the assets at the liquidation of the partnership.

Limited Life

A partnership has a limited life. Many possible events can cause the partnership to be dissolved. The death, bankruptcy, insanity, or other legal incompetence of any partner automatically causes the partnership to dissolve. Any partner may at any time voluntarily withdraw from the partnership, which dissolves the partnership. Of course, this does not mean that the business operated by the partnership must cease to operate. Remaining partners can form a new partnership, but the old partnership exists no longer.

Mutual Agency

Each partner in a partnership is an agent for the partnership. In other words, each partner has the authority to bind the partnership to contracts that are within the scope of the business. This places enormous importance on the careful selection of partners, since each partner has the authority to singly make decisions, without consulting with other partners, that could be of immense importance to the business. For example, if one partner agrees that the partnership will buy assets, the resulting contract is binding on the partnership, even if the other partners knew nothing of the contract. Of course, the partnership can limit the authority of any partner, but such a limitation is not effective with respect to outsiders who have no knowledge of this limitation of authority. Outsiders unaware of this limited authority can successfully bind the partnership to contracts entered into by this partner.

Unlimited Liability

The liability of each partner in a partnership is a *joint and several liability*. This means that if the assets of the partnership are not sufficient to meet the claims of creditors, each partner is personally liable for paying his or her prorata share of the remaining debt out of his or her personal assets. In addition, if one partner has insufficient personal assets to pay all of his or her share of the remaining debt, the fellow partners are liable for the part he or she is unable to pay. Of course, this partner with insufficient assets now owes the fellow partners for the amount of his or her debt they paid, but he or she may never be able to pay them.

DECISION: SHOULD WE ORGANIZE AS A PARTNERSHIP?

The combination of the partnership characteristics of mutual agency and unlimited liability are strong disadvantages to the use of the partnership form of organization. Errors in judgment of partners can have disastrous consequences for each partner. These disadvantages can at least partly be overcome by the careful selection of responsible and capable partners. Strengths of the partnership form of organization can mitigate these disadvantages in some cases. Partnerships are generally easily formed and easily dissolved. The operations of partnerships are much simpler than those of corporations. Mutual agency provides the partnership with greater flexibility, allowing any partner to respond to a crisis rather than requiring that the appropriate corporate officer be located and act for the corporation. In addition, the partnership pays no federal income taxes. Instead, the individual partners report the results of partnership transactions on their personal income tax returns.

The decision as to the best form of organization is not an easy one. It can be made only by carefully examining the objectives of the owners and all the relevant circumstances in each case. It should also be noted that these circumstances may change over time. A business originally formed as a partnership or a corporation may, because of a change in business circumstances or owners' objectives, require reorganization in another form. The owners of the business should periodically review its operations to insure that the most advantageous form of organization is being employed.

ALLOCATING PARTNERSHIP PROFIT AND LOSS

Each partner in a partnership has a capital account and a withdrawals account. Both accounts are usually entitled using the name of the partner, that is, Joan Davis—capital or Joan Davis—withdrawals. At the end of the accounting period, the net income or loss of the partnership is detemined in the usual fashion. Once determined, this net income or loss is then allocated to the partners' capital accounts on some predetermined basis. If the partnership agreement is silent as to the manner in which partnership profis and losses are to be divided, the law provides that they be divided equally among the partners. In the partnership agreement, the partners may agree to divide profits and losses in any way that they choose. The partners may also agree to divide profits on one basis and to divide losses differently.

There are several common methods of dividing profits and losses. Perhaps the most common method of division is the method that allocates a fixed percentage of profits or losses to each partner. Under this method, the partnership agreement establishes a profit-and-loss sharing ratio. For example, a two-person partnership might establish a 60 to 40 percent ratio for the sharing of profits and losses between partners Jim Smith and Joan Davis. If this partnership had a $10,000 profit (i.e., a $10,000 credit balance in the income summary account), the income summary account would be closed to the partners' capital accounts in this entry:

Income summary	$10,000	
Jim Smith—capital		$6,000
Joan Davis—capital........................		4,000
To allocate profits to partners' capital accounts		

Instead of allocating profits on the basis of a fixed sharing ratio, the partners could choose to reward specific partners for investments of time or property by making special allocations to these partners. One agreement might provide, for example, for Joan Davis to receive a special allocation of $5,000 for working in the partnership, with the remaining profits and losses to be divided on a 60 to 40 percent basis between Jim Smith and Joan Davis. If this partnership had $10,000 in profits, the allocation would be determined as follows:

	Allocation to Jim Smith	*Allocation to Joan Davis*	*Amount Remaining to be Allocated*
1. Net income			$10,000
2. Special allocation to Joan Davis		$5,000	
3. General allocation: 60%—Smith 40%—Davis	$3,000	2,000	
Total	$3,000	$7,000	

Although it appears that the partnership is allocating Joan Davis a salary, it is important to note that this amount is not a salary but a division of partnership profits. It should not be recorded in a salary account, but is reflected in the accounts of the partnership in this closing entry:

Income summary	$10,000	
Jim Smith—capital		$3,000
Joan Davis—capital........................		7,000

Another form of special allocation is to provide partners with allocations measured as a percentage of investment in the partnership. Investment could be measured as the amount of the partners' initial investment, or the balance of capital accounts at the beginning of the year, or in other ways. For example, the partnership agreement between Jim Smith and Joan Davis might provide for a special allocation of 8 percent of each partner's initial investment in the partnership, with the remaining profits or losses to be divided in a 60 to 40 percent ratio. If Jim Smith invested $8,000 and Joan Davis invested $2,000 in the partnership, net income of $10,000 would be allocated as follows:

	Allocation to Jim Smith	Allocation to Joan Davis	Amount Remaining to be Allocated
1. Net income			$10,000
2. Special allocation to partners (8% of $8,000 to Smith, 8% of $2,000 to Davis)	$ 640	$ 160	9,200
3. General allocation: 60%—Smith 40%—Davis	5,520	3,680	
Total	$6,160	$3,840	

Special allocations are usually made even if they result in allocating more income than has been earned by the partnership or even in the event that the partnership has a loss in the year. For example, assume the same facts as in the preceding example, except the partnership had a net loss in the year of $3,000. The allocation would be made as follows:

	Allocation to Jim Smith	Allocation to Joan Davis	Amount Remaining to be Allocated
1. Net (loss)			($3,000)
2. Special allocation to partners (8% of $8,000 to Smith, 8% of $2,000 to Davis)	$ 640	$ 160	(3,800)
3. General allocation: 60%—Smith 40%—Davis	(2,280)	(1,520)	
Total	($1,640)	($1,360)	

The entry to reflect this allocation of loss in the partnership accounts would be as follows:

Jim Smith—capital	$1,640	
Joan Davis—capital	1,360	
Income summary		$3,000

A partnership agreement could provide for several special allocations. Since the partners may divide the profit and loss of the partnership in any fashion, an almost unlimited number of possibilities exist for profit or loss division. As a result, it is impossible to detail the various alternatives. The terms of the partnership agreement must be analyzed to determine the exact method or methods to be used. Tiered partnership distribution procedures are established to respond to varying involvements and commitments by the partners.

PARTNERSHIP DRAWINGS

As partners receive cash or property from the partnership, each partner's withdrawal account is debited for the book value of the property or the amount of cash withdrawn, in the same manner as the withdrawals of sole proprietorship. At the end of the accounting period, the withdrawal account of each partner is closed to the partner's capital account. At this point in time, the partner's capital account reflects the equity of each partner in the book value of the partnership assets. The entry to close the withdrawal accounts of Jim Smith with $3,000 in withdrawals and Joan Davis with $4,000 in withdrawals would be as follows:

Jim Smith—capital	$3,000	
Joan Davis—capital	4,000	
Jim Smith—withdrawals		$3,000
Joan Davis—withdrawals		4,000
To close withdrawal accounts to capital accounts		

PARTNERSHIP FINANCIAL STATEMENTS

The financial statements of partnerships are very similar to the financial statements of sole proprietorships. The basic differences are found in the owners' equity section of the balance sheet. For example, the owner's equity section of the balance sheet for the Smith and Davis partnership would be shown as follows:

Smith and Davis Plumbing Co.
Balance Sheet
December 31, 19x1

Owners' equity:			
Jim Smith—capital (January 1, 19x1)		$8,000	
Add: Share of net income	$5,000		
Less: Withdrawals	3,000	2,000	
Jim Smith—capital (December 31, 19x)			$10,000
Joan Davis—capital (January 1, 19x1)		$2,000	
Add: Share of net income	$5,000		
Less: Withdrawals	4,000	1,000	
Joan Davis—capital (December 31, 19x1)			3,000
Total owners' equity			$13,000

In keeping with the adequate disclosure principle, it is not uncommon to find the division of the partnership profits described at the bottom of the partnership income statement, in much the same fashion as earnings per share is shown on the bottom of the corporation's income statement. Where Smith and Davis share profits equally and have $10,000 in net income, their income statement might contain the following.

Smith and Davis Plumbing Co.
Income Statement
For the Year Ended December 31, 19x1

Net income	$10,000
Allocation of net income among partners:	
Jim Smith (50%)	$ 5,000
Joan Davis (50%)	5,000
Total income allocated to partners	$10,000

The adequate disclosure principle also suggests that any other information helpful to the understanding of the financial statements should be included, either parenthetically or as footnotes to the financial statements.

PARTNERSHIP CHANGES AND LIQUIDATIONS

The admission of a new partner, the sale of a partnership interest to an outsider, the retirement of a partner, and the liquidation of a partnership are all material changes that pose significant accounting problems for a partnership. A complete discussion of the accounting treatment of these events is complex and beyond the scope of this introductory text. In each of these events, however, the primary objective is to properly account for the equity of each partner. As noted earlier, the capital accounts of the partners in a partnership measure the claims of each partner to the *book value*—not necessarily the fair market value—of partnership assets. This is true because of the use of the historical cost principle in measuring and recording assets, liabilities, and owners' equity. A material change in the partnership, such as the retirement of a partner, may require that the assets and obligations of the firm be revalued so that the retiring partner may receive his or her fair share of the *fair market value* of partnership assets—not book value. The revaluation may take the form of a complete appraisal of all partnership assets made by professional appraisers or by estimates of the partners. Because appraisals by professional appraisers are relatively expensive, many partnerships estimate the changes in the value of assets themselves.

SUMMARY

We have examined the accounting problems of sole proprietorships and partnerships. A sole proprietorship is an unincorporated business with a single owner, while a partnership is an unincorporated business with more than one owner.

The decision as to the best form of organization for a business—sole proprietorship, partnership, or corporation—is a complex decision. It can be wisely made only after considering the objectives of the owners, the characteristics of each form of organization, and the pertinent advantages and disadvantages of each. Prudent business people will engage professional legal consultation before finalizing partnership agreements.

The basic differences in accounting for sole proprietorships and partnerships lie in the accounting and reporting of owners' equity. A sole proprietorship will have one capital account and one withdrawals account. All changes in owner's equity are ultimately reflected in the sole proprietor's capital account. In a partnership, each partner has a capital account and a withdrawals account. The profits and losses of the partnership are divided among the partners in accordance with the profit-and-loss division method agreed to by the partners, or equally, if there is no agreement. Additional accounting problems are posed by the admission of a new partner, the retirement of a partner, and the liquidation of the partnership. In each of these instances, care must be taken to properly account for the equity of each partner.

QUESTIONS*

12-1 Describe the major characteristics of a corporation.

12-2 Accounting and reporting for partnerships and corporations differ in which respects?

12-3 Describe the attributes of common stock.

12-4 How does preferred stock differ from common stock?

12-5 What is minimum legal capital and what function does it serve?

12-6 Is the minimum legal capital of a corporation disclosed on its balance sheet? How?

12-7 Define the term subscribed stock.

12-8 Identify the attributes of treasury stock.

12-9 How are gains or losses on treasury stock transactions reported?

12-10 What are the principal effects of declaring a stock dividend?

12-11 Distinguish between a stock split and a stock dividend.

12-12 What are the major advantages and disadvantages in operating a business as a corporation?

12-13 What dates are important to accountants in the process of declaring and paying dividends by a corporation?

12-14 What factors must a corporation's board of directors consider in the decision to pay dividends to shareholders?

12-15* Distinguish between a sole proprietorship and a partnership.

12-16* A partnership is distinguished by what characteristics?

*Note: Questions marked wih an asterisk relate to the Appendix.

12-17* What are the accounting differences between partnerships and sole proprietorships?

12-18* When a sole proprietor receives a check from his or her business, is an asset, a liability, or an equity account debited?

12-19* When assets are withdrawn from a sole proprietorship, partnership, or corporation by the owners of the business, what determines the dollar value used to record the transaction?

12-20* Are losses of a partnership usually shared in the same ratio as the profits of the partnership?

EXERCISES*

E12-1 What entry is made to close the income summary account of a corporation if its balance is a credit of $18,000?

E12-2 Record the sale of 6,000 shares of $1 par value common stock and 1,000 shares of $100 par value preferred stock for $5 per share and $105 per share, respectively.

E12-3 Calculate the total dividends paid common stockholders and the total dividends paid preferred stockholders if Homex Corporation, which is one year in arrears in the payment of dividends on its $100 par value 8 percent cumulative preferred stock, 10,000 shares outstanding, declares and pays $240,000 in dividends this year.

E12-4 Calculate the total dividends paid to common and preferred stockholders, given these data:

a. Preferred stock is 6 percent, $100 par value, fully participating, 10,000 shares outstanding.
b. Common stock is $10 par value, 100,000 shares outstanding.
c. No dividends are in arrears.
d. $300,000 in dividends are declared.

*Note: Exercises marked wih an asterisk relate to the Appendix.

E12-5 Record a purchase of 1,000 shares of $10 par value common stock by the issuing corporation for $18 per share and a subsequent sale of this treasury stock for $21 per share.

E12-6 Record the sale of 100 shares of $10 par value treasury stock for $60 per share. The stock was acquired for $90 per share. An account, additional contribution capital from treasury stock transactions, has a credit balance of $600.

E12-7 How would a corporation report the issuance of 1,000 shares of common stock for $13 per share if:

a. The stock has a $10 par value.
b. The stock is no-par-value stock with a stated value of $3 per share.
c. The stock is no-par-value stock without assigned stated value.

E12-8 Record the subscription of 500 shares of $10 par value common stock, $1,000 received in advance and $6,000 to be received three months later in full payment.

E12-9 What entries, if any, are needed to record the declaration and later payment of $3,000 in cash dividends to common stockholders, on these dates:

a. Date of declaration.
b. Date of record.
c. Date of payment.

E12-10 Record the declaration and distribution of a common stock dividend of 1,000 shares of stock with a fair market value of $6 per share and a par value of $1 per share.

E12-11 What entries are required to record a 2 to 1 stock split if 100,000 shares of common stock are outstanding with a par value of $10 per share and a fair market value of $220 per share?

E12-12 The owners' equity section of Hinton Corporation's balance sheet is shown below on December 31, 19x5:

Contributed capital:	
Common stock, $10 par value, 100,000 shares authorized, issued, and outstanding	$1,000,000
Additional contributed capital from common stockholders	110,000
Retained earnings	205,000
Total stockholders' equity	$1,315,000

Net income for calendar year 19x6 was $250,000. The board of directors appropriated $100,000 for contingencies during the year—a big lawsuit looms on the horizon—and declared and paid dividends totalling $40,000 during the year. Prepare the retained earnings statement for Hinton Corporation and the owners' equity section of the corporation's balance sheet for December 31, 19x6.

E12-13 In reviewing the financial records, the following data are discovered, affecting retained earnings:

a. The corporation acquired treasury stock costing $6,000. Local law requires an appropriation of retained earnings equal to the cost of treasury stock.
b. The corporation has decided to appropriate $100,000 in retained earnings for plant expansion to reduce stockholder pressure for dividends.
c. The corporation declared and paid $125,000 in cash dividends.

Required:

Prepare general journal entries to record these events. Prepare the related statement of changes in retained earnings, assuming net income for the year is $400,000 and the beginning retained earnings balance was $665,000.

E12-14 On January 1, 19x7, Wilson, Inc. declared a 5 percent stock dividend when the market value of the common stock was $15 per share. Stockholders' equity before the stock dividend was declared consisted of:

Common stock, $10 par value; authorized 200,000 shares; issued and outstanding 100,000 shares	$1,000,000
Additional paid-in capital on common stock	150,000
Retained earnings	700,000
Total stockholders' equity	$1,850,000

Required:

a. Prepare the journal entry to record the stock dividend.
b. Prepare the stockholders' equity section of a balance sheet immediately after the stock dividend is issued.

E12-15 On Decmeber 10, 19x1, Peacock Co. declared a 20 percent stock dividend. The company had 100,000 shares of $10 par stock outstanding on this date. The market value of the stock was $25 per share. Give the entry to record the dividend declaration assuming:

a. It is viewed as a small stock dividend.
b. It is viewed as a large stock dividend.

E12-16* A sole proprietorship has a net profit of $6,000 for its first year of operation. The owner invested $15,000 to start the business and has withdrawn $7,000 for living expenses during the year. Calculate the balance of the sole proprietor's owner's equity account.

E12-17* Record the investment, withdrawal, and the closing of the withdrawal and income summary accounts in E12-16.

E12-18* Frank and Cindy are partners, sharing profits equally after Frank is allocated a salary share of $5,000. How much is allocated to each partner if the partnership earned $26,600.

E12-19* How much profit is allocated to John Jones and Jim Smith if their partnership earned $16,500 in profits and they divide their profits as follows:

a. Salary shares:
   $3,000 to John Jones
   $2,000 to Jim Smith
b. Eight percent interest on original investments of $10,000 for Jones and $6,000 for Smith.
c. Remainder:
   60 percent to Jones
   40 percent to Smith

E12-20* Record the closing of the income summary account if the total profit (income summary balance) is $18,000, allocating $6,000 to partner A and $12,000 to partner B.

PROBLEMS*

P12-1 Hempstead Corporation was formed this year on March 1 to engage in the manufacture of preassembled roof joists. The charter of the corporation authorized the issuance of 10,000 shares of $5 par value common stock and 1,000 shares of 6 percent, $100 par value, cumulative preferred stock. Hempstead Corporation engaged in the following transactions during its first year of operation.

1. Sold 3,000 shares of common stock for $9 per share.
2. Sold 5,000 shares of common stock on subscription basis receiving $1 per share immediately, with $10 per share to be received in six months.
3. Sold 1,000 shares preferred stock for $103 per share.
4. Declared a dividend of $3 per share on preferred stock.
5. Received $50,000 in full payment for subscribed common stock.
6. Paid $3 per share preferred dividend.
7. Declared a 2 percent stock dividend of common stock to common stockholders. Fair market value of common stock was $13 per share of this date.
8. Issued the stock dividend declared in (7) above.
9. Corporation has net income of $39,000 (close this account).

Required:

a. Give the entries necessary to record these transactions.
b. Prepare the owners' equity section of the balance sheet for Hempstead Corporation.
c. Prepare a retained earnings statement for Hempstead Corporation.
d. Determine the amount of dividends that must be paid preferred stockholders next year before common stockholders may receive any dividends.

P12-2 Mission Candle Corporation has been in business for three years. Although it has barely been profitable in its short history, its business has improved steadily. The owners' equity section of its balance sheet as of December 31, 19x3, is reproduced below:

Stockholders' equity:	
Contributed capital:	
Common stock, no-par-value, 10,000 shares authorized, issued, and outstanding	$300,000
Preferred stock, $2 no-par-value, noncumulative, 2,000 shares authorized, issued, and outstanding	50,000
Retained earnings:	
Unappropriated retained earnings	29,000
Total stockholders' equity	$379,000

Mission Candle Corporation has the following transactions affecting capital this year (19x4):

1. Mission purchases 200 shares of its common stock for $16 per share.
2. A local community gives the corporation three acres of land worth $18,000 for use as a warehouse site in the city's new industrial park.
3. Mission sells 100 shares of treasury stock for $18 per share.
4. The board of directors vote to split the corporations common stock, issuing two shares for each one outstanding, in order to further encourage broad ownership of the stock.
5. The corporation has a profit of $53,000 for the year.
6. The corporation declares $2 in dividends to its preferred shareholders, to be paid early next year.

Required:

a. Give the entries necessary to record these transactions.
b. Prepare the owners' equity section of Mission Candle Corporation's balance sheet.
c. Prepare a retained earnings statement for Mission Candle Corporation.

***Note:** Problems marked with an asterisk relate to the Appendix.

P12-3 The ABC Corporation was formed this year on January 1, 19x3. Its charter authorizes the issuance of 10,000 shares of no par common stock and 10,000 shares of no par cumulative preferred stock. State law requires all proceeds received from the sale of no par stock to be treated as minimum legal capital. The corporation had the following transactions dealing with owners' equity in its first year ended December 31, 19x3:

1. Issued 6,000 shares of common stock for $15 per share.
2. Issued 1,000 shares preferred stock in exchange for land valued at $40,000.
3. Entered into subscription agreements to issue 1,000 shares of common stock at $16 per share, $5 per share received at the signing of the agreement, the remainder to be received in six months.
4. Declared the semiannual dividend of $3,000 on the preferred stock.
5. Paid the preferred dividend.
6. Received the remainder of the subscription payments described in (3) above.
7. Declared a 5 percent common stock dividend at a time when the common stock had a fair market value of $20 per share.
8. Distributed the stock dividend noted above in (7).
9. Declare the semiannual preferred dividend of $3,000.
10. Declare a 20 cent per share annual dividend on common stock.

Required:

a. Give the general journal entries necessary to record these transactions.
b. Prepare the owners' equity section of the balance sheet for this corporation at December 31, 19x3, assuming the corporation had net income of $15,000.

P12-4* Marston's Shoe Shop was formed this year by a capital contribution of $15,000. The business was successful and earned a profit of $22,000 in its first year. During the year, the owner(s) withdrew $16,000 for personal living expenses.

Required:

a. Give the entries to record the initial capital contribution; the withdrawals (assume the entire amount is withdrawn at once); and the closing of the income summary and withdrawal accounts, under the following assumptions. Also, prepare the owner's equity section of the balance sheet under each assumption as of the end of the first year of operation.

   1. The business is a sole proprietorship owned by Joe Marston.
   2. The business is a partnership of Joe and James Marston, making equal ($7,500) capital contributions, sharing profits equally, and each withdrawing $8,000 during the year.
   3. The business is a corporation with 1,000 shares of common stock having a par value of $1 per share, and the $16,000 is declared and paid to shareholders in dividends.

P12-5* Fay Rice and Lise Stone are partners in a plumbing supply business. They made initial capital contributions of $18,000 and $26,000, respectively. Calculate the amount of profit or loss allocated to their respective capital accounts under the following assumptions:

	A	*B*	*C*
Profit and loss sharing ratio (Rice/Stone)	6:4	3:2	1:1
Salary allocated......	None	$3,000 to Rice	$2,000 to Rice $1,000 to Stone
Interest on initial capital contributions	6%	8%	10%
Profit (loss) to be allocated	$8,000	$21,000	($3,000)

P12-6* Bill and Roger Evans, cousins, are partners in a restaurant. The following transactions occurred during the first year of operation:

1. Bill invested $25,000 and Roger invested $37,000 in the partnership on January 1.
2. Bill contributed equipment to the partnership with a fair market value of $6,000 on May 1.
3. Bill and Roger each withdrew $500 per month for living expenses.
4. Roger contributed an automobile to the partnership with a fair market value of $4,000 on July 1.
5. The partnership had a profit of $19,000 for the year, and closed all nominal accounts.

Required:

a. Determine the division of profits between Bill and Roger, assuming they share profits equally after allocating 8 percent interest on the weighted average capital investment of each partner not including allocated profits for the year or withdrawals.

   (**Note:** Weighted average capital investment can be determined by weighting each investment by the number of months it was invested in the business, and dividing the sum of weighted investments for each partner by 12.)
b. Give the necessary entries to record these transactions.
c. Prepare the owners' equity section of the balance sheet.

P12-7 The partnership of Linn & Ward has the following transactions involving capital accounts this year:

1. Because of the increased need for capital, both partners invested an additional $8,000 each in the partnership.
2. Linn manages the business and took an annual salary of $12,000 for his efforts.
3. Ward withdrew an automobile from the partnership, costing $6,000 with a fair market value of $3,000, and accumulated depreciation of $4,000.

An unadjusted trial balance for the firm at year-end on December 31, 19x5, prepared after properly recording these transactions is shown below:

Trial Balance
December 31, 19x5

	Debit	*Credit*
Cash	$ 75,800	
Accounts receivable	100,000	
Inventories	200,000	
Prepaid expenses	36,500	
Equipment	260,000	
Accumulated depreciation		$ 83,000
Accounts payable		34,400
Notes payable		200,000
Linn—capital		116,000
Linn—withdrawals	12,000	
Ward—capital		198,500
Ward—withdrawals	2,000	
Sales		600,000
Cost of goods sold	354,300	
Selling expenses	92,000	
Administrative expense	81,300	
Interest expense	18,000	
	$1,231,900	$1,231,900

4. In addition to the salary paid Linn, the partnership agreement allows each partner an interest allocation equal to 6 percent of January 1, 19x5, capital account balances, and divided profit or loss thereafer equally.

Required:

a. Record the transactions affecting capital.
b. Prepare an income statement.
c. Prepare a balance sheet for the partnership as of December 31, 19x5.

Learning Objectives

Chapter 13 discusses the usefulness of a statement of cash flows and presents a discussion of how to prepare the statement. Studying this chapter should enable you to:

1. Describe how a statement of cash flows is useful in financial statement analysis.
2. Describe the format and content of a statement of cash flows.
3. Prepare a formal statement of cash flows.

13

Statement of Cash Flows

INTRODUCTION

In previous chapters, we have focused primarily on two of the financial statements that must be provided to external financial statement users—the income statement and the balance sheet. The income statement summarizes the results of operations. The balance sheet presented in comparative form indicates the amount of assets, liabilities, and owners' equity, as well as net changes in these amounts between two periods. However, certain information that would be very useful to a variety of financial statement users regarding the financing and investment activities of a firm can be obtained only partially from the income statement and balance sheet. For example, the fact that a corporation acquired machinery with a fair market value of $80,000 for 5,000 shares of its common stock might be deduced by an extremely observant balance sheet reader who notes that the common stock account and machinery account have both increased, but the reader could not be certain that his or her deduction was correct. A variety of other financing and investment activities are obscured by their presentation in the income statement and balance sheet. What were the sources of cash used by the firm this period? How was the firm's cash used? Were there transactions that did not involve cash in the current period but that were, nonetheless, material financing and investment activities of the firm this period? Neither the income statement nor the balance sheet provide the necessary information to allow the investor or creditor to answer these questions. As a result, it may be difficult for the financial statement user to determine the likelihood that dividends will be paid in the future, to determine if the present level of financial recources is sufficient to continue operations at their present of increased levels, or to determine if expansion of the firm will require additional resources.

Because of the perceived value of this information to the financial statement user, the Financial Accounting Standards Board issued *FASB No. 95, "Statement of Cash Flows,"* in 1987. This standard recognized the importance of adequately disclosing the cash flow activities of a firm. It requires that a third statement, called a statement of cash flows, be prepared by accountants and presented to financial statement users along with the income statement and balance sheet. The cash flow statement is intended to assist statement readers in assessing: (a) a company's ability to generate future cash flows, (b) a company's ability to meet future obligations, (c) reasons for differences between net income and cash flows, and (d) the effects on a company's financial position of both its cash and noncash investing and financing transactions. This third major financial statement will be discussed in this chapter.

Definition and Classification of Cash Flows

Cash is defined as cash and cash equivalents. Cash equivalents are short-term, highly liquid investments that are readily convertible into known amounts of cash and are sufficiently near their maturity date that changes in interest rates will not materially affect their value. These include such items as commercial paper, U.S. treasury notes, and money market accounts. Throughout the chapter, any reference to cash or cash flows is intended to include cash equivalents as well.

Cash flows are classified into three types of cash flows (shown in Illustration 1): operating activities, investing activities, and financing activities.

Operating Activities

Cash flows that are directly related to revenue and expense accounts are summarized in this section. Cash inflows include cash sales, collections from customers, cash dividends, and interest received. Cash outflows are cash payments for expenses and payments on accounts payable. The cash outflows are for expense items that normally appear on the income statement such as: cost of goods sold, salary and wages, rent, selling expenses, administrative expenses, interest, taxes, etc.

Investing Activities

Investing activities primarily involve transactions related to the balance sheet accounts classified as investments (including short-term investments other than cash equivalents), plant, property and equipment, intangible assets, and loans to others. Cash inflows result from sale of investments, plant assets, and collections of loans to others. Outflows result from purchase of investments, plant assets, and making loans to others. Note that interest and dividends earned on investments and loans are classified as operating activities, not investing activities.

Illustration 1
Cash Flow Classifications

Cash Inflows	*Cash Outflows*
Operating activities:	
Sales and service revenue	Operating expenses
Collections on account	Payments of accrued and accounts payable
Cash from interest and dividend revenue	
Investing activities:	
Sale of investments	Purchase of investments
Sale of plant assets	Purchase of plant assets
Collection of loan	Lending money
Sale of intangible assets	Purchase of intangible assets
Financing activities:	
Borrowing funds	Repayment of borrowed funds
Sale of additional shares of stock	Repurchase of shares of stock
	Payment of dividends

Financing Activities

Financing activities primarily involve transactions related to balance sheet accounts classified as liabilities (other than accrued payables and accounts payable that relate to expense accounts—these are part of operation activities) and owners equity. Sources of cash come from borrowing money and additional investments by owners in the business. Uses of cash involve repayment of principal on loans and dividends and other cash payments to owners.

Noncash Transactions

Occasionally a company will enter into a significant investing and financing transaction that does not involve immediate cash flows. Since such transactions may affect future cash flows, the FASB indicated that these transactions should be disclosed in a separate section of the statement of cash flows called *schedule of noncash investing and financing transactions.* For example, assume a company acquired a $5 million building in exchange for a long-term mortgage. The transaction does not involve a cash inflow or outflow; however, the company has incurred a significant obligation that will require future cash outflows for interest and principal repayment. Recall that two of the purposes of the statement of cash flows are to help the reader assess the company's ability to generate future cash flows and meet its obligations. Providing information on such noncash activities will assist the statement reader in these areas.

Format of the Statement of Cash Flows

The format of the statement is shown in Illustration 2. The first section shown is the cash flows from operating activities, followed by the cash flows from investing activities and cash flows from financing activities. These are then summed to determine the net increase or decrease in cash during the year. The beginning of year cash is then added to reflect the year-end cash balance. Noncash activities are shown as a separate schedule below the determination of the ending cash balance.

Illustration 2
Company Name
Statement of Cash Flows
Time Period Covered

Cash flows from operating activities:		
Listing of individual inflows	$XXXX	
Listing of individual outflows	XXXX	
Net cash flow from operations		$XXXX
Cash flow from investing activities:		
Listing of individual cash inflows..............	$XXXX	
Listing of individual cash outflows	XXXX	
Net cash flow from investing activities		XXXX
Cash flow from financing activities:		
Listing of individual cash inflows..............	$XXXX	
Listing of individual cash outflows	XXXX	
Net cash flow from financing activities.........		XXXX
Increase (decrease) in cash for period		$XXXX
Beginning cash balance		XXXX
Ending cash balance		$XXXX

Schedule of Noncash Investing and Financing Activities

List of individual transactions	$XXXX

The cash flow from operating activities can be presented in a *direct* or *indirect* format. The two are shown in Illustration 3. In the direct format, actual cash inflows from sales and collections on account are listed first to determine total cash inflows. Cash outflows for expenses is then deducted to get net cash flow from operation. In this format, there is no direct tie-in with the net income figure reported in the income statement. The indirect approach starts with the company's reported net income and adjusts it for

Illustration 3
Direct Versus Indirect Approach
For Cash Flows From Operating Activities

Direct approach:		
Operating activities		
Cash inflows—		
Cash sales	$XXXX	
Collections on account	XXXX	
Cash inflows from interest and dividends	XXXX	$XXXX
Cash outflows—		
Cost of goods sold	$XXXX	
Selling expenses	XXXX	
Administrative expenses	XXXX	
Tax expense	XXXX	XXXX
Net cash flows from operations		$XXXX
Indirect approach:		
Operating activities		
Net income	$XXXX	
Add: Expenses not requiring cash outflow—		
Depreciation	XXXX	
Amortization	XXXX	
Increase in accounts payable	XXXX	
Deduct: Revenues not collected—		
Increase in accounts receivable	XXXX	
Net cash flows from operations		$XXXX

noncash revenues and expenses. For example, if the company has a credit sale of $50,000, it is included in net income because the revenue was earned that year. However, from a cash flow point of view, the revenue is not included because no cash was received from the transaction during the period. Under the direct approach, the $50,000 sale would not appear on the statement. Under the indirect approach, reported net income is the starting point and the $50,000 credit sale is deducted to get the actual cash inflows. In practice, most companies use the indirect format because it provides a direct tie-in to the income statement. For this reason, the indirect format is used throughout the remainder of the chapter.

Preparing Statement of Cash Flows

The statement of cash flows is prepared by first determining the changes in account balances in the balance sheet. Each change is analyzed to determine if the change resulted in a cash inflow or outflow or whether the change had no effect of cash. Changes in all noncash accounts are analyzed. If the change resulted in a cash inflow or outflow, the flow must be properly classified as operating, investing, or financing. Illustration 4 shows a simple balance sheet and indicates where a change in each account would normally by reflected in the statement of cash flows.

Note that the current asset accounts, accounts receivable, inventory, and prepaids, are all operating activities and that changes in these accounts have the same affect on cash flows. When accounts receivable increase, it means that part of the revenues reported in the income statement have not been collected in cash. To convert net income to cash flows, an accounts receivable increase is deducted from sales resulting in lowering the reported net in-

Illustration 4
Cash Flow Classification and Effect of Balance Sheet Changes

Account	Activity Classification	Effect of Change: Account Increase	Account Decrease
Cash			
Accounts receivable	Operating	Decrease income	Increase income
Inventory	Operating	Decrease income	Increase income
Prepaids	Operating	Decrease income	Increase income
Long-term investments	Investing	Cash outflow	Cash inflow
Land	Investing	Cash outflow	Cash inflow
Equipment	Investing	Cash outflow	Cash inflow
Accumulated depreciation	Operating	Increase inflow	N/A
Accounts payable	Operating	Increase income	Decrease income
Accrued payable	Operating	Increase income	Decrease income
Long-term notes payable	Financing	Cash inflow	Cash outflow
Bonds payable	Financing	Cash inflow	Cash outflow
Stock equity	Financing	Cash inflow	Cash outflow
Additional paid-in capital	Financing	Cash inflow	Cash outflow
Retained earnings—beginning	N/A	N/A	N/A
Net income	Operating	Cash inflow	Cash outflow
Dividends	Financing	Cash outflow	N/A

come figure. A decrease in accounts receivable has the opposite effect. In this case, in addition to the sales reported, the company also received additional cash in the form of a payment on accounts receivable. This increases the cash inflow from operations and is added to the net income figure to determine the cash flow from operations.

The logic for the changes in inventory and prepaids is the same. If the account increases, it means that in addition to paying cash for the related expense account in the income statement, additional cash was paid to build up the inventory or the prepaid item. For example, if inventory increases, it means that in addition to the cash flow to pay for the cost of goods sold in the income statement, a cash outflow also was made to increase the inventory account. To adjust the net income to cash flows, the cash outflow for the increase in inventory is added to the cost of goods sold, thereby increasing expenses and having the net effect of decreasing net income.

Long-term investments, land and equipment all relate to investing activities. Unless the change in these accounts resulted from a noncash transaction, increases are assumed to result from the cash purchases of the item, causing a cash outflow. Decreases are assumed to be cash sales of the items, resulting in cash inflows. If a noncash transaction occurred during the period, its effect is eliminated first and any remaining change in the account is viewed as a cash flow item. An example of a noncash transaction is the purchase of land for a long-term note or for common stock.

The change in the accumulated depreciation account will normally result from additional depreciation taken during the year. When depreciation expense is recorded, it will increase expenses in the income statement and increase the accumulated depreciation account in the balance sheet. This expense is a noncash expense since no cash outflow was involved in the current year. To adjust net income to a cash flow figure, the noncash expense is removed, having the effect of increasing net income. Occasionally the accumulated depreciation account will show a decrease. This occurs when a company sells and old asset and its related depreciation is removed from the accumulated depreciation account. When such transactions have occurred, the effect of the transaction on the change in the account balance is removed first. The remaining change in the account should be the increase that resulted from the depreciation expense for the period.

Accounts payable and all accrued payables are operating activities. Changes in these accounts have the same effect on cash flows. For example, if accounts payable increases, it means that part of the goods purchased during the year were not paid in cash. These goods would appear in the income statement as cost of goods sold, an expense. Since part of the expense was not paid in cash, the expense is reduced, having the effect of increasing the reported net income figure to get cash flow from operations. A decrease in one of these liability accounts will have the opposite effect.

Long-term liabilities such as notes, mortgages, and bonds as well as stock and additional paid-in capital accounts are all financing activities. The effects of any noncash transactions are first removed from the net change in these accounts and any remaining net change is assumed to be from a cash transaction. If the account increased, this results in a cash inflow, while a decrease is a cash outflow.

The beginning retained earnings will have no effect on the cash flow since the analysis involves only changes in accounts. The only two items that change retained earnings are net income and dividends; both are analyzed as separate items. Net income is an operating activity and is adjusted to get cash flows from operations. Net income also has to be adjusted to remove any gains or losses from investing activities since these will be shown as part of the cash flow under the investing activity classification. Thus, gains and losses are considered part of investing activities while interest or dividends earned are considered part of operating activities. Dividends paid represent a financing activity. Cash dividends are an outflow of cash, while stock dividends would have no effect on cash flows.

An Example

To demonstrate the preparation of a statement of cash flows, an example will be worked on a step-by-step basis. Illustration 5 presents the balance sheets for Bond Co. for 19x1 and 19x2 and the net changes in each of the accounts. In addition, Bond Co. reported a net income of $64,000 for 19x2. In addition, assume the following:

1. Sold a piece of equipment during the year for $20,000. The equipment originally cost $70,000 and had accumulated depreciation of $60,000.
2. Purchased land during the year in exchange for a $75,000 long-term note.
3. Paid $30,000 in the principal on its outstanding bonds.
4. Paid dividends of $15,000 during the year.

Operating Activities

The operating activities section begins with reported net income and adjusts for changes in current asset and liability accounts, gains and losses, and depreciation. In this example, net income was $64,000. This is then adjusted for changes in current asset accounts. Accounts receivable increased $9,000. Since this increase represents revenues that were not in the form of cash inflows, the increase is deducted from the reported net income. Next inventory increased $5,000. Since this represents an additional cash outflow beyond the cost of goods sold in the income statement, it would increase cash outflows and have the net effect of decreasing cash flow from operations. Therefore, the $5,000 increase is deducted from net income. Prepaids decreased $3,000, meaning that part of the expenses in net income came from prepaids and did not involve a cash outflow this period. These expenses must be reduced to eliminate the noncash portion of the expense. The net effect is that the decrease in prepaids will be added to net income to

Illustration 5
Bond Co.
Balance Sheet

	19x1	*19x2*	*Change*
Cash	$ 15,000	$ 21,000	$+ 6,000
Accounts receivable	43,000	52,000	+ 9,000
Inventory	50,000	55,000	+ 5,000
Prepaids	5,000	2,000	– 3,000
Long-term investments	20,000	25,000	+ 5,000
Land	50,000	125,000	+ 75,000
Equipment	250,000	270,000	+ 20,000
Accumulated depreciation	(84,000)	(34,000)	– 50,000
Building	800,000	800,000	0
Accumulated depreciation	(180,000)	(200,000)	+ 20,000
Total	$969,000	$1,116,000	
Accounts payable	$ 22,000	$ 27,000	$+ 5,000
Accrued payables	12,000	10,000	– 2,000
Long-term note payable	0	75,000	+ 75,000
Bonds payable	200,000	170,000	– 30,000
Common stock	400,000	440,000	+ 40,000
Additional paid-in capital	200,000	210,000	+ 10,000
Retained earnings	135,000	184,000	
Total	$969,000	$1,116,000	

reflect the cash payments for expenses properly. At this point, the operating activities section would appear as follows:

Operating activities:		
Net Income		$ 64,000
Deduct:	Increase in accounts receivable	– 9,000
Deduct:	Increase in inventory	– 5,000
Add:	Decrease in prepaids	+ 3,000

The analysis continues by determing the impact of changes in current liability accounts. The accounts payable increased $5,000 meaning that part of the expenses included in net income were not paid in cash. These are removed, resulting in an increase adjustment to net income. The accrued payables decreased $2,000. Thus, in addition to paying cash for the related expenses deducted to get net income, the company also made additional cash payments to reduce its accrued liability. Since this represents an additional cash payment, it is added to the related expense and results in a *net* decrease in net income. Therefore, the decrease in accrued payables is deducted from net income to get cash flow from operations.

The next item is to remove any gains or losses that are included in net income. The additional information indicates that Bond Co. sold a piece of equipment for $20,000. The equipment had an original cost of $70,000 and accumulated depreciation of $60,000, resulting in a book value of $10,000. Since the sale price was $20,000, a $10,000 gain resulted from the sale and was included in net income. The gain is deducted because it is an investing activity and is included in that section of the statement of cash flows. At this point, the operating activity section would appear as follows:

Operating activities:		
Net income		$ 64,000
Deduct:	Increase in accounts receivable	− 9,000
Deduct:	Increase in inventory	− 5,000
Add:	Decrease in prepaids	+ 3,000
Add:	Increase in accounts payable	+ 5,000
Deduct:	Decrease in accrued payable	− 2,000
Deduct:	Gain on equipment	− 10,000

The only remaining adjustment to net income is for depreciation. Since depreciation is a noncash expense, it is added back to net income to get the cash flow from operations. In this example, there are two accumulated depreciation accounts that must be analyzed. The first is for equipment and the net change in this account for the period was a decrease of $50,000. A decrease in an accumulated depreciation account means there must have been a sale of the related asset during the year. The effect of the sale is first eliminated from the change to isolate the change resulting from depreciation expense. This can be done by analyzing the T-account for accumulated depreciation. The account started with a balance of $84,000 and ended with a balance of $34,000. If the effect of the sale transaction is entered into the T-account, the change resulting from depreciation is isolated. The sale of equipment involved a machine that had accumulated depreciation of $60,000. This amount was debited to the account when the sale was recorded.

Accumulated Depreciation

		Beginning	$84,000
Sale	$60,000		
		Depreciation expense	?
		Ending	$34,000

To get an ending balance of $34,000, the account must have been credited for $10,000 during the year for depreciation expense. This amount is added back to net income as noncash expense.

The other accumulated depreciation account relates to the building. There was no change in the building account during the year and the effect of a sale on accumulated depreciation need not be considered. The accumulated depreciation account increased $20,000 for depreciation expense of the period. This amount is added back to net income. This is the last adjustment for the operating activity section which now appears as follows:

Operating activities:		
Net income		$ 64,000
Deduct:	Increase in accounts receivable	− 9,000
Deduct:	Increase in inventory	− 5,000
Add:	Decrease in prepaids	+ 3,000
Add:	Increase in accounts payable	+ 5,000
Deduct:	Decrease in accrued payable	− 2,000
Deduct:	Gain on equipment	− 10,000
Add:	Depreciation—equipment	+ 10,000
Add:	Depreciation—building	+ 20,000
Net cash flows from operations		$ 76,000

Investing Activities

The next section of the statement of cash flows is the investing section. Preparation of this section involves an analysis of the changes in noncurrent asset accounts. Again, the account changes will be analyzed to determine if they resulted in a cash flow or if they did not affect cash.

The first account is the long-term investments account which increased $5,000 during the year. Since there is no additional information concerning this account, it is assumed that the change resulted from a cash transaction and purchase of investments is shown as a cash outflow in the investing section.

The next noncurrent asset, land, increased $75,000 during the year. A check of the additional information indicates that land was purchased in exchange for long-term debt. Since this transaction did not involve cash, it will not appear in the investing activities section. However, recall that such transactions should be separately disclosed at the bottom of the statement of cash flows.

The equipment account reflects a net increase of $20,000. The additional information indicates that equipment costing $70,000 was sold for $20,000 during the year. This sale represents a cash inflow from investing activities. Since the sale does not account for the total change in the equipment account, one or more other transactions must also have occurred. An analysis of the T-account reflects the following:

Equipment

Beginning	$250,000		
		Sale	$70,000
	?		
Ending	$270,000		

To get the ending balance of $270,000, there must have been a $90,000 debit to the account. A check of the additional information indicates nothing related to a credit purchase, therefore, it is assumed that the company purchased $90,000 of equipment during the year for cash. This represents a cash outflow under investing activities.

The last noncurrent asset account is building. During the year, this account did not change and, therefore, had no effect on investing activities. The investing activities section of the statements of cash flows will appear as follows:

Investing activities:		
Cash inflows—		
Sale of equipment		$20,000
Cash outflows—		
Purchase of investment..................	$ 5,000	
Purchase of equipment	90,000	– 95,000
Net cash flow from investing activities........................		($75,000)

Financing Activities

The financing activities section of the statement of cash flow involves an analysis of the long-term liabilities and the equity accounts other than retained earnings. Bond Co. has two long-term liabilities. The first, a note payable, increased $75,000 during the year. The additional information indicates that this note was used to purchase land. Since no cash was involved in the change in the account, nothing is reflected in the financing activities section. However, as was discussed in the analysis of the change in the land account, this transaction will be disclosed separately at the bottom of the statement of cash flows.

The second long-term liability was a bond payable that decreased $30,000 during the year. The additional information indicates that this resulted from a cash payment of part of the principal. This would be shown as an outflow of cash in the financing activities section.

The common stock and additional paid-in capital accounts increased a total of $50,000 during the year. Since no information is given regarding the source of this change, it is assumed that it was an issuance of stock for cash. This is an inflow of cash in the financing activities section.

The last item in the balance sheet is retained earnings. A change in retained earnings is composed of the net income for the period (which has already been included in the operating activity section) and dividends. The additional information indicated that the company paid dividends of $15,000 during the year. This is an outflow of cash in the financing activities section.

The financing activities section would appear as follows:

Financing activities:		
Cash inflows—		
Issuance of stock		$50,000
Cash outflows—		
Payment of bonds	$30,000	
Payment of dividends	15,000	– 45,000
Net cash flow from financing activities		$15,000

The complete statement of cash flows for Bond Co. appears in Illustration 6. Note that a schedule of noncash investing and financing activities is added to the bottom to reflect the land purchase with long-term debt.

Illustration 6

Bond Co.

Statement of Cash Flows

For the Year Ended December 31, 19x2

Cash flows from operating activities:			
Net income		$ 64,000	
Adjustments for noncash items—			
Increase in accounts receivable		– 9,000	
Increase in inventory		– 5,000	
Decrease in prepaids		+ 3,000	
Increase in accounts payable		+ 5,000	
Decrease in accrued payables		– 2,000	
Gain on equipment		– 10,000	
Depreciation—equipment		+ 10,000	
Depreciation—building		+ 20,000	
Net cash flow from operating activities			$76,000
Cash flow from investing activities:			
Cash inflows—sale of equipment		$ 20,000	
Cash outflows—			
Purchase of investments	$ 5,000		
Purchase of equipment	90,000	– 95,000	
Net cash flow from investing activities			– 75,000
Cash flow from financing activities:			
Cash inflows—issuance of stock		$ 50,000	
Cash outflows—			
Payment on bonds	$30,000		
Payment of dividends	15,000	– 45,000	
Net cash flow from financing activities			5,000
Net increase in cash			$ 6,000
Beginning cash balance			15,000
Ending cash balance			$21,000

Schedule of Noncash Investing and Financing Activities

Issuance of long-term debt for land	$75,000

SUMMARY

The statement of cash flows is intended to compliment the income statement and balance sheet. It provides information on cash flows and assists statement readers in assessing future cash flows.

The statement of cash flows is divided into operating, investing, and financing activities. Operating activities reflect the cash flows from revenue and expense activities of the company. The investing activities comprise purchasing and selling investments and other noncurrent assets. Financing activities involve cash flows from long-term debt and equity transactions. When a company has a significant investing and financing transaction that does not involve cash flows, the transaction should be disclosed at the bottom of the statement of cash flows in a separate schedule.

The preparation of a statement of cash flows involves an analysis of all changes in balance sheet accounts during the period. Each change is analyzed to determine if it impacted cash. If a cash inflow or outflow was involved, it must be properly classified and reported in one of the three activity areas.

KEY DEFINITIONS

Cash equivalents—short-term, highly liquid investments that are readily convertible into known amounts of cash.

Financing activities—cash flows that result form transactions involving long-term liabilities and equity transactions other than net income.

Investing activities—cash flows that result from purchases and sales of investments, and other long term assets.

Noncash transactions—transactions that do not involve an inflow or outflow of cash.

Operating activities—cash flows that relate to revenue and expense items.

Appendix

Work Sheet for Statement of Cash Flows

INTRODUCTION

The chapter illustrated the preparation of a statement of cash flows for a relatively simple company. When accountants are involved with more complex companies, they will use a work sheet to assist in the systematic analysis of all changes in the balance sheet accounts. The Appendix provides an illustration of the work sheet and shows how it is used to analyze account changes when preparing a statement of cash flows.

A work sheet for Trey Co. is presented in Illustration 1. To prepare the work sheet for analysis, the accountant starts by listing the beginning-of-the-year balance of balance sheet accounts. The accounts are listed according to whether they have debit or credit balances. The work sheet then provides two blank column for the analysis of the account changes and then lists the year-end balances as the last column in the work sheet. The debits and credits for both columns are totalled to check for equality. Next, the accountant lists the three major cash flow activities (operating, investing and financing) at the bottom of the work sheet, leaving sufficient space between each category to list specific cash inflows and outflows and adjustments. The work sheet is now ready to use in the analysis of account changes. The analysis of transactions columns are used to analyze each change to determine if it affected cash flows. If the change affected cash flows, it will be classified as an operating, investing, or financing activity and the specific cause of the change is listed at the bottom of the work sheet. If no cash is in-

Illustration 1
Trey Co.
Work Sheet for Statement of Cash Flows
For the Year Ended December 31, 19x2

	Account Balance 12/31/x1	Analysis of Transactions Debit	Analysis of Transactions Credit	Account Balance 12/31/x2
Debits				
Cash	$ 20,000	q $ 5,000		$ 25,000
Accounts receivable	10,000	b 2,000		12,000
Inventory	18,000	c 2,000		20,000
Prepaid insurance	4,000		d $ 1,000	3,000
Investments	15,000	k 5,000		20,000
Land	30,000	g 60,000		90,000
Equipment	100,000	n 100,000	i 80,000	120,000
Building	200,000	h 50,000		250,000
	$397,000			$540,000
Credits				
Accumulated depreciation—equipment	$ 82,000	i 65,000	o 15,000	$ 32,000
Accumulated depreciation—building	60,000		p 10,000	70,000
Accounts payable	8,000		e 3,000	11,000
Accrued wages payble	6,000	f 2,000		4,000
Long-term note payable	0		g 60,000	60,000
Bonds payable	50,000	l 10,000		40,000
Common stock	100,000		{ h 40,000 j 20,000	160,000
Additional paid-in capital	20,000		{ h 10,000 j 15,000	45,000
Retained earnings	71,000	m 13,000	a 60,000	118,000
	$397,000	$314,000	$314,000	$540,000
Cash flow from operations				
Net income		a $ 60,000		
Increase in accounts receivable			b $ 2,000	
Increase in inventory			c 2,000	
Decrease in prepaid insurance		d 1,000		
Increase in accounts payable		e 3,000		
Decrease in accrued wages payable			f 2,000	
Loss on equipment sale		i 3,000		
Depreciation—equipment		o 15,000		
Depreciation—building		p 10,000		
Cash flow from investing activities				
Sale of equipment		i 12,000		
Purchase of investments			k 5,000	
Purchase of equipment			n 100,000	
Cash flow from financing activities				
Issuance of common stock		j 35,000		
Payment on bond payable			l 10,000	
Payment of dividends			m 13,000	
		$139,000	$134,000	
Increase in cash			q 5,000	
		$139,000	$139,000	

volved, the entry to reflect the change would appear only in the top section of the work sheet.

Assume the following additional information is available regarding Trey Co.

1. Net income for the year was $60,000.
2. Issued a long-term note to purchase land.
3. Issued $40,000 of par value common stock to purchase a building valued at $50,000.
4. Sold equipment costing $80,000 for $12,000. The equipment had an accumulated depreciation of $64,000.
5. Issued common stock with a par value of $20,000 for $35,000 cash.
6. Purchased investments for cash.
7. Paid $10,000 principal on bonds.
8. Paid dividends of $13,000.
9. Purchases equipment of cash.

Analyzing Changes

Generally the first change to be entered is net income. Note entry (a) in the work sheet. It debits cash flow from operations—net income in the bottom portion of the work sheet and credits the retained earnings account for the net income of $60,000.

The next step is usually an analysis of the current asset and current liability accounts. The changes are analyzed in entries (b) through (f). In entry (b), the accounts receivable is debited for the $2,000 increase and the cash flow from operations—increase in accounts receivable is credited in the bottom portion of the work sheet. This change has the effect of decreasing the cash flow from operations since net income was entered as a debit. Notice that with each entry in the top portion of the work sheet, the beginning balance is adjusted to get the ending balance. For example, the beginning accounts receivable balance was $10,000 and the adjustment debited the account for $2,000, giving the ending balance of $12,000. In entry (c), inventory is debited and the cash flow from operations—inventory is credited for $2,000. Entry (d) debits cash flow from operations—prepaid insurance and credits prepaid insurance for the $1,000 decrease.

Next, the current liability accounts are analyzed. Entry (e) debits cash flow from operations—accounts payable and credits the accounts payable account for the $3,000 increase. Entry (f) debits accrued wages payable and credits cash flow from operations—accrued wages payable for the $2,000 change.

All of the current asset and liability accounts have now been analyzed. The next step is usually to make entries relating to additional information that is known. The additional information indicated that land was purchased for a long-term note payable. This transaction will not affect cash flows, but an entry must be entered in the work sheet to explain the changes in the accounts. Entry (g) debits land and credits long-term note payable for the $60,000 purchase. The entry fully explains the change in both of these accounts. Notice that the entry did not affect the bottom portion of the work sheet because no cash was involved in the transaction.

The next piece of additional information indicates that the company purchased a $50,000 building by issuing $40,000 of par value stock. Again cash is not affected and entry (h) in the top portion of the work sheet debits building $50,000 and credits common stock for $40,000 and additional paid-in capital for $10,000. Notice that while this entry explains the change in the building account, it explains only part of the change in the common stock and additional paid-in capital account.

Next, the company sold equipment costing $80,000 for $12,000. The accumulated depreciation amounted to $65,000 giving a book value of $15,000. Therefore, the equipment was sold at a $3,000 loss. Entry (i) records the following:

Accumulated depreciation—equipment.........	$65,000	
Cash flow from investing activities:		
Sale of equipment	12,000	
Cash flow from operation activities:		
Loss on sale of equipment	3,000	
Building		$80,000

The entry explains part of the change in the accumulated depreciation and the equipment account and sets up the cash inflow from the sale and removes the loss from the net income.

Common stock with a par value of $20,000 was sold for $35,000. Entry (j) reflects the effect of this transaction. The entry debits cash flow from financing activities—sale of common stock for $35,000 and credits common stock $20,000 and additional paid-in capital $15,000. After this entry, the total change in common stock and additional paid-in capital is explained (i.e. the beginning balance plus the two analysis of transactions entries equal the ending balance in the accounts).

Investments were purchased for cash. This is reflected in entry (k) which debits investments and credits cash flow from investing activities—purchase of investments.

Entry (l) reflects the payment on the bonds. The entry debits cash flow from financing activities—payment on bond payable and credits the bond payable account. Entry (m), which relates to the dividends paid, debits retained earnings and credits cash flow from financing activities—payment of dividends for $13,000.

The last piece of additional information indicates that the company purchased equipment for cash. The equipment account had a beginning balance of $100,000 and entry (i) reduced it by $80,000, leaving a balance of $20,000.

Since the ending balance is $120,000, there must have been a $100,000 purchase during the year. Entry (n) reflects this by debiting equipment for $100,000 and crediting cash flow from investing activities—purchase of equipment for $100,000.

After adjustments have been made for the additional information, the accumulated depreciation accounts can be analyzed to determine the amount of depreciation expense for the year. The accumulated depreciation for equipment started with a balance of $82,000 and was decreased by $65,000 from the equipment sale (entry i) leaving a balance of $17,000. Since the ending balance is $32,000, the account must have been increased during the year by $15,000 for depreciation. Entry (o) debits cash flow from operations—depreciation equipment and credits the accumulated depreciation—equipment. Next entry (p) reflects the change from depreciation on the building. The entry debits cash flow from operations—depreciation building and credits the accumulated depreciation—building account.

At this point, a review of the accounts will show that all changes have been explained by the entries (a) through (p) except the cash account. The change in cash is reflected in entry (q) which debits cash and credits increase in cash at the bottom of the work sheet. At this point, the analysis of transaction debit and credit columns (the top portion of the work sheet) are totalled to check for equality and the possibility of errors. Next, the bottom portion of the work sheet (the cash flows) is totalled and the increase or decrease in cash added to make the column totals equal. The work sheet is now complete and the formal statement of cash flows would be prepared from the bottom portion of the work sheet.

While the work sheet may appear to be difficult and cumbersome, it is a very organized and effective way to prepare a statement of cash flows when complex transactions and numerous accounts are involved.

QUESTIONS

13-1 What is the purpose of the statement of cash flows?

13-2 What are cash equivalents?

13-3 Is it possible to have a positive net income and a negative cash flow for the period? Expain.

13-4 What are the three major classifications of cash flows in the statement of cash flows?

13-5 Describe the difference between the direct and indirect approach to the determination of cash flows from operations.

13-6 What type of transactions are included in cash flows from investing and financing activities?

13-7 Why is depreciation and amortization added back to net income to get cash flows from operations?

13-8 Give an example of an investing/financing transaction that does not affect cash flow. Should it be reported in the statement of cash flows?

13-9 Why are gains and losses eliminated from net income when determining cash flow from operations?

13-10 Can a net change in an individual balance sheet account affect more than one classification (operating, investing, financing) of cash flows? Give an example.

13-11 How are cash flows from the following types of transactions classified in a statement of cash flows: (a) dividend income, (b) gain on sale of investment in stock, and (c) stock dividend received.

EXERCISES

E13-1 For each of the following items indicate: (1) the proper cash flow classification (operating, investing, financing), and (2) whether the item would increase or decrease cash flows.

Assume all purchases and sales transactions are for cash.

	Classification	*Increase/ Decrease*
a. Accounts receivable increase		
b. Accumulated depreciation increase		
c. Accounts payable decrease		
d. Prepaid rent decrease		
e. Office supplies increase		
f. Wages payable increase		
g. Common stock issuance		
h. Purchase of equipment		
i. Sale of investments at a loss		
j. Payment of stock dividend		
k. Payment of cash dividend		

E13-2 What is the cash increase or decrease from operations, if the ABC Company shows a net loss of $8,000 on its income statement and if the following items were included?

Amortization of patents	$ 5,000
Amortization of discounts on bonds payable	3,000
Depreciation expense	22,000

E13-3 Ackey Co. reported a $52,000 profit for the year. Calculate the cash flow from operations given the following changes in the accounts listed:

Account receivable	$+ 5,000
Inventory	+ 7,000
Prepaid insurance	− 3,000
Accounts payable	+ 4,000
Rent payable	− 2,000
Accumulated depreciation	+ 12,000
Patents	− 8,000

Assume no assets were purchased or sold during the year.

E13-4 The balance sheet for the Cooper Company is as follows:

	December 31	
	19x3	19x4
Cash	$ 3,000	$ 4,000
Accounts receivable—net	4,000	8,000
Inventory	9,000	11,000
Permanent investments	2,000	
Fixed assets	15,000	45,000
	$33,000	$68,000
Accumulated depreciation on fixed assets	$ 4,000	$ 6,000
Accounts payable	2,000	4,000
Notes payable short-term—nontrade	3,000	2,000
Long-term notes payable	5,000	17,500
Common stock	15,000	28,000
Retained earnings	4,000	10,500
	$33,000	$68,000

Additional data reflecting changes in the noncurrent accounts:

a. Net income for the year 19x4—$13,000.
b. Depreciation on fixed assets for the year—$2,000.
c. Permanent investments were sold at cost.
d. Dividends of $6,500 were paid.
e. Fixed assets purchased for $10,000 cash.
f. Fixed assets purchased giving a $20,000 long-term note payable.
g. Seven thousand five hundred dollars long-term note payable paid by issuing common stock.
h. Unissued common stock for $5,500.

Required:

Prepare a statement of cash flows

E13-5 For each of the following balance sheet accounts, indicate the proper classification (operating, investing, financing) for any transactions that result in a cash flow.

Account	Classification
Accounts receivable	
Accounts payable	
Supplies inventory	
Bonds payable	
Investment in bonds	
Treasury stock	
Wages payable	
Inventory	
Equipment	
Patents	
Long-term notes payable	
Common stock	
Preferred stock	
Prepaid insurance	
Additional paid-in capital	

E13-6 The following items are descriptions of business transactions and adjustments.

State whether each increases, decreases, or does not effect cash. Explain your answer.

a. Sold common stock for cash.
b. Sold a fixed asset, receiving cash, a short-term note receivable, and a mortgage receivable.
c. Borrowed from the bank, giving a short-term and a long-term note payable.
d. Purchased a fixed asset, giving cash, a short-term note payable, and a mortgage payable.
e. Declared a cash dividend.
f. Paid a cash dividend.
g. Paid debts, debiting both accounts payable and long-term notes payable.
h. Purchased treasury stock for cash.
i. Retired bonds by issuing common stock.
j. Depreciation.

E13-7 Given the following comparative financial statements at December 31 for the Tree Corporation, prepare a statement of cash flows. Income for 19x6 equalled $26,000.

	19x5	19x6
Cash	$ 60,000	$ 75,000
Accounts receivable—net	105,000	91,000
Inventory	87,000	63,000
Machinery	131,000	121,000
Land	73,000	58,000
Accumulated depreciation	(46,000)	(60,000)
Total assets	$410,000	$348,000
Accounts payable	$ 67,000	$ 60,000
Accrued wages	10,000	
Common stock	225,000	200,000
Retained earnings	108,000	88,000
Total liabilities and owners' equity	$410,000	$348,000

Additional data:

a. Machinery was purchased for $10,000 by issuing common stock.
b. Depreciation expense was $20,000.
c. Common stock was retired by giving land worth $15,000.
d. Dividends of $46,000 were paid.
e. Machinery was sold for $14,000 that had originally cost $20,000 (accumulated depreciation for the machinery was $6,000).
f. Common stock of $20,000 was purchased for cash and retired.

E13-8 Given that the accrual-basis net income was $63,000, determine the cash flow from operations.

	19x5	19x6
Currents assets:		
Cash	$ 35,000	$ 50,000
Accounts receivable	21,000	37,000
Inventory	54,000	20,000
Prepaid expenses	17,000	19,000
Noncurrent assets:		
Patents	14,000	10,000
Machinery	330,000	330,000
Accumulated depreciation	(54,000)	(64,000)
Land	163,000	
Total	$580,000	$402,000
Current liabilities:		
Accounts payable	$ 89,000	$ 96,000
Accrued wages	54,000	40,000
Noncurrent liabilities:		
Mortgage payable	300,000	200,000
Owners' equity	137,000	66,000
Total	$580,000	$402,000

E13-9 The following are the equipment and accumulated depreciation account for Lane Co:

Equipment

Beginning	$150,000	Sale	$75,000
Purchase	120,000		
Ending	$195,000		

Accumulated Depreciation

		Beginning	$85,000
Disposal	$60,000	Depreciation	15,000
		Ending	$40,000

In addition to the above, the income statements shows a loss on the sale of equipment in the amount of $7,000. Show how this information would be reported in the cash flow from investing activities section of the statement of cash flows.

E13-10 You are provided the following selected information about Zenith Company for 19x2.

a. Net income—$114,800.
b. Amortization of premium on long-term bonds payable—$2,400.
c. Purchase of equipment—$32,000.
d. Depreciation expense—$8,000.
e. Decrease in accounts receivable—$2,800.
f. Decrease in accounts payable—$5,800.
g. Issuance of long-term notes payable—$60,000.
h. Increase in inventories—$12,000.
i. Gain on sale of land—$16,000.
j. Increase in prepaid insurance—$1,400.
k. Cash dividends paid—$3,000.
l. Increase in wages payable—$1,800.
m. Amortization of patent—$3,000.

Required:

Prepare the cash flow from operating activities section of the statement of cash flows.

PROBLEMS*

P13-1 The Habersham Company's financial records disclose the following:

Sales	$290,000
Beginning accounts receivable	88,000
Ending accounts receivable	80,000
Cost of goods sold	160,000
Beginning inventory	40,000
Ending inventory	45,000
Beginning accounts payable	19,000
Ending accounts payable	20,000
Depreciation expense	16,000
Beginning prepaid expenses	2,000
Ending prepaid expenses	1,000
Beginning accrued liabilities	3,000
Ending accrued liabilities	3,000
Operating expenses and income taxes	70,000

The records also show the following transactions:

1. Issued stock for equipment costing $30,000,
2. Retired $50,000 in bonds for cash.
3. Purchases land for $75,000.

Required:

Prepare a cash flow from operating activities section of a statement of cash flows.

P13-2 The balance sheet of the Saco Company is as follows:

Debits	*December 31 19x5*	*19x6*
Cash	$ 8,000	$ 10,000
Accounts receivable—net	18,000	22,000
Inventory	50,000	48,000
Prepaid expenses	2,000	4,000
Permanent investments	8,000	
Buildings	88,000	118,000
Machinery	38,000	60,000
Patents	5,000	3,000
	$217,000	$265,000
Credits		
Accounts payable	$ 10,000	$ 6,000
Notes payable short-term—nontrade	8,000	12,000
Accrued wages	2,000	1,000
Accumulated depreciation	38,000	37,000
Notes payable—long-term	28,000	34,000
Common stock	120,000	150,000
Retained earnings	11,000	25,000
	$217,000	$265,000

Additional data affecting the noncurrent accounts are:

a. Net income for the year was $20,000.
b. Depreciation of $6,000 was recorded on fixed assets.
c. Patents were amortized—$2,000.
d. Machinery was purchased for $12,000 paying one-half in cash and a seven year interest-bearing note for the balance.
e. Machinery was purchased for $20,000 by issuing common stock.
f. Machinery was sold for $3,000. It originally cost $10,000 ($7,000 depreciated).
g. Added on to building; paid $30,000 cash.
h. Sold $10,000 common stock.
i. Sold permanent investments for $8,000.
j. Cash dividends of $6,000 were paid.
k. Sales on account were $100,000.
l. Accounts receivable collected were $96,000.

Required:

Prepare a statement of cash flows.

Note: Problems marked with an asterisk relate to the Appendix.

P13-3 The following are the financial statements of the Retail Establishment, Inc.

Balance Sheets

	December 31 19x1	December 31 19x0
Assets		
Current assets:		
Cash	$ 150,000	$100,000
Marketable securities	40,000	
Accounts receivable	420,000	290,000
Merchandise inventory	330,000	210,000
Prepaid expenses	50,000	25,000
Land, buildings, and fixtures	565,000	300,000
Less: Accumulated depreciation	55,000	25,000
	$1,500,000	$900,000
Equities		
Current liabilities:		
Accounts payable	$ 265,000	$220,000
Accrued expenses	70,000	65,000
Dividends payable	35,000	
Note payable—due 19x4	250,000	
Common stock	600,000	485,000
Retained earnings	280,000	130,000
	$1,500,000	$900,000

Income Statements

	Year Ended December 31 19x1	Year Ended December 31 19x0
Net sales—including service charges	$3,200,000	$2,000,000
Cost of goods sold	2,500,000	1,600,000
Gross profit	$ 700,000	$ 400,000
Expenses—including income taxes	500,000	260,000
Net income	$ 200,000	$ 140,000

All accounts receivable and accounts payable relate to trade merchandise. Cash discounts are not allowed to customers, but a service charge is added to an account for late payment. Accounts payable are recorded net and always are paid to take all of the discount allowed.

The proceeds from the note payable were used to finance a new store building. Capital stock was sold to provide additional working capital.

Required:

Prepare a statement of cash flows.

P13-4 The comparative balance sheets at December 31 of the Glass Corporation are as follows:

	19x5	19x6
Cash	$ 60,000	$ 65,000
Receivables	78,000	70,000
Inventory	122,000	120,000
Prepaid expenses	18,000	19,000
Fixed assets	227,000	322,000
Accumulated depreciation	(73,000)	(96,000)
Patents	51,000	45,000
	$483,000	$545,000
Accounts payable	$ 93,000	$ 80,000
Taxes payable	75,000	75,000
Mortgage payable	110,000	
Preferred stock		160,000
Additional paid-in capital-preferred		14,000
Common stock	160,000	160,000
Retained earnings	45,000	56,000
	$483,000	$545,000

1. Accumulated depreciation was credited for the period's expense only.
2. The ratained earnings account entries are for cash dividends of $5,000 and net income.
3. The 19x6 income statement is as follows:

Sales	$235,000
Cost of sales	100,000
Gross profit	$135,000
Operating expenses	119,000
Net income	$ 16,000

Required:

Prepare a statement of cash flows.

P13-5 The Greta Corporation's comparative balance sheet accounts for 19x3 and 19x4 are shown below:

	December 31, 19x4		*December 31, 19x3*	
	Debit	*Credit*	*Debit*	*Credit*
Cash	$ 8,400		$ 9,500	
Accounts receivable	26,600		27,300	
Allowance for bad debts		$ 600		$ 800
Inventory	68,700		64,200	
Prepaid expenses	1,100		800	
Equipment	45,000		44,000	
Accumulated depreciation		10,600		7,600
Accounts payable		15,000		14,700
Common stock—no par		105,000		100,000
Retained earnings		18,600		22,700
	$149,800	$149,800	$145,800	$145,800

The firm's financial records indicate the following:

a. Net income for the year totalled $900.
b. Depreciation expense for the year totalled $3,000.
c. Acquired $1,000 in equipment this year.
d. Cash dividends of $5,000 were declared and paid during the year.
e. Sold stock for $5,000 to new investor.

Required:

Prepare a statement of cash flows.

P13-6 Comparative balance sheets for the Mar Corporation are pesented below:

	December 31	
	19x2	19x1
Assets		
Current assets:		
Cash	$ 25,400	$ 23,600
Accounts receivable—net	69,800	66,800
Inventory	171,800	173,400
Supplies	4,000	3,600
Total current assets	$271,000	$267,400
Fixed assets:		
Equipment	$ 10,800	$ 12,200
Accumulated depreciation	(5,000)	(4,800)
Building	80,000	80,000
Accumulated depreciation	(35,000)	(31,000)
Land	20,000	20,000
Total fixed assets	$ 70,800	$ 76,400
Total assets	$341,800	$343,800
Equities		
Current liabilities:		
Accounts payable	$ 39,000	$ 41,000
Notes payable	6,000	7,000
Income taxes payable	6,000	6,200
Total current liabilities	$ 51,000	$ 54,200
Long-term liabilities:		
Long-term notes payable	$ 10,000	0
Total liabilities	$ 61,000	$ 54,200
Owner's equity:		
Common stock—$10 par	$190,000	$180,000
Additional contributed capital—common stock	15,000	15,000
Retained earnings	75,800	94,600
Total owners' equity	$280,800	$289,600
Total equities	$341,800	$343,800

An analysis of the financial records shows the following:

1. Net income for the year totalled $6,200.
2. Equipment costing $1,400 was sold for $200 during the year. Related accumulated depreciation of $1,200 was removed from the account.
3. Depreciation expense for equipment totalled $1,400 and depreciation expense for building totalled $4,000.
4. A two-year $10,000 note payable was taken out on December 30.
5. A 1,000 share stock dividend was declared and distributed when the stock was selling for $10 per share.
6. Cash dividends totalling $15,000 were declared and distributed to stockholders during the year.

Required:

Prepare the statement of cash flows.

P13-7 The management of Braun Co. has provided you with the following comparative analysis of changes in account balances in account balances during 19x2.

	December 31		Increase/
	19x2	19x1	Decrease
Debits			
Cash	$ 39,000	$ 25,150	$13,850
Accounts receivable	36,890	37,740	(850)
Inventory	52,000	42,000	10,000
Prepaid insurance	240	150	90
Land	30,000	0	30,000
Buildings	50,000	35,000	15,000
Equipment	89,500	87,400	2,100
Discount on bonds payable	1,000	0	1,000
	$298,630	$227,440	$71,190
Credits			
Accumulated depreciation—building	$ 10,500	$ 8,000	$ 2,500
Accumulated depreciation—equipment	24,100	26,200	(2,100)
Accounts payable	6,230	9,240	(3,010)
Notes payable—short-term	1,500	2,000	(500)
Dividends payable	8,000	7,000	1,000
Bonds payable	20,000	0	20,000
Common stock—$100 par	137,500	100,000	37,500
Capital in excess of par value	31,250	25,000	6,250
Retained earnings	59,550	50,000	9,550
	$298,630	$227,440	$71,190

The following information was also available:

a. Net income in 19x2 was $17,550; there were no extraordinary items.
b. During January, 19x2, common stock with a par value of $25,000 was exchanged for land, which was recorded at its fair market value of $30,000.
c. On July 1,19x2, 125 shares of common stock were sold for $110 per share.
d. Bonds payable with a face value of $20,000 were issued on December 31, 19x2. The bonds mature in ten years.
e. The only disposal of depreciable assets during 19x2 was the sale of equipment for $2,000. The equipment had an original cost of $7,000 and accumulated depreciation of $5,500.
f. Cash dividends of $8,000 were declared in 19x2.
g. The short-term notes payable relate to the purchase of merchandise.

Required:

Prepare a statement of cash flows.

P13-8* Using the information in P13-6, prepare a cash flow work sheet.

P13-9* Using the information in P13-7, prepare a cash flow work sheet.

Learning Objectives

Chapter 14 discusses common techniques used in analyzing information presented in financial statements. Studying this chapter should enable you to:

1. Describe the process of analyzing financial statements.
2. Identify questions typically asked by financial statement analysts.
3. Perform a comparative historic analysis of financial statements.
4. Perform a common-size analysis of financial statements.
5. Calculate common financial statement ratios and interpret the results of these calculations.
6. Specify the limitations to naive use of each major analytical technique.

14

Financial Statement Analysis

INTRODUCTION

A firm's financial statements, with their accompanying notes, constitute an important source of data for owners, investors, creditors, and others. Financial statement users must generally undertake some analysis to gain full insight from these statements. In this chapter, we focus on financial analysis, concentrating on methods that enhance the interpretability of reported financial information. An understanding of analytical techniques is important for several reasons. Accountants frequently are consulted by clients or other individuals who have little experience with financial statements, but who are required to make financial decisions. Business owners or managers often ask their accountants to analyze business operations and to make recommendations that will improve efficiency. In addition, the accountant's knowledge of financial statement analysis is important in making decisions about the preparation and presentation of financial information. Only by understanding how financial statements are used can the accountant determine whether a particular financial statement presentation will be useful or misleading.

THE ANALYTIC PROCESS

Financial statement analysis is an investigative process. The purpose of the analysis is to *highlight* specific data items, to place data in some *comparative context*, and to *identify* relevant characteristics of the business organization and its financial structure. The process should enhance a decision-maker's ability to evaluate an organization according to some specific objectives. The decision-maker's objectives will influence the type and extent of the analysis to be undertaken.

Users of financial reports may be "internal" or "external" to the firm. Internal users manage the business. Although many management information needs focus on operational data provided by the managerial (internal) accounting system, top management must recognize the potential reactions of owners and creditors to published financial data. External users of financial reports include stockholders, analysts, creditors, and other parties interested in the firm. Their access to data is normally limited to published financial reports. Financial statement analysis serves external users by highlighting and clarifying data included in the report.

Since various users have different goals, the objective of financial analysis depends on the individual needs of the analyst. For example, a stockholder may be concerned about long-term profitability, whereas a short-term trade creditor may be interested in the firm's ability to pay its current obligations. In contrast, a bondholder may be interested in the firm's capital structure and other indicators of long-term solvency.

Most financial statement users are interested in making reasonably accurate predictions about the future. Decision-makers are confronted with alternative courses of action that will produce different consequences. The decision objective is to select that alternative which leads to the most favorable consequence. Because perfect information about the future is not available, the financial statement user must explore the predictive potential of the financial data that are available.

Since financial statements are historical in nature, they contain no specific forecasts. However, accounting data are important inputs into the prediction models of most financial statement users. Many financial analysts rely heavily on financial statement data in making future assessments, and some believe forecasting to be the most important use of financial reports.

Beyond their use in predicting future outcomes, financial statements can be used to evaluate the present position of a business. The debt structure and equity composition of the firm combined with information about its assets to provide a basis for assessing its existing financial position.

PLAN OF ANALYSIS

Financial statement analysis typically follows a series of interrelated steps that leads a user to a meaningful interpretation of financial data. These steps are:

1. Specify the purpose of the analysis.
2. Identify the measurement base.

3. Collect and process the data.
4. Compare the processed data with a standard.

The purpose of financial statement analysis relates to the specific needs of each user. These varying needs address questions of *liquidity*, *solvency*, *profitability*, and *marketability*. Liquidity refers to a firm's ability to meet its current debt obligations. Consequently, it is associated with existing and projected relationships between current liabilities (the debt obligations) and current assets (the means of payment). Liquidity is normally a concern of the short-term creditor.

The ability of a firm to service its long-term debt obligations is called solvency. Solvency relates total liabilities to total assets. In the long run, the asset base must be capable of generating enough liquid resources to meet the demands of maturing debt. Stockholders, as well as long-term creditors (frequently bondholders), have an interest in the solvency of an enterprise.

Profitability measures the success of a business venture. Although operating losses can be sustained in the short run, the organization must generate profitability as a condition for survival. Profitability concerns both long-term creditors and stockholders.

Marketability refers to the resale value of an equity interest (i.e., a share of stock); thus, it measures the current market worth of the stockholder investments. Market analysis attempts to relate reported financial information to price reactions in the stock market. These evaluations are of particular concern to stockholders and potential investors.

Measurement Base

The *absolute data* provided in the financial statements are one common measurement base. These data, the reported dollar amounts, provide a basis for comparison, evaluation, and prediction.

In addition to using an absolute data measurement base, financial statement data are often expressed as *relative data*. Relative data are derived by dividing one number by another number. Two commonly used forms of relative measures are *common-size data* and *ratios*. Common-size data are developed by expressing each number on a financial statement as a percentage of some common base number also found on that statement. For example, analysts frequently express each number on the income statement as a percentage of net sales and each number on a balance sheet as a percentage of total assets. Financial statement ratios are developed by taking two numbers whose relationships is perceived to be important and expressing those two numbers in the form of a ratio. These ratios provide a data base for analysis along with absolute data.

Data Collection

In some cases, computers are used to manipulate great quantities of data into many alternative sets. Some analysts reap greater insights by manually collecting and processing the data. Although collection and processing methods may vary, the purpose is to isolate and highlight relevant relationships from a given body of financial statement data.

Comparison

The key to most financial analysis is comparison. Individual bits of data or ratios became more meaningful when expressed in a comparative format. For example, the fact that current profits are $200,000 has one meaning if last year's profits were $10,000 and another if last year's profits were $1 million. The available data about a firm can be compared in a variety of contexts, including *historic base, like-kind base*, and *goal norm*. Historic, or trend, analysis is most commonly employed. This approach compares the current performance of a firm with historical data from the same firm. Historic analysis isolates trends that have developed over time. Such trends may be projected into the future for prediction purposes if underlying conditions ar expected to remain constant.

A like-kind analysis attempts to gauge one firm's performance against the performance of similar business ventures. In some instances, the target company's data may be compared with industry averages. Financial rating services such as *Moody's, Standard and Poor*, and *Dun and Bradstreet* provide significant quantities of comparative data about a variety of firms and industries. These services allow analysts to determine whether a particular firm is performing more successfully or less successfully than others in the industry. In some cases, analysis may suggest reasons why one firm is more successful than its competition. The analyst may have prespecified a goal, norm, or target about operating performance, solvency, profitability, or marketability. For example, many lending institutions specify minimum standards on selected ratios that are used in setting credit limits. Investors must have established minimum acceptable levels of earnings before an investment is considered. Corporate managers establish profit or solvency goals that they expect to be met. These predetermined goals play a key role in the decision-making process: they establish levels of acceptable performance in the context of the relevant decision-making criteria. Comparison of actual performance with predetermined goals may trigger a final decision.

ANALYTIC TECHNIQUES AND INTERPRETATION

In the rest of this chapter, we review the principal techniques of financial statement analysis. Note, however, that no one technique is clearly superior to others. The success of each technique is a function of the analyst's skill.

Comparative Analysis

In comparative analysis, the financial data for the current year is compared on an absolute or relative basis with the financial data for one or more previous years. In this fashion, the analyst isolates existing trends.

The simplest form of comparative analysis contrasts the absolute amount of each item in the current financial statements with the corresponding item in previous years. To facilitate such analyses, accountants present financial statements in the comparative form shown in Illustration 1. The financial statement user must examine changes to determine if meaningful trends exist. For example, sales and profits of Executrix Corporation, shown in Il-

Illustration 1
Comparative Historic Analysis of Absolute Data

Executrix Corporation
Comparative Income Statements
For the Years Ended December 31, 19x2 and 19x1

	Year Ended December 31	
	19x2	19x1
Sales	$800,000	$600,000
Cost of goods sold	445,000	310,000
Gross profit	$355,000	$290,000
Operating expense:		
Selling expense	$160,000	$110,000
Administrative expense	90,000	105,000
Interest expense	4,000	6,000
Total expense	$254,000	$221,000
Net income before income tax	$101,000	$69,000
Income tax expense	40,000	28,000
Net income	$ 61,000	$ 41,000

lustration, appear favorable since both increased. The trends of administrative expense and interest may be favorable, since both decreased while sales were increasing.

Many accountants anticipate that this form of analysis will be undertaken and therefore prepare financial statements like that shown in Illustration 2. This form highlights changes from the previous year. Percentage analysis of changes in each line item shown in Illustration 2 is called *horizontal analysis*. Note that data from the earliest year's balance (19x1 in the example) are used as a base in a horizontal analysis.

Horizontal analysis can provide important insights into financial trends. For example, Illustration 2 shows that the upward trend of sales is not as sharp as the increase in cost of goods sold. That is, the sales growth was relatively expensive in terms of the cost of goods sold and possibly out of control. Further analysis reveals that cuts in administrative expense and interest expense account for much of the increase in profits. Although the initial comparative analysis of absolute data appeared favorable, subsequent percentage analysis reveals a different situation.

Limitations

Comparative analysis is an important tool in financial statement analysis; however, it is not without limitations. Any trend analysis relies on the assumption that past conditions extend into the future. To the extent that the

Illustration 2
Horizontal Analysis of Both
Absolute and Relative Changes

Executrix Corporation
Comparative Income Statements
For the Years Ended December 31, 19x2 and 19x1

	Year Ended December 31		Increase or Decrease	
	19x2	19x1	Amount	Percent
Sales	$800,000	$600,000	$200,000	33.3
Cost of goods sold	445,000	310,000	135,000	43.5
Gross profit	$355,000	$290,000	$ 65,000	22.4
Operating expense:				
Selling expense	$160,000	$110,000	$ 50,000	45.4
Administrative expense	90,000	105,000	(15,000)	(14.2)
Interest expense	4,000	6,000	(2,000)	(33.3)
Total expense	$254,000	$221,000	$ 33,000	14.9
Net income before income tax	$101,000	$ 69,000	$ 32,000	46.3
Income tax expense	40,000	28,000	12,000	42.8
Net income	$ 61,000	$ 41,000	$ 20,000	48.7

conditions within a business enterprise change (for instance, the development of new products and/or a new management), or that conditions within the business environment change (fluctuations in industry or general economic conditions), evaluation of current data becomes more difficult. Unfortunately, the global economic environment is very dynamic; interpretation of financial trends must consider both industry conditions and general economic conditions. To the extent that current conditions are expected to extended into the future, horizontal financial statement analysis may prove to be extremely effective.

Common-Size Analysis

Common-size analysis, sometimes called *vertical analysis*, emphasizes relationships between data items on the same financial statement. Common-size analysis is relatively simple to effect. Every item on a financial statement is expressed as a percentage of a single base amount. Sales or net sales is commonly used as the base for analysis of an income statement. Total assets is commonly used as the base for the balance sheet. Illustration 3 shows a common-size analysis of the Executrix Corporation income statement. Having expressed a set of financial statements in relative terms, the analyst may compare the results with other firms, or with industry averages. Size differences between firms have been removed by the restatement. Comparative vertical analysis contrasts the increase in cost of goods sold for Executrix

Illustration 3
Comparative Horizontal Analysis of Common-Size Data

Executrix Corporation
Comparative Income Statements
For the Yeas Ended December 31, 19x1 and 19x2

	Year Ended December 31,19x2		Year Ended December 31, 19x1		Increase or Decrease
	Amounter	Percent	Amount	Percent	Percent
Sales*	$800,000	100.0	$600,000	100.0	0
Cost of goods sold	445,000	55.6	310,000	51.6	4.0
Gross profit	$355,000	44.4	$290,000	48.4	(4.0)
Operating expense:					
Selling expense	$160,000	20.0	$110,000	18.3	1.7
Administrative expense	90,000	11.2	105,000	17.5	(6.3)
Interest expense	4,000	.5	6,000	1.0	(.5)
Total expense	$254,000	31.7	$221,000	36.8	(5.1)
Net income before income tax	$101,000	12.7	$ 69,000	11.5	1.2
Income tax expense	40,000	5.0	28,000	4.6	.4
Net income	$ 61,000	7.7	$ 41,000	6.9	.8

*Base amount

vices, such as *Moody's* or *Dun and Bradstreet*. If the industry average for cost of goods sold is reported to be 42 percent, the Executrix percentage of 55.6 is significantly higher than its competition. Reasons for this difference would be investigated further by the analyst. Current relationships of Executrix are highlighted by combining a comparative historic analysis with common-size analysis as shown in Illustration 3. Note that this combination is accomplished by preparing common-size financial statements in comparative format and by calculating the increase or decrease in the percentages over time. Cost of goods sold increased as a percentage of sales 4 percent between 19x1 and 19x2. By comparing this rate of change with industry average rates, the analyst can readily determine whether Executrix's experience during this period differed materially from that of other firms.

Limitations

Common-size analysis suffers from some limitations as does comparative historic analysis. Both evaluations are based on trend assumptions. To the extent that changes occur in the firm or its environment, both forms of analysis may prove poor predictors of the future. In addition, interpretation of relative data may be ambiguous. For example, if operating expense, expressed as a percentage of sales, is materially higher than industry norms, which element presents the problem? Are operating expenses too high, or did expected sales fail to materialize? A thorough analysis of relative data may be required to derive interpretable results.

Ratio Analysis

Ratio analysis is one of the most important and generally used techniques of financial statement analysis. It facilitates pinpoint investigations of specific financial relationships. The needs of the analyst will determine which ratios are selected from the broad variety that can be calculated.

There are four general groups of ratios: profitability ratios, liquidity ratios, solvency ratios, and marketability. Each of these ratio groups relates directly to a particular purpose of financial statement analysis. *Profitability ratios* indicate how successfully the enterprise has been operated during the year. They usually relate some measure of financial success, such as net income, to other financial statement items. This allows the analyst to assess the adequacy of profits and rates of return being generated by business operations. Profitability ratios are of particular interest to existing or potential investors and long-term creditors.

Liquidity ratios address the firm's ability to meet its financial obligations. In general, these ratios relate maturing debt to measures of asset availability. Other liquidity ratios relate the potential of assets to change into more liquid forms to meet business needs. Liquidity ratios are generally useful to all financial statement users, but are particularly useful to short-term creditors.

Solvency ratios measure the extent to which a business utilized debt to finance its operations. These ratios typically relate some measure of debt to either total or long-term capital provided from all sources. The extent to which a firm can service its long-term debt is important to investors and creditors. High-debt firms usually have significant debt service costs that must be paid each year, regardless of the success of operations. Consequently, these firms can present higher risks of insolvency. Solvency ratios provide measures of risk.

Marketability ratios measure the response of the securities markets to published financial data or to other measures that concern investor decisions to purchase securities. Investors and potential investors primarily use these ratios.

AN EXAMPLE

The sections that follow shows the calculation of some common profitability, liquidity, solvency, and marketability ratios. It is important to remember that the mere calculation of financial statement ratios provides little information. Rather, the ratios, or their historic trends, must be compared with industry norms and then must be integrated into a broad framework of analysis before meaningful conclusions can be made. For example, the financial statements of Executrix Corporation are presented in Illustration 4. The percentage equivalent of each ratio will only be extended to one

Illustration 4

Executrix Corporation
Income Statement
For the Year Ended December 31, 19x2

Sales		$ 800,000
Cost of goods sold		445,000
Gross profit		$ 355,000
Operating expense:		
Selling expense	$160,000	
Administrative expense	90,000	
Interest expense	4,000	
Total expense		$ 254,000
		$ 101,000
Net income before income tax		$ 101,000
Income tax expense		$ 40,000
Net income		$ 61,000
Earnings per share (50,000 shares common stock)		$ 1.22

Balance Sheet
December 31, 19x2

Assets		
Current assets:		
Cash		$ 90,000
Accounts receivable (net)		60,000
Inventory		400,000
Prepaid expenses		15,000
Total current assets		$ 565,000
Investments:		
Unimproved land (cost)		50,000
Fixed assets:		
Equipment	$600,000	
Less: Accumulated depreciation	180,000	420,00
Total assets		$1,035,000
Liabilities		
Current liabilities:		
Accounts payable		$ 96,000
Notes payable		52,000
Accrued wages payable		10,000
Total current liabilities		$ 158,000
Long-term liabilities:		
Bonds payable (due 19x9)		150,000
Total liabilities		$ 308,000
Stockholders' Equity		
Common stock ($10.00 par value, 50,000 shares authorized, issued, and outstanding)		$ 500,000
Retained earnings		227,000
Total stockholders equity		$ 727,000
Total liabilities and stockholders' equity		$1,035,000
Other data for 19x2		
Cash dividends paid per share		$ 0.20

Selected data from the previous year's financial statements:

Total assets =	$935,000
Total stockholders' equity =	$706,000
Total number of shares of common stock outstanding =	50,000 shares
Net accounts receivable =	$ 56,000
Inventory =	$320,000

or two decimal places as greater precision is unwarranted. Ratios will be rounded upward when the next digit is 5 or larger.

PROFITABILITY RATIOS

One measure of business profitability is the ratio of profit to sales. It indicates what part of each sales dollar becomes profit. This ratio is calculated by dividing net income by net sales for the period as follows:

Profit Margin on Sales

$$\text{Profit Margin on Sales} = \frac{\text{Net Income}}{\text{Net Sales}} = \frac{\$61{,}000}{\$800{,}000} = 7.6\%$$

If the average profit margin on sales for this industry is 6.6 percent, then Executrix has produced a superior profit margin on sales. This ratio can literally be interpreted to mean that for every dollar of sales, Executrix generates 7.6 cents of profit. The ratio provides information about pricing policy and cost management; it does not indicate how efficiently management utilizes the firm's resources. For example, it does not tell the analyst if the firm has generated adequate sales, given the level of resources at its command.

Rate of Return on Assets

The rate of return on assets ratio highlights the relationship between profit and the resources utilized by the firm to generate profit. It is calculated by dividing net income by average total assets. Net income is found on the current year's income statement. Average total assets must be calculated as the average of total assets at the end of the previous year and the current year as shown below:

$$\text{Average Total Assets} = (\text{Total assets at end of last year} + \text{Total assets at end of current year}) \div 2$$

$$= (\$935{,}000 + 1{,}035{,}000) \div 2 = \$985{,}000$$

$$\text{Rate of Return on Assets} = \frac{\text{Net Income}}{\text{Average Total Assets}} = \frac{\$61{,}000}{\$985{,}000} = 6.2\%$$

This calculation is based on average total assets, because profits are assumed to be earned continually throughout the year.

This ratio may be interpreted to mean that for each $1 of assets utilized by the firm, management succeeded in generating 6.2 cents of profit. When this ratio is compared with industry norms, it gives an indication of how efficiently management utilizes assets in generating profits.

Rate of Return on Common Stock Equity

To measure how effectively the resources provided by common stockholders are being utilized, analysts calculate the rate of return on common stock equity. This ratio can be used by common stockholders or potential investors as a rough indication of the long-run returns they may anticipate. The ratio is calculated by dividing net income (reduced by dividends on preferred stock) by average common stockholders' equity. Net income is reduced by preferred dividends to yield that portion of profits available to common stockholders. This result is then divided by an average of stockholders' equity for the current and previous year-end. Common stockholders' equity represents the sum in the common stock, additional contributed capital, and retained earnings accounts. The rate of return on common stockholders equity for Executrix Corporation is:

$$\text{Rate of Return on Common Stock Equity} = \frac{\text{Net Income Less Preferred Dividends}}{\text{Average Common Stockholders' Equity}}$$

$$= \$61{,}000/(\$727{,}000 + \$706{,}000) \div 2$$

$$= 8.5\%$$

If the industry return was 15 percent, an analyst would conclude that Executrix earns an unusually low return on common investment. Further analysis could pinpoint a cause or causes for this low return.

Earnings Per Share

One of the most widely publicized numbers used in financial statement analysis is the earnings per share ratio, frequently called EPS. This ratio attempts to determine the amount of net income, after payment of preferred dividends, that was earned for the average outstanding common share. It is calculated as follows:

$$\text{Earnings Per Share} = \frac{\text{Net Income Less Preferred Dividends Paid}}{\text{Average Number of Shares of Common Stock Outstanding}}$$

$$= \$61{,}000/(50{,}000 + 50{,}000) \div 2$$

$$= \frac{\$61{,}000}{\$50{,}000} = \$1.22$$

Many corporations have complex capital structures that are composed of additional securities which are similar to common stock or which can be converted into common stock. To insure uniform treatment of these convertible equity interests, the Accounting Principles Board in *Opinion No. 15* prescribes a uniform method of calculating EPS and directs that EPS be explicitly disclosed on the income statement, under net income. Earnings per share is generally perceived by the financial community to be an important indicator of profitability and is widely cited in financial literature.

LIQUIDITY RATIOS

The most commonly used ratio to evaluate the ability of a firm to meet its short-term financial obligations is the current ratio. This ratio is calculated by dividing current assets by current liabilities.

Current Ratio

$$\text{Current Ratio} = \frac{\text{Current Assets}}{\text{Current Liabilities}}$$

$$= \$565{,}000 \div \$158{,}000 = 3.6$$

The relationship of current assets to current liabilities is perceived by analysts as an important measure of a firm's ability to pay its debts. There is no absolute standard by which to judge the adequacy of a firm's current ratio. However, many analysts argue that a current ratio of 2.0 is necessary to ensure liquidity. Comparison with industry norms is probably the most meaningful way in which to evaluate the current ratio. Although a current ratio of less than 1.0 may indicate that a firm has liquidity problems, the opposite case—a current ratio larger than 4—may also be a sign of problems. Assets in an extremely liquid form, for example, cash in bank accounts, may be underutilized and may be earning too little for the firm.

Acid-Test Ratio

Some analysts believe that the current ratio is not a very effective measure of liquidity because the current asset classification contains some assets (for example, inventories) that are not really very liquid. The acid-test ratio addresses this situation by including only assets that can readily be turned into cash, for instance, cash, marketable securities, and net receivables. The acid-test ratio highlights the relationship between these quick assets and current liabilities, revealing how many times current liabilities could be paid with assets that are readily converted into cash.

$$\text{Acid-Test Ratio} = \frac{\text{Cash} + \text{Marketable Securities} + \text{Net Amounts Receivable}}{\text{Current Liabilities}}$$

$$= \frac{\$90{,}000 + 0 + \$60{,}000}{\$158{,}000}$$

$$= 0.95$$

Comparison with other firms in the industry would be necessary to determine if the acid-test ratio is abnormally high or low for Executrix Corporation. An abnormally low acid-test ratio suggests that the firm runs a higher liquidity risk than other firms in the industry. An abnormally high acid-test ratio may suggest that noninterest-bearing cash balances are too high or that problems in collecting receivables have developed. Generally, a rate of 1.0 or higher is considered an acceptable level.

Receivables Turnover

Both the current ratio and the acid test ratio presume that accounts receivable can be converted into cash within enough time to allow the payment of current debts. The receivables turnover ratio indicates how realistic this assumption is by measuring the average length of time receivables are held before collection. This ratio is computed by dividing net credit sales by the average receivables outstanding during the year. Average accounts receivable are calculated by taking the average of the current and previous year-end accounts receivable balances.

$$\text{Accounts Receivable Turnover} = \frac{\text{Total Net Sales or Credit Sales}}{\text{Average Net Accounts Receivable}}$$
$$= \$800{,}000/(\$56{,}000 + \$60{,}000) \div 2$$
$$= 13.8 \text{ Times}$$

This ratio indicates that accounts receivable for Executrix Corporation turn over 13.8 times per year. The average period of time required to collect accounts receivable is obtained by dividing the turnover ratio (13.8) into the number of days in a year (360 is used for simplicity).

$$\text{Average Collection Period} = \frac{\text{Number of Days in Year}}{\text{Accounts Receivable Turnover Ratio}}$$
$$= 360 \div 13.8$$
$$= 26.1 \text{ Days}$$

On average, Executrix Corporation collects its receivables every 26.1 days. This means that Executrix is providing credit to customers for less than a month. If the terms of credit in this industry call for payment within thirty days of sale, a twenty-six day collection period may be viewed as a positive one. Comparison with an inudstry average would help in evaluating these results. A relatively short collection period suggests that most receivables are collectible, since the older a receivable is, the more likely it is to be uncollectible.

Inventory Turnover

Another important liquidity ratio is the inventory turnover ratio. The inventory turnover ratio for Executrix Corporation is calculated by dividing the cost of goods sold by the average inventory balance:

$$\text{Inventory Turnover Ratio} = \frac{\text{Cost of Goods Sold}}{\text{Average Inventory}}$$
$$= \$445{,}000/(\$320{,}000 + \$400{,}000) \div 2$$
$$= 1.24 \text{ Times}$$

The amount of time required to sell the average inventory can be determined by dividing the inventory turnover ratio into the number of days in the year (again, 360 for simplicity).

$$\text{Average Inventory Turnover in Days} = \frac{\text{Number of Days in the Year}}{\text{Inventory Turnover Ratio}}$$
$$= 360 \div 1.24$$
$$= 290 \text{ Days}$$

If the industry average inventory turnover in days is 195, an analyst would conclude that Executrix turns its inventory over too slowly. This could be caused by quantities of obsolete items that may never be sold, items that are rarely needed by customers, or simply by excessive inventories. The inventory turnover ratio addresses two issues: it gives the analyst important information about the liquidity of the inventory, and it also reflects management's effectiveness in utilizing the assets at its disposal.

SOLVENCY RATIOS

Solvency concerns the ability of a firm to service its long-term debt obligations. "Servicing" debt implies that the interest will be paid when due, and that the debtor will continue to satisfy all security and other debt-related contractual obligations. It also implies that the debtor will maintian a credit rating sufficient to allow a refinancing of the debt as an alternative to payment and that the original debt or the refinanced debt will ultimately be paid.

Debt to Total Assets

A common measure of solvency is the ratio of debt to total assets. This ratio indicates what percentage of funds used in a business is provided by creditors. For Executrix, this ratio is calculated as follows:

$$\text{Debt to Total Assets} = \frac{\text{Total Liabilities}}{\text{Total Assets}}$$
$$= \$308{,}000 \div \$1{,}035{,}000$$
$$= 29.75 \text{ Percent}$$

Creditors generally prefer a low debt to total asset ratio, because it indicates that more of the funds invested in the business are provided by owners. The lower the ratio, the lower the creditors' risk that the firm will be unable to pay its debts. For Executrix, creditors can be repaid even if assets are liquidated for only $.30 per dollar of book value.

Times Interest Earned

Another common solvency measure is called the times interest earned ratio. This ratio emphasizes the relationship between annual interest expense and earnings, highlighting the extent to which earnings can fall before the firm will have difficulty serving its debt obligations. The times interest earned ratio is calculated by dividing net income before interest and income taxes by annual interest expense.

$$\text{Times Interest Earned} = \frac{\text{Net Income + Interest Expense + Income Tax Expense}}{\text{Interest Expense}}$$

$$= (\$61{,}000 + \$4{,}000 + \$40{,}000) \div \$4{,}000$$

$$= 26.25 \text{ Times}$$

Executrix has a ratio of 26.25 which tells the analyst that earnings are sufficient to pay creditors' interest 26.25 times. This suggests that the firm has an extensive cushion and that the business earns substantially more than is required to meet interest expenses.

MARKETABILITY RATIOS

Price Earnings Ratio

Perhaps the most common marketability ratio is the price earnings ratio, which is usually referred to as the PE ratio. It is calculated by dividing the market price of a corporation's common stock by its earnings per share. If Executrix common stock was selling for $10 per share on the balance sheet date, its PE ratio would be calculated as follows:

$$\text{Price Earnings Ratio} = \frac{\text{Market Price of Stock}}{\text{Earnings Per Share}}$$

$$= \$10 \div \$1.22$$

$$= 8.2$$

This ratio indicates that the market price of one share of this stock is 8.2 times the earnings per share. The higher this ratio, the more attractive a share of stock is perceived to be by the market. Comparison within the industry is an excellent aid in interpreting the PE ratio. An unusually low PE ratio generally indicates that investors perceive a stock to be fairly risky. An unusually high PE ratio indicates that investors have high expectations for growth in earnings and stock prices.

Payout Ratio

The payout ratio is a different kind of marketability ratio. Instead of measuring the adequacy of profits or the market's response to reported profits, the payout ratio measures the relation of dividends to net income. It is calculated as follows:

$$\text{Payout Ratio} = \frac{\text{Cash Dividends}}{\text{Net Income}}$$

$$= \$10{,}000 \div \$61{,}000$$

$$= 16.4$$

The payout ratio is an important ratio to investors whose primary objective in investing is to generate a current cash return on their investment. This ratio indicates that Executrix paid out 16.4 percent of its net income to its shareholders as dividends. This ratio helps investors determine whether they are interested in investing in a company.

its shareholders as dividends. This ratio helps investors determine whether they are interested in investing in a company.

SUMMARY OF RATIOS

Illustration 5 provides a summary of the ratios calculated in this chapter for Executrix Corporation. A complete analysis of Executrix requires the use of other techniques and a consideration of industry and general economic conditions. With such supplemental consideration, ratio analysis can indicate the strengths and weaknesses of the firm. The capability to pinpoint specific relationships makes it an extremely flexible and unique tool of financial statement analysis.

LIMITATIONS OF RATIO ANALYSIS

Ratio analysis has several recognizable limitations that the user should consider. The interpretation of any relative measure is somewhat confounded by the presence of two elements in the calculation of the ratio. Although a particular ratio may indicate that a problem exists for a firm, the analyst must determine which element in the ratio calculation is responsible for the problem, or if both are responsible. Other forms of analysis frequently must be undertaken to pinpoint the exact nature of the problems highlighted in ratio analysis.

Ratios that measure the relationship between a real account balance and a nominal account balance, or between two nominal account balances, can be misleading if the year-end real account balances are not representative of the balances in those accounts during the remainder of the year. Indeed, some firms, knowing that ratios such as the current ratio will be routinely calculated by analysts, may actually attempt to improve a ratio by paying debts or engaging in other transactions. This later concern may be unfounded in all but rare instances because of the difficulty of materially affecting ratios by year-end transactions.

In addition, ratios only concern historic data; although trend analysis may prove useful in evaluating past events, prediction of future events implicitly assumes that both internal and external conditions and relationships will not change. A ratio, by itself, conveys little information. Only when analyses of ratios are studied as historical trends or are compared with ratios for similar organizations or with expectations will they provide maximum insight.

IMPACT OF ACCOUNTING METHODS

When analyzing financial statements, it is important to recognize that the specific accounting methods used by a company may have a significant impact. When analyzing a company's financial statements over a period of two or more years, it is important to read the footnotes to determine if the company changed any of its accounting methods. Such changes could make comparisons difficult.

Illustration 5
Summary of Ratios
for Executrix Corporation

Ratio	*Formula*	*Calculation*
Profitability Ratios		
1. Profit Margin on Sales	$\frac{\text{Net Income}}{\text{Net Sales}}$	$\frac{\$61,000}{\$800,000} = 7.623\%$
2. Rate of Return on Assets	$\frac{\text{Net Income}}{\text{Average Total Assets}}$	$\$61,000 \div \frac{\$935,000 + \$1,035,000}{2} = 6.3$
3. Rate of Return on Common Stock Equity	$\frac{\text{Net Income Less Preferred Dividends}}{\text{Average Common Stockholders' Equity}}$	$\$61,000 \div \frac{\$727,000 + \$706,000}{2} = 8.5$
4. Earnings Per Share	$\frac{\text{Net Income Less Preferred Dividends}}{\text{Average Number of Shares of Common Stock Outstanding}}$	$\frac{\$61,000}{\$50,000} = \$1.22$
Liquidity Ratios		
5. Current Ratio	$\frac{\text{Current Assets}}{\text{Current Liabilities}}$	$\frac{\$565,000}{\$158,000} = 3.58$
6. Acid Test Ratio	$\frac{\text{Cash + Marketable Securities + Net Accounts Receivable}}{\text{Current Liabilities}}$	$\frac{\$90,000 + 0 + 60,000}{\$158,000} + 0.95$
7. Receivables Turnover	$\frac{\text{Total Net Sales}}{\text{Average Net Accounts Receivables}}$	$\$800,000 \div \frac{\$56,000 + \$60,000}{2} = 13.8$ Times
7a. Average Collection Period	$\frac{\text{Number of Days in Year}}{\text{Receivables Turnover Ratio}}$	$\frac{360}{13.8} = 26.1$ Days
8. Inventory Turnover	$\frac{\text{Cost of Goods Sold}}{\text{Average Inventory}}$	$\$445,000 \div \frac{\$320,000 + \$400,000}{2} = 1.24$ Times
8a. Average Inventory Turnover in Days	$\frac{\text{Number of Days in Year}}{\text{Inventory Turnover Ratio}}$	$\frac{360}{1.24} = 290$ Days
Solvency Ratios		
9. Debt to Total Assets	$\frac{\text{Total Liabilities}}{\text{Total Assets}}$	$\frac{\$308,000}{\$1,035,000} = 29.75\%$
10. Times Interest Earned	$\frac{\text{Net Income + Interest Expense + Income Tax Expense}}{\text{Interest Expense}}$	$\frac{\$90,000 + 0 + \$60,000}{\$4,000} = 26.25$ Times
Marketability Ratios		
11. Price Earnings Ratio	$\frac{\text{Market Price of Stock}}{\text{Earnings Per Share}}$	$\frac{\$10}{\$1.22} = 8.2$ Times
12. Payout Ratio	$\frac{\text{Cash Dividends}}{\text{Net Income}}$	$\frac{\$10,000}{\$61,000} = 16.4\%$

Comparisons to competitors or industry standards must also take into account the accounting methods used. For example, if one company uses FIFO and another uses LIFO for inventory, it will make meaningful comparisons very difficult. In a period of rising prices, the LIFO inventory will be less than FIFO. If a company has been using LIFO for a long period of time, the difference may be substantial. In these cases, comparisons of such items as current ratio and inventory turnover may be misleading. The company on LIFO will show a lower current ratio and a higher inventory turnover. Other items, such as depreciation and amortization, may also cause significant differences between companies.

When analyzing financial statements, care should be taken to make sure the companies are using the same accounting methods or that the data is adjusted where the methods are different and sufficient information is available to determine the proper adjustments. If the methods are different and adjustments cannot be made, the impact of the accounting methods must be considered. As a result, less emphasis may be placed on certain ratios or we might choose another competitor for making the comparisons.

SUMMARY

Financial statements contain a wealth of financial data that can provide exceptional insight into the strengths and weaknesses of a firm. So much data are provided, however, that many relationships are not obvious. Additional analysis must be undertaken to highlight data items, to place these items in a comparative context, and to isolate relevant characteristics or relationships of the business and its financial structure.

Financial statement analysis is an investigative process. A plan of analysis includes four basic steps. The analyst must specify the purpose of the analysis. This is governed by the kinds of decisions to be made and establishes the techniques to be employed in the analysis. The second step is to identify the measurement base. Some analytical techniques use absolute data, whereas others require relative data. The third step in the analytical process is to collect the data needed in the analysis. The final step is to compare the results of the analytical techniques with historical data, like-kind data, or prespecified goals. Comparison is the key to financial statement analysis, providing guides to acceptable performance and helping to establish decision criteria.

Three major analyses are commonly used in studying financial statements. The most common is comparative historic analysis. This technique compares financial data for two or more years in an attempt to discover trends that may serve as a basis for predicting the future. Percentage analysis of changes in comparative data is called horizontal analysis. The second major approach is common-size analysis, sometimes called vertical analysis or component percentage analysis. This form of analysis seeks to determine the relationships between items on the same financial statements. The third major analytical technique is ratio analysis. It pinpoints specific relationships between data items on one year's financial statements, addressing issues such as the adequacy of profits and the liquidity or solvency of the firm. When combined with an analysis of industry and general economic conditions, these techniques can provide the financial statement user with important insights that are difficult to obtain by simple inspection of the financial data.

KEY DEFINITIONS

Horizontal analysis—a comparison of dollar and percentage changes from one year to the next.

Liquidity—a company's ability to meet its current debt obligations.

Marketability—a company's ability to sell equity securities.

Profitability—a company's liability to generate income.

Solvency—a company's ability to meet its long-term debt obligations.

Vertical analysis—common size analysis emphasizing relationships between data items on the same financial statement.

QUESTIONS

14-1 Why must financial statements be analyzed?

14-2 Effective analysis requires that financial data be compared with standards, historical data, or industry data. Why is comparison critical?

14-3 What measurement bases can be used by a financial statement analyst?

14-4 Define the term liquidity. Explain its relevance to financial statement analysis.

14-5 Contrast the concepts of liquidity and solvency.

14-6 How long a period is required for historical analysis? How do conventional financial statements attempt to accommodate this form of analysis?

14-7 What are common-size financial statements?

14-8 Identify ratios that address the issue of profitability.

14-9 For what purpose is the ratio, rate of return on assets, calculated? How does the interpretation of this ratio differ from that of the ratio, rate of return on common stock equity?

14-10 Waltham Corporation reports earnings per share of $.20, and Ridgeland Company reports earnings per share of $2. Is Ridgeland more profitable than Waltham? Explain.

14-11 Is a high inventory turnover preferable to a low turnover? Does this also hold true for a receivables turnover? Explain.

14-12 Wilson Company offers trade terms of 2/10, n/30, and it reports an accounts receivable turnover of 5.2. How do you interpret these facts?

14-13 Sampson Company reports a current ratio of 1.3 to 1. What conclusion can you draw?

14-14 List the two comparative analysis techniques described in the chapter, and explain the differences between them.

14-15 List the categories under which ratios are typically classified.

14-16 What do liquidity ratios attempt to measure?

14-17 What must the analyst know to be able to use ratio analysis properly?

14-18 List the primary user groups of financial statements. State what goals each group has in examining the statements.

14-19 In general, what are the interests shared by all groups who examine financial statements?

14-20 Why are historical comparisons useful to financial statement analysts?

14-21 How can accounting methods affect financial statement analysis?

EXERCISES

E14-1 Data for Wyatt Corporation are shown below:

	19x2	*19x1*
Sales	$60,000	$52,000
Cost of goods sold	41,000	37,000
Gross profits	$19,000	$15,000
Expenses	13,000	11,000
Net income before income taxes	$ 6,000	$ 4,000
Income tax expense	1,200	800
Net income	$ 4,800	$ 3,200

Perform a horizontal analysis of these income statements.

E14-2 Perform: (a) vertical analysis of Wyatt Corporation's income statement for 19x2, using the data in E14-1, and (b) calculate gross margin percentage for Wyatt Corp. in 19x2.

E14-3 Prepare a vertical analysis of North Corporation's balance sheet from these accounts:

	Debits	*Credits*
Cash	$ 16,000	
Accounts receivable	39,000	
Notes receivable	5,000	
Inventory	120,000	
Prepaid expenses	2,000	
Long-term investment	60,000	
Building	80,000	
Equipment	35,000	
Land	10,000	
Accounts payable		$ 29,000
Notes payable		40,000
Mortgage payable		40,000
Bonds payable		100,000
Common stock		100,000
Retained earnings		58,000
	$367,000	$367,000

E14-4 Below are accounts abstracted from Benson Corporation's balance sheet:

	Debits	*Credits*
Cash	$ 18,000	
Marketable securities	40,000	
Accounts receivable	37,000	
Inventory	88,000	
Plant and equipment	155,000	
Land	40,000	
Accounts payable		$ 33,000
Notes payable		21,000
Wages payable		9,000
Property taxes payable		8,000
Long-term bonds payable		100,000

Calculate:

a. Working capital.
b. Current ratio.
c. Acid-test ratio.

E14-5 Calculate the following ratios and give a preliminary interpretation of the results for Jones Corporation:

Ratio	*Industry Average*	*Jones*
(a) Profit margin on sales	5.8%	
(b) Rate of return on assets	5.2%	
(c) Rate of return on common stock equity	7.8%	

Financial data for Jones Corporation:	
Sales	$1,500,000
Net income	96,000
Total assets, current year-end	1,800,000
Total assets, last year-end	1,500,000
Common stockholders' equity, current year-end	1,000,000
Common stockholders' equity, last year-end	920,000

E14-6 The following data are abstracted from the financial statements of ABC, Inc. All sales in the industry in which this firm operates are made on trade terms n/30.

Net sales	$18,000,000
Current year-end net accounts receivable	1,480,000
Previous year-end net accounts receivable	1,260,000

Required:

a. Calculate receivable turnover and the average collection period.
b. What conclusions can be drawn about the liquidity of these receivables and the firm's credit and collection policies if the industry average collection period is twenty-eight days?

E14-7 Smith Company reports the following data with respect to inventory:

Sales	$290,000
Cost of sales	160,000
Year-end inventory balance	60,000
Previous year-end inventory balance	48,000

Required:

a. Calculate inventory turnover and average industry turnover in days.
b. How would you interpret these data?

E14-8 From the data given below: (a) calculate two leverage ratios, and (b) determine the margin of safety for creditors and the ability of the firm to withstand adverse business conditions:

Total liabilities	$6,300.000
Total stockholders' equity	4,600,000
Net income	400,000
Interest expense	380,000
Income tax expense	140,000

E14-9 Below are given some financial data for Apex Company:

Total assets	$1,500,000
Income taxes	60,000
Sales	1,800,000
Interest expense	15,000
Common stockholders' equity	600,000
Preferred dividends	30,000
Net income before income taxes	150,000

Required:

a. Calculate rate of return on total assets.
b. Calculate rate of return on common stock equity.
c. Calculate rate of return on sales.
d. What generalizations can be drawn from your rate of return calculations, if any?

E14-10 Consider the following income statement data from Chairs, Inc.

	Last Year	*This Year*
Sales	$880,000	$1,560,000
Cost of goods sold	660,000	770,000
Selling expenses	79,200	83,600
General expenses	33,000	35,200
Income taxes	52,800	79,200

Required:

a. Prepare common-size income statement for each year.
b. Prepare a comparative income statement.
c. Evaluate these statements.

E14-11 Prepare a horizontal analysis of both absolute and relative changes from the comparative income statements shown below:

AAA Corporation
Comparative Income Statements
For the Years Ended December 31, 19x3 and 19x4

	Year Ended December 31	
	19x4	*19x3*
Sales	$226,000	$219,000
Sales returns and allowances	9,000	6,000
Net sales	$217,000	$213,000
Cost of goods sold	119,000	106,000
Gross profit	$ 98,000	$107,000
Operating expenses:		
Selling expenses	$ 37,000	$ 33,000
General administrative expenses	46,000	42,000
Interest expense	9,000	1,000
Total expenses	$ 92,000	$ 76,000
Net income before income taxes	$ 6,000	$ 31,000
Income taxes	3,000	15,000
Net income	$ 3,000	$ 16,000

E14-12 Prepare a common-size analysis of the comparative income statements shown in E14-11. What insights are provided by this analysis into the firm's problems?

E14-13 Calculate the following ratios from the financial data given below for Webster Corporation:

a. Current ratio.
b. Acid-test ratio.
c. Inventory turnover.
d. Debt to assets.
e. Times interest earned.

Income Statement
For the Year Ended December 31, 19x5

Sales		$290,000
Cost of goods sold:		
Inventory—		
January 1, 19x5	$ 30,000	
Purchases	188,000	
Goods available for sale	$218,000	
Inventory—		
December 31, 19x5	21,000	
Cost of goods sold		197,000
Gross margin on sales		$ 93,000
Operating expenses	$ 57,000	
Interest expense	3,000	
Total expenses		60,000
Net income before income taxes		$ 33,000
Income tax expense		16,000
Net income		$ 17,000

Balance Sheet
December 31, 19x5

Assets	
Cash	$ 4,700
Accounts receivable—net	20,000
Inventory	21,000
Prepaid expenses	1,000
Property, plant and equipment	160,000
Accumulated depreciation	(40,000)
Total assets	$166,700
Equities	
Accounts payable	$ 18,000
Notes payable—due in 10 years	40,000
Common stock—no par	60,000
Retained earnings	48,700
Total equities	$166,700

E14-14 On January 1, 19x6, the River Company's beginning inventory was $400,000. During 19x6, River purchases $1,900,000 of additional inventory. On December 31, 19x6, River's ending inventory was $500,000. What is the inventory turnover for 19x6.

PROBLEMS

P14-1 Given the financial data below, reconstruct the balance sheet and income statement for AAA, Inc. by using ratio formulas to solve for unknowns:

Balance Sheet
December 31, 19x0

Assets	
Current assets:	
Cash	$ 12,000
Accounts receivable—net	?
Marketable securities	28,000
Inventories	?
Total current assets	$?
Long-lived assets:	
Plant and equipment—net	$?
Total assets	$?
Equities	
Current liabilities	$?
Long-term liabilities:	
Bonds payable at 10%	$?
Stockholders' equity:	
Common stock	$240,000
Retained earnings	460,000
Total stockholders' equity	$700,000
Total equities	$?

Income Statement
For the Year Ended December 31, 19x0

Sales—net	$?
Cost of goods sold	?
Gross margin	$560,000
Operating expenses	?
Operating income	$?
Other expenses:	
Interest expense	?
Net income before taxes	?
Income taxes—50%	$112,000
Net income	$?

Other financial data for the year 19x0 include the following:

1. Total debt to common equity was 50 percent.
2. Average number of days to collect accounts receivable was 45 (based on a 360-day year). Beginning accounts receivable balance was $200,000.
3. Inventory turnover was four times during the year. Beginning inventory balance was $120,000.
4. Gross margin was 35 percent of net sales.
5. Times interest earned was 15.
6. Acid-test ratio was 1.60.
7. Operating expenses were 20 percent of sales.

P14-2 The following are the financial statements of the E-Z Company:

Comparative Balance Sheets
December 31, 19x1 and 19x0

	19x1	19x0
Assets		
Current assets:		
Cash	$ 8,000	$ 11,920
Marketable securities	120,000	56,000
Accounts receivable	80,000	64,000
Inventory	160,000	120,000
Total current assets	$368,000	$251,920
Long-term assets:		
Plant and equipment	$320,000	$320,000
Accumulated depreciation	240,000	224,000
Net total long-term assets	$ 80,000	$ 96,000
Total assets	$448,000	$347,920
Equities		
Current liabilities:		
Accounts payable	$120,000	$ 64,000
Taxes payable	40,000	24,000
Total current liabilities	$160,000	$ 88,000
Long-term liabilities:		
Bonds payable—6% interest	$ 80,000	$ 80,000
Stockholders' equity:		
Preferred stock—5% dividend rate	$ 40,000	$ 40,000
Common stock—10,000 shares	80,000	80,000
Capital in excess of par	16,000	16,000
Retained earnings	72,000	43,920
Total stockholders' equity	$208,000	$179,920
Total equities	$448,000	$347,920

Income Statement
For the Year Ended December 31, 19x1

Sales	$648,000
Cost of goods sold	420,000
Gross margin	$228,000
Operating expenses	146,400
Net operating income	$ 81,600
Other expenses:	
Interest expense	4,800
Net income before income taxes	$ 76,800
Income taxes	30,720
Net income	$ 46,080

Required:

a. Calculate the following ratios for the year 19x1:

1. Current ratio.
2. Acid-test ratio.
3. Accounts receivable turnover.
4. Average collection period (assume a 360-day year).
5. Inventory turnover.
6. Number of times interest earned.
7. Earnings per share (common stock).
8. Rate of return on common stockholders' equity.
9. Rate of return on total assets.
10. Total debt to total assets.

b. From the information supplied in (a) above, write out your comments about the condition of the company for the year 19x1.

P14-3 The 19x0 income statement data for two electronics companies, Transistor, Inc. and Computer Company shown below:

Income Statement
For the Year 19x0

	Transistor, Inc.	*Computer Company*
Sales and other income	$294,474	$393,482
Cost of sales	$273,260	$380,870
Pension contributions	2,245	2,956
Depreciation	4,546	2,558
Interest expense	154	469
Miscellaneous taxes	1,195	1,605
Income taxes	6,192	2,214
Miscellaneous expenses	192	0
Total expenses	$287,784	$390,672
Net income	$ 6,690	$ 2,810

Required:

Prepare common-size income statements for the two companies and comment on the results. If Transistor, Inc., used LIFO in valuing inventories and Computer Company used FIFO, what effect, if any, could this have on the reported net income of the two companies.

P14-4 Information selected from the Center Supply Company's financial statements for the current year and the preceding year is presented below:

	Current Year	*Last Year*
Sales—net	$600,000	$375,000
Cost of goods sold	360,000	277,500
Bond interest expense	11,250	11,250
Federal income taxes	13,500	9,000
Net income after taxes	30,000	22,500
Accounts receivable—December 31	67,500	56,250
Merchandise inventory	150,000	90,000
Common stockholders' equity	240,000	225,000
Total assets	450,000	337,500

Required:

Calculate the following ratios for the current year:

a. Inventory turnover.
b. Number of times interest earned.
c. Average collection period.
d. Return on sales.
e. Return on assets.
f. Return on common stockholders' equity.

P14-5 XYZ Company had $300,000 of current assets, a 2 to 1 current ratio, and a 1.5:1 acid-test ratio. The following transactions then took place:

1. Two thousand dollars accounts receivable collected.
2. Sold marketable securities for $34,000 that cost the company $30,000.
3. Allowance for bad debts increased $1,000.
4. Fifteen cents per share cash dividend was declared on 90,000 shares of outstanding common stock, valued at $10 par.
5. The cash dividend was paid.
6. Fifteen thousand dollars was borrowed from a bank for ninety days at 9.5 percent interest.
7. A stock dividend was declared that required 4,500 additional shares to be distributed. Market value of the stock was $14 per share on the declaration date.
8. Merchandise was purchased for $15,000 on credit, and the company uses a perpetual inventory system.

Required:

Prepare a schedule that shows the XYZ Company's current ratio and acid-test ratio after all of the above transactions.

P14-6 Comparative income statements for Boot Company are shown below:

	19x4	19x3
Sales	$945,000	$827,000
Cost of goods sold	650,000	557,000
Gross profit	295,000	270,000
Operating expenses:		
General administrative	48,000	43,000
Selling expense	82,000	77,000
Depreciation	80,000	84,000
Net income from operations	$ 85,000	$ 66,000
Other income	400	250
Net income before income tax	$ 85,400	$ 66.250
Income tax expense	42,700	33,125
Net income	$ 42,700	$ 33,125

Required:

a. Perform horizontal analysis on these income statements. What general conclusions could you gather from a horizontal analysis if you were provided with industry data?
b. Perform vertical analysis on the data provided. What conclusions could you draw from a vertical analysis, given that you had industry data?

P14-7 The BBB Company's comparative income statements for 19x7 and 19x8 are shown below:

	Year Ended December 31	
	19x8	19x7
Sales—net	$8,950	$6,410
Cost of goods sold	4,150	2,500
Gross margin on sales	$4,800	$3,910
Operating expenses:		
Selling expense	950	840
Administrative expenses	2,900	2,600
Total operating expenses	$3,850	$3,440
Net income	$ 950	$ 470

Industry data gathered by a trade association indicate that cost of goods sold averaged 40 percent of sales, selling expenses averaged 18 percent of sales, and administrative expenses averaged 25 percent of sales during this period.

Required:

a. Perform a comparative vertical analysis on these data, similar to that shown in Illustration 3.
b. Using the industry data shown, what observations would you make about the operations of this firm?

P14-8 Comparative income statements for the Evans Company are shown below:

	Year Ended December 31	
	19x8	19x7
Sales	$600,000	$500,000
Sales discounts	11,000	8,500
Net sales	$589,000	$491,500
Cost of goods sold	395,000	268,000
Gross margin on sales	$194,000	$223,500
Operating expenses:		
Selling expense	$ 62,000	$ 55,000
Administrative expenses	88,000	81,000
Total operating expenses	$150,000	$136,000
Net income	$ 44,000	$ 87,500

Required:

a. Prepare a comparative analysis of both absolute and relative changes in the income statements for the Evans Company.
b. What conclusions would you draw from this technique if you independently discovered that the costs of merchandise in this industry have risen, on average, 8 percent during this period? What other trends do you note?

P14-9 The Jenson Marine Company sells boats and accessories. Comparative financial statements for the firm for 19x8 and 19x9 are shown below:

Comparative Income Statements
For the Years Ended December 31, 19x8 and 19x9

	19x9	19x8
Sales	$1,130,000	$887,000
Cost of goods sold	640,000	501,000
Gross margin on sales	$ 490,000	$386,000
Operating expenses:		
Selling expenses	$ 180,000	$141,000
Administrative expenses	140,000	138,000
Interest expense	21,000	4,000
Total expenses	$ 341,000	$283,000
Net income before income taxes	149,000	103,000
Income tax expense	74,500	51,500
Net income	$ 74,500	$ 51,550
Earnings per share—1,000 shares common stock outstanding	$ 7.45	$ 5.15

Comparative Balance Sheets
December 31, 19x8 and 19x9

	19x9	19x8
Assets		
Cash	$ 22,000	$ 18,000
Accounts receivable—net	131,000	89,000
Notes receivable	28,000	3,000
Inventory	239,000	115,000
Prepaid expenses	9,000	10,000
Equipment	62,000	37,000
Accumulated depeciation	(16,000)	(12,000)
Total assets	$475,000	$260,000
Equities		
Liabilities:		
Accounts payable	$ 39,000	$ 14,000
Notes payable—short-term	215,000	65,000
Miscellaneous accrued expenses	3,000	2,500
Bonds payable (due in 10 years)	100,000	100,000
Total liabilities	$357,000	$181,500
Owners' equity:		
Common stock—1,000 shares, $10 par	$ 10,000	$ 10,000
Additional contributed capital, common stockholders	8,000	8,000
Preferred stock—500 shares, $10 par	5,000	5,000
Retained earnings	95,000	55,500
Total owners' equity	$118,000	$ 78,500
Total equities	$475,000	$260,000

Required:

a. Calculate the following ratios for 19x9:

1. Profit margin on sales.
2. Rate of return on assets.
3. Rate of return on common stock equity (a $.60 preferred cash dividend was paid this year).
4. Current ratio.
5. Acid-test ratio.
6. Accounts receivable turnover.
7. Inventory turnover.
8. Debt to total assets.
9. Times interest earned.

b. Compare your results with the following industry data for these ratios:

Profit margin on sales	7.1%
Rate of return on assets	19.7%
Rate of return on common stock equity	29.0%
Current ratio	3.1
Acid-test ratio	1.1
Accounts receivable turnover	12.0 times
Inventory turnover	4.8 times
Debt to total assets	48.0%
Times interest earned	14.3 times

c. If a client were considering an investment in this firm, how would you evaluate the potential risks and rewards associated with this firm?

Learning Objectives

Chapter 15 presents proper accounting for long-term investments in equity securities. Studying this chapter should enable you to:

1. Recognize income from long-term investments under the cost and equity methods.
2. Describe parent-subsidiary relationships.
3. Prepare a worksheet to help consolidate financial statements for parent and subsidiary corporations.
4. Construct consolidated financial statements.

15

Long-Term Equity Investments and Consolidations

INTRODUCTION

In Chapter 9 we introduced accounting for long-term investments in the capital stock of another company. The nature and extent of the financial relationship between two organizations can vary depending on the amount of stock that is owned. Alternatives are available so that the accountant can provide the most relevant information about an investment, consistent with ecomomic reality.

This chapter discusses the cost and equity methods of accounting for long-term investments, principles of business combination and consolidated financial statements.

LONG-TERM STOCK INVESTMENTS

All long-term investments are recorded and valued at their cost on the date of aquisition. Acquisition cost includes all necessary costs to purchase the stock, including brokerage fees and transfer taxes. After acquisition, long-term investments in stock may be accounted for either under the cost method, the equity method, or consolidation.

The three methods do not represent alternatives that may be selected at the investor's option. Rather, they represent methods that must be applied in different economic situations. The primary factor in determining which method should be used is the extent of control or influence over the investee company. Current GAAP may be summarized as follows:

Method	*Conditions Where Applicable*
Cost	Investor has no significant influence—investor owns less than 20 percent of voting stock.
Equity	Investor has significant influence—investor owns 20 to 50 percent of voting stock.
Consolidation	Investor controls investee—investor owns more than 50 percent of the voting stock.

If the investor company does not have significant influence over the investee company, the cost method must be used. If significant influence exists, the equity method is required. To determine when significant influence exists, GAAP assumes that ownership of less than 20 percent of the voting does not result in significant influence and that ownership of 20 to 50 percent of the voting stock does provide significant influence. These percentages are operational guidelines, not hard rules. If a company owns less than 20 percent and can demonstrate that it does have significant influence over the investee, it should use the equity method. This may occur where the investee company's stock is widely held and no single stockholder, other than the investor company, holds a significant percent. Evidence of significant influence can be demonstrated through items such as membership on the board of directors.

Likewise, it is possible that an investor holding more than 20 percent of the stock may not have significant influence and thus, should use the cost method. For example, assume the investor owed 40 percent of the voting stock and one individual, who does not like the investor, owns the remaining 60 percent. In this case, the investor is not likely to have significant influence over the operations of the investee company. The controlling factor is the existence of significant influence.

In cases where the investee owns more than 50 percent of the voting stock, control exists and the investee company should be consolidated. Sometimes an investor may own a majority of the stock but still not have control. For example, if the investee company was in bankruptcy, the courts would control the company. In this situation, the investor company would use the cost method since no control or significant influence would exist.

The *cost method* treats both the investor and investee as separate, distinct entities. The investing company records its acquisition at cost and, as discussed in Chapter 9, values the account on a lower of aggregate cost or market basis. Profits or losses by the investee firm are not reflected in the investor's accounts.

Operations can lead to dividend payments by the investee. In these cases, the owner will recognize dividend income by increasing cash and an appropriate revenue account. For example, if a dividend $1,000 was received, the investor would make the following entry:

Cash	$1,000	
Dividend revenue		$1,000

At the time of sale, any gain or loss from the original cost would be recognized.

The *equity method* assumes a significant economic relationship between the investor and investee. This relationship justifies adjustments to the investment account reflecting net changes in the investee's assets. While initially recorded at cost, the equity method permits the investor to record its proportionate share of changes in the net assets (assets less liabilities) of the investee. Net assets of the investee increase as it earns income, and decrease as it incurs losses or pays dividends. Thus, the investor's account, investment in common stock of X Company, will be adjusted upwards and downwards to reflect events associated with changes in the investee's equity.

Cost and Equity Compared

The mechanics and differences involved in each method can best be illustrated by a comparative example. Assume that Able Company purchased 1,000 of the 4,000 outstanding shares of Baker Company stock for $15,000. The acquisition and subsequent events are shown in Illustration 1. All entries are as they would be made in the books of Able Company.

The acquisition of Baker Company Stock is recorded in the same manner under both the cost and the equity methods. Historical cost is used to record the acquisition.

The report of an operating loss by Baker will lead to no entry if the cost method is used. However, the equity method takes account of the loss. The investment account is reduced and a loss is recognized for the extent of Able's ownership of Baker (1,000 ÷ 4,000 × $2,000). If financial statements were prepared at this time, the investment would be valued at $15,000 under the cost method and $14,500 under the equity method.

Profits are also not recognized under the cost method. In 19x2, the equity method does provide for a proportionate share of net income to be recorded by Able Company (1,000 ÷ 4,000 × $6,000). At this point in time, a balance sheet would disclose an investment in Baker valued at $15,000 under the cost method and $16,000 under the equity method. An income statement for this period would include $1,500 of investment income if the equity method was used.

The payment of a dividend is recognized by increasing cash under each method. The cost method leads to the realization of an equal amount of revenue. Under the equity method, income equal to the earnings of the firm was already recognized. Receipt of a dividend indicates a distribution of some of these earnings by Baker. Therefore, the investment account is reduced.

The entry to record the sale of the investment in Baker Company depends on the investment carrying value. Under the cost method, the cash received exceeds the carrying value, leading to the recognition of a gain. The invest-

Illustration 1

Able Company and Baker Company

Comparison of Cost and Equity Methods

Event	Cost Method			Equity Method		
Able buys 1,000 shares of Baker for $15,000	Investment in Baker	$15,000		Investment in Baker	$15,000	
	Cash		$15,000	Cash		$15,000
Baker reports loss of $2,000 for the period 19x1.	No entry			Loss from investment	500	
				Investment in Baker		500
Baker reports income of $6,000 for the period 19x2	No entry			Investment in Baker	1,500	
				Investment income		1,500
Baker pays dividend of $1,600; Able receives $400 as its share.	Cash	400		Cash	400	
	Dividend revenue		400	Investment in Baker		400
Able sells its investment in Baker for $15,500.	Cash	15,500		Cash	15,500	
	Investment in Baker		15,000	Loss on sale	100	
	Gain on sale		500	Investment in Baker		15,600

ment carrying value under the equity method responded to income and dividends. Since the investment was valued at more than the cash received, a loss is recognized.

Over the total life of this investment, both the cost and equity methods provide for recording the same net results. Differences in the timing of recognition account for the major contrast between them.

OWNERSHIP AND CONSOLIDATION

When more than 50 percent of the outstanding capital stock of a company is acquired by one stockholder, a controlling interest is created: the controlling stockholder can elect a majority of the acquired company's directors. When the controlling interest is held by another corporation, the investing company is called a *parent* and the acquired company is known as a *subsidiary*. Since the stockholders of the parent own the parent, which in turn owns the subsidiary, the stockholders of the parent have an indirect ownership interest in the subsidiary. That is the parent and the subsidiary can be viewed by the parent's stockholders as a single entity. *Consolidated financial statements* report on the financial position and results of operations of a parent and subsidiary. Consolidation involves the combination of like data obtained from the separate financial statements for the parent and subsidiary. For example, combining the cash balances for the parent and subsidiary produces the consolidated cash balance. Consolidated reporting provides readers with a concise summary of the activities and balances for a group of related, but separate, legal entities.

The following sections describe the construction of consolidated financial statements and focus on the related problems of measurement and interpretation. Three events related to consolidation will be considered: creation of a parent-subsidiary relationship, recognition of earnings of the subsidiary, and reporting to the public.

CREATING A PARENT-SUBSIDIARY RELATIONSHIP

A parent-subsidiary relationship may be created whenever one corporation either: (1) acquires more than 50 percent of the outstanding voting stock of an existing corporation, or (2) transfers some assets to a newly organized subsidiary in exchange for a controlling interest in the subsidiary. Both approaches for creating a parent-subsidiary relationship are extremely common. Accounting for parent-subsidiary relationships is relatively complex, since the underlying business transactions themselves are very complex. To simplify the issues, we first discuss only 100 percent owned subsidiaries in this section and deal with partially held controlling interests in a later section. Three cases of 100 percent owned subsidiaries are given in order of complexity. In the first, case the parent gains control by transferring some of its assets to a wholly owned subsidiary. In the second case, the parent acquires all of the subsidiary's stock in exchange for its own common stock and records the investment at the book value of the subsidiary's net assets. In the third case, the parent purchases the subsidiary's stock or assets and values the investment at the market value of consideration given in the exchange.

Transfer of Assets

A parent corporation may create a subsidiary by transferring some of its assets to a newly organized legal entity controlled by the parent. For example, the Major Corporation wishes to create a new subsidiary that will be called the Minor Corporation. Legal counsel for Major obtains a corporate charter for Minor from the secretary of the state of incorporation. The charter specifies that Minor is authorized to issue up to 1,000,000 shares of $10 par common stock. Major then exchanges one-quarter of its cash, accounts receivable, and current liabilities for common stock in Minor. The balance sheets for Major and Minor corporations, both before and after the reorganization, are reflected in Illustration 2.

Major Corporation transfers net assets valued at $45,000 to Minor Corporation 4,500 shares of $10 par (Minor) common stock. This transaction is reflected in Major's journal by the following entry:

Illustration 2
Major Corporation
Before and After Reorganization

	Before Reorganization	*After Reorganization*	
	Major Corp.	*Major Corp.*	*Minor Corp.*
Cash	$ 80,000	$ 60,000	$20,000
Accounts receivable	200,000	150,000	50,000
Plant and equipment	700,000	700,000	0
Investment in subsidiary	0	45,000	0
Total assets	$980,000	$955,000	$70,000
Current liabilities	$100,000	$ 75,000	$25,000
Long-term liabilities	500,000	500,000	0
Common stock—$10 par	55,000	55,000	45,000
Additional paid-in capital	130,000	130,000	0
Retained earnings	195,000	195,000	0
Total liabilities and capital	$980,000	$955,000	$70,000

Investment in Subsidiary	$45,000	
Current liabilities	25,000	
Cash		$20,000
Accounts receivable		50,000

The investment account has a value equal to the net asset value of accounts transferred to Minor Corporation. The 4,500 shares of Minor Corporation common stock provide evidence to support the existence of the investment account. Except for the four accounts affected by the journal entry listed above, the remaining accounts in Major's ledger are totally unaffected by the transaction. For example, the retained earnings account, after reorganization, reflects the same $195,000 balance recognized before the reorganization.

Minor Corporation would record the organization transaction in its journal as follows:

Cash	$20,000	
Accounts receivable	50,000	
Current liabilities		$25,000
Capital stock		45,000

The capital stock account is credited at par: in this case, 4,500 shares of the $10 par stock is valued at $45,000. Illustration 2 presents a balance sheet for the Minor Corporation that reflects this journal entry.

For any number of valid business reasons, management may issue common stock at some dollar value above par. For example, management might attribute a value of $15 per share for Minor common stock used in the reorganization. At this "price," only 3,000 shares are needed to equal the $45,000 net asset value. A journal entry to record the reorganization transaction on Minor Corporation's books at $15 per share is as follows:

Cash	$20,000	
Accounts receivable	50,000	
Current liabilities		$25,000
Common stock—par		30,000
Additional paid-in capital		15,000

Common stock is recorded at par, while additional paid-in capital reflects the remainder (in this case, $5 per share for 3,000 shares). See Chapter 12 for further discussion of accounting for the issuance of common stock.

The example described in Illustration 2 is ideal for comparing consolidated and unconsolidated balance sheets. Stockholders of Major Corporation are interested in the economic reality of the total business entity without regard to internal organizational (and legal) structure; therefore, they would prefer the "before reorganization" balance sheet. A consolidated balance sheet would appear exactly as shown in the "before adjustment" column. To produce a consolidated balance sheet, the accountant would start with balance sheets prepared for the parent and all subsidiaries. Those balances that reflect unique information would then be added together. Thus, the consolidated cash of $80,000 would be determined by adding together the cash of Major and Minor corporations ($6,000 + $20,000). *Reciprocal accounts* would be ignored in consolidation since one account reflects a debit balance for the same amount as the other account reflects a credit balance. For example, the investment in subsidiary account (debit) and the common stock of Minor (credit) both refer to 4,500 shares of Minor common stock par value $10. Neither of these $45,000 balances would be reflected in the consolidated balance sheet since they offset each other.

In contrast, an unconsolidated balance sheet is reflected in the middle column of Illustration 2, "Major Corp after reorganization." The balance associated with the account, "investment in subsidiary," clearly indicates that the accounts of the subsidiary have not been combined with those of the parent. An unconsolidated balance sheet would interest the creditors of Major Corporation: those creditors associated with the $75,000 current liabilities only have recourse against the assets of Major Corporation and have no claim against the assets of Minor Corporation. (Remember, the corporate form of organization is recognized by the courts as having limited legal liability.) All of the asset and liability accounts of the subsidiary are summarized in the investment account in unconsolidated parent-company balance sheets.

Stock-for-Stock Exchange

Some parent-subsidiary relationships are created when a parent acquires all of the capital stock of a subsidiary in exchange for its own capital stock. This form of business combination is commonly known as a *pooling of interests*. A business combination resulting from a pooling if interests is viewed by the accounting profession as a modification in existing reporting entities rather than as an accounting transaction requiring revaluation of assets and liabilities. Financial statements after a pooling of interests will maintain the same book values for assets and liabilities for the entities as existed before the business combination.

A pooling of interests may best be described with reference to an example. Part A of Illustration 3 presents summarized balance sheets for two companies: Pater, Inc. and Sunco. Although the common stock of both companies has a $10 par value, no single stockholder owns stock in both companies. Managers for both companies agree on a pooling of interests in which Sunco stockholders will receive one newly issued Pater share for each Sunco share they hold. The stockholders of both companies agree to the plan and the stock-for-stock exchange occurs.

Assuming that Sunco operations will be merged into those of Pater, Inc. and that Sunco will cease operating as a separate legal entity, the following entry will be recorded in Pater's journal to reflect the pooling of interests:

Illustration 3
Pater, Inc. and Sunco
Before and After Pooling of Interests
Balance Sheets
(Assuming Merged Operations)

	Part A *Before Pooling*		*Part B* *After Pooling*
	Pater, Inc.	*Sunco*	*Pater, Inc*
Assets	$700,000	$200,000	$900,000
Liabilities	$400,000	$ 50,000	$450,000
Capital stock—$10 par	100,000	25,000	125,000
Additional paid-in capital	35,000	110,000	145,000
Retained earnings	165,000	15,000	180,000
Total liabilities and equities	$700,000	$200,000	$900,000

Assets	$200,000	
Liabilities		$ 50,000
Capital stock—par		25,000
Additional paid-in capital		110,000
Retained earnings		15,000

The first two lines of the journal entry carry over to Pater's books the balances that had been recorded in Sunco's individual asset and liability accounts. Obviously, if Sunco had hundreds of such accounts, the journal entry would be quite extensive. The last line of the journal entry carries forward to Pater (the surviving entity) all of the accumulated Sunco retained earnings: in effect, this is a retroactive recognition of Sunco's prior earnings history. The capital stock credit reflects the par value of new Pater stock issued to the old Sunco stockholders. Since this pooling of interests involved a one-for-one exchange of shares with identical par values, the equity accounts after the pooling represent the sum of the prepooling balances for both Pater and Sunco. Thus, the equity accounts were summed because of the nature of the exchange and the equality of par values. Part B of Illustration 3 presents a postpooling balance sheet for Pater, Inc. In contrast to the previous example, if it is assumed that Sunco would continue to operate as a separate legal entity after the pooling of interest, the Pater journal entry, to record the pooling, appears as follows:

Investment in Subsidiary	$150,000	
Capital stock—par		$ 25,000
Additional paid-in capital..............		110,000
Retained earnings		15,000

The investment in Subsidiary account receives a balance equal to the net assets carried on Sunco's books. After the exchange of stock, all of the outstanding Sunco shares would be held by Pater and would serve as evidence to support the investment account. No journal entry would be required by Sunco, since the exchange of stock occurred between the shareholders of Sunco and Pater, Inc. Postpooling balance sheets for Pater, Inc. and Sunco are displayed in Part A of Illustration 4. Part B of Illustration 4 presents a consolidated statement, which would be most meaningful to stockholders, since all stockholders hold Pater, Inc. stock. Notice that the consolidated balances reflect the sum of all accounts for both companies, except the $150,000 investment in Subsidiary account of Pater and the three equity accounts of Sunco, which total $150,000, are eliminated as shown in the accounts eliminated column. This elimination prevents double-counting of assets and equity. (Also note that Part B of Illustrations 3 and 4 contain identical balances: the former balance sheet reflects the actual combination of Pater and Sunco, while the latter reflects the consolidation of the two.)

Illustration 4
Pater, Inc. and Sunco
After Pooling of Interests
Balance Sheets
Unconsolidated and Consolidated
(assuming separate operations)

	Part A Unconsolidated		*Accounts Eliminated*		*Part B Consolidated*
	Pater, Inc.	*Sunco*	*Debit*	*Credit*	*Pater, Inc.*
Investment......................	$150,000	$ 0		$150,000	$ 0
Assets	700,000	200,000			900,000
Total assets....................	$850,000	$200,000			$900,000
Liabilities......................	$400,000	$ 50,000			$450,000
Capital stock—10 par	125,000	25,000	$ 25,000		125,000
Additional paid-in capital	145,000	110,000	110,000		145,000
Retained earnings	180,000	15,000	15,000		180,000
	$850,000	$200,000			$900,000

Whenever the par value of stock given by the parent differs from the par value of stock received from stockholders of the subsidiary, the equity accounts after a pooling of interests will not be identical to the sum of the separate equity accounts of the parent and subsidiary. Full discussion of this point is well beyond the scope of this book. Interested readers are directed to any standard advanced accounting textbook.

Purchase Transactions

A parent-subsidiary relationship can be created whenever a parent purchases the stock or assets of a subsidiary. Stock would be acquired from the subsidiary's stockholders, while assets would be acquired directly from the subsidiary.

As compensation for its acquired investment, the parent may distribute cash, marketable debt securities (bonds), or newly issued common stock. In any event, the market value of compensation given in the purchase of a subsidiary determines the value of the investment. Obviously, the investment account is most easily valued when a parent makes a cash purchase. It is less easily valued when the parent acquires the subsidiary for its own common stock, since stock values tend to change on a day-to-day basis. Most often, the managers of the parent and subsidiary agree on a method for valuing the stock, such as a one-month average of the daily closing prices. Once the method is agreed on, the valuation itself is relatively easy.

For example, the Gramp Company acquires all of the assets of the Junior Company for $4,675,000 in cash. The purchase would be recorded in Gramp's journal by the following entry:

Investment in Subsidiary.................	$4,675,000	
Cash		$4,675,000

If Gramp issued new common stock having a market value $4,675,000 to acquire Junior's assets, the specific journal entry used would depend on the market price per share, par value per share, and the number of shares issued. If the market price per share was $50, par value was $20, and 93,500 shares were issued, Gramp's journal would reflect the following entry:

Investment in Subsidiary.................	$4,675,000	
Common stock—par		$1,870,000
Additional paid-in capital		2,805,000

Several comments should be made about these journal entries used to record the purchase of Junior by Gramp. First the investment in subsidiary account is always valued at the market value of consideration that is given to consummate the purchase. Second, the common stock account always reflects the par value of securities issued, and the additional paid-in capital account reflects the difference between par value and market value: the retained earnings account is never credited as part of a purchase transaction. Third, the acquisition journal entry is not affected by the means in which the parent gains control over the subsidiary; an acquisition of assets or of subsidiary common stock would be recorded with journal entries. Finally, it is highly unlikely that the value attributed to the investment in subsidiary account is equal to the values of the underlying subsidiary net assets. Further elaboration of this final point appears in the following section.

A parent can acquire a subsidiary in exchange for newly issued parent company stock. The market price of parent company stock is determined by many factors, including the parent's earnings, dividends, and financial leverage (associated with liquidity and solvency risks). In addition, interest rates, inflation, economy growth, and other enviromental factors also affect the price of common stock. In other words, much of the day-to-day change in the price of the parent's stock are associated with elements beyond the control of the parent.

At the same time, the individual assets and liabilities of the subsidiary reflect historical cost altered by accounting adjustments. For example, inventories are reflected at LIFO, FIFO, and/or lower of cost or market adjustments. Net plant and equipment valuations reflect estimated project lives and alternative depreciation methods. Few of the assets or liabilities reflect changed market conditions, such as inflation or supply/demand factors associated with current replacement costs or disposal values. The accounting convention of "conservatism" generally tends to understate asset market values.

Additionally, accountants face the problem of valuing the total package consisting of the subsidiary's separate assets and liabilities. For many elements of the package, the total value is not equal to the sum of the values of the separate parts. For example, the value of a fleet of cars is not the same as the sum of the value of the individual cars; the value of the individual parts of an automobile are not equal to the value of the automobile. Even if the accountant could determine the value of the subsidiary's individual assets, the sum of these probably would not equal the total value of the subsidiary.

Excess Cost Over Net Book Value

Whenever the acquisition price for a subsidiary is larger than the market value of the subsidiary's net assets, goodwill may be recognized when the transaction is recorded as a purchase. Accountants presume that a difference between the price and book value indicates that the individual acquired assets are undervalued and/or that some positive goodwill is associated with the subsidiary. Goodwill is an intangible asset that is recognized under the account name *goodwill*. For example, if Parent Company acquires a 100 percent interest in Sub Corp. for $100,000 when the net assets of Sub are appraised to only $80,000, the transaction may be journalized as follows:

Investment in subsidiary	$100,000	
Cash		$100,000

Goodwill will be separated and recognized in the consolidated statements.

This excess cost over net book value may reflect the fact that the parent has acquired two elements in one package, the net assets of the subsidiary and an additional intangible asset that had not been previously recognized on the subsidiary's book. Generally accepted accounting procedures require that the excess cost over net book value must first be assigned to specific undervalued assets of the acquired subsidiary (to revalue them at their current purchase value). That is, the excess cost is used to correct any undervaluation that may appear on the subsidiary's book. The remaining excess will be labeled goodwill. Goodwill is amortized by systematic charges against income for a period not to exceed forty years. Revaluation of acquired assets and recognition of goodwill occur as part of the consolidation process, a subject discussed in the following section. That is, these two types of accounting events may not be reflected in the subsidiary's records.

Consolidation of a Purchased Subsidiary

Consolidation of a purchased subsidiary is best described with reference to a specific case. For example, the Parent Company acquires (from Subsidiary's stockholders) all of the outstanding common stock of Subsidiary, Inc. for $200,000. Immediately preceding the acquisition, the financial position of each company appeared as follows:

	Parent	Subsidiary
Current assets	$230,000	$ 15,000
Plant and equipment	200,000	95,000
Total	$430,000	$110,000
Current liabilities	$ 5,000	$ 10,000
Common stock	130,000	20,000
Additional paid-in capital	120,000	5,000
Retained earnings	175,000	75,000
Total	$430,000	$110,000

Parent's journal would reflect the following entry to record the acquisition transaction:

Investment in Subsidiary	$200,000	
Cash		$200,000

This $200,000 acquisition price is $100,000 larger than the net assets recognized on Subsidiary's books. For the sake of this illustration, assume that the excess $100,000 is attributable to a $65,000 undervaluation of plant and equipment and the remaining $35,000 is associated with goodwill. In other words, the account, investment in Subsidiary, reflects a whole host of factors.

Balance sheets for the Parent Company, Subsidiary, Inc., and the Consolidated Entity are presented in Illustration 5. Note that the entry to eliminate the investment and the sub's equity accounts also adjusts the plant and equipment for a $65,000 increase and records goodwill of $35,000. These

Illustration 5
Parent Company, Subsidiary, Inc. and Consolidated Entity
Consolidation of a Purchased Subsidiary
Balance Sheets
(immediately after the acquisition)

	Parent Company	Subsidiary Inc.	Accounts Eliminated or Adjusted: Debit	Accounts Eliminated or Adjusted: Credit	Consolidated Entity
Current assets	$ 30,000	$ 15,000			$ 45,000
Plant and equipment	200,000	95,000	$65,000		360,000
Goodwill	0	0	35,000		35,000
Investment in Subsidiary	200,000	0		$200,000	0
Total assets	$430,000	$110,000			$440,000
Liabilities	$ 5,000	$ 10,000			$ 15,000
Common stock	130,000	20,000	20,000		130,000
Additional paid-in capital	120,000	5,000	5,000		120,000
Retained earnings	175,000	75,000	75,000		175,000
	$430,000	$110,000			$440,000

eliminations and adjustment are then reflected in the Consolidated Entity column.

The consolidated balances of current assets and liabilities are determined by adding the separate Parent and Subsidiary balances. Half of the investment in Subsidiary balance, $100,000, relates to (and offsets) the three Subsidiary equity accounts. The remaining $100,000 in the investment in Subsidiary account is allocated to plant and equipment, and goodwill. Thus, consolidated plant and equipment represents the sum of $200,000, $95,000, and $65,000. The consolidated equity accounts are identical to Parent's equity accounts since the owners of the parent are the direct and indirect owners of the consolidated entity,

The underlying events in this case were relatively simple; yet the consolidated balances are not intuitively obvious. Accountants often prepare worksheets to aid in the preparation of consolidated financial statements. The following section describes consolidation worksheets.

CONSOLIDATION WORKSHEETS

The accountant who prepares consolidated financial statements usually develops a worksheet to help determine the correct consolidated balances. First the year-end parent and subsidiary financial statements are entered in parallel columns, as shown in Illustration 6, columns P and S. The accountant then compiles information about the extent of intercompany activity and the methods used by the separate entities to record this activity. This additional information is used to prepare adjustment entries that eliminate intercompany balances, as shown in the middle set of columns in Illustration 6. These adjustment entries suppress balances associated with interfirm activities that do not involve transactions with independent parties outside of the consolidated group. The numbers across each row of the worksheet are then combined (giving proper recognition to debit and credit balances) to derive consolidated balances. The last column of Illustration 6 lists consolidated balances that will appear in the consolidated balance sheet.

The worksheet in Illustration 6 is keyed to the following explanations:

1. Scan the list accounts from top to bottom. The first account, which contains reciprocal balances, is notes receivable. S owes P $6,000. This balance is reflected in the S notes payable as well as in the P receivables but

Illustration 6
P and S
Consolidated Worksheet
December 31, 19x1

	Separate Balance Sheets		*Adjustments*		*Consolidated Balance Sheet*
	P	*S*	*Debit*	*Credit*	
Debits					
Cash	$ 2,200	$ 1,500			$ 3,700
Accounts receivable	9,800	7,600			17,400
Notes recievable	15,000	10,000		$ 6,000 (a)	19,000
Dividends receivable	8,000	0		8,000 (b)	0
Investment in bonds of P	0	9,800		9,800 (c)	0
Investment in stock of S	110,000	0		110,000 (d)	0
Inventory	50,000	25,000			75,000
Other assets	252,000	77,100			329,100
Total	$447,000	$131,000			$444,200
Credits					
Accounts payable	$ 23,000	$ 7,000			$ 30,000
Notes payable to P	0	6,000	$ 6,000 (a)		0
Dividends payable	0	8,000	8,000 (b)		0
Bonds payable	98,000	0	9,800 (c)		88,200
Capital stock	105,000	30,000	30,000 (d)		105,000
Additional paid-in capital	50,000	10,000	10,000 (d)		50,000
Retained earnings	171,000	70,000	70,000 (d)		171,000
Total	$447,000	$131,000			$444,200

affects no party outside the consolidated entity; the consolidated entity owes itself the $6,000. Since the final consolidated balance in both accounts is produced by the process of cross-footing, the workseet adjustment is as follows:

Notes payable	$6,000	
Notes receivable		$6,000

This entity eliminates the redundant reciprocal balances.

2. The dividend receivable account of P is directly related to the dividend payable account of S: the directors of S have declared, but have not yet paid, and $8,000 dividend. P owns all of the stock of S: it will be the sole recipient of the dividend. The intercompany dividend receivable and payable are offset by the following entry:

Dividends payable	$8,000	
Dividends receivable		$8,000

3. The investment in bonds of P account on the S books relates directly to the bonds payable account on the P books. An adjustment would remove all of the investment and a like dollar amount of the payable as follows:

Bonds payable	$8,800	
Investment in bonds		$9,800

If S had acquired its investment in bonds of P from third parties, the cost of the investment might well differ from the original issuance price. However, discussion of this additional complexity is beyond the scope of this text.

4. An adjustment to the investment in stock of S account offsets $110,000 against the equity accounts of S: capital stock, additional paid-in capital, and retained earnings. The entry to record the offset is:

Capital stock(s)	30,000	
Additional paid-in capital(s)	10,000	
Retained earnings(s)	70,000	
Investment in stock of S		110,000

Worksheets are not absolutely necessary; in simple cases where little intercompany activity has occurred, the accountant may prepare consolidated reports directly from the original separate company reports. However, there are several advantages in preparing worksheets for all consolidations. By preparing worksheets, accountants are forced to formalize their thinking and to explicitly state any necessary adjustments. Worksheets allow for a division of labor, so that more than one person may be engaged on the project. They also facilitate review of the consolidating work by others. Finally having a worksheet will help in next year's preparation, since it represents a model to be followed.

CONSOLIDATED INCOME STATEMENT

Consolidated income statements are prepared by combining balances for like accounts from the parent and all subsidiaries. The revenue account balances for all units would be accumulated to determine consolidated revenue. Similarly, the expense account balances would be accumulated to produce consolidated expense. However, consolidated balances would have to be adjusted to eliminate the double-counting effects of intercompany transactions. Two types of intercompany transactions are commonly found when preparing consolidated income statements: recognition by the Parent of subsidiary earnings and intercompany sales of goods or services.

Consolidation adjustments for reciprocal income statement transactions are best described with reference to an example. The S Company is a wholly owned subsidiary of the P Corporation. Income statements for both companies are presented in Part A of Illustration 7. The account, income from subsidiary—$20,000 (disclosed on the P income statement)—clearly indicates that P recognized income from the subsidiary under the equity method. This $20,000 balance should not be disclosed in the consolidated income statement since all of the separate revenue and expense items underlying the $20,000 will be reflected in the statement. That is, including this $20,000 would constitute double-counting. Therefore, the $20,000 is eliminated with the following entry:

Income from Subsidiary	$20,000	
Net income		$20,000

Additional information about the relationship between P and S might indicate that one unit sold goods or provided services to the other unit at a profit. For example, assume that S Company provided maintenance services to P Corporation. Actual costs to S Company of labor and supplies for these services amounted to $5,000, but S charged P $9,000 for these sevices. That is, the S revenue account reflects $9,000 while its expense account reflects $5,000. Since P acquired these services from S, the P expense account also reflects $9,000. From a consolidated entity point of view, total expense for maintenance should be $5,000 rather, than $14,000 ($5,000 + $9,000). Furthermore, revenue will be overstated by $9,000 if no adjustment is made for the intercompany service. The intercompany sale is eliminated as follows:

Revenue (S)	$9,000	
Expense (P)		$9,000

Part B of Illustration 7 presents a consolidation income statement worksheet. The accounts have been reordered so that all credit balance accounts appear together. The total of the debit balance accounts is set equal to the total credit balance by including a line item for net income. The two adjustments are reflected on the worksheet. Neither of these adjustments change the $48,000 net income that accrues to the benefit of the P stockholders.

Illustration 7
P Corporation and S Company
Separate Company Income Statements
and Consolidated Worksheet

Part A
Separate Company Statements
Period Ended December 31, 19x1

Income Statement	*P Corporation*	*S Company*
Sales revenue	$1,000,000	$500,000
Cost of sales	850,000	325,000
Gross profit	$ 150,000	$175,000
Expenses	(122,000)	(155,000)
Income from Subsidiary	20,000	0
Net profit	$ 48,000	$ 20,000

Part B
Consolidation Worksheet

	Separate Income Statements		*Adjustments*		*Consolidated Income Statement*
	P	*S*	*Debit*	*Credit*	
Revenue	$1,000,000	$500,000	$ 9,000 (a)		$1,491,000
Income from Subsidiary	20,000		20,000 (b)		
	$1,020,000	$500,000			
Cost of sales	$ 850,000	325,000			
Expenses	122,000	155,000		$ 9,000 (a)	(1,175,000)
Net income	48,000	20,000		20,000 (b)	(268,000)
Total	$1,020,000	$500,000			$ 48,000

After the adjustments, however, the consolidated revenue and expense accounts only reflect transactions that involved third parties: no intercompany transactions are reflected in the income statement.

Additional adjustments are required whenever intercompany sales of goods occur. These adjustments become quite complicated whenever some of these goods remain within the consolidated group at the end of the accounting period, that is, when they have not been sold to third parties. Additional complexities arise whenever a subsidiary involved in these intercompany transactions is not completely controlled by the parent, that is, when the parent owns less than 100 percent of the outstanding common stock of the subsidiary. Other than noting the existence of these adjustment problems, further discussion is well beyond the scope of this book, Interested readers are referred to any standard advanced accounting textbook.

REPORTING PARENT-SUBSIDIARY RELATIONSHIPS

Parent-subsidiary relationships can be reported to the public in a number of ways. First, consolidated financial statements may be prepared and issued. Second, financial statements might be prepared for each separate legal entity. Third, the parent might issue its own unconsolidated financial statement. Each of these alternatives has been persuasively defended (and also attacked) in the financial literature.

Consolidated reporting is the predominant mode in the United States. The American financial community presumes that consolidated financial statements are more meaningful than separate legal entity or unconsolidated parent company statements. Consolidation is necessary for fair presentation of operating results and the financial position for groups of entities organized in parent-subsidiary networks. The widespread acceptance of consolidated reporting amply demonstrates the usefulness of this form of financial reporting. Primary beneficiaries of consolidated reporting are the stockholders of the parent company.

Not all corporations within the parent-subsidiary relationships should be consolidated. To be considered for consolidation, the parent must currently control and plan to have continued control over the subsidiary management.

MINORITY INTERESTS

Whenever a parent acquires less than 100 percent ownership of a subsidiary, consolidated financial statements will reflect a subordinated ownership claim commonly labeled minority interest. *Minority interest* represents ownership rights in the subsidiary held by parties other than the parent. The dollar balance in minority interest is determined by multiplying the subsidiary's net assets by the percentage of stock held by minority stockholders.

For example, consider a case in which the parent acquires 90 percent of the outstanding stock of Subco for $900,000. Subco had net assets of $100,000 on the day of the acquisition, so no goodwill is associated with the acquisition. The parent would journalize the transaction in summary form as follow:

Investment in Subsidiary	$90,000	
Cash		$90,000

Immediately after recording the acquisition entry, balance sheets for the parent and Subco would appear as in the first two columns of the consolidation worksheet presented in Illustration 8.

The consolidation adjustment offsets the investment in Subsidiary balance of $90,000 against the equity accounts of Subco, common stock, additional paid-in capital, and retained earnings, for a total of $100,000. Ob-

Illustration 8
Consolidation Worksheet Disclosure of Minority Interest

	Parent Inc.	Subco	Debit	Credit	Consolidated Entity
Current assets	$ 50,000	$ 15,000			$ 65,000
Plant and equipment	200,000	95,000			295,000
Investment in Subsidiary	90,000	0		$90,000	0
Total	$340,000	$110,000			$360,000
Liabilities	$ 35,000	$ 10,000			$ 45,000
Common stock	40,000	20,000	$20,000		40,000
Additional paid-in capital	120,000	55,000	55,000		120,000
Retained earnings	145,000	25,000	25,000		145,000
Minority interest	0	0		10,000	10,000
Total	$340,000	$110,000			$360,000

viously, an additional credit of $10,000 is required to maintain the equality between debits and credits. The $10,000 credit is attributed to the account, minority interest. In retrospect, it can be seen that the original $100,000 net asset value of the subsidiary was claimed as $90,000 by the parent and $10,000 by the minority stockholders.

The account, minority interest, usually is disclosed on consolidated balance sheets between the liability and owners' equity section. In theory, minority interest is not a liability, since there is no legal obligation for the parent to ever pay the minority shareholders any amount at any known future date, for any services rendered.

SUMMARY

A controlling interest is acquired whenever more than 50 percent of the common stock of a corporation is acquired by one stockholder. Where the one stockholder is a corporation, parent-subsidiary relationship if created. From the viewpoint of the parent's stockholders, both the parent and the subsidiary can be viewed as a single economic entity. Consolidated financial reports do present the financial position and results of operations for parent-subsidiary relationships as if they represented a single economic entity.

Parent-subsidiary relationships can be created by having the parent transfer assets to a newly created subsidiary or by acquiring the controlling interest directly from the subsidiary's stockholders. Alternately, the parent might acquire a controlling interest by obtaining the assets of a subsidiary in exchange for cash, debt securities, or its own common stock. Acquired subsidiaries may result from the pooling of interests or a purchase transaction.

In a pooling, assets of the subsidiary are valued at existing book value and retained earnings of the subsidiary are carried forward to the surviving entity. Under the purchase method, the acquired assets are recorded at market value, while any additional excess of cost over book value is recognized as an intangible asset, goodwill. Goodwill must be amortized periodically in income over the period not to exceed forty years.

Consolidation is the process of aggregating parent and subsidiary account balances into a single set of asset, liability, owners' equity, revenue, and expense accounts. While combining accounts, care is taken to exclude reciprocal balances that only relate to activities or relationships within the parent-subsidiary group. Worksheets can be prepared to facilitate the consolidation process. Consolidated financial reporting is appropriate in most instances and is the most commonly used method of reporting parent-subsidiary relationships in the United States.

KEY DEFINITIONS

Cost method—accounting for investments in equity securities by valuing them at the lower of aggregate cost or market.

Equity method—accounting for investments originally at cost with future adjustments for changes in the net assets of the investee company.

Goodwill—the excess of the purchase price of a company over the market value of its net assets.

Parent—the company that owns a majority of another company's voting stock.

Pooling of interest—a business combination formed when one company issues its stock in exchange for the stock of another company. Book values of the acquired company are recorded by the acquiring company.

Subsidiary—a company where the majority of its stock is owned by another company.

QUESTIONS

15-1 Describe the conditions under which the cost method, the equity method, and consolidation should be used.

15-2 Why are the stockholders of a parent considered indirect owners of subsidiary companies, in contrast to being considered direct owners?

15-3 By what two methods are parent-subsidiary relationships created?

15-4 Identify the most frequent types of intercompany transactions encountered in preparing consolidated financial statements.

15-5 What does a controlling interest refer to? Describe the relationship between a corporation that exercises controlling interest and the controlled corporation.

15-6 Why might the price paid to acquire a controlling interest in a subsidiary be different from the book value of the equity acquired?

15-7 What determines the value of an investment of a subsidiary acquired by a pooling of interests, as reflected on the book of the parent?

15-8 Wood Sales, Inc. has an 80 percent ownership interest in Oak Corp., a 100 percent interest in Maple Co., and a 50 percent interest in Lumber Ltd. Which entities may Wood consolidate for financial reporting purposes?

15-9 List and describe two criteria that must be satisfied before a subsidiary may be consolidated in the financial statements.

15-10 How is goodwill determined?

15-11 Company A owns a 100 percent interest in corporation B, acquired in a purchase transaction. Which account on A's balance sheet will indicate that B has not been consolidated assuming that it has not been consolidated? If B is included within the consolidated financial statements, the presence of which account may reflect the fact of consolidation?

15-12 Company B acquired a 100 percent interest in corporation C through a purchase transaction at a cost in excess of book value. What is the accounting disposition of the cost in excess of book value in current and future consolidated financial statements?

15-13 How is the value of a minority interest determined when preparing consolidated financial statements?

15-14 Should an account identified as minority interest be classified as a liability?

EXERCISES

E15-1 Lee Company paid $480,000 cash for all of the capital stock of Mob Corp. At the date of acquisition, Lee's total stockholders' equity consisted of $1,700,000 capital stock and $1,100,000 retained earnings, while Mob reflected $460,000 capital stock and $20,000 retained earnings. Prepare the stockholder's equity section for a consolidated balance sheet immediately after the acquisition.

E15-2 Kar Corporation purchased all the outstanding shares of Lab Co. for cash of $2,800,000. At that time, Lab's accounts reflected total assets of $3,400,000 and total liabilities of $1,400,000. In consolidation, Lab's assets will be reflected at what dollar amount?

E15-3 Total assets of S Company reflect a book value of $200,000, even though their fair market value is $280,000. S also has liabilities of $10,000. P Corporation purchases all the outstanding shares of S for cash of $270,000. Prepare a journal entry to record the acquisition of S by P, assuming you are P's bookkeeper.

E15-4 Prepare the stockholders' equity section for a consolidated balance sheet, assuming that a 100 percent equity in the subsidiary was acquired in a pooling of interests transaction.

	Unconsolidated Account Balances	
	Parent	*Subsidiary*
Investment in Subsidiary	$600,000	$ 0
Capital stock—$10 par	800,000	480,000
Additional paid-in capital	150,000	70,000
Retained earnings	160,000	50,000

E15-5 Okay Company entered Into an agreement with ABC Company whereby Okay acquired all 3,000 shares of ABC's $50 par value stock. In return, Okay transferred 1,200 shares of its $100 par value stock (currently selling for $200 per share). Before the agreement, the two firms had the following balance sheets:

	Okay	*ABC*
Net assets	$600,000	$180,000
Common stock	$480,000	$150,000
Retained earnings	120,000	300,000
	$600,000	$180,000

Required:

a. Prepare a consolidated balance sheet immediately after the transaction, assuming that the acquisition will be treated as a purchase.
b. Prepare a consolidated balance sheet immediately after the transaction, assuming that the acquisition will be treated as a pooling of interests.

E15-6 a. Circle Corp. acquired 90 percent of the outstanding stock of Fan Company for $270,000. The net assets of Fan Company on the day of acquisition were $200,000. What is the dollar balance in minority interest? Where is this balance recorded on the balance sheet?
b. Thunder Company owns all of the voting shares of Wall Company. During the year, Thunder earned $80,000 (including its share of Wall's earnings) while Wall earned $50,000. Determine the amount of consolidated net earnings for the year.

E15-7 The Pears Company acquired the Sunny Company for $80,000, Immediately after acquisition, an appraisal of the fixed assets for Sunny established their fair market value at $90,000. Nonconsolidated balance sheets for the two companies are as follows:

Balance Sheets
Immediately After Acquisition

	Pears Company	*Sunny Company*
Cash	$ 15,000	$ 13,000
Note receivable from Pears Company		5,000
Investment in Sunny Company—100%, at cost	80,000	
Fixed assets	105,000	85,000
Total	$200,000	$103,000
Liabilities	$ 25,000	33,000
Note payable to Sunny Company	5,000	
Common stock—$1 par	130,000	50,000
Retained earnings	40,000	20,000
Total	$200,000	$103,000

Required:

Prepare a consolidated balance sheet, assuming that the transaction was as a purchase.

E15-8 On January 1, Carr Corp. purchased 100 percent of the common stock of Motor Company. At the end of the year, Carr's general ledger reflected revenue—$150,000, cost of goods sold—$100,000, expenses—$40,000, and income from investments (in Motor Company)—$10,000. Motor's general ledger reflected revenue—$80,000, cost of goods sold—$40,000, and expenses—$30,000. Motor Company had performed services for Carr Corp., billing $14,000 for services that cost Motor only $8,000 to perform. Prepare a consolidation worksheet similar to those described in the text. Complete the worksheet. Explain the adjustments.

E15-9 On January 1, Stemm Company purchased 60 percent of the outstanding common stock of Dodd Company for $160,000 cash. The fair-market value of the assets equalled their book values. Immediately after the acquisition the balance sheets reflected the following:

Balance Sheets
Immediately After Acquisition

	Stemm Company	*Dodd Company*
Cash	$ 80,000	$ 30,000
Accounts receivable	200,000	80,000
Investment in Dodd Company	160,000	0
Fixed assets	300,000	150,000
Total	740,000	$260,000
Liabilities	$ 65,000	$ 20,000
Common stock—$5 par	100,000	25,000
Additional paid-in capital	300,000	125,000
Retained earnings	275,000	90,000
Total	$740,000	$260,000

Required:

Prepare calculations to determine the amount of goodwill purchased.

E15-10 On January 1, the Martin Corp. acquired 100 percent of the outstanding shares of stock of Dixe, Inc. in a transaction treated as a pooling of interests. After the acquisition, Dixe, Inc. will cease operations and be merged into the Martin Corp. Immediately before the transaction, a balance sheet of Dixe, Inc. showed the following:

Cash	$ 15,000
Accounts receivable	95,000
Service trucks	100,000(Fair market value, $120,000)
Current liabilities	85,000
Common stock—$5 par	55,000
Retained earnings	70,000

Required:

Journalize the acquisition transaction for Martin Corp. assuming that Martin exchanges one share of $5 par stock for each share of Dixe's common stock.

E15-11 The following information relates to P Company and its subsidairy, S Company, one year after consolidation:

	P Company	*S Company*	*Consolidated*
Assets			
Cash	$ 60,000	$ 25,000	$ 85,000
Accounts receivable	90,000	75,000	80,000
Inventory	280,000	170,000	450,000
Investment in S	500,000	0	0
Long-term assets	750,000	350,000	1,100,000
Excess of cost over book	0	0	20,000
Value of investment in S	$1,680,000	$620,000	$1,735,000
Liabilities and Stockholders' Equity			
Accounts payable	$ 75,000	$ 30,000	$ 20,000
Long-term payables	420,000	110,000	530,000
Capital stock	800,000	300,000	800,000
Additional paid-in capital	210,000	60,000	210,000
Retained earnings	175,000	120,000	175,000
	$1,680,000	$620,000	$1,735,000

For some accounts, the sum of the balances for P and S equals the balance reflected in the consolidated statement. Cash is determined as follows: $60,000 + $25,000 = $85,000. This relation does not exist for other accounts. Please explain the nature of each adjustment required to reconcile the sum of balances for P and S to the Consolidated balance.

E15-12 River Company and Current Company have entered into a contract to pool their firms into a single company. Using the following data, answer the questions below.

	River	Current
Total assets	$1,600,000	$1,300,000
Total liabilities	500,000	600,000
Capital stock—par value $10 for each	700,000	500,000
Additional paid-in capital	100,000	100,000
Retained earnings	300,000	100,000

a. Prepare a journal entry for River Company that will account for a pooling of interests, assuming that 50,000 shares of River are exchanges for all of the stock of Current.
b. Prepare a consolidated balance sheet that reflects the transaction recorded in requirement (a).

E15-13 The Penn Corporation owns all of the outstanding common stock of the Sawyer Corporation. During 19x0, Sawyer declared a $10,000 cash dividend payable in 19x1. In addition, in 19x0 Penn borrowed $5,000 from Sawyer. The loan and $300 interest was repaid at the end of 19x0. Record the adjusting entries to eliminate these intercompany balances for 19x0.

E15-14 During the course of the year 19x4, Glen Corporation, a 100 percent subsidiary of Ross Corporation, engaged in the following transactions with its parent:

a. Sold assets costing $600,000 to Ross Corporation at a $100,000 loss.
b. Loaned Ross Corporation $250,000, earning $12,500 in interest income.
c. Leased from Ross Corporation equipment (on an operating lease contract) for $50,000.

Required:

Record these transactions by Glen Corporation, then give the entries necessary to adjust these intercompany balances.

E15-15 On November 30, 19x7, Ace Incorporated purchased all 300,000 shares of the outstanding common stock of Moon Company for cash of $25 per share. Moon's balance sheet at November 30, 19x7, reflected net assets of $6,000,000. Additionally, the fair value of Moon's property, plant and equipment on November 30, 19x7, was $800,000 in excess of its book value. What amount, if any, will be shown in the balance sheet caption "goodwill" in the November 30, 19x7, consolidated balance sheet of Ace Incorporated and its wholly-owned subsidiary, Moon Company.

E15-16 On January 1, 19x6, Sanders Corporation acquired as a long-term investment for $130,000 a 40 percent common stock interest in Amo Company. On that date, Amo had net assets of $300,000. During 19x6, Amo reported net income of $60,000 and declared and paid cash dividends of $15,000. (a) What is the maximum amount of income that Sanders can report this investment for the calander year 19x6? (b) Determine the balance in Sanders investment account at the end of 19x6.

PROBLEMS

P15-1 Ham Company owns 100 percent of the stock of Son Company. Below are the two income statements for the year after consolidation.

	Ham Company	*Son Company*
Sales	$900,000	$450,000
Cost of goods sold	600,000	300,000
Gross margin	$300,000	$150,000
Operating expenses	(94,000)	(45,000)
Interest expense	(6,000)	(11,000)
Interest income	12,000	0
Tax expense	(90,000)	(38,000)
	$122,000	$ 56,000

Son sold merchandise to Ham for $40,000 which cost $32,000. None of this merchandise is included in Ham's ending inventory. Son paid $11,000 interest charges to Ham during the year. Ham's income statement does not include its equity interest in the subsidiarys' income.

Required:

Prepare a consolidated income statement for the year just ended.

P15-2 On January 1, the Cosgrove Company exchanged one-third of its cash, one-fourth of its inventory, one-fourth of its current liabilities for all of the outstanding common stock of Nills Corporation, a new entity created by Cosgrove on this date. The number of shares received by Cosgrove is determined by the book value of assets transferred to Nills. Nills Corporation is authorized to issue up to 1,000,000 shares of $10 par value stock. Management attributes a value to Nills common stock of $20 per share. The balance sheet for Cosgrove Co., immediately before the exchange, is as follows:

Balance Sheet
Immediately Before the Exchange

Cash	$ 90,000
Accounts receivable	260,000
Inventory	160,000
Plant and equipment	550,000
Total assets	$1,060,000
Current liabilities	$ 120,000
Long-term liabilities	400,000
Common stock—$10 par	150,000
Additional paid-in capital	255,000
Retained earnings	135,000
Total liabilities and capital	$1,060,000

a. Is the transaction a pooling of interests, a purchase, or neither? Explain.
b. Prepare an entry made by Cosgrove Company to record the exchange.
c. Prepare an entry made by Mills Corp. to record the exchange.
d. Prepare unconsolidated balance sheets for Cosgrove Co. and for Nills Corp. after the above exchange. Prepare a consolidated balance sheet.

P15-3 The unconsolidated balance sheets of the Ladd Corp. and King Company, immediately after the Ladd Corp. acquired King, are given below:

Balance Sheets
Immediately After Acquisition

	Ladd Corp.	*King Company*
Cash	$ 80,000	$ 40,000
Accounts receivable	40,000	15,000
Inventory	170,000	80,000
Investment in King Company—cost	240,000	0
Plant and equipment	160,000	130,000
Total assets	$690,000	$265,000
Current liabilities	$ 25,000	$ 45,000
Bond payable—7%	100,000	20,000
Common stock—$10 par	450,000	150,000
Retained earnings	115,000	50,000
Total liabilities and capital	$690,000	$265,000

After Ladd Corp. acquired King Company, it was determined that King Company's inventory was overstated by $6,000 and plant and equipment was understated by $31,000.

Required:

a. Was this a pooling of interests or a purchase? Explain.
b. Determine the amount of goodwill that would be reflected on the consolidated balance sheet after considering all adjustments.
c. At what amount will the assets of King Company be included in the consolidated balance sheet? Explain.

P15-4 The Rass Company acquired a 100 percent interest in Tass Company from Tass's stockholders for $850,000. The fair market value of Tass' long-term assets are $900,000, even though their book value is $700,000. Balance sheets for the two companies immediately before the acquisition are presented below.

	Rass Company	*Tass Company*
Assets		
Current assets	$1,800,000	$ 400,000
Long-term assets	2,100,000	700,000
Total assets	$3,900,000	$1,100,000
Liabilities and Stockholders' Equity		
Current liabilities	$ 300,000	$ 250,000
Long-term liabilities	850,000	350,000
Capital stock	1,100,000	380,000
Retained earnings	1,650,000	120,000
Total	$3,900,000	$1,100,000

Required:

Prepare a consolidated balance sheet.

P15-5 On January 1 the Vast Company acquires 100 percent of the assets of the Mite Company from Mite's stockholders for $900,000 cash. The balance sheets of both companies before the acquisition are as follows:

Balance Sheets
Immediately Before the Exchange

	Vast Company	*Mite Company*
Cash	$1,100,000	$100,000
Accounts receivable	600,000	200,000
Plant and equipment	900,000	600,000
Total assets	$2,600,000	$900,000
Current liabilities	$ 400,000	$150,000
Long-term liabilities	1,300,000	400,000
Common stock—$1 par	100,000	50,000
Additional paid-in capital	500,000	250,000
Retained earnings	300,000	50,000
Total liabilities and equity	$2,600,000	$900,000

On the date of acquisition, an appraisal determined the fair market value of Mite's plant and equipment to be $720,000.

Required:

a. Should the transaction be recorded as a pooling of interests or a purchase? Explain.
b. Prepare the entry required by Vast Company to record the acquisition.
c. Analyze the acquisition to determine the amount of goodwill associated with the purchase.
d. Prepare a consolidated balance sheet.

P15-6 Assume the same facts as in P15-5, except that Vast Company acquired 100 percent of the assets of Mite Company in exchange for 45,000 shares of newly issued stock. The market price of Vast's common stock on the date of the acquisition was $20 per share.

Required:

a. Is the acquisition a purchase or pooling of interests?
b. Record the acquisition.
c. Prepare a consolidated balance sheet as of the date of acquisition.

P15-7 Condensed uncosolidated balance sheets at December 31, 19x2, for Boyd and Wynn Corporations prior to Boyd's acquisition of 100 percent of the stock of Wynn Corporation, are shown below:

	Boyd Corporation	*Wynn Corporation*
Assets		
Current Assets	$2,800,000	$ 600,000
Long-term assets	3,100,000	1,000,000
Total assets	$5,900,000	$1,600,000
Equities		
Current liabilities	$ 500,000	$ 300,000
Long-term liabilities	900,000	500,000
Capital stock	1,000,000	500,000
Retained earnings	3,500,000	300,000
Total equities	$5,900,000	$1,600,000

On December 31, 19x2, Boyd acquired 100 percent of the stock of Wynn Corporation for $1,200,000, paid out of current assets. Wynn Corporation's long-term assets had a fair market value on the date of purchase of $1,400,000.

Required:

a. Record the acquisition of the stock by Boyd Corporation.
b. Prepare a consolidated balance sheet for these corporations immediately after the acquisition.

P15-8 On July 14, 19x8, Pitt and Brown Corporations entered into a pooling type combination in which Pitt acquired all of Brown's 50,000 shares of $10 par value common stock by issuing 10,000 shares of its own $10 par value common stock. The fair market value of Pitt's common stock on the day of the transfer was $80 per share. Balance sheets for these two corporations on the day of the transaction before pooling are shown below:

Balance Sheet
July 14,19x8

	Pitt Corporation	*Brown Corporation*
Assets		
Current assets	$ 200,000	$300,000
Long-term assets	1,000,000	400,000
Total assets	$1,200,000	$700,000
Equities		
Current liabilities	$ 100,000	$ 50,000
Long-term liabilities	500,000	100,000
Total liabilities	$ 600,000	$150,000
Common stock	$ 400,000	$500,000
Retained earnings	200,000	50,000
Total stockholders' equity	$ 600,000	$550,000
Total equities	$1,200,000	$700,000

Required:

a. Record the acquisition of Brown's stock by Pitt Corporation.
b. Prepare a consolidated balance sheet for these corporations immediately after the acquisition.

Learning Objectives

Chapter 16 reviews footnote disclosures for annual reports and reporting for international operations. Studying this chapter should enable you to:

1. List other information included with the financial statements.
2. Describe the content and interpretation of the auditor's opinion.
3. Explain requirements for interim reporting and business segment reporting.
4. Discuss the accounting problems in reporting on foreign operations.
5. Make basic foreign currency translations for financial reporting.

16

Analysis of Other Disclosures and International Operations

INTRODUCTION

The first part of this chapter examines several disclosures included as a part of comprehensive financial reports in addition to the basic financial statements discussed in previous chapters. We will review five additional subjects:

1. Accounting policy disclosures.
2. Footnote and other information disclosures.
3. Auditor's report.
4. Interim reports.
5. Reporting for segments of a business.

The second part of this chapter focuses on the proper accounting for international operations.

PART I: ANALYSIS OF OTHER DISCLOSURES

Management of each organization has considerable flexibility in selecting from alternative generally accepted accounting methods. The accounting methods selected by a firm can significantly affect the determination of financial position, changes in financial position, and results of operations. A hypothetical example of the effects of alternative accounting methods is provided in Illustration 1. In this example, earnings per share could range from $1 to $1.95, depending on accounting methods, given one set of underlying economic circumstances. Therefore, the usefulness of the financial data will be enhanced if disclosure includes information regarding the methods used by the firm. When financial statements are supplemented by such information, the financial data of different firms can be adjusted for differing accounting alternatives to make them comparable.

Those accounting principles and methods of applying the principles selected by management are referred to as the *accounting policies* of the entity. *Accounting Principles Board No. Opinion 22, "Disclosures of Accounting Policies"* requires that a "description of all significant accounting policies of the reporting entity should be included as an integral part of the financial

Illustration 1

Effects of Alternative Generally Accepted Accounting Principles (with identical economics events)

	A Company	B Company
Sales revenues—net	$10,000,000	$10,000,000
Expenses:		
Cost of goods sold[1]	$ 6,000,000	$ 5,600,000
Depreciation[2]	400,000	300,000
Pension and post retirement costs[3]	200,000	50,000
Salaries and bonuses[4]	400,000	200,000
Miscellaneous expense	2,000,000	2,000,000
Total expenses	$ 9,000,000	$ 8,150,000
Income before taxes	$ 1,000,000	$ 1,850,000
Income tax expense	500,000	875,000
Net income	$ 500,000	$ 975,000
Earnings per share (500,000 shares outstanding)	$1.00	$1.95

[1] A Company uses the last-in, first-out method for pricing inventories. B Company uses the first-in, first-out method.

[2] A Company uses accelerated depreciation for book and tax purposes. B Company uses the straight-line method for financial accounting and accelerated depreciation for tax purposes.

[3] A Company accrues post retirement health costs while B Company does not.

[4] A Company pays incentive bonuses to officers in cash. B Company grants stock options to officers.

statement." Such disclosure should describe the accounting principles followed by the reporting entity and the method of applying those principles that materially affect the determination of financial position and results of operations. In general, the disclosure should identify principles and describe methods peculiar to the industry or other unusual or innovative applications of accounting principles. Accounting policy disclosure would include such items as the basis of consolidation, depreciation methods, amortization of intangibles, inventory cost-flow assumptions, income realization on long-term contracts, and recognition of revenue from franchising or leasing operations. The opinion did not require a specific format for accounting policy disclosures, but it did recommend that the disclosures could appear in a separate "summary of significant policies" preceding the notes to the financial statements or as the initial note. In recent years, most large business enterprises have included in their annual reports a separate summary of their significant accounting policies.

FOOTNOTE DISCLOSURE

The information used in financial analysis is basically derived from the financial statements. Normally, however, the statements alone cannot provide all the information needed to understand the subtleties impounded in the financial position and results of operations. Consequently, *footnotes* are an important means of disclosing additional quantitative and qualitative information required for a proper interpretation of the statements. These footnotes are considered an integral part of the financial statements. Although footnote disclosures tend to be detailed and lengthy, they generally represent a vital input to the analysis process. Some of the more important topics covered by footnotes are the following:

1. Significant accounting policies.
2. Changes in accounting principles and retroactive adjustments.
3. Contingent assets and liabilities.
4. Description of liabilities oustanding and credit agreements.
5. Information regarding stockholders' equity.
6. Long-term commitments.
7. Subsequent events.
8. Other useful disclosures.

These subjects are discussed and illustrated in the following paragraphs.

Significant Accounting Policies

As indicated previously, APB Opinion No. 22 requires that the accounting principles followed and methods of applying those principles be described within the financial statements, preferably as the initial footnote or as a separate summary preceding the norms to the financial statements. Frequent disclosures concern the consolidation basis, depreciation methods, interperiod tax allocation, inventory cost flow assumptions, translation of foreign currencies, and revenue recognition. Illustration 2 shows the accounting policies footnote from a recent annual report of H.J. Heinz Company.

Changes in Accounting Principle

APB Opinion No. 20 "Accounting Changes," concluded that a change in accounting may significantly affect the financial statements, and therefore disclosures should be made to facilitate financial analysis. For most changes in principle, footnotes to the financial statements generally disclose the nature of and justification for the change as well as the effect of the change on net income and the related earnings per share. Footnotes are also frequently used to disclose the effect on income of a change in estimate. The excerpts from actual annual reports, shown in Illustration 3, show both types of footnotes.

Contingencies

A contingency involves circumstances shrouded in a considerable degree of uncertainty that may result in gains or losses through potential effects on asset or liability balances. Contingent liabilities arise from current or prospective litigation against the company, guarantees or indebtedness, and tax reassessments. Contingent assets may arise from loss carryforwards, claims for tax refunds, and patent infringement suits against other parties. The usual means of disclosing contingencies is in the footnotes to the financial statements. An example of a footnote disclosure of a contingent liability is shown in Illustration 4.

Description of Liabilities Outstanding—Credit Agreements

Tyically, footnotes are used to disclose supplementary information regarding the nature of current liabilities, long-term debt, and loan commitments for future loans or extensions of existing loans. In addition, footnote disclosure is often used to describe imputed interest on long-term payables not bearing interest or bearing an interest rate lower than the prevailing rate.

Information Regarding Stockholder's Equity

Companies present some information in the body of the balance sheet regarding the nature of equity securities. However, additional disclosure is usually presented in footnote form. The need for disclosure in connection with the capital structure of a corporation is stated *APB Opinion No. 15, "Earnings Per Share"* as follows:

> ". . . financial statements should include a description in summary form, sufficient to explain the pertinent rights and privileges of the various securities outstanding. Examples of information which should be disclosed are dividend and liquidation preferences, participation rights, call prices and dates, conversion or exercise prices or rates and pertinent dates, sinking fund requirements, unusual voting rights, etc."

Illustration 2

Example of Accounting Policies Footnote

H.J. HEINZ COMPANY

NOTES TO CONSOLIDATED FINANCIAL STATEMENTS

1. Significant Accounting Policies

Fiscal Year: The company operates on a fiscal year ending the Wednesday nearest April 30. However, certain foreign subsidiaries have earlier closing dates to facilitate timely reporting. Fiscal years for the financial statements included herein ended April 27, 1988, April 29, 1987 and April 30, 1986.

Principles of Consolidation: The consolidated financial statements include the accounts of the company and its domestic and foreign subsidiaries. Certain fishing vessel operations were consolidated in 1988 as a result of certain restructurings and the adoption of FASB Statement No. 94, "Consolidation of All Majority-owned Subsidiaries." The consolidation of these subsidiaries did not have a material effect on the consolidated financial results of the company.

All significant intercompany accounts and transactions were eliminated. Certain reclassifications were made to prior years' amounts to conform with the 1988 presentation.

Translation of Foreign Currencies: The financial position and results of operations of the company's foreign subsidiaries are measured generally using local currency as the functional currency. Assets and liabilities of these subsidiaries are translated at the exchange rate in effect at each year-end. Income statement accounts are translated at the average rate of exchange prevailing during the year. Translation adjustments arising from the use of differing exchange rates from period to period are included in the cumulative translation adjustment account in shareholders' equity.

Inventories: Inventories are stated at the lower of cost (principally the average cost method) or market.

Depreciation: For financial reporting purposes, depreciation is provided on the straight-line method over the estimated useful lives of the assets. Accelerated depreciation methods are generally used for income tax purposes.

Income Taxes: Deferred income taxes result primarily from timing differences between financial and tax reporting. The company has not provided for possible U.S. taxes on the undistributed earnings of foreign subsidiaries that are considered to be reinvested indefinitely. Where it is contemplated that earnings will be remitted, credit for foreign taxes already paid generally will offset applicable U.S. income taxes; in cases where they will not offset U.S. income taxes, appropriate provisions are included in the Consolidated Statement of Income. The investment tax credits are accounted for under the "flow-through" method, which recognizes the benefit in the fiscal year in which the asset was placed in service.

In December 1987 the FASB issued Statement No. 96, "Accounting for Income Taxes." The statement requires the use of the liability method of accounting for deferred income taxes and must be implemented no later than Fiscal 1990. The company is in the process of determining the impact of the statement's implementation.

Net Income Per Common Share: Net income per common share has been computed by dividing income applicable to common shareholders by 132,705,945 in 1988, 136,834,666 in 1987, and 137,315,701 in 1986, the weighted average number of shares of common stock outstanding and common stock equivalents during the respective years.

Intangibles: The excess of investments in consolidated subsidiaries over net assets at acquisition and other intangibles arising from acquisitions are being amortized on a straight-line basis over periods not exceeding forty years. The company regularly reviews the individual components of the balances and recognizes, on a current basis, any diminution in value.

Business Segment Information: Information concerning business segment and geographic data is on page 31 in the Financial Review.

Illustration 3
Example of Accounting Changes Footnote

CHANGE IN PRINCIPLE:

JOHNSON CONTROLS, INC.

NOTES TO CONSOLIDATED FINANCIAL STATEMENTS

Note 1. Change in Accounting Method
Effective October 1, 1987, the company changed the controls segment's method of accounting for long-term contracts from the completed-contract method to the percentage-of-completion method. The company believes the percentage-of-completion method more fairly presents the results of current period economic activity of the controls segment. Financial statements of prior years have been restated to apply the new method retroactively. The accounting change increased (decreased) net income, primary earnings per share and fully diluted earnings per share for each of the five years in the period ended September 30, 1988 as follows:

	1988	1987	1986	1985	1984
(in millions, except per share data)					
Net income	$7.5	$(4.1)	$(9.8)	$(9.9)	$1.0
Earnings per share					
Primary ...	$.20	$(.11)	(.26)	(.31)	.04
Fully diluted ..	$.19	$(.10)	(.24)	$(.31)	—

Shareholders' equity at October 1, 1986 increased $43.6 million due to the cumulative effect of the accounting change on prior years' earnings.

CHANGE IN ESTIMATE:

CROWN CENTRAL PETROLEUM CORPORATION

NOTES TO CONSOLIDATED FINANCIAL STATEMENTS

Note M. Change in Accounting Estimate
In the second quarter of 1987, the Company increased the estimated remaining useful lives of its refinery units based upon available technology and anticipated severity of service. Remaining asset lives which averaged 9 years were increased to an average of 20 years. The change in accounting estimate increased the Company's 1988 net income approximately $2,601,000, or $.36 per primary share, ($.26 per fully diluted share). The change in accounting estimate increased 1987 net income by approximately $1,799,000, or $.25 per primary share, ($.18 per fully diluted share).

This disclosure should also include a description of stock options or purchase plans outstanding. In addition, it is important to disclose the nature of any restrictions such as the amount of retained earnings available for cash dividends.

Long-Term Commitments

Many businesses make various types of commitments for future performance. Such commitments include long-term lease agreements and pension and retirement plans. Some of these events are typically not reflected in their entirety in the accounts, but they are sufficiently important so that disclosures should be made in the notes to financial statements. Certain disclosures are required for pension plans and for long-term leases. Illustration 5 provides a typical footnote disclosure relating to operating type leases.

Illustration 4
Example of Contingencies Footnote

GUILFORD MILLS, INC.

NOTES TO CONSOLIDATED FINANCIAL STATEMENTS

9. Contingencies:
In May 1988 a jury awarded $5.2 million to a former employee of the Company for an alleged breach of contract and wrongful termination of employment. The Company has appealed the judgmednt on the basis of errors in the judge's instructions to the jury and insufficiency of evidence to support the amount of the jury's award. The Company is vigorously pursuing the appeal.

The Company and its subsidiaries are also involved in various other litigation arising in the ordinary course of business.

Since it presently is not possible to determine the outcome of these matters, no provision has been made in the financial statements for their ultimate resolution. The resolution of the appeal of the jury award could have a significant effect on the Company's earnings in the year that a determination is made; however, in management's opinion, the final resolution of all legal matters will not have a material adverse effect on the Company's financial position.

Illustration 5
Example of Long-Term Commitments Footnote

OMNICOM GROUP INC.

NOTES TO CONSOLIDATED FINANCIAL STATEMENTS

11—Commitments
At December 31, 1988, the Company was committed under operating leases, principally for office space. Certain leases are subject to rent reviews and require payment of expenses under escalation clauses. Rent expense was $80,053,000 in 1988, $70,136,000 in 1987, and $57,175,000 in 1986 after reduction by rents received from subleases of $9,088,000, $6,715,000, and $3,197,000, respectively. Future minimum base rents under terms of non-cancellable operating leases, as reduced by rents to be received from existing non-cancellable subleases, are as follows:

	(Dollars in Thousands)		
	Gross Rent	Sublease Rent	Net Rent
1989	$ 76,477	$15,082	$ 61,395
1990	73,118	13,812	59,306
1991	69,038	12,792	56,246
1992	63,150	9,189	53,961
1993	55,487	4,764	50,723
Cumulative thereafter	363,062	17,626	345,436

Subsequent Events

Events or transactions that occur subsequent to the end of the accounting period but prior to the issuance of financial statements and which have a material effect on the financial statements should be disclosed in the statements. Examples of subsequent events that may require disclosure are business combinations pending or affected, litigation settlements, issues of sale of bonds or capital stock, and catastrophic loss of plant or inventories. A footnote disclosing a subsequent event is presented in Illustration 6.

Illustration 6
Example of Subsequent Events Footnote

COOPER INDUSTRIES, INC.

NOTES TO CONSOLIDATED FINANCIAL STATEMENTS

Note 14: Subsequent Event

On February 23, 1989, Cooper commenced a cash tender offer for all outstanding shares of Champion Spark Plug Company at a price of $21 a share. Champion's Board of Directors approved the offer and agreed to recommend that its shareholders accept the offer and tender their shares. Champion Spark Plug is a world leader in the manufacture and distribution of spark plugs for automotive, industrial and aviation markets. Based on Champion's outstanding Common stock, debt to be assumed and acquisition expenses, the total cost would be approximately $800 million. The acquisition would be financed with borrowings from commercial banks pursuant to existing and a newly established $750-million credit facility, or the issuance of debt securities, including commercial paper. The acquisition is not expected to affect adversely the Company's overall liquidity. For the year ended December 31, 1988, Champion had revenues of $738 million and net income from continuing operations of $22 million.

Other Useful Disclosures

Footnote disclosure is often used to provide any other information relevant to the understanding and interpretation of the financial statement data. Examples of such information relate to foreign operations, product lines, sales backlogs and inventory profits.

THE AUDITOR'S REPORT AS AN INFORMATION DISCLOSURE

Financial statements are representations of the management of an entity to interested parties. Although management has a responsibility to disclose sufficient information to ensure that financial statements are not misleading, an independent auditor may evaluate these statements to express an opinion to third parties about the fairness of presentation of the statements. This independent audit provides confidence to readers of the financial statements about the quality of information provided to them. Consequently, the report prepared by the auditor may serve as an important input to the financial reporting process. However, readers must understand the meaning of the auditor's opinion and the implications of the opinion for financial statement analysis.

The *auditor's report* is written after the auditor has undertaken an extensive and objective study of the accounting process and the financial statements prepared by management. Auditors indicate in a report to the stockholders the scope of their examination and then express an opinion regarding the fairness of the financial statements. The standard format of a report that indicates no qualification as to the fairness of the financial statements is as follows:

[Date]

INDEPENDENT AUDITOR'S REPORT

We have audited the accompanying balance sheets of X Company as of December 31, 19x2 and 19x1, and the related statements of income, retained earnings, and cash flows for the years then ended. These financial statements are the responsibility of the Company's management. Our responsibility is to express an opinion on these financial statements based on our audits.

We conducted our audits in accordance with generally accepted auditing standards. Those standards require that we plan and perform the audit to obtain reasonable assurance about whether the financial statements are free of material misstatement. An audit includes examining, on a test basis, evidence supporting the amounts and disclosures in the financial statements. An audit also includes assessing the accounting principles used and significant estimates made by management, as well as evaluating the overall financial statement presentation. We believe that our audits provide a reasonable basis for our opinion.

In our opinion, the financial statements referred to above present fairly, in all material respects, the financial position of X Company as of [at] December 31, 19x2 and 19x1, and the results of its operations and its cash flows for the years then ended in conformity with generally accepted accounting principles.

[Signature]

This report is referred to as an *unqualified (clean) opinion* because the auditor has not qualified his or her opinion in any way.

Scope of the Audit

In the second paragraph (preferred to as the scope paragraph), the statement "We conducted our audits in accordance with generally accepted auditing standards" relates to both general standards and standards of field work. Conformance to general standards implies that the examination was performed by adequately trained, proficient auditors who maintained an independent mental attitude and who exercised due professional care. Conformance to field standards implies that the work was properly planned, that assistants were adequately supervised, and that a sufficient study and evaluation of the internal control (of the business) was made. The audit includes an examination of evidence supporting reported dollar amounts and assessing accounting principles used and significant estimates made by management. The audit must have a sufficient basis upon which to form an opinion concerning the financial statements.

The Opinion

The opinion paragraph of the auditor's report requires the auditor to express an opinion on the financial statements; or if he or she cannot express an opinion, to clearly indicate so and state all the reasons. The four reporting standards are listed below:

1. The report shall state whether the financial statements are presented in accordance with generally accepted principles of accounting.
2. The report shall state whether such principles have been consistently observed in the current period in relation to the preceding period.
3. Informative disclosures in the financial statements are to be regarded as reasonably adequate unless otherwise stated in the report.
4. The report shall either contain an expression of opinion regarding the financial statements, taken as a whole, or an assertion to the effect that an opinion cannot be expressed. When an overall opinion cannot be expressed, the reasons therefore should be stated. In all cases where an auditor's name is associated with financial statements, the report should contain a clear-cut indication of the character of the auditor's examination, if any, and the degree of responsibility he or she is taking.

Thus, if an auditor's examination is made in accordance with generally accepted auditing standards, and if the financial statements are fairly presented in conformity with generally accepted accounting principles, applied on a consistent basis, and include all necessary disclosures, the auditor will issue a "clean" (unqualified) opinion. In all other circumstances, the auditor must give either a qualified opinion, an adverse opinion, or disclaim an opinion.

In a *qualified opinion*, the auditor expresses certain reservations in his or her report concerning the scope of his or her examination and/or the financial statements. When the auditor's reservations are more serious, an adverse opinion or a disclaimer of opinion is given. In an adverse opinion, the auditor indicates that the financial statements do not present fairly the financial position and results of operations of the company. A disclaimer of opinion indicates that the auditor is unable to express an opinion. The inability to express an opinion usually occurs because of limitations in the scope of the audit.

The five major types of conditions that require the auditors to express an opinion other than unqualified opinion are as follows:

1. The scope of the auditor's examination is limited by:
   a. Conditions that prevent the application of auditing procedures considered necessary in the circumstances.
   b. Restrictions imposed by the client.
2. The financial statements do not present fairly the financial position or results of operations because of:
   a. Lack of conformity with generally accepted accounting principles or standards.
   b. Inadequate disclosure.
3. Accounting principles are not consistently applied in the financial statements.
4. Uncertainties exist concerning the future resolution of material matters whose effects canot be reasonably estimated.
5. There is doubt about the entity's ability to continue operations as a going concern.

The auditor's report shown in Illustration 7 shows qualified opinions based on litigation and going concern problems.

It should be apparent that information very relevant to the process of financial analysis may be revealed in the auditor's report. Consequently, the user of financial statements should carefully examine the auditor's opinion in relation to the other financial data in the annual report.

INTERIM REPORTING

Interim financial reports, usually issued on a quarterly basis, are designed to provide more timely information than annual reports. Interim financial information may include data on financial position, results of operations, and changes in financial position, and it may take the form of either complete financial statements or summarized financial data. The publication of interim reports is required by companies listed on both the New York Stock Exchange and the American Stock Exchange. The Securities and Exchange Commission also requires all listed companies to file quarterly reports on Form 10-Q.

Because the ultimate results of operations cannot be known with certainty until the business is finally liquidated, many problems are incurred when allocating costs and revenues to relatively short time periods. Consequently, interim reports are subject to even more significant limitations than annual reports.

Given the problems inherent in determining interim financial results, it is important that the user fully understand the limitations of such data. However, the pronouncements of the APB and the FASB should serve to enhance the comparability of interim reports. When analyzed with the proper cau-

Illustration 7
Example of Qualified Opinions

Litigation

INDEPENDENT AUDITORS' REPORT

The Board of Directors and Stockholders
Murphy Oil Corporation:

We have audited the accompanying consolidated balance sheets of Murphy Oil Corporation and Consolidated Subsidiaries as of December 31, 1988 and 1987, and the related consolidated statements of income, stockholders' equity and cash flows for each of the years in the three-year period ended December 31, 1988. These consolidated financial statements are the responsibility of the Company's management. Our responsibility is to express an opinion on these consolidated financial statements based on our audits.

We conducted our audits in accordance with generally accepted auditing standards. Those standards require that we plan and perform the audit to obtain reasonable assurance about whether the financial statements are free of material misstatement. An audit includes examining, on a test basis, evidence supporting the amounts and disclosures in the financial statements. An audit also includes assessing the accounting principles used and significant estimates made by management, as well as evaluating the overall financial statement presentation. We believe that our audits provide a reasonable basis for our opinion.

In our opinion, the financial statements referred to above present fairly, in all material respects, the financial position of Murphy Oil Corporation and Consolidated Subsidiaries at December 31, 1988 and 1987, and the results of their operations and their cash flows for each of the years in the three-year period ended December 31, 1988 in conformity with generally accepted accounting principles.

As discussed in Note D to the consolidated financial statements, Mentor Insurance Limited (MIL), a Bermuda subsidiary of Ocean Drilling & Exploration Company (ODECO), a 61 percent owned subsidiary of the Company, is currently in liquidation under the supervision of the Supreme Court of Bermuda. In March 1986, the liquidators of MIL filed suit asserting various claims against ODECO. The ultimate outcome of the litigation cannot presently be determined. Accordingly, no liability, and loss, that may result upon adjudication has been recognized in the accompanying consolidated financial statements.

* * * * * *

Going Concern

REPORT OF INDEPENDENT CERTIFIED PUBLIC ACCOUNTANTS

To The American Ship Building Company

We have audited the accompanying consolidated balance sheets of The American Ship Building Company and subsidiaries as of September 30, 1988 and 1987, and the related consolidated statements of operations, stockholders' equity and cash flows for each of the three years in the period ended September 30, 1988. These financial statements are the responsibility of the Company's management. Our responbility is to express an opinion on these statements based on our audit.

We conducted our audits in accordance with generally accepted auditing standards. Those standards require that we plan and perform the audits to obtain reasonable assurance about whether the consolidated financial statements are free of material misstatement. An audit includes examining, on a test basis, evidence supporting the amounts and disclosures in the consolidated financial statements. An audit also includes assessing the accounting principles used and significant estimates made by management, as well as evaluating the overall financial statement presentation. We believe that our audits provide a reasonable basis for our opinion.

In our opinion, the financial statements referred to above present fairly, in all material respects, the consolidated financial position of The American Ship

Illustration 7 Continued:

Going Concern Continued:

REPORT OF INDEPENDENT CERTIFIED PUBLIC ACCOUNTANTS

To The American Ship Building Company

Building Company and subsidiaries as of September 30, 1988 and 1987, and the results of their operations and their cash flows for each of the three years in the period ended September 30, 1988, in conformity with generally accepted accounting principles.

As discussed in Note 8 to the consolidated financial statements, the Company is a defendant in a lawsuit alleging that excess pension plan assets, which reverted to the Company when the plan was terminated, should have been distributed to the plan participants. This litigation is in the early stages of discovery, and the ultimate outcome cannot presently be determined. Accordingly, no provision for any liability that may result upon adjudication has been made in the accompanying consolidated financial statements.

The accompanying consolidated financial statements have been prepared assuming that the Company will continue as a going concern. The Company has sustained significant losses in the last two years and, as discussed in Note 9 to the consolidated financial statements, the Company has given notice to its lenders of events which constitute default under its credit agreement. In addition, the Company does not currently have any signficiant long-term contracts. These factors raise substantial doubt about the Company's ability to continue as a going concern. The consolidated financial statements do not include any adjustments that might result from the outcome of this uncertainty.

tion, it appears that the information contained in interim reports can be used to improve the user decision-making process.

REPORTING FOR SEGMENTS OF A BUSINESS

In the 1960's, conglomorates were formed. These are companies that operate in several line of business. For example, Tenneco has operations in pipelines, heavy and farm equipment manufacturing, ship building, and agricultural products. The purpose of the diversification is to hedge against downturn's in any one area of business activity. Such diversified companies are required to disclose financial information concerning the activities of individual segments of the business. The term *segment* generally is used to describe a component of an entity whose activities relate to a separate major class of customer or product. Individual segments of a diversified company may be uniquely affected by economic conditions and have different rates of profitability, degrees of risk, and opportunities for growth. Therefore, segment financial data can help financial analysts and other users of financial statements learn about and make informed decisions regarding such companies. Some of the more important specific uses of segmented data include the following:

1. To provide information regarding the nature of the businesses a company is involved in and the relative size of the various segments.

2. To use the sales and contributions toward profit as an input to the evaluation and projection of corporate earnings.
3. To appraise the ability of management in making aquisitions.
4. To make credit decisions by using information concerning the sources and use of funds by the various segments.

Problems in Providing Segment Data

There are several potential problems in providing financial data for diversified companies on a segment basis. The three main problems that occur in developing financial data on a segment basis are: (1) allocation of common costs to two or more segments, (2) pricing transactions between segments, and (3) determining segments to be used for reporting purposes. Each problem must be addressed if meaningful information is to be reported.

Disadvantages of the Reporting Company

Concern has been expressed by corporate management that disclosure of segment financial information may cause difficulties harmful to the reporting company. The disadvantages cited often include confidential information that would be revealed to competitions, technical problems inherent in the preparation of the data that might result in misleading information users, and, the cost of providing the data that could be significant.

Usefulness of Segment Data

Diversified companies present special problems in financial analysis and decision-making. Since these companies may have varying degrees of profitability, uses, and growth potential for individual components, the analyst needs financial information regarding the components to make meaningful decisions. Despite the potential usefulness of segment information, however, the analyst must use extreme caution in assessments and evaluations of the data.

PART II: ACCOUNTING FOR INTERNATIONAL OPERATIONS

The accounting system for multinational business organizations is designed to record business transactions that subsequently will be reflected on the balance sheet, the income statement, and the statement of cash flows. Accounting for multinational organizations introduces three complexities above and beyond those encountered by domestic businesses. This discussion highlights three major areas of international accounting complexities: differences in generally accepted accounting principles, international transaction gains and losses, and international translation of foreign balances.

Foreign Accounting Principles

Accounting principles differ from nation to nation, and reflect each nation's economic system, business environment, and its social and legal traditions. Some nations require that accounting systems in their countries must formerly recognize the impact of inflation, and that this impact must be reflected in publicly distributed financial statements. Businesses in other nations are allowed to artifically smooth year-to-year net income by creating discretionary "reserves" that can be expanded or contracted at will. Thus, income in these nations takes on a different meaning than income reported in the United States. Companies that are organized into several subsidiaries are not required to prepare consolidated financial statements in some countries, while comparable operations by U.S. concerns are required to do so. Depreciation policy in some countries permits immediate write-off of the cost of fixed assets, or requires depreciation in excess of amounts that would be recognized by domestic United States concerns. In addition, inventory methods, goodwill amortization, treatment of stock dividends, and the accounting for pension plans or leases differs dramatically from country-to-country.

These differences between domestic and foreign generally accepted accounting principles produce financial statements that are not directly comparable from country-to-country. Differences in principles affect the assets, liabilities, owners' equity, revenues, and expenses reflected in balance sheets and income statements. Before a domestic United Satates business consolidates accounts of foreign subsidiaries or evaluates their financial statements, adjustments must be made to the financial statements to correct for differences in accounting principles.

Accounting for Multinational Transactions

Whenever a domestic United States firm engages in international transactions, accounting problems are liable to occur. In particular, importing involves the purchase of goods or services from foreign suppliers while exporting involves the sales to foreign customers. Importing or exporting transactions may require that the monetary measurement be denominated in a currency other than the U.S. dollar. An American corporation may purchase goods from a foreign supplier and promise to pay for the purchase with the foreign currency. Between the time of purchase and the time of payment, the relationship between the value of the foreign currency and the value of the dollar may change, thus creating an opportunity for gains or losses on foreign transactions. For example, assume that the ABC Corporation purchases some merchandise from a foreign supplier on May 1 for 10,000 Deutschmarks (DM). Each DM can be exchanged for $.60 on May 1. The following journal entry could be used to record the purchase:

Purchases	$6,000	
Accounts payable		$6,000
To record a purchase for 10,000 DM when the exchange rate is $.60)		

Suppose that the exchange rate on August 1, the date of payment, is DM = $.62. At that exchange rate, the 10,000 DM debt will require ABC Corporation to pay $6,200 in satisfaction of the debt. The journal entry to record payment at the rate of 62 cents is as follows:

Accounts payable	$6,000	
Foreign exchange transaction loss	200	
Cash..................................		$6,200
To record payment of 10,000 DM debt when exchange rate is $.62		

That is, a change in the exchange rate exposes an international trader to a foreign exchange loss that goes above and beyond the normal risks of business carried on domestic corporations. At the same time, changes in exchange rates may enable domestic concerns to recognize gains on international transactions. For example, assume that the exchange rate on August 1 is DM = $.58. Then, ABC Corporation will save 2 cents on each Deutschmark that is spent to satisfy the foreign debt. The entry to record payment at a rate of 58 cents is as follows:

Accounts payable	$6,000	
Cash..................................		$5,800
Foreign exchange transaction gain		200
To record payment of 10,000 DM debt when the exchange rate is $.58		

Similar types of foreign exchange gains and losses can be recognized in a foreign sale that is denominated in terms of the foreign currency. Foreign exchange losses will be recognized whenever a sale is made at one exchange rate, and the payment occurs after the exchange rate has fallen. For example, if a sale had been made on July 1 for 10,000 DM when the exchange rate was 65 cents, and the collection occurs on August 1 when the exchange rate is 60 cents, then a $500 foreign exchange loss would be recognized as part of the collection transaction. Alternately, foreign exchange gains may be recognized on a sale transaction, whenever the sale is denominated in the foreign currency and the exchange rate rises. For example, a sale for 10,000 DM when exchange rates are DM = 65 cents will generate an accounts receivable balance of $6,500. If the exchange rate increases to DM = 70 cents at the time of settlement, cash receipts will be $7,000, and a foreign exchange gain of $500 will be recognized.

Translation of Foreign Balances

Multinational corporations commonly organize foreign subsidiaries to facilitate an international transaction. Domestic American corporations will reflect these foreign subsidiaries on the domestic financial statements either as long-term investments, or as a consolidated element in the consolidated financial statements. To accomplish either of these practices, however, the account balances of the foreign subsidiaries must be translated in terms of dollars. A problem results whenever exchange rates fluctuate over time, so that the foreign account balances were incurred at different exchange rates. The translation adjustment will depend on the type of foreign operation involved. If the foreign subsidiary is self-contained and its operations are integrated into the economy of the foreign country, we will call it a type A subsidiary. A type B subsidiary is one that is mainly a direct or integral part or extension of the parent company's operations. For example, a type A may be a subsidiary that manufactures and markets products in a foreign country. A type B subsidiary would be one that merely markets products of the parent that are produced in the U.S. Translation rules for these two types of subsidiaries are summarized in Illustration 8. For the type A subsidiary, all balance sheet accounts, except equity accounts, are translated at the current exchange rate on the date of the financial statements. Contributed capital accounts are translated at the rate that existed when the capital arose, called the historical rate. Retained earnings are not adjusted. Income statement items are translated at the average translation rate during the period covered by the statement. Since exchange rates are constantly changing, the translated value of the parents investment may appear to be changing. Changes that result from changes in the exchange rate are called *translation adjustments*. Since these changes are not likely to affect cash flows or net income, they are reported as part of owner's equity in the consolidated balance sheet.

For type B subsidiaries, the translation process differs and it is called a restatement. Current assets and all liabilities are translated at current rates, while the other balance sheet accounts, other than retained earnings, are translated at historic rates. Retained earnings are not adjusted. Income statement items are generally translated at the average rate for the period. Exceptions include depreciation, amortization, and cost of goods sold, which are translated at historical rates. Translation gains and losses are likely to

Illustration 8

Restatement Rates for Foreign Subsidiaries

Accounts	*Type A*	*Type B*
Cash and receivables	Current	Current
Inventories and prepaids	Current	Historical
Plant assets and intangibles	Current	Historical
Liabilities	Current	Current
Contributed capital	Historical	Historical
Retained earnings	N/A	N/A
Revenues	Average	Average
Cost of goods sold	Average	Historical
Depreciation and amortization	Average	Historical
Other expenses	Average	Average

affect future cash flow and net income and, therefore, are reported as part of income for the current period.

Illustration 9 shows the translation process for both types of subsidiaries. The following information is assumed regarding rates of exchange between the British pound and the U.S. dollar:

Year-end rate	$1.90
Average for year	1.85
Historic rates:	
Inventory and cost of goods sold	1.95
Plant assets	2.05
Common stock	2.10

Illustration 9

Restatement of Subsidiaries Financial Statements

		Type A Subsidiary		*Type B Subsidiary*	
	Pounds	*Exchange Rate*	*U.S. Dollars*	*Exchange Rate*	*U.S. Dollars*
Balance Sheet					
Cash	$ 10,000	$1.90	$ 19,000	$1.90	$ 19,000
Accounts receivable	20,000	1.90	38,000	1.90	38,000
Inventories	25,000	1.90	47,500	1.95	48,750
Plant assets	150,000	1.90	285,000	2.05	307,500
Total assets	$205,000		$389,500		$413,250
Accounts payable	$ 8,000	1.90	$ 15,200	1.90	$ 15,200
Long-term note	10,000	1.90	19,000	1.90	19,000
Common stock—no par	150,000	2.10	315,000	2.10	315,000
Retained earnings	37,000		92,500		64,050
Translation adjustment			(50,200)		
Total liabilities and equity	$205,000		$389,500		$413,250
Income Statement					
Sales	$ 80,000	1.85	$148,000	1.85	$148,000
Cost of goods sold	$ 45,000	1.85	$ 83,250	1.95	$ 87,750
Depreciation	7,000	1.85	12,950	2.05	14,350
Other expenses	18,000	1.85	33,300	1.85	33,300
Exchange gain or loss					(5,000)
Total expenses	$ 70,000		$129,500		$130,400
Net income	$ 10,000		$ 18,500		$ 17,600

Retained earnings are not translated because it is made up of many elements of income and dividends over the years. It is usually calculated as the beginning adjusted balance plus income, less dividends. For illustration purposes, we will assume the beginning adjusted balance for type A was $74,000 and for type B $46,450.

The translation adjustment in type A translations is the amount necessary to balance the balance sheet and represents the accumulation of several years of adjustments. The translation gain or loss shown in the type B income statement is also an assumed figure. The calculations of such adjustments are beyond the scope of this text.

Note that the two types result in different dollar amounts being reported in the financial statements. Before the FASB issued Statement No. 52, all translations were made as in type B. This method was highly criticized because it caused significant fluctuations in income from year-to-year. Many believed that when a type A subsidiary was involved, the fluctuations would not be realized in the near future in the form of cash payments from the subsidiary to the parent. The subsidiary frequently reinvests its profits into its own operations. Since this currency fluctuation was not going to be realized in the near future, it was believed that it should not be included as part of income.

SUMMARY

Footnotes are an integral part of the financial statements. They provide information that is essential for developing an understanding of the information presented in the statements. The footnotes contain information on specific accounting methods or policies adopted by the company, detail regarding account information, and information regarding commitments and contingencies. The auditors report indicates the scope of the auditors' investigation and their opinion regarding whether the financial statements are a fair presentation of the results of operations and the financial position of the company.

Accounting for multinational operations introduces three additional complexities not found in the accounting for domestic operations: differences in generally accepted accounting principles, gains and losses on foreign exchange transactions, and foreign exchange translation gains and losses. Accountants who deal with multinational organizations must be thoroughly familiar with the accounting implications of each of these events. Multinational operations require a degree of sophistication and expertise of accounting that is not easily gained without extensive study and research.

KEY DEFINITIONS

Accounting changes—changes in accounting principles, accounting estimates, and reporting entities.

Accounting policies—the particular accounting methods adopted by a company in preparing its financial statements.

Auditors report—the auditor's letter that indicates the scope of his or her audit and their opinion regarding the fair presentation of the financial statements.

Interim reports—the quarterly financial reports that are issued during the time period between the annual reports.

Qualified opinion—an audit opinion that has reservations regarding scope of the audit, uncertainties or going concern.

Segment information—information presented in the footnotes to the financial statements regarding specific product lines and/or customers.

Translation gains and losses—gains and losses that result from settlement of claims when exchange rates have changed between the date the claim arose and its settlement date.

QUESTIONS

16-1 What disclosures and reports, besides financial statements, are large businesses (such as large publicly held corporations) required to prepare or publish?

16-2 Describe the accounting policies section of footnotes found in financial statements.

16-3 Why are accounting policies required to be disclosed?

16-4 What kind of information should be included in the footnotes to the financial statements?

16-5 List some topics commonly covered in the footnotes to the financial statements.

16-6 Describe a typical auditor's report.

16-7 Is the management of a firm responsible for preparing the auditor's report on that firm's financial statements?

16-8 What kinds of opinions may an auditor express in an auditor's report regarding the fairness of a firm's financial statements?

16-9 Of what use is the auditor's report to the financial statement user?

16-10 How does an interim financial report differ from the annual financial report?

16-11 Why do the major stock exchanges require corporations listed on those exchanges to publish interim financial statements?

16-12 What limitations exist to the preparation and use of interim financial statements?

16-13 Define the term business segment.

16-14 Of what benefit is it to a financial statement user to be provided with financial reports that separately report business segment activities for diversified businesses?

16-15 Providing financial data for segments of a business is more complex than providing data for the whole business. List some additional accounting problems associated with segment reporting.

16-16 What accounting problems do companies with foreign subsidiaries encounter?

16-17 What is the difference between what the text referred to as a type A and B subsidiary?

16-18 How do the translation adjustments differ for type A and B subsidiaries?

16-19 When a company has a foreign obligation which is settled for less than anticipated because of favorable changes in the exchange rate, how should the difference be reported?

EXERCISES

E16-1 Ace Co. sold merchandise to Canadian Supply Company for $15,000 Canadian. On the date of sale, the exchange rate was $1 U.S. = $1.15 Can. Ace paid the account two months later when the exchange rate was $1 U.S. = $1.13 Can.

Required:

Give the entries to record the purchase and payment.

E16-2 Swindle Co. purchased merchandise from LeSalle Co. for 10,000 francs. On the date of purchase, the exchange rate was 1 Franc = $.19. When Swindle paid the account, the exchange rate was 1 Franc = $.21.

Required:

Give the entry to record the purchase and payment.

E16-3 Global Co. has international subsidiaries that market its products in foreign countries. Global produces all the products in the U.S. and makes shipments directly to customers. The foreign subsidiaries are basically just sales offices. In the spaces below, indicate the type of exchange rate (current, average in current year, historic) that Global should use in translating the subsidiaries accounts.

Account	*Type of Rate*
Cash	
Accounts receivable	
Supplies inventory	
Land	
Buildings	
Accounts payable	
Common stock	
Retained earnings	
Sales	
Depreciation	
Other expenses	

E16-4 International Co. has a subsidiary in Australia. The subsidiary manufactures products and markets them in the local economy. The subsidiary was an independent company before International purchased them two years ago. In the spaces provided below, indicate the exchange rate (current, average of current year, historic) International should use in translating the subsidiary's accounts.

Account	*Type of Rate*
Cash	
Accounts receivable	
Inventory	
Equipment	
Land	
Buildings	
Accounts payable	
Long-term notes	
Common stock	
Additional paid-in capital	
Retained earnings	
Sales	
Cost of goods sold	
Depreciation	
Other operating expenses	

E16-5 Pasta Co. operates a subsidiary in Italy. The following is a partial listing of account balances of the subsidiary as of the end of the year.

Cash	$ 50,000
Equipment	400,000
Building	2,500,000
Accounts payable	200,000
Common stock	2,000,000
Retained earnings	300,000
Sales	4,000,000
Cost of sales	3,000,000
Depreciation	275,000
Other expenses	400,000

Assume the following are the translations rates:

	$1 U.S. =
Current	.0005
Historic	.0020
Average	.0006

Assume the single historic rate applies in all cases where the historic rate should be used.

Required:

Translate the above amounts into U.S. dollars assuming the subsidiary is a type A subsidiary.

E16-6 Using the information in E16-5, translate the amounts into U.S. dollar assuming a type B subsidiary.

E16-7 The following information relates to Birkett Co.

Cash	$ 15,000
Accounts receivable	30,000
Inventories	37,500
Plant assets	225,000
Total	$307,500
Accounts payable	$ 12,000
Long-term note	15,000
Common stock—no par	220,000
Retained earnings	60,500
Total	$307,500
Sales	$120,000
Cost of goods sold	67,540
Depreciation	10,500
Other expenses	27,000

Birkett is a Canadian subsidiary. Assume the following exchange rates apply.

	$1 Canadian = $ U.S.
Current year-end	$.86
Average for the year	.84
Historic rates:	
Inventory	.80
Plant assets	.70
Common stock	.75

Assume the beginning adjusted retained earnings equalled $43,630 and that the translation adjustment was $20,000. Prepare the translated balance sheet and income statement for Birkett Co. assuming it is a type A subsidiary.

E16-8 Using the data in E16-7, prepare a translated income statement and balance sheet for the Birkett subsidiary assuming it is a type B subsidiary. Assume the beginning adjusted balance for retained earnings was $18,980 and that there was a $2,230 exchange gain in the current year.

Index

—A—

Absolute data, 385
Acid-test ratio, 399
Accounting:
  accrual basis, 80
  cash basis, 79
  cost, 18
  defined, 4-5
  environment, 26-27
  managerial, 10
  model, 5
  not-for-profit, 18
Accounting cycle, 51
Accounting entity, 6
Accounting equation, 30-32
Accounting policies, 444
Accounting Principles Board (APB), 40
Accounts, 7, 34
  closing entries, 63-65
  contra, 85
  control, 137
  drawing, 338
  income summary, 64
  ledger, 51
  normal balances, 53-54
  T-format, 53
Accounts payable, 265
Accounts receivable:
  aging, 161
  defined, 190
  turnover, 395
Accruals, 93
Adjusted trial balance, 97
Adjusting entries, 96-97
Age of receivables, 161
Allowance for doubtful accounts, 161
American Institute of Certified Public Accountants (AICPA), 17, 89
Amortization:
  bond discount, 297-300
  bond premium, 300-301
  defined, 248-49
  intangible assets, 247-49
  straight-line method, 298-99
Annuity, 273
APB Opinion No. 15, 446
APB Opinion No. 20, 446
APB Opinion No. 22, 444

Assets:
deferred charges, 250
defined, 8
fixed, 229
goodwill, 248, 424
intangible, 247-49
Assumptions (*see* Accounting policies)
Auditing, 17
Auditor's report, 451
Average collection period, 395
Average cost method, inventory, 209-10, 213
Average inventory turnover in days, 396

—B—

Bad debts:
defined, 159-60
expense, 160
estimating, 160
Balance sheet, 11-12, 36, 80, 97
Bank checking account (*see* Checking account)
Bank reconciliation statement, 180-85
Bank statement, 180
Bonds, 294
coupon, 294
debentures, 294
discount, 297-98
mortgage, 291
par value, 294
premium, 300-01

—C—

Capital, 37
Capital expenditures, 243
Capitalizing retained earnings, 331
Cash:
control, 177-78
defined, 177
sales, 124
Cash discounts, 126-29
Cash equivalents, 256
Certified Public Accountants (CPA), 17
Charter of incorporation, 318
Checking account, 179-80
Clarity, 14
Closing process, 63-65
Common-size data, 385
Common stock (*see* Stock)
Comparability, 14, 29
Compound entry, 62
Compound interest, 272-74
table of an amount, 276, 278
table of an annuity, 277, 279
Conciseness, 14
Consistency, 29, 243
Consolidated statements, 417
Contingent assets, 446
Contingent liabilities, 260, 446
Contra account, 85
Contributed capital, 338
Control accounts, 137
Corporations:
defined, 69-70, 318-19
Cost:
defined, 27
incurred, 57, 80
inventory, 207
Cost benefit, 29
Cost method, 414, 417
Cost of goods sold, 121, 154-55
CPA (*see* Certified Public Accountant)
Credit memorandum, 179
Credits, 54
Current liabilities, 261
Current ratio, 264-65, 394

—D—

Debit memorandum, 179
Debits, 54
Debt to total assets ratio, 396
Deferrals, 93
Deferred charges, 250
Deferred revenues, 260, 271
Deferred taxes, 307-08
Depletion, 247
Depreciation:
defined, 85
double-declining-balance, 237-38
expense, 233
partial year's, 242
straight-line, 235-37
sum-of-the-years'-digits, 238-40
units-of-production, 241
Discount:
amortization, 297
bond, 297
effective-interest amortization, 297
Discounted note, 274

Discounted present value, 274
  table of an amount, 276, 278
  table of an annuity, 277, 279
Discounting, 192-93
Discounts:
  cash, 126-29
  notes receivable, 192-93
  trade, 127
Dishonored notes, 191-92
Dividends, 332-35
  declaration date, 332
  in kind, 332
  payment date, 332
  property, 332
  record date, 332
  stock, 333
Double-entry recording, 54-55
Drawing account, 338
Dun and Bradstreet, 386, 389

—E—

Earnings, 12
Earnings per share, 121, 183, 393
Effective-interest amortization, 300
Entity, 6
EPS (*see* Earnings per share)
Equities, 10
Equity method, 414-17
Errors, 81-82
Expense, 12, 28, 32, 57-58
  accounts, 58
  accrued, 93
  administrative, 163
  prepaid, 84
  recognition, 57
Extraordinary items, 129-30
Extraordinary gains, 129-30
Extraordinary losses, 129-30

—F—

FASB (*see* Financial Accounting Standards Board)
Fair market value, 215, 232
Feedback value, 29
FIFO (first-in, first-out), 210-11
Financial Accounting Standards Board (FASB), 17, 39
Financing activities, 357, 366-67
Financing leases, 305
Fiscal year, 28
FOB (free on board), 205
Footed, 53, 94
Foreign accounting principles, 456-57
Foreign balances, 458-61
Freedom from bias, 14

—G—

GAAP (*see* Generally accepted accounting principles)
Generally accepted accounting principles (GAAP), 16, 25-26
Going concern assumption, 27
Goodwill, 298, 424
Gross margin, 36, 156
Gross profit method, 216-18

—H—

Historical costs, 27, 215 (*see also* Cost)
Horizontal analysis, 387

—I—

Income, 12
Income statement, 12-13
  multiple-step form, 133
  single-step form, 133
Income summary, 64
Inflow, 120
Information, 24
Intangible assets, 247-49
Interest bearing notes, 265-66
Interim financial reports, 453
Internal auditing, 18
Internal control, 178, 261-63
Inventory:
  account, 154
  available for sale, 154
  average cost, 209-10, 213
  beginning, 154
  closing entries, 163
  defined, 203
  ending, 154
  estimation, 216-18
  FIFO, 210-11
  LIFO, 211, 213-14
  lower of cost or market, 216

periodic, 156, 207
perpetual, 156, 205-06
specific identification, 208
Inventory turnover, 395-96
Investing activities, 356, 365-66

—J—

Journal:
cash disbursements, 141-42
cash receipts, 140-41
defined, 59
format, 59-60
sales, 137-40
special, 137

—L—

Land, 230
Lease liabilities, 305-06
Ledger:
defined, 52
format, 52-54
general, 52-54
subsidiary, 136-37
Legal capital, 321
Legal title, 204
Leverage, 292
Liabilities, 9, 259-61
current, 261
fixed, 291
long-term, 291
LIFO (last-in, first-out), 211, 213-14
Liquidity, 264, 385
Long-term investments, 249-50
Lower of cost or market, 188, 216

—M—

Manual systems, 51-52
Marketability, 385
Marketable securities, 187
Matching, 120
Matching concept, 28
Materiality, 30
Measurement scale, 27
Minority interest, 431-32
Monetary-unit-of-measure-concept, 27
Moody's financial rating service, 386, 389
Multinational transactions, 457-58

—N—

Natural resources, 246-47
Net book value, 87
Net income, 10, 32
Net owners' investment, 32
Neutrality, 29
Noncash activities, 357
Noninterest bearing notes, 266
Notes payable:
discounted, 267-68
interest bearing, 265-66
noninterest bearing, 266
Notes receivable, 191-93
NSF check, 182, 185

—O—

Operating activities, 256, 362-65
Operating leases, 305
Organizational costs, 70
Outflow, 120
Owners' equity, 9, 320

—P—

Par value, 294, 321
Partnerships:
defined, 68, 340-46
Payout ratio, 397-98
Payroll:
deductions, 268-70
defined, 268
recording, 269-70
taxes, 270
Pension liabilities, 307-08
Periodicity, 27-28
Petty cash, 185-86
Plant and equipment, 230
acquisition, 231-32
disposition, 243-46
Pooling of interests, 420
Posted, 59
Predictive value, 29
Preferred stock (*see* Stock)
Premium:
amortization, 300
bond, 300
effective-interest amortization, 300
Prepayments, 83-85
Price earnings ratio, 397
Prior-period adjustments, 331-32

Profit, 10, 12
Profitability, 385
Profit margin on sales, 392
Proprietorships:
  defined, 68, 338-40
Purchase discounts, 157
Purchase order, 204
Purchase returns and allowances, 157
Purchases, 156

—Q—

Qualified opinion, 452

—R—

Rate of return on assets, 342
Rate of return on common stock equity, 343
Ratios:
  accounts receivable turnover, 395
  average inventory turnover in days, 396
  acid-test, 394
  average collection period, 395
  current ratio, 264, 394
  debt to total assets, 396
  earnings per share, 163, 393
  inventory turnover, 395-96
  liquid ratios, 394
  marketability ratios, 397
  payout, 397-98
  price earnings, 397
  profit margin on sales, 392
  profitability ratios, 392
  rate of return on assets, 392
  rate of return on common stock equity, 393
  receivables turnover, 395
  solvency ratios, 396
  times interest earned, 396-97
Realization principle, 128
Receivables turnover, 395
Reciprocal accounts, 420
Relative data, 385
Relevance, 14, 29
Reliable, 29
Representational faithfulness, 29
Residual value, 87, 233
Retained earnings:
  account, 330-31
  defined, 330
  statement, 162-64, 331
Retained earnings statement, 163-64, 331
Revenue, 12, 28, 32, 57-58
  accounts, 58
  expenditures, 243
  realization, 121
Reversing entries, 103-08
  expense accruals, 105-06
  revenue accruals, 106-08

—S—

Sales, 12, 121
  (*see also* Revenue)
Sales returns, 125-26
Schedule of noncash investing and financing transactions, 357
Securities and Exchange Commission (SEC), 17, 39-40
Segment reporting, 455-56
Separate entity assumption, 6
Solvency, 385
Source documents, 124
Specific identification, inventory, 208
Standard and Poor, 386
Statement of cash flows, 358
  direct format, 358-59
  indirect format, 358-59
  worksheet, 369-73
Statement of financial position, 11
  (*see also* Balance sheet)
Stock:
  common, 322
  discount, 322
  dividend, 332
  dividend preference, 323
  issuance, 325-28
  legal capital, 321
  liquidation preference, 325
  no-par value, 322
  partially participating, 324
  participating, 324
  par value, 321
  preferred, 323-25
  premium, 322
  splits, 335
  subscribed, 328
  treasury, 328-330
Straight-line, 87-88, 235-37
  amortization, 248-49, 298-99
Subscribed stock (*see* Stock)
Subsequent events, 450

—T—

T-accounts, 53
Taxation, 17
Temporary investments, 186-89
Timeliness, 14, 29
Times interest earned, 396-97
Time value of money, 271
Trade discounts, 127
Trade receivables, 190
Transactions, 6, 59
Transaction adjustments, 459
Treasury stock, 328-30
Trial balance, 62-63

—U—

Underwriters, 244
Unearned income, 90-91, 123-24
Unqualified opinion, 451

—V—

Verifiability, 14, 29
Vertical analysis, 388-89

—W—

Working capital, 264
Worksheet:
  consolidated, 426-31
  defined, 93
  illustrated, 93-98
  statement of cash flows, 369-73